PARENTS AND CHILDREN

The Law of Parental Responsibility

FOURTH EDITION

Brenda M. Hoggett, Q.C., M.A.

*Law Commissioner, Visiting Professor,
Kings College, London*

LONDON
SWEET & MAXWELL
1993

First Edition   1977
Second Edition   1981
Third Edition   1987
Fourth Edition   1993

Published in 1993 by
Sweet & Maxwell Ltd, of
South Quay Plaza, 183 Marsh Wall, London E14 9FT.
Typeset by York House Typographic Ltd., London.
Printed in Great Britain by Butler and Tanner Ltd.,
Frome and London.

No natural forests were destroyed to make this product.
Only farmed timber was used and replanted.

A catalogue record for this book is available from the British Library

ISBN 0421 48320 2

The index was prepared by Patricia Baker.

PREFACE

This book is about the legal relationship between parents and their children and what can go wrong with it. It was originally written mainly for social workers and other people who are professionally concerned with the care of children, but over the years it has also found friends amongst lawyers and law students, and I hope that it will continue to do so. I have tried to write about the law in a way which is accessible and interesting to people who have not studied it before and may even be reluctant to study it now. These aims have not changed since the last edition, but for better or worse the law itself has changed dramatically, and so the whole book had to be re-written. This is mainly the result of the work of the Law Commission and the Review of Child Care Law, which together led to the Children Act 1989, and so I can hardly complain. It was a great privilege to be involved in both those reviews and to have the opportunity of making some contribution to such a fundamental reform of the law. I learned a great deal from everyone else who took part, just as in earlier years I had learned so much from my students and colleagues at Manchester University. I am grateful to everyone who has helped in so many different ways towards the contents of this book: but it is nobody's fault but my own if I have got anything wrong.

Brenda Hoggett

June 1, 1993

CONTENTS

CONTENTS

CONTENTS

TABLE OF CASES

TABLE OF STATUTES

TABLE OF STATUTORY INSTRUMENTS

INTRODUCTION

Most people would probably still define a family as a mother and a father and their children. This unit is still thought to provide the best upbringing for children. All children have physical needs which must at first be supplied by someone else if they are to survive at all and society usually looks to the mother to do this and to the father to protect and support her while she does so. All children also have complex emotional and psychological needs which are usually best supplied if they are brought up throughout their childhood by a couple who are warmly and deeply committed to one another and to their children. Society also has an interest in the welfare of children. Stable, happy children are likely to grow up into stable, happy adults, ready to play their part in society and also to found families of their own. A free society can accept many different styles of family and family life but it depends upon families to bring up the next generation. So parents have responsibilities, not only to their children, but also towards the rest of us.

This book is about these responsibilities. It begins by trying to define what they are, who has them, and how long they last. It then looks at the different sorts of parent, married or unmarried, genetic or social, and how this affects their relationships with their children. After that come the ways in which those relationships can be affected by later events, mainly the separation, divorce, death or remarriage of the parents, but also the intervention of other important individuals in the child's life. But public authorities can also intervene to reinforce parental responsibility. Mainly this is to offer help and services to families who need them, either because the children have special needs or because their families do. The authorities also have to protect the welfare of children looked after away from home and sometimes to remove children from homes where they may otherwise come to harm. And children who themselves cause harm may attract the attention of the criminal law. Finally the authorities may arrange new families for children whose parents are unable to look after them.

Most of this law is now set out in the Children Act 1989. The principles are quite clear and simple. Parents share responsibility for their children and should be left to get on with it until things go wrong or they need help. If things go wrong, most children still need both their parents. Disputes between them should be judged solely by what is best for the child. The wider family can also play an important part. Public authorities should help parents rather than undermine them. But they may need to take over if the children are going to suffer harm. Even so they should try to act in partnership with the family unless and until the children have to be found a new one. But the reason for all this activity is that children are people too, with a right to a voice in decisions about their lives and a developing right to take some of those decisions for themselves.

PART I: PARENTHOOD AND CHILDHOOD

Chapter 1

PARENTAL RESPONSIBILITIES AND CHILDREN'S RIGHTS

It is much easier to define what we mean by a family than it is to define the legal rights and responsibilities of the people in it. Statutes used to mention parental "rights", "powers", or "duties", and now they refer to "parental responsibility", but nowhere does the law provide us with a neat little list of what this contains. The concept of parental responsibility recognises that legal relationships between parents, children and others with an interest in a child's future can never be quite like those between adults. We can assume that parents have some special standing in relation to their children. However, a legal "right" assumes that someone else has a corresponding duty to respect or comply with it and that the courts will always enforce that duty if the right-holder asks. Nowadays, the courts will refuse to force anyone, whether it is another parent, another adult, or even the child himself, to comply with a parent's wishes if this conflicts with the child's best interests. We can also assume that parents owe some special duties towards their children. But who has the right to enforce these? Their whole object is to provide for the upbringing of someone who is not only too young to bring himself up but also too young to force others to do it for him.

The enforcement of parental duties therefore depends mainly on the powers and duties of others to oblige parents to adopt acceptable standards of child care. Sometimes the only way they can do this is by taking over, or even taking the child away. But children are people too and their needs and wishes change and develop as they grow older. The duty of parents and others is to provide the things to which the child is thought to have a right, but the child normally has to accept what others think good for him. Increasingly, however, the law is being asked to decide when a child should be allowed to make his own decisions, whether or not these are not in his own best interests.

Parental responsibility therefore involves a complicated tripartite relationship between parents, children and outsiders, which contains elements of both the private law (governing legal relations between private persons) and the public law (governing legal relations between private persons and state authorities).

5

1. THE LAW'S DEVELOPMENT

Early private law had little interest in how children were brought up. It was designed mainly to serve the dynastic needs of the landed classes and so concentrated on the identification of reliable heirs (through the concept of legitimacy) and the transmission and preservation of property (through succession, guardianship and the control of marriage). Even so, in the eighteenth century, Blackstone (1765) recognised something of the reciprocity of the relationship between generations:

> "The duty of parents to provide for the *maintenance* of their children is a principle of natural law; an obligation . . . laid on them not only by nature herself, but by their own proper act, in bringing them into the world: . . . And thus children will have a perfect *right* of receiving maintenance from their parents. . . . The *power* of parents over their children is derived from the former consideration, their duty; this authority being given them, partly to enable the parent more effectually to perform his duty, and partly as a recompense for his care and trouble in the faithful discharge of it. . . . The *duties* of children to their parents arise from a principle of natural justice and retribution. For to those, who gave us existence, we naturally owe subjection and subsistence during our minority, and honour and reverence ever after; they, who protected the weakness of our infancy are entitled to our protection in the infirmity of their age; . . . "

Blackstone did not suggest that English law was, even then, perfect in its recognition of this contract. He did, however, point out the differences between mothers and fathers:

> " . . . the establishment of marriage in all civilised states is based upon this natural obligation of the father to provide for his children; for that ascertains and makes known the person who is bound to fulfil this obligation: whereas in promiscuous and illicit conjunctions the father is unknown; and the mother finds a thousand obstacles in her way . . . that stifle her inclinations to perform this duty: and besides, she generally wants ability."

That "want of ability" generally applied just as much in marriage. The husband enjoyed a great deal of practical, financial and legal power over his wife and his children. By the early nineteenth century, the courts recognised this by translating it into legal rights which they would enforce against the wife, the child and the outside world in almost every case. Moreover, not only was he the children's sole natural guardian in law, but he could also rule his children from the grave by appointing a testamentary guardian who, although rather more subject to the courts' control, took precedence over the mother. The courts recognised that fathers had corresponding obligations to their children but were baffled by the problem of enforcing them.

Some limits were recognised. A child came of age at 21. *Habeas corpus* would not be issued to help a father regain possession of an unwilling child who had reached the "age of discretion", apparently fixed at 14 for boys and 16 for girls. Although the father had the right of "reasonable chastisement" a child could sue, through a next friend, for injury caused by excessive punishment. The father never became entitled to his child's property and although he had some powers of management, the child could sue for misuse of these. The Court of Chancery, exercising the Crown's powers as *parens patriae* to protect minor children, would usually uphold the father's wishes, but occasionally it might refuse to do so because he had behaved so badly as to forfeit his rights. Children of unmarried parents, of course, having no fathers, were outside the scheme of things and belonged to no-one.

Private law came gradually to recognise both the interests of children and the claims of mothers, but hand in hand with one another. At first, the courts would only grant a mother's claim, even to see her children, if the father had behaved so badly as to forfeit his right to object. Then from 1839 until 1886, statutes extended her rights to apply to the courts for access and even custody and in 1886 she was given guardianship rights after the father's death. From 1857 onwards, the courts also acquired powers to grant divorce, separation and maintenance orders and at the same time to deal with the children of the marriage. In 1925, the courts were expressly told to ignore the question of whether the father's rights were technically superior to those of the mother (or even *vice versa*) and she was given the same rights as him both to act as a guardian after his death and to appoint a guardian to act with him after hers. She had to wait until 1973, however, to be given equal "rights and authority" with the father *before* there was any court order or death. Long before then, the courts had given an unmarried mother much the same position as a married father. Unmarried fathers were first given statutory rights to apply for custody and access in 1959; by 1987 they could apply to be put in the same position as married fathers; and under the Children Act 1989 they can agree to this. They are now in much the same position that married mothers were in before 1973.

Having acquired these powers to intervene between parents, the courts needed a principle upon which to decide disputes. At first, they remained more sympathetic to the father's wishes, not only because of his common law rights but also because Victorian judges believed that he was usually the best judge of what was right for his children. However, they did develop the principle that the child's welfare could *override* his wishes and in 1886 statute required them to put this *first*, before the conduct and wishes of the parents. In 1925, the child's welfare was made the *first and paramount* consideration in any proceedings in any court where a child's custody or upbringing is in question.

That essentially is still the law today. As explained by Lord MacDermott in the leading House of Lords' decision in *J.* v. *C.* [1970] A.C. 668 at 711 (see page 124, below), the welfare of the child is "the first consideration because it is of first importance and the paramount consideration because it rules on or determines the course to be followed". *J. v. C.* also decided that this principle applied, not only to disputes between parents whose claims are equal, but to any dispute about a child's future between private individuals, whether they are parents, relatives, foster parents or, of course, the child himself.

However, the courts are much prone to quoting, and sometimes applying, the well-known words of Lord Templeman in *Re K.D. (A Minor) (Ward: Termination of Access)* [1988] 1 A.C. 806 at 812:

> "The best person to bring up a child is the natural parent. It matters not whether the parent is wise or foolish, rich or poor, educated or illiterate, provided that the child's moral and physical health is not in danger. Public authorities cannot improve on nature."

Where the intervention of public authorities was concerned, the law had developed quite differently. The private law's notions of parental rights had little relevance for families without property, where attempts to enforce parental responsibility were more prominent. The state intervened first through the criminal law, which tried to punish concealment, abandonment and neglect. The object was to prevent children becoming a burden to the public rather than to protect the children themselves. The poor law was the first to provide procedures for forcing parents, including unmarried fathers, to provide for their children. But once the poor law authorities took over the child, they tended to do so at the expense of both the children's welfare and their parents' "rights".

However, just as the private law began to recognise the need of children for tender loving care during the nineteenth century, so the public law became more and more concerned with their protection and their "rights". The control of child labour and the provision of universal education were obviously part of this. The responsibilities of local social services authorities have developed piecemeal from several sources, including the former poor law and health service responsibilities for providing substitute care for children whose parents were unable to provide it themselves; the control of baby-farming and other private arrangements made by parents, and the compulsory supervision or care of children whom the courts had found to be delinquent, troublesome or at risk of harm in their own homes. Each of these had their own criteria and powers of intervention, whether compulsory or voluntary, none of which rested solely upon the child's welfare.

All of this led to a complex rag-bag of statutes in both the private and public law. In private law, there was the underlying common law of paternal guardianship, overlaid with statutory provisions dealing with guardianship and parental rights and with the powers of the courts to rearrange this either in free-standing proceedings about the child's custody, access or mainten-ance, or in proceedings between married parents about their separation or divorce. In the public law, separate statutes dealt with the supervision of private day-care and private fostering, with the provision of substitute care to the needy and to the mentally or physically disabled, with the compulsory care and supervision of those brought before the court in care or criminal proceedings and those caught up in their parents' problems. The main purpose of the Children Act 1989 was to bring all this law together into a single statutory framework which would reflect a coherent set of legal concepts and principles.

2. PARENTAL RESPONSIBILITY

"Parental responsibility" is both the fundamental *concept* of the Children Act 1989 and one of its most important underlying *principles*. The old rule of law that a father is the natural guardian of his legitimate child is abolished (1989 Act, s.2(4)). Where a child's mother and father were married to each other at the time of his birth, they each have parental responsibility for him automatically (s.2(1)). References to a child whose mother and father were (or were not) married to one another "at the time of his birth" have been given a slightly wider meaning by the Family Law Reform Act 1987 (1989 Act, s.2 (3)). The 1987 Act was designed to remove the legal differences between *children* of married and unmarried parents and, in doing so, to avoid using any sort of adjective ("legitimate", "marital" or their opposites) to describe the *child*. However, the 1987 Act did not remove all the differences between the *parents*: it retained the rule, which is now in the 1989 Act, that where a child's mother and father were not married to one another "at the time of his birth", only the mother has parental responsibility automatically, although the Act also provides several ways in which the father may acquire it (1989 Act, s.2(2)). This is all discussed in Chapter 2. Throughout the law, however, it is important to remember that there is a distinction between a "parent" and a "parent with parental responsibility".

Obviously, more than one person may have parental responsibility for a child at the same time (1989 Act, s.2(5)). And a person who has parental responsibility does not stop having it just because someone else acquires it (1989 Act, s.2(6)). Thus, the mother does not lose her responsibility just because the father has it or is later given it too; nor do either of them lose responsibility when a third party is given it as a result of an order that the child is to live with him or to go into care. Unlike parents, however, third parties, whether they are private individuals or local authorities, only have parental responsibility for as long as the order giving it to them lasts (1989 Act, ss.12(2), 33(3)(a)). Parents with parental responsibility, on the other hand, can only lose it altogether if the child dies, or leaves the family through being adopted or freed for adoption (see Chapter 12), or reaches the age of majority, which is now 18 (Family Law Reform Act 1969, s.1), although exceptionally an unmarried father can revert from being a "parent with parental responsibility" to being simply a "parent" (see Chapter 2).

Where more than one person has parental responsibility for a child, each of them may act alone and without the other (or others) in meeting that responsibility (1989 Act, s.2(7)). This crucial rule is designed to allow each parent, but particularly the one with whom the child lives or who is doing most of the work of looking after and bringing up the child, to carry out that work and make decisions without having to consult or get the consent of the other parent. The other parent can, of course, object, but if he does so, and there is a dispute, it is the parent who wishes to prevent something being done who must take the matter to court, rather than the other way about. The Law Commission (1988) thought this the most sensible and practical way to ensure that children were properly looked after, but others would prefer there to be a duty to consult or even obtain consent on major issues.

In any case, there are two general qualifications to the rule allowing independent action. First, it does not affect any statutory provision requiring the consent of more than one person in a matter affecting the child, for example to his marriage or adoption (1989 Act, s.2(7)). Secondly, the fact that a person has parental responsibility does not entitle him to act in any way which would be incompatible with an order about the child made under the 1989 Act (1989 Act, s.2(8)). So, if there is an order that the child is to live with his mother, his father cannot send him away to boarding school; or if there is an order that the child is to go to a particular school, the mother cannot change this unilaterally.

A person cannot surrender or transfer any part of his parental responsibility to someone else (1989 Act, s.2(9)). He can of course arrange for another person to meet some or all of it on his behalf (1989 Act, s.2(9)), and that other person could be someone who already has parental responsibility (1989 Act, s.2(10)); but making such arrangements does not affect any liability which he may have for failing to meet his own responsibility for the child (1989 Act, s.2(11); see 3. (iii) below). So, for example, a parent may still be liable for neglecting his child if he chooses an inadequate child-minder or baby-sitter.

But if someone does not have parental responsibility, this does not mean that he cannot do anything to help the child. Anyone who has care of a child may do what is reasonable in all the circumstances to safeguard or promote the child's welfare (1989 Act, s.3(5)). Obviously, it is not reasonable for a baby-sitter to arrange major surgery without consulting the parents, but it is reasonable to call the doctor or go to casualty if an accident happens. People with actual care of a child have the same criminal liability for ill-treating, abandoning or neglecting the child as parents do (see 3. (iii) below). They also have to educate him properly (see 3. (vii) below); but they do not have the same duty to go on looking after him, or to see that others do so.

3. BUT WHAT IS PARENTAL RESPONSIBILITY?

So far, the rules about "parental responsibility" are almost exactly the same as the rules about "parental rights" before the Act. And "parental responsibility" means "all the rights, duties, powers, responsibility and authority which by law a parent of a child has in relation to the child and his property"

(1989 Act, s.3(1)). There is still no neat little list of these, so in a moment we shall have to do our best to devise one. But why change from rights to responsibilities at all? There were several reasons.

One was to reflect the philosophy, outlined in the passage from Blackstone quoted earlier, and adopted by Lord Scarman in *Gillick* v. *West Norfolk and Wisbech Area Health Authority* [1986] A.C. 112 at 184:

"The principle of the law . . . is that parental rights are derived from parental duty and exist only so long as they are needed for the protection of the person and property of the child."

If so, the responsibilities of parents are the reason for any rights they have and the law's language should reflect this. The Scottish Law Commission (1992) prefers to refer to both responsibilities and rights but the English (1988) preferred to emphasise the first. Does it matter?

Another reason was to reflect the everyday reality of parenthood. Bringing up a child can be a great joy and delight; but it also involves a great deal of practical work, in feeding, washing, clothing, stimulating, educating, supervising, controlling and generally safeguarding the child from harm. The parent will think first of her responsibility to do these things, rather than her "right" to choose how to do them. Although she undoubtedly has that right, it is only within the limits set by society and the law.

If parental "responsibility" reflects both the philosophy and the reality of the relationship between parent and child, it also reflects both the philosophy and reality of the relationship between parents and the rest of society. Parental responsibility is owed, not only to children, but also to society. We expect parents to bring up their own children and, so long as they meet our expectations to a reasonable standard, we will respect their right to do so. But we do interfere in a number of ways to help or persuade them to meet their responsibilities, and we will only relieve parents of the whole burden in the most extreme circumstances.

Thus "parental responsibility" refers the collection of tasks, activities and choices which are part and parcel of looking after and bringing up a child. Hence, having, or not having, parental responsibility does not affect (a) any legal obligation in relation to the child (such as a statutory liability to maintain the child) or (b) any rights which, in the event of the child's death, he or any other person may have in relation to the child's property (1989 Act, s.3(4)). In other words, the liability to support a child financially and any rights of succession or inheritance to this estate are not part of parental responsibility. But what does it consist of?

(i) Before birth

The extent of the parents' responsibilities towards their as yet unborn children is by no means clear. There are complex conflicts of interest between mother and child which require very careful consideration. The criminal law gives the child some protection against deliberate killing. Once the unborn child is "capable of being born alive", it is an offence intentionally to cause the child's death before he has an existence independent of his mother, except where this is done in good faith in order to save the mother's life (Infant Life (Preservation) Act 1929, s.1(1)). This indicates that the mother's life takes priority over the child's and also that doctors may take steps to protect the mother's health even at some risk to the baby, provided that there is no intention that the baby should die.

Where an unborn child is not capable of being born alive, of course, the pregnancy may be terminated if the risk to the mother's life or health would be greater in letting it continue (Abortion Act 1967, s.1(1)(a)). Neither a married nor an unmarried father has the right to prevent a mother from having a lawful abortion (*Paton* v. *British Pregnancy Advisory Service Trustees* [1979] Q.B. 276; *C.* v. *S.* [1988] Q.B. 135, C.A.). Otherwise, an unborn child is not a person with legal rights and status until he is born (or, it now seems, on the point of birth).

Once born, however, he may sue for injuries wrongfully caused before his birth. A father may be sued just like any other person for causing harm, but a mother may only be sued for injuries caused by careless driving during pregnancy and not, for example, by drug-taking or refusing medical treatment (Congenital Disabilities (Civil Liability) Act 1976). Further an unborn child cannot be made a ward of court so as to protect him from the harm which his mother's behaviour may do to him (*Re F.* (*in Utero*) [1988] Fam. 122, C.A.). However, the High Court has granted permission for a baby to be delivered by caesarian section against the mother's will in a case where it was certain that not only the baby but also the mother would otherwise die (*Re S.* (*Adult: Refusal of Treatment*) [1993] Fam.123; see also Lord Donaldson M.R. in *Re T.* (*Adult: Refusal of Treatment*) [1993] Fam.95, C.A.). It seems unlikely that the courts would develop this highly controversial principle much, if at all, further without legislation.

(ii) Name

It is a parental responsibility to register the child's birth within six weeks (Births and Deaths Registration Act 1953, s.2) and in doing so to state the name by which it is intended that the child will be known. Unlike many countries, we have no rules about family names; an adult's name is that by which is generally known and it is for the parents to choose the surname by which their child is known. It used to be said that this was an aspect of the father's common law guardianship (*Re T.* (*orse H.*) (*An Infant*) [1963] Ch. 238) but it must now be a matter for which there is equal parental responsibility. Each parent is therefore free to make a choice and disputes can be decided (by a specific issue or prohibited steps order) according to what is best for the child. The same applies to changes of name. However, problems are most likely to arise if the parents are separated or divorced and the parent with whom the child lives adopts a new surname which she wishes the child to share or if the child goes into care and lives with a foster family for a long time. The 1989 Act provides that, where there is a residence order or a care order in force, no person may cause the child to be known by a new surname without either the written consent of every person who has parental respons- ibility or the leave of the court (1989 Act, ss.13(1)(a),33(7)(a)). The courts' approach is discussed in Chapters 6 and 7.

(iii) Care and upbringing

Parents are responsible for looking after their children, either personally or by arrangement with others. The offence of "cruelty to a child" imposes criminal liability for abandonment, neglect or ill-treatment upon any person of 16 or over who is "responsible" for a person under 16 (Children and Young Persons Act 1933, s.1(1)). Anyone who has parental responsibility for the child or is otherwise legally liable to maintain him is not only presumed to be responsible for this purpose (1933 Act, s.17(1)(a)) but does not stop being responsible simply because he does not have care of the child (1933 Act, s.17(2)). Carers are also responsible (1933 Act, s. 17(1)(b)), but cease to be so once they no longer have care.

The defendant must be shown to have wilfully assaulted, ill-treated, neglected, abandoned or exposed the child. These are not watertight compartments and a particular case could be described in more than one way. Conduct of all five types must have been "in a manner likely to cause unnecessary suffering or injury to health". This can define what is meant by "exposes" but it also limits the scope of, say, abandonment if the child is left with people or in a place where no harm is likely to come to him. But the fact that harm which was likely has been prevented by the act of someone else is no defence (1933 Act, s.1(3)(a)). A parent or other person legally liable to maintain is deemed to have neglected the child in a manner likely to cause unnecessary suffering or injury to health if he has failed to provide the child with adequate food, clothing, medical aid or lodging, or being unable to do so, has failed to seek the assistance of the state (1933 Act s.1(2)(a)). Parents cannot, therefore, escape their responsibility to see that their children's basic needs are met, if not by them then by someone else.

However, the conduct must be "wilful". A person accused of neglect or ill- treatment must have been aware of the risk of harm to the child or simply not have cared about any possible danger. In *R.* v. *Sheppard* [1981] A.C. 394, the majority of the House of Lords rejected the idea that this should be an offence of strict liability to be judged on the objective standard of the "reasonable parent". Criminal penalties are there to deter, and they cannot deter people who have genuinely not foreseen the harm which their conduct may cause. An ignorant or inadequate parent may therefore have a defence. However, a parent who is well aware of the risk but takes it because of a sincere religious belief, for example that medical aid is sinful, has no defence (*R.* v. *Senior* [1899] 1 Q.B. 283).

Whatever the offence charged, if the prosecution cannot prove how the child came to harm or which parent was responsible, then both must be acquitted (*R.* v. *Lane and Lane* (1985) 82 Cr.App.R. 5). The best way of avoiding liability for this or any other crime against a child who is dead or unable to speak for himself is to refuse to give any explanations at all. Some people think the "right to silence" should be removed in such cases. Sometimes, however, it can be shown that they must have acted together, even if one caused the injuries and the other encouraged or failed to protect the child when she could reasonably have done so (*Marsh and Another* v. *Hodgson* [1974] Crim.L.R. 35).

These problems do not arise in care proceedings, which are designed to protect the child from harm (see further in Chapter 10). Parents may also be held liable in damages to their children if they cause them harm by failing to take the care of them that a reasonable parent would take, and the child can usually sue within three years of reaching 18, but such proceedings are hardly ever brought. As Sir Nicholas Browne-Wilkinson said in *Surtees* v. *Kingston-upon-Thames Royal Borough Council*, [1991] F.L.R. 559, C.A.

"the responsibilities of a parent, normally the mother, looking after children in addition to a myriad other duties far exceeded those of other members of society. The court should be slow to characterise as negligent the care which ordinary loving and caring mothers were able to give to children, given the rough and tumble of home life."

In return, the parents' claim to look after their children does receive some protection from the criminal law. It is an offence for a non-parent to remove or keep a child under 16 from the "lawful control" of the person entitled to it, but only if this is done without lawful authority or reasonable excuse (Child Abduction Act 1984, s.2). Refuges for runaways may be given exemption by the Secretary of State for Health (see Chapter 8). Parents no longer have the right to sue others for damages for enticing away or harbouring their children or any other interference with their parental "rights" (Law Reform (Miscellaneous Provisions) Act 1970, s.5; see *F.* v. *Wirral Metropolitan Borough Council* [1991] Fam.69; *Re S. (Minor) (Parental Rights)*, *The Times*, March 30, 1993). They may resort to self-help to recover a child from a third party, but if they have to use legal procedures the courts will only support them if it is in the child's best interests to do so.

The child also has a voice in this. Lord Denning described the parents' claim as a "dwindling right which the court will hesitate to enforce against the wishes of a child, the older he is" (*Hewer* v. *Bryant* [1970] 1 Q.B. 357, C.A.). The House of Lords took the same view in *Gillick* v. *West Norfolk and Wisbech Area Health Authority* [1986] A.C. 112. Under the Children Act 1989, the court must not make residence or other private law orders in respect of children who have reached 16, or provide for orders to continue beyond that age, unless the circumstances are exceptional (1989 Act, s.9(6),(7)). Care proceedings remain possible until the age of 17 and a child may be made a ward of court until 18. In practice, therefore, a child may leave home at 16, unless he is or is likely to come to harm. Under the

Children Act 1989, he may also ask the court's leave to apply for an order about his upbringing (see 5. below).

(iv) Discipline

It is a parental responsibility to set reasonable boundaries to a child's behaviour and to attempt to maintain these. Parents may be called to account for the criminal behaviour of a child aged 10 or more (see further in Chapter 11) and care proceedings may be brought if a child is or is likely to suffer significant harm because he is beyond parental control (see further in Chapter 10). This responsibility is still reflected in the parental right to administer "lawful chastisement". This is a defence, not only to the offence of cruelty under the Children and Young Persons Act 1933 (1933 Act, s.1(7)) but also to any other offence against the child's person, as well as to civil liability.

However, the punishment must be most moderate and reasonable and perceptions of what is reasonable have undoubtedly changed. It is no defence that the parent comes from a different country or culture in which harsher punishments are acceptable (*R.* v. *Derriviere* (1969) 53 Cr.App.R. 637). The punishment must have been imposed for a good reason, that is because the parent genuinely believed that the child had broken a fair and reasonable rule; it must be in proportion to the child's "offence"; it must take into account the child's age, understanding and physique; and it must not be imposed for an ulterior motive, such as the "gratification of passion or of rage" (*R.* v. *Hopley* (1860) 175 E.R. 1027) or perverted sexuality. This concept of punishment should probably be distinguished from the equally lawful physical restraint which is necessary to save a very young or handicapped child from danger or to teach him to save himself.

This still leaves the law in an uncertain and to many an unacceptable state. The Scottish Law Commission (1992) considered the psychological evidence and competing arguments and opinions with some care. They concluded that "it would be going too far to criminalise ordinary safe smacks of the sort occasionally resorted to by many thousands of normal affectionate parents" (para. 2.95) but recommended that it should be unlawful to strike a child with a stick, belt or other object or in such a way as to cause, or to risk causing, injury, or in such a way as to cause, or to risk causing, pain or discomfort lasting more than a very short time. Interestingly, Penelope Leach had argued in her evidence that the sort of moderate punishment allowed by the law and practised by many parents was particularly likely to be ineffective. No such proposals have yet been made in English law, and not all corporal punishment is severe enough to be condemned as "degrading punishment" under Article 3 of the European Convention on Human Rights (*Costello-Roberts* v. *United Kingdom, The Times*, March 26, 1993, E.C.H.R.). However, judicially ordered corporal punishment has been held degrading (*Tyrer* v. *United Kingdom* (1978–79) 2 E.H.R.R. 1) and corporal punishment is now prohibited in all state schools (Education (No. 2) Act 1986, s.47), in all residential homes for children and in local authority foster placements (see further in Chapter 8).

(v) Medical treatment

It is a parental responsibility to provide adequate medical aid for a child. Failure to do so may result in criminal liability (see (iii) above) and in proceedings to ensure that the child is given the treatment he needs. In an extreme case where it is necessary for the local authority to have parental responsibility, this could be by care proceedings. Usually a specific issue order will be more appropriate (*Re H.G. (Specific Issue Order: Sterilisation)* [1993] 1 F.L.R. 589; *Re R. (A Minor) (Blood Transfusion), The Independent,* June 9, 1993; *cf. Re O. (A Minor) (Medical Treatment), The Times,* March 19, 1993). A private individual may make the child a ward of court and a local authority may invoke the inherent jurisdiction if a specific issue order is not available (see further in Chapters 4 and 10). In an emergency or where the parents have disappeared or abandoned the child, doctors may proceed without either the parent's or the child's consent (*Gillick* v. *West Norfolk and Wisbech Area Health Authority* [1986] A.C. 112).

Normally, of course, parents consent to their children's treatment. Consent is usually required to medical treatment, not because it would otherwise be an invasion of the parents' rights, but because it would be an invasion of the rights of the child. This means that a child who is old enough to understand a treatment proposal may give his own consent to it, at least if it is designed for his benefit and not for other purposes, such as research or the benefit of others. By statute, the consent of a 16-year-old is as good as if he were 18 (Family Law Reform Act 1969, s.8(1)) and a 16-year-old may be informally admitted for psychiatric treatment without reference to his parents (Mental Health Act 1983, s.131(2)). The 1969 Act does not affect the validity of any other consent (1969 Act, s.8(3)) and a younger child who is capable of understanding fully what is proposed may give his own consent, at least to treatment which is in his best interests (*Gillick*, above).

But while a capable child can override his parents' objections to treatment, it is more doubtful whether his objections can override the parents' consent. Lord Scarman in the *Gillick* case said that the parents' right to decide whether or not their child should have treatment ends if and when the child becomes mature enough to decide for himself. Recently, however, the courts have held that they have power, as part of their inherent parental jurisdiction, to override the child's objections even when he does have sufficient understanding and has reached 16. They will start with a preference for respecting his views, but will not allow him to die, or probably to suffer serious harm, through lack of treatment, especially if his illness is distorting his judgment (*Re W. (A Minor) (Medical Treatment: Court's Jurisdiction)* [1993] Fam.64, C.A.; see also *Re R. (A Minor) (Wardship: Medical Treatment)* [1992] Fam.11, C.A.). Lord Donaldson M.R. has gone further and said that a person with parental responsibility can also override the child's views (and see *Re K., W. and H. (Minors) (Consent to Treatment)* [1993] 1 F.C.R. 240). It is an unattractive prospect that parents might have power to oblige a capable child to accept forcible treatment against his will and without any of the safeguards attached either to legal proceedings or to the procedures under the Mental Health Act 1983.

But the courts may also prevent parents from taking a treatment decision. Thus in *Re D. (A Minor) (Wardship: Sterilisation)* [1976] Fam.185, an educational psychologist made a child a ward of court in order to challenge the decision of a mother and a paediatrician that an 11-year-old girl should be sterilised. She suffered from sotos' syndrome, a rare congenital handicap which might affect her capacities as a mother, and she was fast approaching puberty. The judge held that the operation was not in the child's best interests; it would deprive her of a normal adult life when it was not yet known how severely her handicap would affect her and she would suffer no immediate harm if the operation were not performed. In *Re B. (A Minor) (Wardship: Sterilisation)* [1988] A.C. 199, the House of Lords allowed a severely handicapped 17-year-old girl to be sterilised. However, Lord Templeman thought sterilisation so drastic that it could only be done with the leave of a High Court judge. If so, it could be argued that sterilisation, at least for contraceptive rather than for therapeutic purposes (the latter to not require leave: *Re E. (A Minor) (Medical Treatment)* [1991] 2 F.L.R. 585), falls outside the scope of parental responsibility, but this was not accepted in *Re H.G.*, p. 16 above. The court cannot, however, order a doctor to treat a child in a manner inconsistent with his clinical judgment (see *Re J. (A Minor) (Child in Care: Medical Treatment)* [1993] Fam. 15, C.A.).

(vi) Leaving the country

It is a parental responsibility to decide whether a child may leave the country (which for this purpose means the United Kingdom), either temporarily or permanently. The Crown requires the consent of a parent before issuing a passport to a child under 16. However, the normal power of independent action is modified in several ways.

First, under section 1(1) of the Child Abduction Act 1984, it is a criminal offence for a "person connected" (which means a parent or person with parental responsibility; 1984 Act, s.1(2)) with a child under 16 to take or send the child out of the country without the appropriate consent. This means the consent of each other person with parental responsibility or the leave of the court (1984 Act, s.1(3)). However, it is not an offence if;

(a) the connected person believes that a person whose consent is required either has consented or would do so if aware of all the relevant circumstances, or;

(b) he has taken all reasonable steps to communicate with the other but been unable to do so, or;

(c) the other has unreasonably refused to consent (1984 Act, s.1(5)).

Secondly, if the child is the subject of a residence order or a care order under the Children Act 1989, no-one may remove him from the country without either the written consent of every person who has parental responsibility for him or the leave of the court (1989 Act, ss.13(1)(*b*), 33(7)(*b*); when the court makes a residence order it can give the required leave either generally or for specified purposes; 1989 Act, s.13(3)); however, this rule does not prevent the person in whose favour the residence order is made, or the local authority in whose care the child is, from removing him for a period of less than one month (1989 Act, ss.13(2), 33(8)(a); unless, of course, the court has specifically prevented this) and in that case there is no offence under the Child Abduction Act 1984 (1984 Act, s.1(4)).

The object of all this is to prevent even parents with parental responsibility snatching their children and taking them out of the other parent's reach. The exception for people with residence orders is to allow them to take the child abroad on short holidays and trips without having to get the other parent's agreement or return to court. The rules can always be modified by the court if the circumstances warrant it. Their approach to disputes between parents is discussed in Chapter 4.

Child abduction is undoubtedly a serious and growing problem. When a child is wrongfully taken or kept out of this country, it may be possible to recover him summarily through the central authorities if he has been taken to another country which is a party either to the Hague Convention on Child Abduction (which is concerned with abduction in breach of custody rights generally) or to the European Convention on the Enforcement of Orders concerning Children (which is concerned with the reciprocal enforcement of court orders). In turn, however, a child who has been brought here in such circumstances may have to be returned to the country from which he was taken. The operation of these Conventions (provided for in the Child Abduction and Custody Act 1985) is outside the scope of this book. If they do not apply, the only remedy is to take action in the country to which the child has gone.

If a child is in compulsory care, the local authority also has power to arrange for him to live outside England and Wales (Children Act 1989, s.33(8)(b); Sched. 2, para. 19), but only if the court approves. The court can only approve the arrangement if it is in the child's best interests to live outside England and Wales, suitable arrangements have been made for him in the country to which he is to go, the child himself consents to living in that country (or if he lacks the understanding to decide, if he is to live in that country with a parent, guardian or other suitable person), and every person with parental responsibility has either given his consent or cannot be found, is incapable of consenting or is withholding his consent unreasonably. Where a child is being looked after by a local authority but is not in compulsory care, the authority may arrange for him to live outside England and Wales provided that every person with parental responsibility approves.

These provisions may appear elaborate and even unnecessary in the case of children who have been effectively abandoned in care by their parents. However, there is a long and often unhappy history, which continued until surprisingly recently, of voluntary organisations and some local authorities arranging the emigration of children in their care, generally to Canada, Australia or Southern Africa (Wagner, 1981; Bean and Melville, 1988).

It is important to notice the distinction between taking a child out of the United Kingdom and taking the child out of England and Wales. Scotland and

Northern Ireland are separate jurisdictions with different courts and legal systems. However, the law generally allows children to be taken there because there is now machinery for each country to recognise and enforce the orders made in the other (Family Law Act 1986, Pt. I).

(vii) Education

It is a parental responsibility to educate the child properly. If he is of compulsory school age, parents have a duty to cause him to receive efficient full-time education suitable to his age, ability, and aptitude and to any special educational needs he may have. (Education Act 1944, s.36), whether by going to school or in other ways. "Parent" in this context includes, not only everyone with parental responsibility, but also anyone with care of the child disregarding temporary absences, for example in hospital or at boarding school (1944 Act, s.114 (1D),(1E)).

The present provisions for enforcing school attendance (1944 Act, ss.37, 39, 40; Education Act 1980, ss.10, 11) will soon be replaced by the very similar provisions in the Education Bill 1993, Pt. IV. Briefly, the local education authority (L.E.A.) may require a parent to satisfy them that the child is being suitably educated, whether by regularly attending school "or otherwise"; if not satisfied, they can make a school attendance order, requiring the parent to register the child at a particular school or schools; however, they must first give notice allowing the parent to try to find a preferable school which is prepared to have the child; that school will then be named in the order. A parent who disobeys a school attendance order is guilty of an offence unless he can show that the child is indeed being suitably educated outside school. A parent also commits an offence if a registered pupil fails to attend school regularly, whether this is the parent's or the child's fault, for example because he has been excluded for arriving late or breaking school rules. The only excuses are days set aside for religious observance, or where the authority does not provide transport (or boarding or a different school) for children living outside walking distance, or where the child is sick, has leave of absence, or is prevented by some "unavoidable cause"; but this must affect the child, not the parents. Older girls cannot be kept at home to look after the family when the mother is ill, at work, or away (*Jenkins* v. *Howells* [1949] 2 K.B. 218).

Instead of, or even as well as, prosecuting the parent, the L.E.A. may seek an education supervision order, on the ground that a child of compulsory school age is not being properly educated (1989 Act, s.36(3)). This is assumed if there is a breach of a school attendance order or failure to attend regularly, unless the contrary is proved (1989 Act, s.36(4)). The L.E.A. must first consult the social services department, and an order cannot be made if the child is in care (1989 Act, s.36(6),(8)). The order places the child under the supervision of the L.E.A. (1989 Act, s.36(1)). The supervisor must advise, assist, befriend and direct both the child and his parents so as to secure that the child is properly educated (1989 Act, Sched. 3, Pt. III). The parents must tell the supervisor the child's address and allow him reasonable contact with the child (the order may also require the child to do this). The parents' rights and duties under the 1944 Act (and 1993 Bill) are then replaced by a duty to obey the supervisor's directions; persistent failure is a criminal offence, unless the parent can show that he tried to comply, or the direction was unreasonable, or incompatible with a requirement contained in an ordinary supervision order with which he has complied. The order lasts initially for a year but can be extended for periods of up to three years at a time, ending when the child reaches school leaving age or goes into care.

If the child persistently fails to comply with the supervisor's directions, the L.E.A. must tell social services who must then investigate (1989 Act, Sched. 3, para. 19). They might then bring care proceedings and in really bad cases of truancy or school refusal, or where educational problems are a symptom of wider difficulties in the family, a care order may be appropriate at the outset (see *Re O. (A Minor)* (*Care Proceedings: Education*) [1992] 1 W.L.R. 912). But one aim of the 1989 Act was to stop social services departments being used to pick up the pieces after the schools and education authorities had failed, so it is for them and not the L.E.A. to decide whether or not to apply.

In return, sufficient and suitable schools must be made available for all the children in the area (the 1993 Bill allows the Secretary of State for Education to transfer all or some of this responsibility in a particular area from the L.E.A to the new funding authority). The authorities must also have regard to the general principle that, so far as efficient education and use of public money allow, children are to be educated in accordance with their parents' wishes (1944 Act, s.76). This does not give the parent the right to insist on being provided with what he wants (*Watt* v. *Kesteven County Council* [1955] 1 Q.B. 408); instead, parents have to be given an opportunity of expressing a choice, together with information to help them make it. The authority must respect that choice, unless it prejudices efficient education or use of resources, or it is incompatible with the admission procedures for that school, or they have chosen a selective school for which the child is not qualified. Parents have a right of appeal to an appeal committee, against their child's allocation to, or refusal by, a particular school (Education Act 1980, ss.6 to 8, Sched. 2). The committee has to balance the parents' wishes against the L.E.A.'s prescribed admission policies, but otherwise there are no fixed criteria and the authority is bound by the committee's decision.

Children with special educational needs should normally be educated in ordinary schools (Education Act 1981, s.2). The 1993 Bill, Pt.III, contains a new system for assessing and providing for special educational needs. The L.E.A. will have a duty to identify and assess those children for whom it is necessary for the authority to determine the special educational provision called for by any learning difficulty they may have. If after assessment it proves necessary to do so, the authority must make a statement of the child's needs and of the provision to be made for him. Unless the parents make suitable arrangements themselves, the authority must then make that provision. Parents will be able to appeal to a special educational needs tribunal against a refusal to make an assessment if they ask, or a refusal to make a statement, or the content of the statement itself. It is not appropriate to make the child a ward of court for this purpose (*Re D. (A Minor)* [1987] 1 W.L.R. 1400, C.A.).

Thus children have the right to some education, but parents have the right to choose how to educate them, within the limits of what the local schools and education authorities are prepared to offer or what they can afford to pay. Although the state is allowed to prescribe the elements of a national curriculum, under Article 2 of the First Protocol to the European Commission on Human Rights, it must respect the right of parents to ensure that their children's education conforms to their own religious and philosophical convictions. Parents who are fighting for the best school available at public expense will have their case decided by the local appeal committee; parents who are fighting for provision for their child's special educational needs will soon have this decided by the special educational needs tribunal; and parents who are fighting to educate their children at home will usually have this decided by the local magistrates' courts, either in criminal or in family proceedings. If parents are fighting between themselves, their choices will still be confined to what is on offer and what they can afford, but the court will make a specific issue order (see Chapter 4) on the basis of what will be best for the child.

(viii) Religion

Freedom of religion, like freedom of education, plays an important part in the diversity of life-styles and beliefs which is the hall-mark of a free society. Parents have no legal responsibility to bring their children up in any religious faith, although they may choose to do so. The authorities can only intervene, in criminal or civil proceedings, if the parents' choice of religion causes or is likely to cause harm to the child; a blood transfusion will be authorised for a Jehovah's Witness but circumcision of a Jewish boy will not be prevented. However, social services authorities must give "due consideration" to the child's religious persuasion, racial origin and cultural and linguistic background when making any decision about a child they are or are proposing to look after (Children Act 1989, s.22(5)(c))) and a care order gives them no right to cause the child to be brought up in a different religion from the one in which he would otherwise have been reared (1989 Act, s. 33(6)(a)). A parent can no longer impose a religious condition upon her agreement to adoption, but adoption agencies must so far as possible respect her wishes when choosing a placement for the child (Adoption Act 1976, s.7). When parents or others are in dispute about what the child's religion should be, the courts will decide what is in the child's best interests. They will rarely disturb a settled faith that the child has acquired. Hence the law respects the child's right to practise his own religion, rather than the parents' right to pass their own on to him, even if in practice this usually amounts to the same thing.

(ix) Finance and property

Parents are responsible for maintaining their children, although the state gives them some help towards this. Usually, they meet their responsibility by providing a home for the child, rather than by paying others to look after him. But payment may be required if they are living apart from one another or from the child. As we have seen, financial liability can exist independently of parental responsibility. Under the Child Support Act 1991, both parents, whether or not they have parental responsibility, are liable to support their children. This will be assessed and enforced through the Child Support Agency, leaving only a residual jurisdiction for the courts, and both parents will be expected to cooperate in enforcing one another's liabilities (see further in Chapter 4).

Parents have no claim on any money or property which belongs to their child, but they have some power to administer his assets and his income, and the duty to do so honestly and carefully. Parental responsibility now includes all the powers of a guardian of the child's estate, which includes the power to give a valid receipt, for example for legacies (Children Act 1989, s.3(2),(3)). Quite how much control this gives them over what the child does with his own money or property is not clear. Where the child has substantial assets, of course, it is usual for these to be held by trustees for his benefit until he grows up. Occasionally, however, the child will receive a gift, legacy or compensation which it would not be proper for the parent to receive and administer on his behalf. Although guardianship of the estate has generally been abolished, it may become possible for the Official Solicitor to be appointed such a guardian for this limited purpose (1989 Act, s.5(11),(12); see page 101, below).

(x) Representation

The rules of court normally insist that civil litigation be conducted by someone else on a child's behalf and parents are usually responsible for doing this, acting as next friend on behalf of a child plaintiff or applicant and as guardian *ad litem* on behalf of a child defendant or respondent. However, the court is able to appoint someone else and parents cannot represent their children in cases where there is a conflict of interest between them. The most important example of this is in care proceedings, where there is a special system of qualified guardians *ad litem* to represent the child (see further in Chapter 10).

(xi) Marriage

It is a parental responsibility to decide whether a child of 16 or 17 should be allowed to marry. Marriages by people under 16 in this country (or elsewhere if they are domiciled here) are absolutely void (Matrimonial Causes Act 1973, s.11(a)(ii)). If a child is 16 or 17, but not a widow or widower, the consent (or, in the case of a Church of England marriage to be solemnised after banns, the absence of dissent) of each parent with parental responsibility and each guardian is generally required; however, if there is a residence order in force then the consent of each person with the benefit of the residence order is required instead; and if there is a care order in force, the consent of the local authority is required in addition to the parents' and guardians' consent (Marriage Act 1949, s.3(1),(1A),(2)). In the case of a marriage to be solemnised after publication of banns, it is enough that none of these people actively objected (1949 Act, s.3(3),(4)).

The Registrar (or ecclesiastical authority) may dispense with the consent of a person who is absent, inaccessible or incapable (1949 Act, s.3(1)(a)). If consent is refused, the child can apply to the High Court, a county court or a family proceedings court for permission to marry (1949 Act, s.3(1)(b)). Most applications are made to magistrates' courts and, while it appears that most are successful, it is not known what criteria the courts use; no doubt they will do their best, but is this a matter of "upbringing" in which the child's welfare is the paramount consideration (see 1989 Act, s.1(1))? In any case, it is not impossible to get married without the required consent and such marriages are valid, although there may be criminal penalties for lying to a Registrar. Making the child a ward of court automatically brings with it a prohibition on the child's marriage, which it is a contempt of court to disobey; but if the couple succeed in doing so, the court may hesitate to make matters worse by sending either of them to prison. Some might think that the consent requirement (which does not exist in Scotland) serves no useful purpose, but the Government did not accept the Law Commission's (1988) proposal to abolish it.

4. HOW DOES PARENTAL RESPONSIBILITY END?

Parents remain responsible until their children reach 18, although the extent to which they can meet it may be severely limited by court orders and by the child's own developing power to decide for himself. It only comes completely to an end when the child or the parent dies or the child is adopted or freed for adoption.

Parents may feel that it is part of their responsibility to provide for their children's upbringing in the event of their death. Under the 1989 Act a parent with parental responsibility may appoint another individual to be the child's guardian after the parent's death and a guardian may also do so (1989 Act, s.5(3)(4); see further in Chapter 5). However, other people with parental responsibility, such as relatives with residence orders or local authorities with children in care, have no power to appoint a guardian (1989 Act, ss.12(3)(c), 33(6)(b)(iii)). It is, therefore, a means of transmitting parental responsibility rather than an aspect of responsibility as such.

Similarly, parents with parental responsibility may decide whether or not their child is to be adopted or freed for adoption, although their agreement may be dispensed with in certain circumstances (see further in Chapter 12). This is also part of a guardian's responsibilities. It is not, however, a responsibility which is assumed by non-parents or local authorities when a residence order or care order is made in their favour (1989 Act, ss.12(3)(a),(b), 33(6)(b)(i)(ii)). Once again, therefore, this is part of a method of transmitting parental responsibility than an aspect of that responsibility itself.

5. CHILDREN'S RIGHTS

The discussion of parental responsibility also illustrates quite clearly the different categories of children's rights. The first category, and for much of their childhood the most important category, consists of what are sometimes known as "rights of recipience" or welfare rights. These are rights to be provided with goods or services which they are unable to provide for themselves. Children have the right to have their basic needs for food, shelter, clothing and medical aid met, to be protected from significant harm, and to receive a full-time education during their school years. It is, of course, the parents' responsibility to see that all this is provided and it is also the parents' responsibility to decide how much further they will go beyond the minimum standard of "good enough" parenting and material support that the law requires.

But society, in the shape of the law and public authorities, also accepts responsibility for its children, in several ways. In the first place, society lays down the minimum standards of what can be expected of parents and these are obviously changing all the time. Secondly, society accepts that some things, principally education and health care, should be provided for children at public expense, whether or not their parents can afford them, although we retain the right of parents who can afford to do so to make alternative private provision if they wish. Thirdly, it is accepted that if parents cannot provide properly for their children, society must help them to do so, initially by providing financial and other assistance for children living with their families but if need be by providing them with an alternative home, whether temporarily or permanently. This includes removing children, compulsorily if need be, from homes where they are at risk of significant harm. Finally, society accepts that we all have a responsibility, greater than that which we have towards adults, to refrain from harming children. Hence we have laws prohibiting or restricting child labour, and protecting them from sexual exploitation and a number of other activities, such as drinking and smoking, which we are prepared to tolerate in adults.

But as the whole point of this is to enable children to develop into healthy adult members of society, we also have to recognise that children are human beings with their own wishes and feelings. When should the law accept that children have the same freedom to make their own decisions as is enjoyed by adults? In this respect, unlike the earlier type of rights, children cannot expect to have any more rights than adults do and in some respects they may have fewer. The greatest restriction on anyone's freedom is the limited number of choices in fact available to him.

This can readily be illustrated by the recent cases concerning children who wish to "divorce" their parents. The Children Act 1989 has done several things to recognise the child's status as a person in his own right. First, a child who has sufficient understanding to make an application for an order about his upbringing may be given leave to do so (1989 Act, s.10(1)(a)(ii), (2),(8); see further in Chapter 4). He may ask for an order about where he is to live,

---

whom he should visit, stay with or otherwise be allowed to have contact with, or what should be done about a particular aspect of his upbringing. He does not have the right to demand that these be provided for him: only his parents and, failing them, the state have any obligation to look after him. The child simply has the right to ask the court to choose between the alternative homes, schools or whatever else, which others are prepared to offer. Alternative homes, or even schools, are sometimes offered (and the fact that one or both parents might then be made to pay could be an inducement). The prospect, however unlikely, of children who are going through the natural turmoil of adolescence running to the courts to solve all their battles with their parents has caused some alarm. Applications by children for leave to apply for their orders must now be made or transferred to the High Court (*Practice Direction* [1993] 1 All E.R. 820).

Secondly, once an issue comes before a court, whether or not on the child's application, the court must take into account the ascertainable wishes and feelings of the child, considered in the light of his age and understanding (1989 Act, s.1(3)(*a*); see further in Chapter 4, section 3.(ii)(a)); but it must regard the child's welfare as paramount (1989 Act, s.1(1)). The older the child, the more powerful his views are going to be, not only because he is more likely to know what is best for him and have good reasons for it, but also because it becomes more and more futile to force a different choice upon him. This is why the Act accepts that private law orders should not be made (or made to last) beyond the age of 16 unless the circumstances are exceptional (1989 Act, s.9(6),(7)). Public law orders can be made up to the age of 17 and last up to the age of 18 (1989 Act, ss.31(3), 91(12)).

Thirdly, the Act provides for several ways of putting the child's views before the court. In private law cases, he will be a full party with a right to his own lawyer (usually on legal aid) if he has applied for an order; he can be made a party in other cases, but this is rare; commonly his views emerge through the welfare officer's report (see Chapter 4, sections 3.(ii)(a), 4(i)). In public law cases, he is usually represented by a specialist guardian *ad litem* and a lawyer (see Chapter 10, section 6). Each system has a different solution to the dilemma between putting forward the child's best interests and advocating his views. If these conflict, should the child have the right to have both put before the court?

The same dilemma arises when the child is not asking for something to be provided but simply for the right to decide what is to happen to his body. The courts are understandably reluctant to allow a child to choose to die, or to suffer serious harm to his health or development, by refusing medical treatment or education or by running away from home. But we do recognise that, although he may have to be locked up in his own interests, he is entitled to a hearing before being deprived of his liberty (see Chapter 8).

In the criminal law, we are much more prepared to put children in the same position as adults. Their welfare may mean that they escape punishment altogether, but recent legislation has gone a long way towards providing that sanctions should only be imposed upon them in accordance with the same procedural safeguards and substantive principles (including proportionality) as apply to adults (see Chapter 11).

Child law is always struggling with these dilemmas, but the clearest message to emerge from recent events is that "the child is a person not an object of concern" (Butler-Sloss, 1988).

Chapter 2

UNMARRIED PARENTS

The proportion of live births outside marriage rose steeply in the swinging sixties, fell off a little after the Abortion Act 1967, and then resumed a climb which became steeper still during the 1980s. By 1991 it had reached 30 per cent. Many of these children are born into relationships which are as stable as many marriages. Of the children of unmarried parents born in 1958 (and included in the National Child Development Study of all births in a single week) who were not adopted by strangers, two in five were living with both natural parents at the age of 11 (Lambert and Streather, 1980). Of all the children of unmarried parents born in 1991, three-quarters were registered by both parents and a half had parents living at the same address (*Social Trends*, 1993). Only a tiny proportion are now adopted. Among the reasons suggested for these changes are better contraceptive and abortion facilities making it more likely that the child is wanted; fewer financial and social pressures upon the mother; diminishing stigma and disability for the child; and an increasing tendency either to postpone marriage or to reject it altogether in favour of cohabitation.

The institution of marriage may well have been devised by early societies in order to establish a relationship between man and child (Mair, 1971). A man would derive spiritual, emotional and material advantages from having children, but whereas motherhood could easily be proved, fatherhood could not. A formal ceremony between man and woman, after which it was assumed that any children she had were his, was the simplest method of establishing a link. It also enabled him to limit his relationships to the offspring of a suitable selected mate. A legal system which concentrates on the orderly devolution of property and status within patrilineal families therefore places great emphasis on the institution of marriage and the concept of legitimacy. A legal system which is no longer so concerned about material provision for future generations of the few, and is far more concerned about the welfare of all young children, is likely to find the discrimination involved in the concept of legitimacy more and more distasteful. Abolishing it for the sake of the children, however, presents a problem. If the main distinction is that a child of married parents has an automatic legal relationship with both his mother and his father, while a child of unmarried parents does not, abolishing the distinction might be thought to require the law to confer automatic parental responsibility on all fathers (as has happened in some countries) (Law Commission, 1979 and 1982). Some people believe that this would be in the best interests, not only of the fathers, but also of the children themselves (Scottish Law Commission, 1992). Others take a different view, mainly because most of these children are still brought up by their mothers alone, and they have enough to contend with apart from the additional pressures and problems which the father's parental responsibility might bring (One Parent Families, 1980; Law Commission, 1982 and 1986; Deech, 1992).

The Family Law Reform Act 1987, therefore, tried to remove all those differences which affected the child's legal position. It also improved the position of the father, but without giving him automatic responsibility for the child's upbringing. Much of the 1987 Act has now been superseded by the Children Act 1989, which follows the same policy. However, the 1987 Act is still the source of the important rule that in any legislation and legal documents passed or made after it came into force, there is no need expressly to include children of unmarried parents, or relationships traced through unmarried parents. All references to a relationship between two people (such as "father", "mother", "child", "parent", "grandparent" or "relative") now include these unless a contrary intention appears (1987 Act, s.1(1)).

1. SHEEP OR GOAT?

Where the law does have to draw distinctions, it now tries to avoid using any adjective (such as "illegitimate" or "non-marital") to describe the *child*. Instead, it refers to whether or not the *parents* were married to one another at the relevant time. So legislation can refer to "a person whose father and mother were married to each other at the time of his birth" (1987 Act, s.1(2)(a)). This phrase has, however, been given a special meaning, to cover all the people who were or were regarded as legitimate under the existing law.

The time of a person's birth includes any time between the insemination or conception which resulted in his birth and his birth (1987 Act, s.1(4)). This covers anyone whom the common law regarded as legitimate: it was sufficient if your mother and father were married either when you were born (even if you had been conceived before marriage) or when you were conceived (even if your parents had been divorced or your father had died before you were born) or (probably) at any time in between your conception and birth. The proportion of conceptions outside marriage is far higher than the proportion of births, although the trend is for fewer and fewer parents to see a hasty marriage as the best solution.

The term "person whose father and mother were married to one another at the time of his birth" also includes four other kinds of people. First are those treated as legitimate by virtue of section 1 of the Legitimacy Act 1976 (1987 Act, s.1(3)(a)). This refers to people whose parents' purported marriage is legally void (for example because one of them was already married or was under 16); logically, their parents are not married and so they should not be included. However, since 1959, statute has provided that if at the time of the act of intercourse or insemination leading to the conception, or at the time of the marriage if this was later, either or both of the parents reasonably believed that their marriage was valid, the child is legitimate (Legitimacy Act 1976, s.1; the father must have been domiciled in England and Wales at the date of birth); mistakes of law, for example as to the recognition of a foreign divorce decree, are permissible if reasonable (1987 Act, s.28). It may well be difficult to establish what your parents thought before you were born, particularly for succession purposes after the parent in question has died. The section only applies to dispositions of property made after it was first introduced in 1959, but (unlike legitimation) it can allow succession to peerages and other titles.

Second are people who have been legitimated within the meaning of section 10 of the Legitimacy Act 1976 (1987 Act, s.1(3)(b)). The common law insisted that the marriage take place before the birth, hence the need to get out the shotgun. However, in 1926 statute provided that a person became legitimated if his parents married after his birth, but only if they could have been married when he was born; it was thought that to include children of extra-marital as opposed to non-marital unions would encourage adultery; this limitation was removed in 1959. The parents should then re-register the birth as though they had been married when the child was born; unless the husband was originally registered as the father, some verification of his paternity will be required (Legitimacy Act 1976, ss.2 and 9). If the child has previously been adopted by his mother or father alone, he can still be legitimated and they may apply for the adoption order to be revoked (Adoption Act 1976, s.52).

Legitimated people have the same rights as any others, except for succession to peerages and other titles. For dispositions of property made *before* January 1, 1976, however, these rights only apply if the legitimation took place before the disposition. For later dispositions it does not matter when the legitimation took place, except that if the disposition itself depends upon the date of birth ("to all my legitimate grandchildren born before I die"), the person is taken to have been born at the date of his legitimation rather than his actual birth, unless he was already entitled to the property in any event ("to all my grandchildren born before I die") (Legitimacy Act 1976, ss.5, 6 and Sched. 1).

It was estimated that about 20 per cent. of the children born to unmarried parents between 1951 and 1968 would eventually be legitimated (Leete, 1978). Before the reform of divorce law in 1971, one of the arguments for allowing an "innocent" spouse to be divorced against her will after five years of separation was the supposed existence of many children who might then be legitimated. But there seems to have been no dramatic increase in legitimations since then and indeed the rate appears to have gone down. This could indicate that there are fewer long term "stable illicit unions" than had been supposed or that fewer couples are choosing to marry even when they are free to do so.

Also included in the definition of people whose parents were married at the time of their birth are adopted children (see Chapter 12) (1987 Act, s.1(3)(c)) and any other people who are treated in law as legitimate (1987 Act s.1(3)(d)). This last category was included in case there were any other people, usually with a foreign connection, whose status as the child of married parents would be recognised in law, even though they were neither born to married parents, nor legitimated, nor adopted. References to someone whose parents were not married to each other at the time of his birth cover everyone else (1987 Act, s.1(2)(b)).

The upshot of all of this is that, to almost all intents and purposes, you are the child of married parents if you are adopted or *if your mother and father have been married to one another at any time since your conception*. It is a shame that the 1987 Act did not review the Legitimacy Act 1976 and try to find a simpler way of saying so. In any event, as the law now refers to the relationship between the parents rather than to the child as such, and as parents' marriage is almost always irrelevant to the child's legal position, the idea of legitimacy as a special legal status for the child has virtually ceased to have any meaning and it ought to be removed from the statute book altogether (Scottish Law Commission, 1992).

2. PROVING PARENTAGE

Marriage has always been the most convenient way of proving fatherhood. The law presumes that every child born to a married woman is her husband's child until the contrary is shown. This applies even though the child must have been conceived before the marriage, or if the birth takes place within the normal period of gestation after the marriage has ended by death or divorce. These presumptions can conflict, for example when the mother is widowed or divorced less than nine months before the birth and remarries while pregnant. A court would choose the most likely father (*Re Overbury* [1955] Ch. 122), but perhaps until then we should assume that she did not commit adultery? The presumption does not apply if at the time of conception the husband and wife were living apart under a decree of judicial separation (or under the now-discontinued magistrates' "non-cohabitation clause"); but it may have to be rebutted if they are simply living apart without any sort of court order. Apparently the presumption does not apply if paternity is disputed for the purposes of the Child Support Act 1991 (see Chapter 4).

The presumption may be rebutted by evidence which shows that it is "more probable than not" that the husband is not the father (Family Law Reform Act 1969, s.26). Such evidence is of two types; one seeks to show that the husband and wife did not or could not have intercourse at the relevant time (and in the past the main difficulty was to identify the relevant time); the other seeks to show that even if they may have had intercourse, the child was not the product of it. The usual way of doing this is by blood or other tissue tests. Conventional blood tests now have up to a 99 per cent. chance of excluding a man from paternity. Recently developed D.N.A. profiling, however, can provide conclusive evidence one way or the other (see Webb, 1986).

It is always possible for the parties and the person with parental rights over a young child to agree that tests shall be taken. A statutory power to direct in civil proceedings that blood samples be taken from the child or any party and tested to see whether a man was excluded from paternity was first introduced in 1969 (1969 Act, s.20). In 1987 this was expanded to allow the taking and testing of bodily samples for the purpose of determining maternity or paternity (1987 Act, s.23; but this is not yet in force). The court simply directs. The person concerned, or if he is a child under 16 (or is mentally incapable) the person who has care and control of him, may still refuse to provide a sample (1969 Act, s.21). If so the court may draw such inferences from this as seem proper (1969 Act, s.23) and no doubt these will usually be unfavourable. Anyone who is seeking a remedy from a court in reliance on the presumption of legitimacy may be denied that remedy if he refuses to undergo a test, even though there is no other evidence to rebut the presumption.

The court has a discretion whether or not to direct a blood test. But the House of Lords has said that this is not simply a matter of the child's upbringing, so that the child's welfare is not necessarily the paramount consideration; the interests of justice would normally require that the truth be told, and in general this would usually be better for the child as well (*S.* v. *S.*; *W.* v. *Official Solicitor* [1972] A.C. 24). Where there is a conflict, however, the court may refuse to order a blood test if this would be positively detrimental to the child's welfare; for example where the child had been brought up by his mother and her husband since birth and the stability of their family might be put at risk if it turned out that the mother's former lover was the father (*Re F. (A Minor: Paternity Test)* [1993] 1 F.L.R. 598, C.A.). It might, however, be different if husband and wife had separated and a test would set the husband's mind at rest (*T.* v. *T.*, *The Times*, July 31, 1992). In both recent cases, much depended upon the mother's attitude and the court doubted whether a test should be ordered if she, as the person with care and control of the child, would refuse to allow a sample to be taken from him.

Although the presumption of a husband's paternity may be rebutted on the simple balance of probabilities, it may require rather more to prove that a particular man is the father if there is any dispute about it: "the degree of probability in an issue of paternity should . . . be commensurate with the transcending importance of that decision to the child" (Heilbron J., approved by Ormrod L.J. in *Re J.S.* [1981] Fam.22). There are no presumptions to help. Technically, a conventional blood test only excludes; if a man is not excluded, the fact that only one in, say, 100,000 men could be the father is not conclusive, but is certainly relevant alongside the other evidence pointing to him (see *W.* v. *K. (Proof of Paternity)* [1988] 1 F.L.R. 86). Once again, D.N.A. profiling should provide the answer. A finding of paternity in any proceedings in which it is necessary to establish that a person is the father before making orders about parental responsibility, upbringing, maintenance or support is evidence in any later civil proceedings (Civil Evidence Act 1968, s.12; amended by 1987 Act, s.29).

A person may also apply to the High Court for a declaration, which will be binding on the whole world, either that a particular person is his parent, or that he is the legitimate child of his parents, or that he has or has not become a legitimated person (Family Law Act 1986, s.56; amended by 1987 Act, s.22; the applicant must be domiciled in England and Wales or have been habitually resident here for a year beforehand).

The most common method of "official" recognition, however, is through registering the child's birth. It is possible to register, or re-register, the birth so as to show the father's name in three circumstances; first, at the joint request of mother and father; second, at the request of mother or father, if each makes a declaration that he is the father; and third, at the request of mother or father, on production of an order naming him as father, and, if the child is 16 or over, the child's written consent (Births and Deaths Registration Act 1953, s.10; 1987 Act, ss.24 and 25). Thus the father may only be registered without the mother's co-operation if there is a court order based on a finding of his parentage. However, he is now named in roughly three-quarters of registrations and this is increasing all the time.

3. PARENTAL RESPONSIBILITY

The common law regarded the child born outside the legally approved family unit as "nobody's child." He scarcely enjoyed a legal relationship with his mother, let alone his father. However, case law and statute gradually accorded her similar powers of upbringing to those of the father of a legitimate child. The Children Act 1989 now makes it quite clear that where a child's mother and father were not married to each other at the time of his birth, the mother has parental responsibility for the child automatically; but the father does not, unless he acquires it in accordance with the provisions of the Act (1989 Act, s.2(2)).

This does not mean that he has no relationship with the child. He is the child's "parent" whether or not he has parental responsibility; this means that he is liable to support the child (see Chapter 4); he may also be punished for neglect or ill-treatment (see Chapter 1); but he may succeed to the child's estate (see 5. below); he is normally entitled to be consulted by the social services and to have contact with a child they are looking after (see (iv) below and in Chapters 8 and 10); and he can always go to court for an order about his child's upbringing. The Act also provides for several ways in which he may assume full parental responsibility, sharing it with the mother.

(i) Parental responsibility orders and agreements

Until 1959, the only thing that an unmarried father could do to try and obtain some voice in his child's upbringing was to make the child a ward of court.

Then he was allowed to apply like any other parent for legal custody or access, but this did not allow him to share legal custody with the mother even if they wanted him to do so. The 1987 Act allowed him to apply for all the parental rights and duties, sharing these with the mother in the same way that married couples do. This has been taken over into the Children Act 1989 which provides that "the court may, on the application of the father, order that he shall have parental responsibility for the child" (1989 Act, s.4(1)(a)).

This still requires them to go to court. In 1979, the Law Commission provisionally proposed that all fathers should automatically have parental rights, but organisations representing one parent families opposed this because most mothers remained solely responsible for their children's care and upbringing. They did, however, suggest that there should be some way in which mother and father could agree to share responsibility without having to go to court. One solution might have been to link parental responsibility to birth registration; but either parent might want there to be an official record of the child's parentage, whether for their own or the child's sake, without wanting to share responsibility for his upbringing. Hence the 1989 Act provides that "the father and mother may by agreement . . . provide for the father to have parental responsibility for the child" (1989 Act, s.2(1)(b)).

These agreements have no effect unless they are made in the form prescribed in regulations made by the Lord Chancellor (1989 Act, s.4(2)(a)) and recorded in the manner (if any) which he has prescribed (1989 Act, s.4(2)(b)). A simple form has been devised which is relatively straightforward to complete but warns both mother and father that they should seek independent legal advice because making it has important legal effects for both of them. The agreement must be recorded in the Principal Registry of the Family Division which will then send a sealed copy to each parent (see Parental Responsibility Agreement Regulations 1991). In the first eight months after the Act came into force, 1,510 agreements were recorded, which was thought to be a great success (Booth, 1992).

It is important for parents to understand that a parental responsibility agreement has exactly the same legal effect as a parental responsibility order made by a court. The fact that the father assumes responsibility does not mean that the mother loses hers (1989 Act, s.2(6)) and each is able to act alone in meeting that responsibility (1989 Act, s.2(7)) unless this is incompatible with a court order under the Act (1989 Act, s.2(8)) or some statutory provision requiring them both to consent (1989 Act, s.2(7)). This probably makes little difference to the ordinary work of bringing up a child. The main impact is when the parents come into contact with other agencies, where the law does distinguish between parents who have, or have not, parental responsibility for the child (see (iv) below).

Parents making such agreements should also realise that, although they can easily be made, they cannot easily be brought to an end. Both an agreement and an order under section 4 continue in force until the child reaches the age of 18, unless they are brought to an end earlier (1989 Act, s.91(8),(7)). This can only be done by an order of the court, made on the application of any person who has parental responsibility for the child or, with the leave of the court, the child himself (1989 Act, s.4(3)). This means that either the mother or the father himself might apply, and so might a guardian, or anyone else who has a residence order or care order (or even an emergency protection order) is in force in their favour; but the court cannot act of its own motion and it may only grant the child leave to apply if satisfied that he has "sufficient understanding" (1989 Act, s.4(4)).

It might be thought controversial that the mother has to go to court to get an agreement ended, even if she has been tricked or pressurised into signing it. On the other hand, there is no way, short of adoption or freeing for adoption, that a mother or a married father can be deprived of their parental responsibility and it might be thought that once he has become responsible an unmarried father should be in the same position. The reason given for allowing any revocation (by the Law Commission, 1986) was that the courts might be reluctant to make these orders at all unless they could revoke those which turned out badly. This would be unfortunate, if the aim is to encourage both parents to play as large a part as possible in the upbringing of their child. As it turns out, the courts have shown no reluctance at all to make these orders: 1,282 were made in the first eight months after the 1989 Act (Booth, 1992).

The Act does not lay down any criteria for making or ending parental responsibility orders. If the court can be regarded as determining a question with respect to the child's "upbringing", or the administration of his property or application of his income, the child's welfare is the paramount consideration (1989 Act, s.1(1)). Upbringing and administration are undoubtedly included within the question of parental responsibility; but it could be argued that, as parental responsibility is wider than that, so the court is entitled to go wider and look at other factors, including the interests of the parents as well as those of the child. The court is not *required* to consider the welfare "checklist" when considering whether to make or end a parental responsibility order or agreement (see 1989 Act, ss.1(3),(4); see Chapter 4).

It was originally thought that orders would be sought in three situations. The first, where the parents were living together and wanted to share responsibility, is now catered for by parental responsibility agreements. The second was where the mother had died without appointing the father guardian and in that case he could instead apply to be appointed guardian himself (the relative merits are discussed at (iii) below). The third was where the child was to live with the father after the parents' separation and the father wanted full parental status (Law Commission, 1982). In such a case the father will no doubt apply for a residence order, to which the welfare principle and checklist undoubtedly apply, and if he is successful the court must also make a parental responsibility order (1989 Act, s.12(1); see (ii) below).

The cases decided before the Children Act, however, were about a very different situation. In *D.* v. *Hereford and Worcester County Council* [1991] Fam.14, the parents had separated, the child had been taken into care, and the father's contact had been ended by the local authority. He applied for a parental responsibility order so as to give him standing to challenge that

decision. He now has that standing whether or not he has parental responsibility (1989 Act, s.34(1)). The judge's approach, however, was to ask "Can
this respondent show that he is a father to the child, not in the biological
sense but in the sense that he has established or is likely to establish such a
real family tie with the boy that he should now be accorded the corresponding legal tie." This approach was taken even further by the Court of Appeal in
Re H. (Minors) (Local Authority: Parental Rights) [1991] Fam.151. Here it
was held that the father should have been granted an order so as to give him
standing to oppose an application to free a child in care for adoption, even
though the court then held that his agreement should be dispensed with on
the ground that it was unreasonably withheld.

Asking whether the father has anything to offer the child (see *Re D.*, above)
is not quite the same as asking whether the order will be in the child's best
interests. Given the extent to which the Children Act recognises the father's
standing in relation to local authorities, whether or not he has parental
responsibility, there is not quite the same need to award it to him. The courts,
however, appear to be taking the same approach to cases between parents.
They have given parental responsibility to fathers who will have no contact
with the child, and thus no opportunity of meeting it, because of opposition
either from the child's mother or from his step-father (*Re C. (Minors) (Parental
Rights)* [1992] 1 F.L.R. 1, C.A.; *Re H. (A Minor) (Parental Responsibility)*,
[1993] 1 F.L.R. 484, C.A.). Before the 1989 Act, there was a view that joint
custody orders should only be made with the agreement of the parent with
whom the child was to live, or at least where there was no active disagree-
ment. However, shared parental responsibility is different from joint custody:
it does not give one parent a veto over the other's activities and its purpose is
to recognise and encourage a relationship rather than to confer rights. The
courts can show sympathy for fathers who have established a relationship
with their children without interfering too much in the relationship between
mother and child.

(ii) Section 8 orders

The 1989 Act provides for several orders, collectively known as "section 8
orders", designed to resolve the practical questions which may arise about
the care and upbringing of any child (see further in Chapter 4). These consist
of a "residence order", a "contact order", a "specific issue" order, a
"prohibited steps" order, and orders varying or discharging any of these
(1989 Act, s.8(1),(2)). They are mainly intended for use between private
individuals, particularly parents. Any parent, whether or not he has parental
responsibility, is always entitled to apply for any section 8 order (1989 Act,
s.10(4)(a)).

If a court has ordered that the child is to live with his father for some or all of
the time, it would be wrong for the father not to have full parental responsibility for him. Hence, if the court makes a residence order in favour of a
father who does not already have parental responsibility, it must also make a
parental responsibility order (1989 Act, s.12(1)). That order cannot be

brought to an end for as long as the residence order remains in force (1989 Act, s.12(4)) and it can stay in being even if the residence order changes. Once a court has decided that it is in the child's interests for him to live with his father, there is likely to be a considerable relationship between them and the law should continue to recognise this. It would only be right to end the order if the father had nothing to offer the child.

Section 8 orders are matters of "upbringing" in relation to which the child's welfare is paramount. The "checklist" applies in any disputed case and will also influence the conduct of any negotiations towards an agreed order. It used to be thought that the courts were unsympathetic to the claims of unmarried fathers. However, where the dispute is between a mother and a father who have lived together with their child, the more recent reported cases suggest that the courts will treat married and unmarried parents very much alike (see, for example, *B.* v. *T.* (*Custody*) [1989] 2 F.L.R. 31). The principles are fully discussed in Chapter 4.

Where the parents have never lived together, or only did so for a short while or some time ago, the issues in contact and other applications may be more complex. The courts now attach great importance to the benefit to the child in maintaining links with both sides of his family. They have said for a long time that the child's right to do this applies whether or not his parents were married (*S.* v. *O.* (*Illegitimate Child: Access*) (1977) 3 F.L.R. 15) but this does not mean that they will always make a contact order in his favour (*M.* v. *J.* (*Illegitimate Child: Access*) (1977) 3 F.L.R. 19; *B.* v. *A.* (*Illegitimate Children: Access*) (1981) 3 F.L.R. 27). Much depends upon the length and strength of the real relationship between them, but also upon the length and strength of any new relationship formed by the mother and the extent to which the child is now integrated into a different family. The courts used to give greater weight to the advantages of cementing the new family, particularly if the mother had married, when the child's parents had not been married to one another than they did when married parents were separated or divorced. The case of *Re F.* (page 31, above) suggests that they may still do so. In *Re R.* (*A Minor*) (*Access*), *The Times*, March 29, 1993, however, the Court of Appeal found that there was an urgent need for a five-year-old girl, brought up to believe that her mother's cohabitant was her father, to be told the truth and re-introduced to her real father as soon as possible.

Where the issue is not between mother and father but between the father and other people who want to look after the child, the courts undoubtedly give great weight to the advantages for any child in being brought up by his own parent rather than by anyone else, however close. This goes back at least as far as the case of *Re C.* (*M.A.*) [1966] 1 W.L.R. 646, C.A., in which the father obtained custody of a 17-month-old child whose mother had arranged at birth for him to be placed for adoption with eminently suitable adopters with whom he had lived since he was two months old. The court considered a good deal of psychiatric evidence about the nature of the parent-child relationship and the extent to which this might be strengthened by the parental commitment stemming from the knowledge of a blood tie and concluded that the move would be in the best interests of the child. The same conclusion was reached in a similar situation in the more recent case of *Re O. (A Minor) (Custody: Adoption)* [1992] 1 Fam.73, although in that case the child was still with short term foster parents when the father applied; and in *Re K. (A Minor) (Custody)* [1990] 1 W.L.R. 431 (page 125, below), the Court of Appeal upheld the claims of the father against those of the maternal relatives in the strongest possible terms (quoting Lord Templeman in *Re K.D. (A Minor) (Ward: Termination of Access)* [1988] A.C. 806, 812, page 126, below). It seems that parents, including unmarried fathers, are to be preferred to strangers or even other relatives, unless the placement is "doomed to failure" or otherwise clearly not what is best for the child.

(iii) Guardianship

If the child's mother has died, an unmarried father could alternatively assume parental responsibility by becoming the child's guardian. The mother may appoint him guardian (1989 Act, s.5(3)); this is usually done by will, but can now be done by any properly signed written document (1989 Act, s.5(5)). Where unmarried parents are on reasonable terms but not living with one another, the mother might prefer to have sole responsibility while she is alive but be glad for the father to have take responsibility in the event of her death. She could also appoint some-one else to share it with him.

If the mother has not appointed him guardian, he could apply for the court to appoint him, because the court has power to appoint guardians for children who have no parent with parental responsibility (1989 Act, s.5(1)). However, he might just as well apply for a parental responsibility order (1989 Act, s.4(1)(a), see (i) above). There is very little difference between the two. Guardians have the same parental responsibility as parents (1989 Act, s.5(6)); they now have power to appoint guardians to take their place if they die (1989 Act, s.5(4)); and their agreement to the child's adoption is required unless it can be dispensed with (see Chapter 12). The only real difference is that the appointment can be brought to an end, not only on application by a person with parental responsibility or with leave by the child, but of the court's own motion in any family proceedings (1989 Act, s.6(7)). However, it is much more appropriate both legally and psychologically for the father's status as a father to be recognised by way of a parental responsibility order (which will have incidental benefits in establishing the relationship as a fact).

(iv) Parental responsibility and other agencies

A parent with parental responsibility can at any time remove a child from accommodation provided by a local authority (1989 Act, s.20(8)). Indeed, the authority cannot provide accommodation if the parent is willing to provide or arrange it himself and objects to the authority doing so (1989 Act, s.20(7)). A parent without responsibility must if practicable be consulted about any decision the authority make about a child they are looking after or are proposing to look after, and his views must be given due consideration, but that is scarcely the same (1989 Act, s.22(4)(b), (5)(b)).

If the child is in compulsory care, the authority have a duty to allow him reasonable contact with both his parents, whether or not they both have parental responsibility (1989 Act, s.34(1)) and they can apply to the court for a contact order (s.34(3)). A parent with parental responsibility can simply apply for a care order to be discharged (1989 Act, s.38(1)(a)); without responsibility he would have to apply for a residence order (1989 Act, s.10(4)(a)), although in practice this would amount to much the same thing. A parent with parental responsibility can apply for a supervision order to be varied or discharged (1989 Act, s.38(2)(a)); without responsibility he can only apply to vary requirements imposed upon him where the child is living with him (1989 Act, s.38(3)).

Most important of all, if a parent has parental responsibility his agreement to the child's adoption is required, unless it can be dispensed with on the defined grounds (see Chapter 12). However, before a court frees a child for adoption, it must be satisfied either that the father has no intention of applying for a parental responsibility or residence order or that if he did so he would be likely to fail (Adoption Act 1976, s.18(7)). We have already seen (see (i) above) how the Court of Appeal has supported a father who wished to have parental responsibility in order to oppose a freeing application.

Without parental responsibility, the father's agreement is not required but he does have some standing in the adoption proceedings. Where the adoption agency knows his identity, it must treat him in the same way as any other parent, so far as it considers this reasonably practicable and in the interests of the child (Adoption Agencies Regulations 1983, reg. 7(3)). However, the courts cannot force the agency to approach him, particularly where he does not know about the child and to do so might put at risk an adoption which is otherwise clearly in the child's best interests (*Re L. (A Minor) (Adoption: Procedure)* [1991] 1 F.L.R. 171). The courts' rules provide that if he is liable by virtue of an order or agreement to maintain the child, he must be made a respondent to the application and he may always be made a respondent in any other case (Adoption Rules 1984, r.15(2)(h), (3)). As a respondent he has the right to attend court and be heard on whether or not the order should be made (1984 Rules, r.23(1)).

But this is not the same as a right to be told, or to be made a respondent, still less to refuse consent. Nor will these rights be of much use unless the father can offer a better alternative. Thus some fathers opposing adoption also apply for a residence order, which they may now do even if the child is in care (Children Act 1989, s.9(1)), or simply for contact. If so, the applications should be heard together, so that a proper choice between them can be made (see *G.* v. *G., The Times*, December 24, 1992).

The issue arises in several different contexts. If the mother has decided to place the baby with strangers for adoption at an early age, the father may not have been able to prevent her. The court's choice may be between the prospective adopters, who are no doubt suitable in every way and have been caring for the child almost since birth, and the father, who is related to the child by blood but has had no opportunity of forming an emotional bond with him, and is unlikely to have either such a good home or such a good mother-substitute to offer (*Re Adoption Application 41/61* [1963] Ch. 315; *Re O.* (*An Infant*) [1965] Ch. 23). Even in this situation, the father may be able to convince the court that the child will be better with him (in *Re C.* (*M.A.*) [1966] 1 W.L.R. 646, page 36, above, he was now reconciled with his wife, who made an excellent impression on the judge, and they could offer a good home) and this is more likely if an adoption placement has not yet been found (*Re O.* (*A Minor*) (*Custody: Adoption*) [1992] 1 Fam.73).

There has probably been an even greater change in relation to adoptions by the mother and the step-father she has since married. The courts used to give great weight to the legal, social and psychological advantages of becoming the child of married parents (*F. v. S.* (*Adoption: Ward*) [1973] Fam.203). In some cases, the unmarried father may not want or be able to offer the child an alternative home, but his objections to the total severance of ties are just as valid as those of a divorced parent. In *Re E.* (*P.*) (*An Infant*) [1968] 1 W.L.R. 1913, C.A., these were thought to be frivolous, compared with the advantages of wiping out the "stigma of bastardy" and enabling the child to become "so far as possible" a respectable member of society. Nowadays, the courts are likely to take a more balanced view, as all step-parent adoptions are regarded with some suspicion (see Chapter 6). Exceptionally, the courts might require the adopters to allow him contact (*Re S.* (*A Minor*) (*Adoption Order: Access*) [1976] Fam.1) but the normal approach has been that this should only be done if everyone agrees (*Re C.* (*A Minor*) (*Adoption: Conditions*) [1989] A.C. 1; see further in Chapter 12). As adoption proceedings are "family proceedings", the courts now have power to make section 8 orders either on application or of their own motion in the course of them. They could, therefore, add a contact order to the adoption order or make a residence order in favour of mother and step-father instead.

Different again is adoption by the mother on her own. This deprives the child of a legal relationship with his father's family and now that the short form birth certificate is in general use, such adoptions rarely serve any useful purpose. The courts are prohibited from granting an adoption on the sole application of the child's mother or father, unless the other natural parent is dead or cannot be found or there is some other special reason to exclude him (Adoption Act 1976, s.15(3)).

4. FINANCIAL SUPPORT

Of all the problems facing the mother who decides to bring up her baby on her own, money is probably the most serious. All one-parent families are likely to be materially less well-off than their two-parent counterparts, but unmarried mothers are the least well-off of this already disadvantaged group (Finer, 1974; Ferri, 1976; Bradshaw and Millar, 1991). Unlike divorced or separated spouses, they cannot turn to the father for support for themselves as well as the child. While the child is so young that his mother has to give up work to care for him, her needs might be taken into account in deciding how much should be ordered for the child (*Haroutunian* v. *Jennings* (1977) 1 F.L.R. 62). Despite that, most orders were extremely low, apparently lower than those for children of married parents (McGregor, Blom-Cooper and Gibson, 1970; Bradshaw and Millar, 1991), perhaps because the fathers were usually both younger and poorer and all were aware that the order would benefit the D.S.S. rather than the mother and child. Unlike widows, unmarried mothers cannot turn to the state or their husbands' employers for a pension. Yet they are more likely than either widows or married mothers to be left unsupported at the very time when they are unable to support themselves because the baby is so young. Thus the main source of income, at least after any maternity allowance has come to an end, is likely to be means-tested benefits. These will be reduced by the full amount of any provision made by the father.

The law of child maintenance has always had close links with the Poor Law. Single mothers were first given a private right of action against the father in 1844, in fact shortly before married mothers were given such rights on divorce or separation. This was because, until the New Poor Law of 1834, there had been a right to take action against the father, but only in order to spare the Poor Law authorities expenditure. The abolition of this had led, somewhat to the authorities' surprise, to an increase rather than a decrease in births outside marriage (Finer and McGregor, 1974). The single mother's action, in what became known as affiliation proceedings, always betrayed its origins in the Poor Law; it could only be brought in a magistrates' court, and the orders were strictly limited; there were also time limits and above all the mother's evidence had to be corroborated. The provision available for the child was therefore much more limited than that which could be made for married parents and their children.

The Family Law Reform Act 1987 abolished this discrimination and provided a uniform scheme, under which either parent of a child, whether married or not, could claim secured or unsecured periodical payments and property adjustment orders from the other parent for the benefit of their child. That scheme was consolidated with other powers in the Children Act 1989. As from April 1993, however, the courts' powers to assess and collect periodical payments for the support of children are being progressively overtaken by those of the Child Support Agency under the Child Support Act 1991 (see Chapter 4).

The role of the courts will then be limited to making lump sum and property adjustment orders and, where resources are very substantial, to ordering "top up" periodical payments. Where an unmarried couple have been living together and their relationship breaks down, the courts do not have the same powers that they have on divorce (or judicial separation) to adjust the strict property rights of each party in order to achieve a fair distribution of their marital property and make proper provision for the needs of the parties, not only of the children, but also of each other (Matrimonial Causes Act 1973, s.24). Nor do they have the power under the Matrimonial Homes Act 1983 (1983 Act, s.7 and Sched. 1) to transfer a protected, statutory, assured or secure tenancy from one to the other or from their joint names into the name of one of them. Under the Children Act 1989, however, they can make lump sum and transfer or settlement of property orders for the benefit of the children (1989 Act, Sched. 1, para. 1(1)(c)(d)(e)(f)). The courts' general approach used to be that children were entitled to be housed, maintained and educated while they were young, but did not have "expectations" of capital settlements from their parents, however rich (*Chamberlain* v. *Chamberlain* [1973] 1 W.L.R. 1557, C.A.; *Lilford (Lord)* v. *Glyn* [1978] 1 W.L.R. 78, C.A.). However, preserving a home for the children, at least until they grow up, has always been an important consideration in divorce settlements. If the only way this can be done where the parents are unmarried is by ordering a transfer or settlement for the benefit of their children, the courts may be prepared to do it. In *K.* v. *K. (Minors) (Property Transfer)* [1992] 1 W.L.R. 530, C.A., it was held that the court could order an unmarried father to transfer his share of a joint council tenancy to the mother for the benefit of their children. The Law Commission (1992) have drawn attention to the technical difficulties associated with such transfers and proposed that the courts should have express power to transfer tenancies between cohabiting or formerly cohabiting couples instead.

Instead of going to the Child Support Agency or to the courts, the mother and father can make an agreement for the child's maintenance which will be enforced by the courts (*Ward* v. *Byham* [1956] 1 W.L.R. 496). However, the agreement does not prevent the mother from bringing court proceedings later (*Follit* v. *Koetzow* (1860) 121 E.R. 274) or the Child Support Agency from making an assessment whenever it has power to do so (see Chapter 4). Lawyers are therefore beginning to draft agreements on the basis that capital settlements will be repaid if a Child Support Act assessment is later made, but whether these are contrary to public policy remains to be seen.

The parents may always agree things which the court would not have power to order, as long as a trust or the essential ingredients of a contract can be shown. Thus, for example, in *Tanner* v. *Tanner* [1975] 1 W.L.R. 1346, C.A., a man who bought a house for the mother and their twin daughters to live in was held to have granted her a contractual licence to stay there until the girls had finished school, in return for her agreeing to give up her own flat to look after the children and the house, some of which was let. Once upon a time such agreements would have been regarded as tainted by immorality; nowadays, the courts are likely to uphold those in which each party promises something to the other, as long as it is not simply the supply of sexual services.

5. PROPERTY AND SUCCESSION

It is quite extraordinary that, while still denying the relationship between father and child when the father was alive, the law was prepared to recognise it when he died. The discriminatory rules of succession developed for the dynastic purposes of the propertied classes were in fact abandoned (in the

1969 Act; see Russell, 1968) before those about the upbringing of a growing child. It has always been possible to leave property to a named person, whatever that person's birth, but a general gift to "children" or "issue" was originally presumed to exclude people born outside marriage (or relationships traced through them) unless the contrary was stated. Dispositions since 1969 are presumed to include not only them, but relationships traced through them, unless a contrary intention appears (1969 Act, s. 15; replaced by 1987 Act, s.19). Succession to peerages and other titles is still excluded.

Before 1970, a child of unmarried parents could not claim anything if his father or his father's relatives died intestate (*i.e.* without leaving a will), and he could only claim from his mother if she had no legitimate children (this was one of the main reasons for her to adopt him if she got married). After 1969, he could share in the intestate estate of either parent, equally with any legitimate children (1969 Act, s.14). The parents might also share in his, if he died without leaving a spouse or children of his own. Otherwise the rules remained as they had been. Since the 1987 Act, however, the rules of intestacy apply irrespective of whether any person's parents were married to one another (1987 Act, s.18). All are to be regarded as relatives and treated alike, but there is a rebuttable presumption that the father and his relatives died before the child.

Lastly, the courts have discretionary powers to adjust the dispositions made under a will or intestacy, if these do not make reasonable provision for the maintenance of (among others) the children (minor or adult, but adults usually do not require maintenance) of the deceased (see Chapter 5). Since 1970, these have applied to all the deceased's children, irrespective of whether the parents were married to one another. The courts can also award damages for all the deceased's children if a parent is wrongfully killed (Fatal Accidents Act 1976, s.1(3) and (5)(a)).

The only thing that the child of unmarried parents still cannot inherit from his father is a title or his nationality (British Nationality Act 1981, s.50(9)(b)). The latter is a serious discrimination, as British nationality now depends upon descent rather than birth here; the child of married parents can acquire it through mother or father, the child of unmarried parents only through his mother.

6. COMMENTARY

The laws of both England and Scotland have now removed almost all legal distinctions between people whose parents were and were not married to one another. They have done their best to remove the offensive labels as well, but for as long as these remain on the statute book in legislation passed before 1987 they are likely to remain in use. The 1987 Act gives the Lord Chancellor power to amend previous legislation by statutory instrument in order to adopt the new terminology but he has not yet done so.

The burning issue is still whether or not the remaining legal distinctions should be removed by giving all fathers the same legal relationship with their children (or all children the same legal relationship with their fathers). The old stereotypes undoubtedly do not work; there are many deeply committed unmarried fathers who have or would like to have just as close a relationship as any married father. It is easy to see the mothers who resist this as callous or selfish. But the other crucial difference is that unmarried parents have no financial responsibilities towards one another. Whenever parents part, and unmarried parents do so more often than married, it is far more likely than not that the mother will continue to look after the children, usually because she has carried the major burden of doing this in the past, and she will not have the same claim to be compensated for this as her married sister does. Should the law's powers to adjust matters between the parents be improved before the father's position is improved?

Chapter 3

GENETIC AND SOCIAL PARENTS

In the olden days, there was no need to define what was meant by a "parent". Before the Family Law Reform Act 1987, however, it did have a technical meaning; only the mother and a father who was married to the mother at the relevant time was regarded as a "parent" so if it was intended to include a father who was not married to the mother it was necessary either to use the term "father" or to say so expressly. The 1987 Act, as we have seen, changed all that: the word "parent" now includes all mothers and all fathers, although a distinction may now be drawn between a "parent" and a "parent with parental responsibility".

But it was still assumed that there was no need to define what we meant by a "parent", a "mother" or a "father". There was no statutory definition and it could be taken for granted that these expressions referred to the man and woman who were genetically responsible for the child's conception and birth. Of course, a man who was not in fact the child's genetic father might well be taken as such, with or without his knowledge. But that did not affect our understanding of what the words meant. So the fact that a man has lived with the child's mother for many years and been regarded as her child's father does not make him a "parent" in the eyes of the law.

By 1990, however, the development of assisted conception had made it necessary for the law to be a little more precise, not only about what it means to be a "father" but also about what it means to be a "mother".

1. WHO IS MY MOTHER?

It is now entirely possible, though not common, for a woman to give birth to a child who has been produced from another woman's egg. Eggs are collected from the donor; they may then be fertilised outside the body, by mixing them with sperm in a dish or other vessel, in the technique known as *in vitro* fertilisation (I.V.F.), and the resulting embryo transferred to the recipient, "carrying" mother, in the hope that implantation will take place; alternatively, eggs and sperm may be placed together in the recipient's fallopian tube, in the technique known as gamete intra-fallopian transfer (G.I.F.T.), in the hope of fertilisation and implantation; in the intermediate technique known as zygote intra-fallopian transfer (Z.I.F.T), eggs and sperm are mixed outside the body and transferred while fertilisation is taking place.

The success rates (in terms of healthy live births) with these techniques vary considerably with the individual characteristics of the people involved and the expertise of the practitioners. I.V.F. has some advantage over G.I.F.T., because fertilisation at least is assured, although implantation is not. Also, embryos can be successfully frozen for use at a later date, whereas it is not yet possible to preserve eggs; synchronising the egg collection from a suitable donor and the transfer to a suitable recipient is not always easy. Donated eggs are, understandably, in short supply. The woman may be given superovulatory drugs which stimulate her ovaries into releasing more than one egg in her menstrual cycle; these may then be collected, either in the course of a sterilisation operation in which the ovaries are removed or by removing them from the ovaries, through a needle either by laparoscopy or guided by ultrasound. Both are invasive procedures involving some risk to the woman's health. Although some donation is for purely altruistic reasons, perhaps by a woman who knows the recipient, most is an incidental advantage of the donor's own sterilisation or infertility treatment. It is usually thought unethical to offer a woman any financial or other inducement to donate her eggs.

Donation usually takes place because a woman wishes to have a child but is unable to produce eggs herself. In this case, it is intended that the mother who carries the child will also become his "real" mother and bring him up. Occasionally, however, it is part of a surrogacy arrangement, in which the woman who wishes to have a child is able to produce eggs but unable to conceive or carry a child. Then it is intended that the carrying mother will give him to his genetic mother to bring him up (see further 5. below).

The Warnock Committee on Human Fertilisation and Embryology recommended that the law should always regard the carrying mother as the child's real mother; the donor should have no rights or duties with respect to the child (*Warnock Report*, 1984, para. 6.8). Hence the Human Fertilisation and Embryology Act 1990 provides that "the woman who is carrying or has carried a child as a result of the placing in her of an embryo or of sperm and eggs, and no other woman, is to be treated as the mother of the child" (1990 Act, s.27(1)). An embryo for this purpose includes an egg in the process of fertilisation (1990 Act, s1(1)(*b*)). This applies whether or not the treatment (I.V.F., Z.I.F.T. or G.I.F.T.) took place in the United Kingdom (1990 Act, s.27(3)). The carrying mother then becomes the child's mother for all legal purposes (1990 Act, s.29(1)). References to any relationship in legislation or other legal documents are to construed accordingly (1990 Act, s.29(3)). The only exception is for succession to peerages and other dignities and property devolving along with them (1990 Act, s.29(4)). No exception is made for other respects in which the law normally regarded blood relationship as crucial, such as the rules prohibiting marriage or sexual intercourse between certain close relatives. The rule does not apply if and when the child is adopted (1990 Act, s.27(2)).

The reason given by the Warnock Committee for adopting this approach was certainty. A clear and simple rule produces, not only legal certainty but also factual certainty. It is almost always apparent who has given birth to a child, but (as fathers have always known) it cannot always be proved whose genetic material has been used to create him. The carrying mother is on the spot. More often than not, this rule also reflects the parties' intentions and the social reality: the object is to produce a child for the carrying mother to bring up. It may well reflect the psychological reality, if the relationship which develops between mother and child through the prolonged period of pregnancy and the experience of childbirth is likely to be closer than the purely genetic relationship, at least until the genetic relationship is combined with a nurturing one.

Special provision was made for surrogacy cases (as we shall see at 5. below). A perhaps more fundamental objection is that, if knowledge of one's genetic parentage is important to adopted children, it may be just as important to a child born of egg donation. Again (as we shall see at 4. below), the 1990 Act seeks to address this concern, not only for egg but also for sperm donation.

2. WHO IS MY FATHER?

Egg donation is a recent development which was only made possible by the invention of I.V.F., Z.I.F.T. and G.I.F.T.. Sperm donation has always been possible, because it can take place either naturally (as when a woman has intercourse with a man who is not her husband or partner) or artificially (as when she is artificially inseminated with sperm from a donor other than her husband or partner or donated sperm is used in the course of I.V.F., Z.I.F.T. or G.I.F.T. treatment). Even artificial insemination is a very simple process and has certainly been practised for a very long time.

Under the common law, any resulting child was not the child of the mother's husband and was therefore illegitimate, unless and until they adopted him. The donor, if he could be identified, was still the child's father and could theoretically have been made financially liable for his mainten-ance. In practice, doctors who practised donor insemination under the guidelines laid down by the Royal College of Obstetricians and Gynaecolo-gists guaranteed the donor anonymity. The mother and her husband might well be tempted, or even advised, to rely upon the presumption that every child born to a married woman is her husband's child and register the child as his. It might even be suggested that they lend colour to this presumption by continuing to have intercourse at the relevant time or by using a mixture of the husband's and the donor's sperm.

It was obviously tempting to leave the law as it was, for many people still found the whole idea of donor insemination intrinsically distasteful and did not wish to give it any encouragement by legislating about it (Feversham, 1960). On the other hand, doctors increasingly regarded it as a "treatment" for male infertility (although of course it is no such thing). It was always possible that the marriage would later break down and disputes arise. Blood tests could show with increasing accuracy whether or not the husband was not the father (should either want to challenge the matter). Finally, as the Law Commission said in their Working Paper on *Illegitimacy* (1979, para. 10.8), "Couples should not be put into a position, as they now are, where they are strongly tempted (and perhaps even advised) to make a false declaration on registering the birth; it brings the law into disrepute if it is believed that it can safely be defied . . . " The Commission (1979 and 1982) therefore recommended that the mother's husband should be treated for all purposes as if he were the child's father, unless it was proved that he had not consented to the insemination. This recommendation was supported by the Warnock Report (1984, para. 4.17) and first implemented in section 27 of the Family Law Reform Act 1987.

There are, however, several arguments against this. The analogy between the mother's husband in donor insemination and the carrying mother of a donated egg is not very close; the process of conceiving, carrying and bearing a child must bind the mother to her baby, whatever his genetic make-up, in a way which the process of watching, waiting and helping simply cannot do. Individuals differ in their ideas of what parenthood is all about; some women want a pregnancy and a baby as much as if not more than they want a child to look after and bring up; this is not an option for men. Some men also want a child to look after and bring up, others want their wives to have a child to look after and bring up, and others want their "own" children, heirs and successors. "Deeming" the husband to be the father obscures the genetic truth, not only from society (in the shape of the birth register) but also from the parents (who can deceive themselves into thinking the position to be something other than it is) and, most importantly, from the child himself. The information in the birth register is often in fact false, but it does not follow from the fact that some people tell lies that the law should not only permit but actually insist upon their doing so.

The Human Fertilisation and Embryology Act 1990 retains and expands the concept in the 1987 Act, while making some attempt to meet these concerns. The 1990 Act rules apply whenever a woman carries a child as a result of embryo transfer following I.V.F., or of Z.I.F.T. or G.I.F.T., or of artificial (but not natural) insemination (1990 Act, s.28(1)), whether the woman was in the United Kingdom or elsewhere when the treatment took place (1990 Act, s.28(9)).

If the child is the legitimate child of the parties to a marriage, as a result of the ordinary common law rules, then no special rules apply (1990 Act, s.27(5)(a)); so, if the mother was at the relevant time (see page 28, above) married to the man whose sperm was used, even if by the time of the birth she was married to or cohabiting with someone else, the sperm provider is the father. The rules also do not apply if and when the child is adopted (1990 Act, s.28(5)(c)).

Otherwise, if at the time of the embryo transfer, Z.I.F.T., G.I.F.T. or insemination, the mother was married to a man whose sperm was not used to create the resulting child, her husband is regarded in law as the father of the child, unless it is shown that he did not consent to the treatment (1990 Act, s.28(2)) or there was a judicial separation (including a legal separation obtained in another country but recognised here) in force at the time (1990 Act, s.28(7)(*a*), (9)). Marriage for this purpose includes a void marriage if either or both of the parties reasonably believed at the time of the treatment that the marriage was valid; and it is presumed that one of them did so unless the contrary is proved (1990 Act, s.28(7)(*b*)).

The husband need not give his positive consent to the treatment. Both the Law Commission (1979 and 1982) and the Warnock Committee (1984, para. 4.24) recommended that his consent should be assumed; the legal status of the child should not have to depend upon proof of his consent or the existence of some special document evidencing his consent. Even so, both the Warnock Committee (1984, para. 4.23) and the Human Fertilisation and Embryology Authority (H.F.E.A.) in their Code of Practice (1991, para. 5.7) stress the practical importance of obtaining the husband's written consent. The Code also advises that if his views should always be discovered if possible and written evidence obtained even if he does not consent to the treatment; the object is to clarify the child's parentage at the outset so as to prevent or resolve any later disputes (Code, para. 5.6). To disprove parentage the husband must show that he did not consent to the treatment; it is not enough to show that he consented to the treatment but not to becoming the child's father (no doubt there are natural fathers who also wish that it were).

If the child does not have a father under the above rules (because the mother was not married, or her husband was not the genetic father and did not consent to the treatment, or she was judicially separated from him) but the treatment with donated sperm took place "in the course of treatment services provided for her and a man together" then that man is regarded in law as the child's father (1990 Act, s.28(3)). Unlike the rule about husbands, this rule only applies to treatment carried out by a person covered by a licence under the 1990 Act (which therefore excludes do it yourself or foreign treatment). The rule does not depend upon the man's actual or presumed consent, but upon whether or not the couple are being treated together, a vague concept which the Act does not define. The Code of Practice (1991, para. 5.8) advises centres to record at each appointment whether or not the man was present and to try and obtain his written acknowledgment that they are being treated together and that donated sperm is to be used.

If these rules apply, the man becomes the child's legal father for all purposes (1990 Act, s.29(1)); references to any relationship in any legislation or legal document are to be construed accordingly (1990 Act, s.29(3). An exception is made for succession to titles and to property devolving along with them (1990 Act, s.29(4)) but not for incest or the prohibited degrees of marriage. If the man deemed father by these rules is married to the mother, then he is treated like any other married father and has parental responsibility automatically (Children Act 1989, s.2(1)). If he is not married to her, he does not have parental responsibility automatically (1989 Act, s.2(2)) but will be able to acquire it in any of the ways provided under the 1989 Act. Perhaps it would be good practice for infertility treatment centres to advise unmarried couples whom they are treating together to consider whether or not they wish to make a parental responsibility agreement (see page 33, above) when the child is born.

3. FATHERLESS BY LAW

If a particular man (or woman) is treated as the child's father (or mother) by virtue of these rules, then no-one else can be (1990 Act, s.29(2)). The child will always have a legal mother, even if she dies in childbirth. But the 1990 Act provides that in two circumstances a man cannot be the child's father, whether or not there is another father available.

The first is where a sperm donor has given his consent in the terms required by the Act for his sperm to be used for the treatment of others and it has been used in accordance with that consent; the donor is not then to be treated as the father of the child (1990 Act, s.28(6)(a)). The Warnock Committee (1984, para. 4.22) had recommended that the donor should have no "parental rights and duties" in relation to the child, but this takes the logical further step of providing that they are not to be treated as related in any way at all (1990 Act, s.29(2)).

Thus where treatment is given to an unmarried woman with no male partner the child will have no father and no paternal relatives at all. The Act does not prohibit the treatment of single women or those in lesbian relationships. It is possible that doing so would be an unjustified discrimination in the law's respect for family life or the right to found a family which are guaranteed under Articles 8 and 12 of the European Convention on Human Rights. However, treatment requiring a licence under the Act (which includes any treatment involving donated gametes) cannot be given "unless account has been taken of the welfare of any child who may be born as a result of the treatment (including the need of that child for a father) . ." (1990 Act, s.13(5)). The Code of Practice (1991, para. 3.16b.) advises that in all cases where the child will have no legal father, centres should pay particular attention to the prospective mother's ability to meet the child's needs throughout his childhood and where appropriate to whether there is anyone else within the prospective mother's family and social circle who is willing and able to share responsibility for meeting those needs and for bringing up, maintaining and caring for the child.

The second situation in which the child will have no legal father is where a man's sperm, or an embryo created with his sperm, is used (which must mean placed in a woman) after his death (1990 Act, ss.28(6)(b), 29(2)). This does not mean that the embryo or sperm cannot be used—simply that the resulting child will be fatherless by law unless and until he is adopted. Now that embryos and sperm can be frozen and kept for long periods, it may seem hard to prevent widows from having their husbands' or partners' children. The reason is purely pragmatic, to do with the complexities which would otherwise be caused in property and inheritance law, and the mother may wish to go ahead with treatment in any event. The dilemma for those treating her, however, is the same as that with would-be single or lesbian mothers: they may be able to bring the child up very well indeed, but is it in the interests of any child to be born with only one legal parent and only one set of legal relatives?

4. WHAT ABOUT THE CHILDREN?

The main task of the 1990 Act is to regulate any treatment or research which involves the creation, keeping or using of human embryos outside the body, or the storage or donation of human eggs and sperm (gametes). It does not attempt to control all kinds of infertility treatment, but only those involving donation or I.V.F., including Z.I.F.T. for this purpose (1990 Act, s.1(2)(a)), which were thought to raise special ethical and social problems. G.I.F.T. is not included, unless donation is also involved, although there is power to do so by regulations (1990 Act, s.4(3)).

The Act set up a licensing system administered by the H.F.E.A., which is also required to maintain a Code of Practice giving guidance on the "proper conduct" of the licensed activities (1990 Act, s.25). Its purpose is to help and protect the would-be parents and their prospective children. Both are protected by seeing that the staff are properly qualified, that the premises and equipment of a suitable standard, and that high standards of scientific and clinical practice are observed. Rigorous selection and screening of gamete donors is essential, not only to increase the chances of success, but also to protect parents from infection and children from inherited defects and diseases. Would-be parents are helped and protected by the requirements that they be given proper information, and offered counselling about the implications of what is proposed, before and during treatment.

The children are protected in two other ways. The first is the requirement to consider their welfare (and that of the parents' existing children) before deciding whether to offer treatment (1990 Act, s.13(5)). The Code of Practice (1991, paras. 3.12 to 3.27) advises centres to discover who will be the legal parents of any resulting child and who will be bringing him up. They should then assess the prospective parents, taking into account their commitment to having and bringing up a child; their ages and medical histories and that of their families; the needs of any children who may be born (including the implications of any possible multiple births) and the prospective parents' ability to meet those needs; any risk of harm to the child, including the risk of inherited disorders, problems during pregnancy or neglect or abuse; and the effect of a new baby on any existing child of the family. Where donated gametes are to be used, centres should also take into account a child's potential need to know about his origins and whether the prospective parents are prepared for any questions which may arise while he is growing up; the possible attitudes of other members of the family towards the child and his status in the family; the implications if the donor is personally known within the child's family and social circle; and any known possibility of dispute about the child's legal fatherhood.

The Code advises centres to make enquiries of the prospective parents, and if they agree of their G.P., and to go further if there is cause for concern, for example because the prospective parents have had children removed from their care. It suggests that the views of everyone at the centre who has been involved with the family should be taken into account, although members of the team (particularly counsellors) should not share information given them in confidence without the clients' consent unless it is so serious that confidentiality cannot be maintained.

The Code is struggling hard to do what the Act asks, but this is a difficult and controversial task. Is the object to protect the child's physical or psychological welfare? How close is the analogy with choosing adopters (Brandon and Warner, 1977)? Is it about rationing and choice at all? From the parents' point of view, is it fair to assess their suitability for treatment on anything other than medical and scientific grounds? It can well be argued that assessments of prospective parenting ability are notoriously unreliable even at the best of times (Blyth, 1990). No-one has to be licensed to produce children by the ordinary method, so why should their eligibility be scrutinised and judged simply because they require one (or both) of two particular kinds of medical help? It is difficult to answer this in the case of ordinary couples seeking ordinary I.V.F. treatment. One argument is the need to ration the scarce resources available for such highly specialist treatment, but this is unconvincing given that most I.V.F. is provided privately rather than by the National Health Service. The treatment does present some ethical problems, mainly because it is likely to produce "spare" embryos which may have to be allowed to perish or used for research; this may justify regulating the treatment itself, but does not logically justify rationing it on the basis of the welfare of any resulting child. It is easier to see the justification for assessing the prospective parents when donated gametes are to be used, for here couples are competing for the scarce resource of donated gametes and the analogy with adoption is much closer.

From the point of view of any resulting child, it is easier to see why some assessment of his prospective home and family is justified. Although the Code (1991, para. 3.12) insists that no more than three eggs of embryos are replaced, both I.V.F. and G.I.F.T. bring a greater than normal risk of multiple pregnancy and births (but so does any treatment involving super-ovulation) and new techniques using micro-manipulation of sperm and egg may turn out to bring other risks. Provided that the gametes are properly screened, donation does not bring physical risks but it could bring psychological and social problems. Even so, the choice does not lie between two or more upbringing options offered for an existing child but between being born to these parents or not being born at all. However, if it is reasonable to try to prevent a child being born with an inherited disease or disability, is it also reasonable to try to prevent a child being born into a family where he is likely to suffer harm?

In practice, centres are unlikely to want or be able to carry out the sort of assessments normally carried out in fostering or adoption cases. Although the Code advises multi-disciplinary assessment, the ultimate decision rests with the doctor and the clinical team, to whom such assessments do not come easily. They are more likely to rely upon rather simple moral or social judgments of how "deserving" the would-be parents are. Single women and lesbian couples may be rejected or scrutinised carefully, whereas married or unmarried heterosexual couples may not. After all, the latter are infertile and can easily be regarded as "patients" in need of medical treatment or cure. The former are not infertile but simply want to have a child in this way (see Douglas, 1992). However if they are denied licensed treatment, they may well choose more dangerous, unscreened sources of sperm (and the donor will then technically become the child's father). The Code (1991, paras. 3.13, 3.23, 3.26) points out that everyone seeking treatment is entitled to a fair and unprejudiced assessment of their situation and needs; that they should be given an opportunity of stating their views and meeting any objections raised; and that if treatment is refused, they should be given reasons and an explanation of the options which remain open to them.

The Act's emphasis on the child's welfare may be more important in the long run, not in deciding eligibility for treatment, but in focusing attention on the needs of the child once born. Centres whose main objective is to help people who desperately want to become parents can easily lose sight of the help which the child may also need. There has been a tendency to condone and even promote the parents' natural inclination to keep the circumstances of the child's birth a secret, particularly where donation is involved. They may be so successful that the child never knows, but the truth may easily emerge, perhaps in particularly traumatic and distressing circumstances. This is one reason why the Act and the Code emphasise the importance of offering the parents counselling so that they can explore whether or not they propose to tell the child and when and how to do so.

The Act also requires the H.F.E.A. to set up a register. On this will be recorded all the treatment given, in such a way that it can show who has been or may have been born as a result of treatment, and whose gametes have been used (1990 Act, s.31(1),(2)). The person born, when grown up, will be able to apply to the Authority to be told whether or not he has been born as a result of donation and whether or not he is or might be related to a person he proposes to marry. Provided that he has been offered "proper counselling", he must be told the answer and also given any further information about the donor specified in regulations (1990 Act, s.31(3),(4)).

These regulations have not yet been made (for the children involved are still very young) but they will not be able to allow disclosure of the identity of donors who made their donations at a time when the regulations did not provide for this (1990 Act, s.31(5)). While donors are thus protected against retrospective withdrawal of the anonymity they have been promised, it can be argued that their children have a right to know their identity (Bruce, 1990). At all events, the Authority is now collecting names as well as other interesting information about donors; but the object is to satisfy the child's basic and natural curiosity about his genetic parentage, rather than to provide a link which could lead to tracing and meeting.

5. SURROGACY

Surrogacy is where a woman (the surrogate mother) agrees to carry a child to be handed over to someone else (the commissioning parent(s)) who is to meet the parental responsibility for him (see Surrogacy Arrangements Act 1985, s.1(2)). This definition applies whether or not the child is in any way related to the commissioning parents, but in practice there are two types of surrogacy: partial, where the surrogate mother is artificially inseminated with sperm from the commissioning father, and full, where an embryo, or sperm and eggs, coming from both the commissioning parents are used.

Surrogacy arouses strong feelings and the Warnock Committee (1984; see paras. 8.10 to 8.16) were divided. It was thought "inconsistent with human dignity" for a woman to use her womb for profit and treat it as an incubator for someone else's child; a distortion of the relationship between carrying mother and child and the wrong way to approach pregnancy; damaging for the child who has strong bonds with his carrying mother whatever his genetic make-up; degrading for a child to be bought and sold; and unethical to induce a woman to undertake the risks of pregnancy and child-birth in return for money or to put any pressure on her to give up the child against her will. On the other hand, this may be the only hope for some couples to have a child; little is known about the bonds which develop between the child and his mother during pregnancy and these do not prevent adoption or fostering; and why should a woman who can have children be prevented from such an act of generosity towards one who cannot, or indeed from using her body in whatever way she chooses, provided that her choice is properly informed and freely made?

Some members of the Warnock Committee wanted an outright ban and others wanted only to prohibit profit-making agencies. The Surrogacy Arrangements Act 1985 makes it an offence to negotiate surrogacy arrangements on a commercial basis (1985 Act, s.2) or to advertise surrogacy services or a willingness to take part (1985 Act, s.3). The H.F.E.A. Code of Practice was revised in 1993 to advise that a surrogate pregnancy should only be initiated where it is impossible or undesirable for medical reasons for the commissioning mother to carry a child and never just because she would find it inconvenient or distasteful to do so.

The Code also advises that when considering the welfare of the child (for the purposes of section 13(5) of the 1990 Act; see 4. above) the centre should consider the circumstances of both families, because it is possible that either of them will eventually bring him up. This is because a section inserted in the 1985 Act by the 1990 Act provides that "no surrogacy arrangement is enforceable by or against any of the persons making it" (1985 Act, s.1A). The mother is not automatically obliged to hand over the child; nor can she sue for any payment promised, although she can keep any payment given. The commissioning parents could bring proceedings (either under the High Court's inherent jurisdiction or the Children Act 1989) but the court is unlikely to consider it in the child's best interests to be parted from his mother (see *A. v. C.* [1985] F.L.R. 445, C.A.).

If she keeps the child, she is of course his mother (1990 Act, s.27; see 1.above) and unless it is shown that her husband did not consent to the treatment, he is the father (1990 Act, s.28; see 2. above). If, as might have been thought sensible, he indicated out the outset that he did not consent, the commissioning father will be the father, because he has not donated his sperm in the manner provided by the 1990 Act (see 3. above). The problems this could cause, for example under the Child Support Act 1991 (see Chapter 4) may easily be imagined.

The same rules apply if she does hand over the child, so that although the commissioning father may be the legal father, the commissioning mother cannot be the legal mother. They could adopt the child (and the court could authorise any payment retrospectively; see *Re Adoption Application* [1987] Fam.81); but they may well not want to do this if they see the child as their own.

Hence, the 1990 Act provides for a court to make an order for the child to be treated in law as the child of their marriage, provided that artificial methods of conception with the gametes of one or both of them were used in the arrangement (1990 Act, s.30(1); otherwise it could be used as a substitute for adoption). They must apply within six months of the birth and the child must be living with them at the time (1990 Act, s.30(2),(3)). The agreement is required, not only of the child's mother but also of his father if he has one (unless it is the commissioning father), except where they cannot be found or are incapable of giving agreement (1990 Act, s.30(5),(6); there is no provision for "unreasonable withholding"). The court must be satisfied that no money or other benefit (apart from expenses) has changed hands in return for the order, the agreement, handing the child over, or making any arrangement with a view to making the order, unless the court authorises this (1990 Act, s.30(7)). Regulations can provide for some of the law relating to adoption to apply to these orders, including the rules as to their effect upon the child' status and relationships afterwards (1990 Act, s.30(9)). The draft Parental Orders for Gamete Donors Regulations 1993 provide for a guardian *ad litem* to be appointed to safeguard the child's welfare and ensure that parental agreement is freely given. The child will have to be registered as a member of the birth family in the usual way but after an order he will be re-registered in a separate register and the link between them kept confidential. The draft would allow the link to be disclosed by court order but does not give the child the same right as an adopted child to obtain a copy of the original birth certificate when grown up (see Chapter 12). After consultation on the draft regulations and rules, the section is likely to be brought into force during 1993.

6. COMMENTARY

Assisted conception tells us a great deal about our perceptions of parenthood. Just as our attitude to surrogacy (and primarily the surrogate mother but also the commissioning mother) probably reveals how each of us feels about pregnancy and motherhood, our attitude to donor insemination (again primarily the social father but also the donor) reveals how each of us feels about fatherhood. It is worth thinking about the relative weight of parental claims based on a genetic link, or on carrying and bearing the child, or on looking after and bringing him up, before we turn to the courts' approach to disputes between parents and others in the chapters which follow.

PART II: REARRANGEMENT—
THE PRIVATE LAW

Chapter 4

PARENTAL SEPARATION AND DIVORCE

Marriage breakdown is not, of course, the same as divorce but it must have increased almost as dramatically. The rate of divorce per thousand married people in England and Wales rose from 2.1 in 1961, to 6.0 in 1971, to 11.9 in 1981, and has since levelled off at around 12.7. Part of the rise may be explained by legal and procedural changes, which have allowed a higher proportion of already broken marriages to be dissolved. But this cannot be the whole explanation, for the underlying trend was established before the law was radically changed by the Divorce Reform Act 1969. The law may have contributed to a climate of opinion in which divorce is a more acceptable solution to an unhappy marriage, but many other factors are at least as significant. Among these are smaller, consciously planned families, which release women earlier from their demands; improvements in the social and economic status of women, which have liberated them from traditional restraint and their husbands from traditional responsibility; and far higher expectations of personal fulfilment and happiness from relationships (Law Commission, 1988a; Phillips, 1988; Reibstein and Richards, 1992). It has been argued that a higher rate of marriage breakdown reflects a healthier and more positive attitude than in the days when marriage was the only respectable career for a woman (Fletcher, 1973; Mortlock, 1972). People still marry in large numbers and with high hopes (Mansfield and Collard, 1988). But the pain, grief and bitterness suffered by those whose expectations of life-long happiness are shattered may well be even greater (Vaughan, 1987; Elliott, 1991).

More and more couples are seeking to avoid some of the perceived pitfalls of marriage, and probably the pain of divorce, by living together without marrying, at least for a while. For many, this is a preliminary or transitional phase before marriage. Around 50 per cent. of those marrying in 1987 were already living together, compared with less than 10 per cent. in 1971. Many of these were second marriages for at least one partner, where the rates of living together beforehand and of divorce are higher than average. Couples who never marry are unlikely to be counted in official statistics either at the beginning or the end of their relationship.

There must still be grave concern about the effects upon the increasing

---

numbers of children involved. Prolonged one-parent status (particularly for mothers) often brings financial stringency, housing problems and downward social mobility, and these all tend to be worse where the marriage was broken by divorce rather than death (Finer, 1974; Ferri, 1976; Maclean 1991). Significant links have been found between marriage breakdown and delinquency, emotional disturbance and poorer educational achievement in the children (Rutter, 1971; Ferri, 1976; Wallerstein and Kelly, 1980; Maclean and Wadsworth, 1988; Elliott and Richards, 1991). It is not known, however, how far these are caused by economic disadvantages, or social stigma, or parental bitterness and disharmony, or by the separation itself. The outcome may be rather different now that divorce is more widespread and possibly more amicable. The effects do vary with such things as the level of conflict before and after the divorce (Emery, 1982, 1988), the age and character of the children, the social position of the family and the living arrangements afterwards. It is argued that those children who are able to maintain satisfactory links with both parents after the break tend to do better, psychologically and materially, than those who cannot (Richards and Dyson, 1982; Maidment, 1984a; Richards 1986, 1991).

1. WHERE DO THE COURTS COME IN?

If parents separate, some decision must be reached about the children. Many now feel that it is better for the children if the parents can agree the arrangements for themselves even if what they agree is not ideal. The function of family mediation is to help them do this and on the whole this seems more effective if it is conducted as far away from the courts as possible (Newcastle, 1989). Even without mediation, contested cases about where the children are to live are remarkably rare, although disputes about contact with the other parent and his family are much more common (Maidment, 1976; Eekelaar and Clive, 1977; Eekelaar, 1982). But if there is no contest, is there any need for the courts to be involved at all?

(i) The courts' duty to consider the children

In proceedings about the children, it should be impossible for the court to overlook their interests. But in divorce and other proceedings about the adults' relationship, where the parties are agreed about what is to happen to the children, the children's interests will only be specifically addressed if the court has a positive duty to do this. Parents going through the trauma of separation and divorce are not always in the best position to make rational decisions about their own interests, let alone their children's. The Royal Commission on Marriage and Divorce (Morton, 1956) recommended that divorce courts should have a duty to vet the arrangements made for their children and a similar idea was extended to magistrates' courts in 1978. It does not apply in proceedings dealing with domestic violence or occupation of the family home, where priority is given to the victim's need for protection.

In any proceedings for a decree of divorce, nullity of marriage or judicial separation, the court must first consider whether there are any "children of the family" to whom this duty applies (Matrimonial Causes Act 1973, s.41(1)(a), as substituted by the Children Act 1989, Sched. 12, para. 31). A "child of the family" is not only a natural or adopted child of the marriage, but also any other child who has been treated by both parties as a child of their family, apart from one who is (currently) placed with them as foster parents by a local authority or voluntary organisation (1973 Act, s.52(1); the same definition appears in the Children Act 1989, s.105(1)). The obvious example is step-child, including a wife's extra-marital child who the husband thinks is his own, but privately fostered children or orphans being cared for by relatives are also covered. The essential criterion is that the child is regarded and treated by both husband and wife as a member of their common household, so that it is as much his home as anyone else's which is breaking up.

The court's duty applies to (a) any child of the family who is under 16 when the court considers the case under this section, and (b) any child of the family who has reached 16 and in relation to whom the court specifically directs that the duty shall apply (1973 Act, s.41(3)). The previous version of this provision applied to 16- and 17-year-olds who were still being educated or trained (even if, like apprentices, they also had a job). This was difficult to apply, as so many young people move in and out of various types of education, employment and youth training schemes these days. Nevertheless, the Family Proceedings Rules 1991 (r.2.2(2)) still require petitioners to list these children and to provide particulars to the court about them.

The arrangements which have been, or are proposed to be made for the upbringing and welfare of these children must be described at some length in a separate document which is filed with the petition. The court must then examine this and decide whether it should exercise any of its powers under the Children Act 1989 in respect of any of the children (1973 Act, s.41(1)(b)). If the court thinks that the circumstances do or are likely to require it to exercise its powers; and it is not in a position to do so without giving further consideration to the case; then it *may* direct that the decree of divorce or nullity is not to be absolute, or that the decree of judicial separation is not to be granted, until the court allows it; but this power to postpone the decree can only be exercised where there are exceptional circumstances which make it desirable in the interests of the child that the court should do so (1973 Act, s.42(2)). Normally, there is no reason why the divorce or other decree should not go ahead anyway. This power is not supposed to be used in every case where final decisions about the children's future have not yet been made, but only where there is some special reason to think that holding up the divorce will help them.

Under the previous law, the judge had positively to approve of the parties' arrangements; if he did not, the parties did not get their decree until they had made arrangements of which he did approve unless he made a special exception. This sounds excellent, but there were real problems. The judge was asked to perform a "welfare" rather than an adjudicatory function and it was a matter of chance whether he was any good at it. If he was troubled by anything, he could call for a welfare officer's report; but judges varied considerably in the things which troubled them and in their readiness to ask for reports (Hall, 1968; Davis, MacLeod and Murch, 1983; Dodds, 1983). They had little time in the course of their few minutes with the petitioner to find out whether there were real problems. Even if a judge was unhappy with what was proposed, he could only make the parents think again. He could not force an unwilling parent to take the child and the alternative of putting him in care would usually be much worse than leaving things as they were. Once the decree had gone through, the only way of monitoring the approved arrangements and ensuring that they were kept was to make a supervision order, which could not be done in every case. Increasingly, it was questioned whether these children should be singled out for the courts' special attention and whether it was right for a judge to try to impose his preferred solution upon parents (Maidment, 1984b; Law Commission, 1986). However, abolishing the court's duty altogether would have sent the wrong messages to parents, who ought to be encouraged to think about the arrangements for their children before they are divorced (Booth, 1985; Law Commission, 1988). Hence the court's obligation to approve was replaced with an obligation to investigate and decide whether there was anything that it needed to do—a much more appropriate task for a court.

There is no such procedure in matrimonial proceedings in magistrates' courts, but where there is any child of the family under 18, the court must not make a final order for financial provision until it has decided whether to exercise any of its powers under the 1989 Act (Domestic Proceedings and Magistrates' Courts Act 1978, s.8(1); the definition of "child of the family" is the same as in the 1973 and 1989 Acts; 1978 Act, s.88(1)).

(ii) When orders about the children can be made

The 1989 Act provides two main types of order about the care and upbringing of children. The "public law" orders are designed to be used by public authorities for the protection of children from harm (see Chapter 10). The "private law" orders are designed to be used mainly by private individuals, and in principle anyone can apply for or obtain one, although some people need the court's leave to do so. These are known as "section 8 orders" after the section which defines them (see 2.(i) below) and can be made in three situations:

(1) on an application made independently of any other proceedings, by someone who is either entitled under the Act or who has obtained the court's leave (1989 Act, s.10(2)); any parent, whether or not he has parental responsibility, and any guardian of the child is always entitled to apply for such an order (1989 Act, s.10(4)(a));

(2) on an application made in the course of some other "family proceed-

ings", again by someone who is either entitled to do so or has obtained the court's leave (1989 Act, s.10(1)(a)); and

(3) of the court's "own motion" in any "family proceedings" in which "a question arises as to the welfare of any child and the court considers that an order should be made" even though no-one has applied for it (1989 Act, s.10(1)(b)). Usually, a court does not make an order unless the person who is to benefit has asked it to do so. But one object of the 1989 Act was to give all courts in family cases powers which were as similar as possible to those of the High Court in wardship proceedings (see (iv) below). In theory, the court becomes guardian of its ward and must search, as any good parent does, for the solution which will be best for him (*Re E. (S.A.) (A Minor)* [1984] 1 W.L.R. 156, H.L.). If it becomes apparent, as a case progresses, that a particular solution is available which will be best for the child, the court now has power to make the order, without requiring a formal application and the extra paperwork and costs.

Most private law orders will therefore be made in the course of other family proceedings by whatever court is hearing those proceedings, whether it is the High Court, divorce or county court, or a magistrates' family proceedings court. Independent applications can be made to whichever level of court the applicant wants and can afford.

(iii) The definition of "family proceedings"

Section 8 orders can now be made, whether on application or of the court's own motion, in almost all proceedings which are usually thought of as part of family law. The Act does not lay down any particular connection between the child and the parties to the proceedings, other than that a "question arises with respect to the welfare" of the child concerned (1989 Act, s.10(1)). Specifically, "family proceedings" for this purpose means (1989 Act, s.8(3)) proceedings under "the inherent jurisdiction of the High Court in relation to children" (usually wardship; see (iv) below) or any of the following statutory provisions (1989 Act, s.8(4)):

(a) *Parts I, II and IV of the Children Act 1989 itself*

This covers most cases about children, but only under Part I (dealing with parental responsibility and guardianship orders), Part II (dealing with section 8 orders), and Part IV (dealing with care and supervision orders, including interim orders, education supervision orders and orders about contact with children in care). Part III (which includes secure accommodation orders) and Part V (dealing with child assessment and emergency protection orders) are not included. This gives the court flexibility in both private and public law cases to do what is best for the child, but not in the limited or emergency situations with which Parts III and V are concerned.

(b) *The Matrimonial Causes Act 1973*

This covers proceedings in the divorce courts between husband and wife not only for divorce (1973 Act, s.1), nullity (1973 Act, ss.11, 12) and judicial separation (1973 Act, s.17), and their related "ancillary relief" dealing with the couple's property and finances, but also for a decree of presumption of death and dissolution of marriage (1973 Act, s.19) or for financial provision unconnected with anything else (1973 Act, s.27). Divorce proceedings are far and away the most common family proceedings and children under 16 are involved in roughly two-thirds of them. Until the 1989 Act, orders of some sort would be made about the children in almost all of these cases. The other types of case under the 1973 Act are comparatively rare.

(c) *The Domestic Violence and Matrimonial Proceedings Act 1976*

This covers proceedings in the county courts between husband and wife, or between a man and woman who are living with each other as if they were husband and wife (1976 Act, s.1(2)), for injunctions prohibiting one from molesting the other or any child living with the applicant or excluding one of them from the family home (1976 Act, s.1(1)). These cases are often brought *ex parte* (that is, without notice to the other side) or on short notice and it may well be necessary to make orders about where the children are to live, or how much contact the respondent is to have with them, at the same time. Apart from cases brought under the Children Act, however, these are the only "family proceedings" available to cohabitants; they have no way of sorting out their affairs except by the ordinary laws of property, contract and tort.

(d) *The Adoption Act 1976*

This includes applications to adopt, or to free a child for adoption, or for a provisional adoption order (see Chapter 12). The court can consider and make a section 8 order, such as an order that the child is to live with rather than be adopted by the prospective adopters, or is to live with his father, instead of an adoption order; but the court may also make a section 8 order, such as an order that the adopters are to allow the child to have contact with particular members of his birth family as well as the adoption order.

(e) *The Domestic Proceedings and Magistrates' Courts Act 1978*

This covers applications to magistrates' family proceedings courts between husband and wife, either for financial provision (1978 Act, ss.1, 6, or 7) or for personal protection or exclusion orders where there has been violence, or the threat of violence, against the applicant or a child of the family (1978 Act, s.16). Previously it was only possible to make orders about the children in financial provision cases, but as in the higher courts, it may be just as necessary to deal with the children's immediate future in cases of domestic violence.

(f) *Sections 1 and 9 of the Matrimonial Homes Act 1983*

These are proceedings in the county courts between husband and wife relating to the occupation of the matrimonial home, whether they are jointly entitled to it as owners, tenants or the like (1983 Act, s.9) or only one of them is entitled (1983 Act, s.1). The House of Lords has decided that the criteria in this Act govern all applications to oust one partner from the family home, whether made under the 1976 Act or under this Act, and whether or not in the course of divorce or other proceedings (*Richards* v. *Richards* [1984] A.C. 174). This means that although the children's needs are relevant, alongside the parties' conduct and their own needs and resources, the children's welfare is not the paramount consideration. It still makes sense to be able to deal with their future at the same time.

(g) *Part III of the Matrimonial and Family Proceedings Act 1984*

This refers to applications in the divorce courts between formerly married partners for financial relief or property adjustment under the law in England and Wales after they have been divorced in a country outside the United Kingdom.

(iv) Wardship and the inherent jurisdiction of the High Court

The powers of the High Court in respect of children who are in need of its protection stem from the ancient notion that the King was *parens patriae*, or father of his people. They have never been defined (although they have now been curtailed) by statute. The most usual way of invoking them is to make a child a ward of court, but it seems clear that this can be done in other ways, for example by applying for an injunction to protect a child (*Re N. (Infants)* [1967] Ch. 512). Traditionally, wardship was the preserve of rich families, usually preoccupied with controlling the marriage or property of heiresses and orphans.

However, its use mushroomed in the 1970s and 1980s, largely because anyone might bring proceedings. Social services departments who found their statutory powers to protect children unduly restrictive were encouraged by the courts to do so; the 1989 Act was designed to make this unnecessary and so they can now only invoke the inherent jurisdiction in very limited circumstances (see Chapters 8 and 10). Relatives, foster parents and other interested people had no other way of getting a case into court; now they may be able to apply for section 8 orders instead (see Chapter 7). Parents who were trying to enforce their wishes against a rebellious older child or who were battling between themselves might also want to use the more flexible powers and greater authority of the High Court, particularly where there was a risk that the child would be taken abroad (Law Commission, 1987b).

A child automatically becomes a ward of court immediately an application is made for him to become one (Supreme Court Act 1981, s.41(2)). No important move can then be made without the court's leave, and the notice specifically prohibits marriage, leaving the country or changing his educational arrangements; other orders can be obtained very quickly if needed. The child will automatically cease to be a ward after 21 days unless steps have been taken to arrange a hearing date or if the court does not continue it at the hearing (Family Proceedings Rules 1991, r. 5.3(1)). The object of this rule was to prevent children becoming or remaining wards of court by accident rather than to speed up what can be a very slow process. It is slow because it is so careful; all interested parties are usually represented by lawyers; exceptionally, if the court thinks an independent or expert view on the child's behalf is needed, the Official Solicitor may be asked to represent him separately; and although judges can quickly be found in an emergency, the Family Division of the High Court is not large and it can take months to arrange a full hearing; but decisions other than to ward or deward can now be taken in a county court. Unless the child is dewarded, the court retains control of the case, while giving someone day to day "care and control" of the child and making other orders as and when appropriate. Any "important step" in the child's life, however, must be referred back to the court (*Re S.* (*Infants*) [1967] 1 W.L.R. 396).

The 1989 Act does not prevent private individuals using wardship or the inherent jurisdiction if they want and can afford to do so. Occasionally, what they want is only available in the High Court, for example if extra protection against publicity (e.g. *Re M. and N.* (*Minors*) (*Wardship: Publication of Information*) [1990] Fam.211, C.A.), or kidnapping, or unwarranted sterilisation is needed. But there is now almost always an alternative available to them under the 1989 Act, which can be brought in the most convenient court and transferred to a higher court if this is in the child's interests. Where a case has been concluded in another court, the High Court is unlikely to allow a party to use wardship as a "second bite at the cherry" but it may be prepared to intervene to take over a particularly difficult or sensitive case from a lower court. Wardship should not, however, be used to deprive a mature child of the right to bring Children Act proceedings and instruct lawyers on his own account (*Re T.* (*A Minor*) (*Wardship: Representation*), *The Times*, May 10, 1993, C.A.). Because the High Court's inherent jurisdiction is within the definition of family proceedings, the court may make orders under the Children Act instead of the usual orders over its wards. There is often no real need for the court to retain control (or it could do so by means of a prohibited steps order under the 1989 Act) and it would be simpler and cheaper to dispose of the case by an order under the 1989 Act, which can always be varied or discharged if the need arises.

2. THE ORDERS AVAILABLE

(i) Section 8 orders

In the Children Act 1989, a "section 8 order" means any of the following orders and any order varying or discharging such an order (1989 Act, s.8 (1),

(2)). Unlike the old public law orders, orders for custody, access or care and control under the old law were not automatically converted into the new orders when the 1989 Act came into force (because there were not exact equivalents for many of them); but they could be replaced by orders under the new law if the family come back to court.

(a) A residence order

This "means an order settling the arrangements to be made as to the person with whom the child is to live" (1989 Act, s.8(1)). Basically, it decides where the child is to make his home, but it is flexible enough to accommodate a wide variety of living and sharing arrangements. The singular includes the plural (Interpretation Act 1978, s.6(c)) so two or more people could be named in the order. They might be a parent and step-parent sharing a household or they might be a mother and father who live apart. If an order is made in favour of two or more people who do not all live together the order may specify the periods during which the child is to live in the different households concerned (1989 Act, s.11(4)). This was meant to reverse the view that time-sharing of this sort should not be allowed (*Riley* v. *Riley* [1986] 2 F.L.R. 429, C.A.); but courts will probably go on thinking that it should be exceptional (*Re J. (A Minor)* [1991] 2 F.L.R. 385, C.A.). In practice, if separated parents are getting on well enough for such a shared care arrangement to work, it is probably better for the child to have no order at all.

The order only decides where the child is to live. It does not award "custody" or any other bundle of proprietorial rights in the child. If both parents have parental responsibility, they continue to do so, and each may act independently in meeting it, as long as this is not inconsistent with the order. In practice, most parental responsibilities are met by looking after the child, not only while he is at home but also while he is visiting or being visited by the other parent. Each can choose how to look after the child while he is with them.

The situation is therefore quite different from the "joint custody" order which had become increasingly popular in some courts before the 1989 Act (Priest and Whybrow, 1986). A joint custody order gave each parent a power of veto over the other's actions (see Children Act 1975, s.85(3)). In practice, this meant that the parent who was not looking after the child most of the time had some sort of control over the parent who was; although the courts insisted that this did not affect day to day matters, it was not clear exactly what amounted to a serious decision over which the other had a veto; but it did include education, despite the fact that the parent looking after the child would carry all the responsibility of implementing the decision. Under the 1989 Act, each parent retains the power of independent action, so that it is the one who wishes to challenge the other's decisions who has to take the matter to court.

There are, however, two exceptions. While a residence order is in force, no-one can change the child's surname or take him out of the United Kingdom without the consent of everyone with parental responsibility or the leave of the court (1989 Act, s.13(1)). Change of name usually comes up when the mother remarries and is discussed in Chapter 6. Going abroad can be an even bigger problem; the residential parent is allowed to take the child away for up to a month without getting permission (1989 Act, s.13(2)), although the court may prohibit this if there is a risk that she will not return. If she wants to emigrate, the courts will not usually interfere with the reasonable and realistic plans of the parent with whom the children have their home (*Poel* v. *Poel* [1970] 1 W.L.R. 1469; *Barnes* v. *Tyrrell* (1981) 3 F.L.R. 240; *Lonslow* v. *Hennig* [1986] 2 F.L.R. 378). But they will not allow her to take the children away against the other parent's wishes if her plans are unrealistic (*Re K. (A Minor) (Removal from the Jurisdiction)* [1992] 2 F.L.R. 98) or if it will damage the children (*M.* v. *M. (Minors) (Removal from the Jurisdiction)* [1992] 2 F.L.R. 303, C.A.). The courts' respect for the children's need for both their parents is certainly growing.

(b) A contact order

This means an order "requiring the person with whom a child lives, or is to live, to allow the child to visit or stay with the person named in the order, or for that person and the child otherwise to have contact with one another" (1989 Act, s.8(1)). It is sometimes argued that children cannot relate properly to two parents who are not living or in close touch with one another; a clean break from the distressing associations of the past will be better for them and remove a damaging source of worry for the parent with whom they live, who should be left to decide for herself what will be best (Goldstein, Freud and Solnit, 1973). Others feel that a complete severance of ties may do serious harm to the child and his later sense of identity and personal worth, particularly if he is of the same sex as and grows up closely resembling the absent parent who, he has always been told, treated his mother so badly. Children who have lost a parent on divorce continue to grieve for them for a long time afterwards (Wallerstein and Kelly, 1980).

Majority expert opinion (Richards, 1982) supports the second view, as do the courts, for they have described access as a right of the child rather than a right of the parent (*M.* v. *M. (Child: Access)* [1973] 2 All E.R. 81; and see *Re H. (Minors) (Access)* [1992] 1 F.L.R. 148, C.A.). They are particularly likely to take this view where the child is of mixed racial, ethnic or religious origin. The courts are also aware that a parent who is allowed some contact with his child may be more likely to respect his financial obligations towards them, although in theory one is not a *quid pro quo* for the other. But many parents find contact so difficult that they lose touch within a remarkably short time (Maidment, 1976; *cf.* Murch, 1980; Richards, 1982; Bradshaw and Millar, 1991). Contact is notoriously difficult to enforce if the parent carer objects, for sending her to prison or changing the children's residence will not usually help anyone. But for every parent carer who obstructs contact between the child and the other parent there are probably many more who would love there to be some way of forcing the absent parent to keep in touch.

(c) A specific issue order

This means an order "giving directions for the purpose of determining a specific question which has arisen, or which may arise, in connection with any aspect of parental responsibility for a child" (1989 Act, s.8(1)). In the past, the only way in which a court could decide such questions was in wardship or by giving one parent or the other the right to make decisions over a particular area of the child's life. The object of a specific issue order is to enable the court itself to decide a particular dispute about a child's upbringing—where he should go to school, whether he should have an operation, whether he can leave the country, and so on. The "directions" are not therefore simply procedural, to do with how the court is to go about making the decision, but about how the decision of the court is to be put into effect (Donaldson M.R. in *Re B. (A Minor) (Residence Order: Ex Parte)* [1992] Fam.157 at 168, C.A.). The issue must relate to parental responsibility (see chapter 1). Although one recent case held that a specific issue order could not be used *ex parte* to order a blood transfusion for a Jehovah's Witness child (*Re O. (A Minor), The Times,* March 19, 1993) a more recent case has decided that they can and should be used in such cases, although *inter partes* if at all possible (*Re R. (A Minor) (Blood Transfusion), The Independent,* June 9, 1993). Specific issue orders cannot be used as a substitute for residence or contact orders (1989 Act, s.9(5)(*a*)).

(d) A prohibited steps order

This means an order "that no step which could be taken by a parent in meeting his parental responsibility for a child, and which is of a kind specified in the order, shall be taken by any person without the consent of the court" (1989 Act, s.8(1)). This too is modelled on the wardship jurisdiction, where no important step can be taken in the ward's life without leave of the court. In this case, however, the step(s) in question must be specified so that everyone knows where they stand. They must, of course, fall within the scope of parental responsibility. These orders are no substitute for injunctions or orders prohibiting abuse or molestation which cannot possibly be part of parental responsibility. Nor can they be used as a substitute for ouster orders, so as to compel a parent to leave the home (*Nottinghamshire County Council v. P., The Times,* April 8, 1993, C.A.) or to prevent the parents from contacting one another (*Croydon London Borough Council v. A. and Others* [1992] Fam.169). The definition is drafted as if these orders operate against the whole world ("any person") although even in wardship no-one could be punished for disobeying an order of which he was unaware. Support for this interpretation is provided by the contrast with the reference to "the person named in the order" in the definition of a contact order. There is no doubt, however, that courts are finding prohibited steps orders against named persons very useful. As with specific issue orders, however, they cannot be made "with a view to achieving a result which could be achieved by making a residence or contact order" (1989 Act, s. 9(5)(*a*)). As contact orders deal with the contact which is to be allowed, it may be that a prohibited steps order could be used to prevent a parent who has left home from having any contact with his children, but it was not designed for that purpose.

(e) *Supplementary provisions*

There are restrictions on the use of section 8 orders by local authorities (see Chapter 10) and by local authority foster parents (see Chapter 7). The only type of section 8 order which can be made in respect of a child who is subject to a care order is a residence order (1989 Act, s.9(1)). This will bring the care order to an end (1989 Act, s.91(1); see Chapter 10). It is therefore only likely to be used where the child is to go and live with someone other than his parents, for they will normally simply apply for the care order to be discharged (1989 Act, s.39(1)).

Section 8 orders can be made for a limited period of time (s.11(7)(c)) or indefinitely if appropriate. They cannot be made or made to last beyond the child's 16th birthday, unless the circumstances are exceptional (1989 Act, s.9(6)). They will also end automatically on that date unless specially extended in any event when the child reaches 18 (1989 Act, s.91(10),(11)). Section 8 orders are normally made in proceedings between adults to which the child is not a party, but he is just as much a person as they are; it would be wrong to force him to comply with an order once he has reached an age when he is entitled to leave school, seek employment and otherwise try to live an independent life. In any case, it will usually be futile to attempt to do so.

All section 8 orders are in one sense "interim", especially between parents, who both still have parental responsibility and, it is hoped, will remain interested and involved with their children. But some are made to conclude the case after a full hearing or an agreement; others are deliberately made for a short time because the proceedings have not yet been completed; and some relate to the children while other matters remain outstanding. Whenever a court has power to make a section 8 order, it may do so at any time in the course of the proceedings even though it is not yet in a position to dispose of them finally (1989 Act, s.11(3)).

A residence order which provides for the child to live with one (but not both) of two parents who each have parental responsibility for him will come to an end automatically if those parents live together for a continuous period of more than six months (1989 Act, s.11(5)). Similarly, a contact order which requires a parent with whom the child lives to allow the child to have contact with the other parent (whether or not they each have parental responsibility) will come to an end if the parents live together for a continuous period of more than six months (1989 Act, s.11(6)).

Section 8 orders are intended to be very flexible. They may contain directions about how they are to be put into effect (1989 Act, s.11(7)(a)); they may impose conditions to be complied with, not only by the person in whose favour the order is made but also by any parent or person with parental responsibility or anyone else with whom the child is living (1989 Act, s.11(7)(b)); the order itself or any provision in it can have effect for a specified period (1989 Act, s.11(7)(c)); and the court may make such incidental, supplemental or consequential provision as it thinks fit (1989 Act, s.11(7)(d)). These very wide powers are not designed to impose impossible conditions or restrictions on people who are looking after children; an element of common sense and restraint is needed; but they are the counterpart of the rule that people with parental responsibility can usually act alone in deciding how their responsibilities are to be met (1989 Act, s.2((7)). Sometimes it is necessary for a decision to be challenged or conditions imposed, for example, if the child is to live with a parent who has conscientious objections to blood transfusions it may be sensible to insist that the other parent is consulted, so that he or she can consent should the need arise.

(ii) Ancillary injunctions

The High Court has an inherent power to grant injunctions to protect the welfare of children; this, like wardship and the power to appoint guardians, is another aspect of its *parens patriae* jurisdiction in relation to children. The High Court and county courts also have a general power to grant injunctions which are ancillary to any other cause or matter within their jurisdiction. Hence divorce courts may grant injunctions to protect either spouse or children from molestation pending or even after the hearing of a divorce or other matrimonial cause; and county courts may grant injunctions to protect children who are involved in Children Act proceedings from molestation or abuse. County courts also have statutory power to grant injunctions protecting a spouse, or a person who is living with the other as a spouse, or a child living with that person, from molestation and dealing with the short-term occupation of the family home (Domestic Violence and Matrimonial Proceedings Act 1976, s.1(1)).

An injunction is like a prohibited steps order, in that both generally forbid a person to do something, on pain of punishment for contempt of court. But a prohibited steps order prevents a person from taking steps which are within the scope of parental responsibility, and which a parent would otherwise have every right to do; an injunction prevents a person doing something which he would not otherwise have the right to do—it is a fundamental principle that an injunction can only be granted to protect the victim's legal rights. Most types of molestation are also invasions of the victim's legal right not to be assaulted or harmed, but there is no general right not to be molested in other ways. In divorce cases, the courts developed the principle that spouses had the right not to be "kicked or kissed" out of their remedy, which has led to the statutory power to grant protection against molestation. Children, also, have the right to have their welfare protected, but not necessarily at the expense of other rights which the law respects. Hence, a person suspected of harming a child cannot be ousted from the family home which he has a right to occupy unless there is power to do so under the Domestic Violence, Matrimonial Homes, or Domestic Proceedings Acts (see 1. (iii) above). In those Acts, the child's welfare is an important but not the paramount consideration.

(iii) Family assistance orders

The power to make supervision orders in matrimonial cases was first introduced in 1958 as a way of following up and monitoring the arrangements approved in divorce cases (see 1. (i) above). Orders were usually made as a result of a welfare officer's report. Reports became very common in disputed cases, but courts varied in their readiness to call for them where there was no dispute (Eekelaar and Clive, 1977; Eekelaar, 1982). Officers also varied in their readiness to recommend supervision (James and Wilson, 1984). Surprisingly, perhaps, some courts with particularly high rates of joint custody also had high rates of supervision orders (Priest and Whybrow, 1986). It was possible to appoint either a probation officer or the local social services authority as supervisor, but the criteria, duration and effects of a "matrimonial" supervision order were never clearly defined. Its purposes had become much broader than originally envisaged (Law Commission, 1987a).

The purpose might be to provide support for the children or the parent with whom they were living after the trauma of divorce; or to reassure the losing parent in a difficult contested case; or, perhaps most frequently, to help the parents to learn to co-operate with one another and to manage continued contact with their children. These purposes were relatively specific and short term and the supervisor was usually the court welfare officer who had been involved in the report (Booth, 1985; Law Commission, 1987a). Where there was a need for long term protection of the child from possible abuse or neglect, or for access to the social services department's resources, it might be more appropriate for the local authority to be appointed supervisor. But in that case, confusion was caused by the difference between these orders and orders under the child protection legislation. There was also a risk that children might be stigmatised as having been in need of supervision when it was often their parents and not they who needed expert help.

The 1989 Act provides two different orders to meet these two situations. In child protection cases where social services involvement is required, the case should be referred for a possible supervision order under section 31 (see (iv) below). If shorter term assistance is needed to help the family through the trauma of separation or conflict about their children, a family assistance order under section 16 may be more appropriate.

A family assistance order may be made of the court's own motion in any family proceedings in which it has power to make a section 8 order, whether or not it does make such an order (1989 Act, s.16(1)). The order requires either a probation officer to be made available, or a local social services authority to make a social worker available, to "advise, assist and (where appropriate) befriend" anyone named in the order (1989 Act, s.16(1)). The people named may be any parent or guardian of the child, anyone with whom the child is living or who is named in a contact order, or the child himself (1989 Act, s.16(2)). The circumstances have to be exceptional and everyone named in the order, other than the child, has to consent (1989 Act, s.16(3)). The consent of the probation service or local social services authority is not required; the probation officer is selected in accordance with arrangements made by the local probation committee for the area where the child lives or is to live (1989 Act, s.16(8); if the one selected dies or is unable to act another will be selected in the same way; s.16(9)); the local social services authority is the one for the area where the child lives or will live—unless another local authority has agreed to act (1989 Act, s.16(7)).

A family assistance order lasts for six months or a shorter specified period (1989 Act, s.16(5)), but the court could always make another order if the circumstances were still exceptional. The order may direct anyone named in it keep the officer informed, in whatever way is specified, of his address and to allow him to visit the person named (1989 Act, s.16(4)). While the order is in force, the officer also has power to refer to the court the question of whether any section 8 order about the child should be varied or discharged (1989 Act, s.16(6)). Although intended as a private law measure, it looks as though courts are mainly finding these orders useful in public law cases (Booth, 1992).

(iv) Referral to the local social services authority

Before the 1989 Act, children might be compulsorily committed to care in the course of family proceedings. This again was first introduced to give teeth to the divorce court's duty to approve the arrangements made in divorce cases and was later extended to other proceedings. Some local authorities would deliberately intervene in divorce proceedings in order to apply for children to be committed to care; in this way a care case could be transferred from the magistrates' to the divorce or High Court. The criteria were simply that the circumstances were exceptional; no special grounds or pre-conditions were laid down; there was no provision for a guardian *ad litem* or similar protection for the child; and the effect on the legal position of the child, his parents and the local authority was by no means clear. It was wrong that children could end up in compulsory care without any of the usual safeguards, even if in practice this only happened in very serious cases. Children committed to care in family proceedings tended to remain there for a very long time.

The 1989 Act ensures that the criteria, procedures and effects of committal to care are the same, no matter how the child came to the authority's attention. If a court in any family proceedings (see 1. (iii) above) considers that it may be appropriate for a care or supervision order to be made, it may direct the local authority to undertake an investigation of the child's circumstances (1989 Act, s.37(1)). The authority is the one for the area where the child is "ordinarily resident" or otherwise the one where the circumstances arose (1989 Act, s.37(5)). The authority must then investigate and consider whether to apply for a care or supervision order; or to provide services or assistance for the child or his family; or to take any other action about the child (1989 Act, s.37(2)). If they decide not to apply for an order, they must inform the court of their reasons, of the services they do or intend to provide for the child or his family, and any other action they propose to take (1989, Act, s.37(3)). This must be done within eight weeks of the direction, unless the court directs otherwise (1989 Act, s.37(4)). The authority must also decide at that time whether to review the case later and if so set a date (1989 Act, s.37(6)).

This means that the courts can no longer make a care or supervision order of their own motion, effectively forcing the authority's hand. However, if when giving a direction under section 37 (1), the court finds that there are reasonable grounds for believing that the threshold criteria for making a care or supervision order are made out (see Chapter 10), it may also make an interim care order or an interim supervision order (1989 Act, s.38(1)(b), (2)). It then has all the usual powers associated with an interim care order. If the court gives a direction and makes or is considering making an interim order, it must appoint a guardian *ad litem* for the child unless satisfied that this is not necessary in order to safeguard his interests (1989 Act, s.41(1)(6)(b)). The child is therefore as well protected as he is in any other care proceedings. Although an interim order can be made whether or not the local authority have asked for one, the authority are under no obligation to take over the proceedings and apply for a full care or supervision order when the interim order comes to an end.

3. THE PRINCIPLES

(i) The welfare principle

"When a court determines any question with respect to—(a) the upbringing of a child; or (b) the administration of a child's property or the application of any income arising from it, the child's welfare shall be the court's paramount consideration." (Children Act 1989, s.1(1)).

This was meant to repeat the existing law, although not in exactly the same words. The provision which it replaced (Guardianship of Minors Act 1971, s.1, itself replacing the Guardianship of Infants Act 1925, s.1, where it first appeared) required the court to make the child's welfare its "first and paramount" consideration. A "first" consideration may be the most important but could leave room for other considerations to be taken into account. In *J.* v. *C.* [1970] A.C. 668, however, the House of Lords said that the "paramount" consideration was the one which "rules on or determines the course to be followed". Later cases decided that this ruled out balancing the child's welfare against other considerations such as "justice" between his parents (*Re K. (Minors) (Wardship: Care and Control)* [1977] Fam.179, C.A.; *S. (B.D.)* v. *S. (D.J.) (Infants: Care and Consent)* [1977] Fam.109, C.A.). The Law Commission (1988) therefore recommended making this crystal clear in a provision that the child's welfare should be the court's "only concern". But is it likely that the courts will now say that making the child's welfare their "paramount consideration" rather than their only concern means that other things can be weighed in the balance against it? Mostly, the other things which the courts might want to take into account are also relevant to assessing the child's welfare.

The courts have often said that each case is an exercise of their discretion in its own individual circumstances and that there are no "rules" or even "principles" as to what is best for children. The appeal court will only interfere with the decision of the court which heard the evidence and saw the people involved if it was "plainly wrong" (*G. v. G. (Minors: Custody Appeal)* [1985] 1 W.L.R. 647, H.L.). One recent example, however, comes close to laying down a rule. In *Re W. (A Minor) (Residence Order)* [1992] 2 F.L.R. 332, unmarried parents made a parental responsibility agreement intending that the father would bring the baby up. The mother allowed the father to collect the newborn baby from hospital but soon changed her mind. The Court of Appeal held that there was a "rebuttable presumption of fact" that a baby was better with the mother and made a residence order in her favour.

(ii) The checklist

The Children Act 1989 refused to lay down general rules, whether that young children were better with their mothers, or that siblings should not be separated, or that all children need to keep in touch with both their parents. But it does contain a "checklist" of factors to which the court must have regard whenever it is considering whether to make, vary or discharge a section 8 order and this is opposed by any party to the proceedings (1989 Act, s.1(3),(4)). The object is to encourage courts to consider all the factors which are likely to be relevant in a systematic way; this may lead to greater predictability and consistency and also to fewer contested cases. Limiting the court's duty to "opposed" cases does not mean that these factors are otherwise ignored, merely that the court does not laboriously have to consider them when the parties are agreed. But the parties are likely to take them into account when negotiating their own arrangements. Checklists can be a great help to solicitors or mediators in helping them to focus the parties' minds on the things that the court is going to find relevant rather than on other things—such as the rights and wrongs of their own relationship—which are only indirectly relevant to the children's welfare. The court is required to have regard "in particular" to the following seven factors:

(a) *"the ascertainable wishes and feelings of the child concerned (considered in the light of his age and understanding)"*

This mirrors a provision which has been part of adoption law for some time but had never before been expressly stated in other proceedings. Two questions arise: first, how much weight will the court give to the child's views; and secondly, how can it find out what these are?

A court will hardly ever make an order if the child is 16 or over in any event. Below that age, it will take his views into account, the more so the older he is, and if he is adamant it may have little other option (*M. v. M. (Minor: Custody Appeal)* [1987] 1 W.L.R. 404 C.A.); but it will also bear in mind that he may be influenced by the spite of one parent, the bribery of another, or the natural preferences of a young person who is not yet able to judge his own long term best interests (*Re S. (Infants)* [1977] 1 W.L.R. 396; *Re D.W.* (1983) 14 Fam.Law 17). Children change their minds at least as often as adults do. There is a distinction between their "wishes", which can be variable or ambivalent or under undue influence, and their "feelings", which are a significant part of the relationships around them. It is also important that the child is not made to feel responsible for choosing between his parents (*Adams* v. *Adams* [1984] F.L.R. 768). But whether or not the court does what the child wants, it should always pay proper attention and respect to his views and they may well tip the balance in a difficult case (*Re P. (A Minor) (Education)* [1992] 1 F.L.R. 316, C.A.).

How then are the child's views to be ascertained and put before the court? Discovering and assessing a child's true wishes and feelings is a difficult task requiring different skills from those commonly possessed by lawyers. The court may order that the child be made a party to the proceedings in his own right. He or his representative can then take a full part in the proceedings, calling and cross-examining witnesses, addressing the court, and appealing. This is very rarely done in private law proceedings, unless the child is making an application on his own behalf. Generally, the courts take the view that the realistic options, evidence and arguments are likely to emerge fully from the cases presented by the adult parties, so that it would be a waste of scarce time and resources to insist upon another party. If the child is made a party, the case is normally conducted on his behalf by a guardian *ad litem*, usually the Official Solicitor (Family Proceedings Rules 1991, r. 9.2). Guardians from the panel used in public law cases (see Chapter 10) cannot be used in private law proceedings. The guardian must conduct the case in what he thinks are the child's best interests, rather than how the child wants. If the child asks, or if his solicitor thinks he is capable, he can be allowed to conduct the case without a guardian (1991 Rules, r. 9.2A). This will depend upon how mature he is thought to be. The courts have upheld the right of a 13-year-old girl (*Re T. (A Minor) (Wardship: Representation), The Times,* May 10, 1993) but refused to allow an 11-year-old boy to instruct his own solicitor (*Re S. (A Minor) (Representation), The Times,* March 2, 1993, C.A.

It will rarely be in the child's interests to call him as a witness and subject him, not only to the strains and formalities of a court appearance, but also to the prospect of cross-examination on behalf of one or both of his parents. In the High Court and county courts the judge may interview the child in private, but this is not encouraged and magistrates are not allowed to do so. Although it may appear a humane and sensible solution, it is difficult to reconcile with our traditional court procedures, which depend upon the open exchange of evidence which can be challenged or rebutted by any party. The child cannot be given an assurance that any confidences will be respected, because his parents must obviously be told of anything relevant which they might want to challenge or rebut (*Elder* v. *Elder* [1986] 1 F.L.R. 610). Nor are all judges comfortable with the idea of seeing and talking to children, but many will do so if the child asks and some will ask to do so themselves.

Hence one of the welfare officer's most important tasks (see 4.(i) below) is to canvass the child's own "wishes and feelings". Here again, the child cannot be given a guarantee of confidentiality, but the welfare officer can choose what to put into the report which will go before the court and be made available to the parties, thus avoiding some of the "due process" problems of the court seeing the child in private. Many will regard this compromise solution as unsatisfactory—should not the child always have a right to be heard if he wishes? And should not the court at least have an obligation to meet the child's whose future it is to decide?

(b) *"his physical, emotional and educational needs"* which is perhaps most easily considered along with (*d*) *"his age, sex, background and any characteristics of his which the court considers relevant"* and (*f*) *"how capable each of his parents, and any other person in relation to whom the court considers the question to be relevant, is of meeting his needs"*

These three factors go together. It is the needs of the particular child which are in question, and these obviously vary according to his age, sex and developmental state. They may also vary according to his "background", which includes his racial, ethnic and religious background, as well as more controversially his social-economic class. And although the court is not in terms engaged in evaluating the parents, or anyone else, in the "good parent" stakes, if choices have to be made it is the comparative merits of the parents in meeting their child's needs which will determine what will be best for him. The court will also have to take into account the merits of other significant people in the child's life, particularly any new partners, proposed substitute carers or helpers, and other members of the family.

The child's physical needs were the courts' major preoccupation in earlier days and even now that other factors loom larger, their mundane importance should not be over-looked. How suitable is the accommodation offered? How are the child's basic needs for food, clothing, hygiene to be supplied? How will a working parent cope with school holidays, late afternoons, or a pre-school child? It is not a question of which family is the better-off, for the courts may find it easier to believe that a woman can provide better physical care, especially for a young child, than can a man (*e.g. Re K. (Minors) (Children: Care and Control)* [1977] Fam.179, C.A.; *cf. B. v. B. (Custody of Children)* [1985] F.L.R. 166, C.A.). Full-time care, even on income support, may be preferred to variable or impracticable arrangements made by a working parent. But where there is a substantial disparity in material standards between otherwise equally suitable homes, the courts may not be able to ignore it. However, in the matter of physical care, as in so many things, the mother usually enjoys a built-in advantage.

The courts realised long ago that children had more than physical needs, but at first this tended to be reflected in concern for their "moral" welfare. The parents' behaviour towards one another is no longer of much significance in itself (*Re K.* again; see (iv) below), but its effects upon the children can be crucial. The courts realise that adultery does not make a woman a bad mother, but they may consider whether there will be adverse effects if she were a prostitute or a lesbian or the children have previously been brought up on the strictest moral principles. Cases involving lesbian mothers depend a good deal on what the experts say; an expert called on behalf of the child may carry more conviction in persuading the court that there is little evidence of harm to children brought up in lesbian households than an expert called on behalf of the mother (*cf. C.* v. *C.* (*A Minor*) (*Custody: Appeal*) [1991] 1 F.L.R. 223, C.A. and *C.* v. *C.* (*No. 2*) [1992] 1 F.C.R. 206). A criminal or violent history or homosexuality in the father will also be taken into account.

Religion may be a factor. Although the courts do not prefer one religion above another they may prefer some religious or moral guidance to none at all, and may prefer the (perhaps stricter) values of one parent to those of the other (*May* v. *May* [1986] 1 F.L.R. 325, C.A.). There are some religious sects which they recognise may do positive harm to the children, particularly if they have only recently been espoused by one of the parents (*Re B. and G.* (*Minors*) (*Custody*) [1985] F.L.R. 493). Apart from those rare cases, where a child has already acquired a settled religious faith they will be reluctant to disturb it but there is no rule or principle against doing so (*Re R.* (*A Minor*), *The Times*, November 3, 1992, C.A.).

Recently, these considerations have been over-shadowed by concern for the child's emotional well-being. At best, the court should make a close investigation of the quality of the relationships surrounding the child, and of the strength of his attachments, not only with his natural parents but also with the people offered as parent substitutes (*e.g. Stephenson* v. *Stephenson* [1985] F.L.R. 1140, C.A.). This led the courts to abandon the old practice of deciding cases entirely on affidavit evidence; now all the adults involved should be seen as witnesses and an attempt made to assess their characters and qualities as parents (see Thorpe, 1993). In practice, however, the court may be tempted to rely on rather stereotyped ideas of a child's emotional needs. Here again the mother can enjoy a built-in advantage, for the courts have tended to assume that the natural mother is best for a young child (*Re W.* (*A Minor*) (*Custody*) (1982) 4 F.L.R. 492, C.A.; *Re W.*, page 75, above; *cf. B.* v. *B.* and *Stephenson* v. *Stephenson* above). On the other hand, it is sometimes assumed that older boys need a father's firm hand and guidance (*e.g. May* v. *May* above).

In a sense this is part of a child's educational needs—to be brought up not only with the knowledge and skills necessary to play a proper part in adult life but also with the social and behavioural skills needed to become a mature and law-abiding member of society. The courts will look at the schooling and other educational opportunities available to the child both inside and outside the home in the light of the circumstances of the family and of any particular needs the child himself may have.

(c) *"the likely effect on him of any change in his circumstances"*

A vital factor is the need to cause as little disruption as possible to the child's already disrupted life. The court will certainly try to preserve the status quo in the immediate stress of parting and to discourage one parent from snatching the children away (*Re B. (Minors) (Residence Order)* [1992] Fam.157, C.A.). But eventually the court may conclude that the parent best suited to supply the child's needs is the one who is not at present looking after him. Where the parents have not been separated long, the court will not be deterred from ordering a transfer (*Allington* v. *Allington* [1985] F.L.R. 586, C.A.). It would not be right if the one who happened to retain the children at the separation enjoyed too great an advantage. The court may also be able to order that the parent with whom the child is to live returns to the matrimonial home. The problem becomes most acute when the parents have been separated from some time. Gone are the days when the court could contemplate with equanimity the transfer of a child aged seven from the only home she had ever known (*Re Thain* [1926] Ch. 676). Nowadays they are well aware of the child's need for stability and continuity, not only in relationships with parents, but also in physical surroundings, school, friends, and above all, brothers and sisters (*Re C. (A Minor) (Custody of Child)* (1980) 2 F.L.R. 163, C.A.; *B.* v. *B.* above). A reading of the reported decisions of the Court of Appeal suggests that the courts are sometimes prepared to disturb a long-standing and quite satisfactory status quo, particularly if the children have been with their father (Maidment, 1981), yet the empirical evidence suggests that transfer of the child from one parent to another as a result of a court order is rare; it is far more likely to result from a parents' own arrangements (Eekelaar and Clive, 1977). Their arrangements are also the main reason why the mother ends up looking after the child in around 90 per cent. of cases (see Priest and Whybrow, 1986).

(e) *"any harm which he has suffered or is at risk of suffering"*

"Harm" in this provision has the same meaning as it has for the purpose of care proceedings (1989 Act, s.105(1)). Hence it means "ill-treatment or the impairment of health or development"; "ill-treatment" includes sexual abuse and forms of ill-treatment which are not physical; "development" means physical, intellectual, emotional, social or behavioural development; and "health" means physical or mental health (1989 Act, s.31(9); see Chapter 10). Generally, however, the actual or possible risk of harm will be part of considering the child's needs and how best the adults involved can meet them.

(g) *"the range of powers available to the court under this Act in the proceedings in question"*

This is the only factor in the checklist which is relevant, not to assessing the child's welfare, but to how best to provide for it. The court is not bound to accept the proposals put forward by the parties but can suggest others, provided, of course, that it has behaved in a properly judicial way. There is no point in considering alternatives which may well be better but which the court cannot oblige anyone to provide; there is no point in forcing the child or an order relating to the child upon someone who does not wish it; and it is wrong for the court to devise a solution which it has not at least canvassed in court with the parties so that they can comment upon it.

(iii) The "no order" principle

"Where a court is considering whether or not to make one or more orders under this Act with respect to a child, it shall not make the order or any of the orders unless it considers that doing so would be better for the child than making no order at all" (Children Act 1989, s.1(5)).

The object is to stop the court making orders which will be of no benefit to the child. It puts the burden on the person who wants an order to explain to the court why an order would be better than leaving things as they are. In divorce and other cases between the child's parents, it used to be assumed that some order had to be made about the children, whether or not the parents wanted one and whether or not it would do any good. That attitude was understandable in the days before the Guardianship Act 1973, because until then the child's mother had no parental rights and authority unless and until there was a court order. Once that Act had given married parents equality, as does the 1989 Act (1989 Act, s.2(1)), there was no need to make an order simply to give the mother status. Making an order can make one parent look like a winner, the other a loser, one important and one insignificant in the child's life. The hope is to keep them both involved if at all possible.

However, the section does *not* say that it is usually better for children to make no order. It must be better for the child to make an order if there is a dispute between his parents, or if a likely dispute may be forestalled. Even if they have agreed, the child may benefit from the security which an order gives both him and his carer. The courts have already recognised this for maintenance orders (*K.* v. *H.*, *The Times*, December 31, 1992). An order also brings other benefits, such as the residential parent's right to take the child abroad on holiday or to appoint a testamentary guardian (see Chapter 5), or the other parent's right to see the child. Often, the parents are not really agreed but simply not prepared to fight about things, knowing how much harm it will do both to them and their children. Just as there may be a risk of one parent feeling left out if there is a residence order in favour of the other, there may also be a risk of his feeling even less wanted if there is no formal arrangement for him to retain contact.

There is already some evidence (Booth, 1992; Bainham, 1993) that the courts have been more than enthusiastic in espousing the so-called "no order" principle, believing quite rightly that it is better for the child to retain as full a relationship as possible with both parents, without considering the impact on the absent parent and also on the one who has the main burden of bringing up the child. Shared parental responsibility is all very well, but the practical responsibility is very rarely shared equally and the child's interests are closely tied up with those of the parent with whom he has his home.

(iv) The non-delay principle

"In any proceedings in which any question with respect to the upbringing of a child arises, the court shall have regard to the general principle that any delay in determining the question is likely to prejudice the welfare of the child" (Children Act 1989, s.1(2)).

This is the one value judgment contained in the 1989 Act about what is likely (though not certain) to be best for a child. The courts often used to urge that children cases should be tried as quickly as possible and need not wait for the solution of other issues between the parents (*Jones* v. *Jones* [1974] 1 W.L.R. 1471, C.A.); but there were no rules requiring cases to be heard according to a particular timetable and views differed about whether this would be practicable (Booth, 1985; Law Commission, 1987a). The speed of litigation depends mainly on the parties, who do not normally include the child. In cases about children, delay is almost always to the advantage of one of the adult parties, and it is not necessarily unprofessional for their legal advisers to do all they can to exploit this. Professional convenience is a considerable factor in the "culture of delay" which affects so many court proceedings (Murch *et al.*, 1987, 1992). The whole adult world tends to forget that a child's sense of time is entirely different from its own and what may seem a short time to parents, professionals and courts may have been an age for the child (Goldstein, Freud and Solnit, 1973).

Hence the Act not only lays down a general principle, but backs it up with a duty upon the court, in any proceedings where the question of making (or any other question relating to) a section 8 order arises, to draw up a timetable with a view to determining the question without delay and to give directions to ensure so far as is reasonably practicable that the time-table is kept (1989 Act, s.11(1)). This is done at a directions hearing; the court rules also provide set time limits which can only be extended by the court and insist that the court fixes a return date whenever the case is adjourned (Family Proceedings Rules 1991, rr. 4.14, 4.15).

Some delays can be beneficial. Time taken in investigation may be well spent, but only if the information derived from the investigation is going materially to increase the court's chances of making the right decision without prejudicing the question at issue (*Re C. (A Minor) (Custody of Child)* (1980) 2 F.L.R. 163, C.A.). Time taken in positive work with the family to improve their relationships or enable them to arrive at sensible conclusion for themselves may be even better spent, but not if it is used tactically by one side. Other delays may not be beneficial but could be unavoidable. Each party has normally to be given notice and a reasonable time within which to prepare their case. Welfare officers have to be given time to investigate and report. This can be a major source of delay which can be attributed to resources rather than ill-will or inefficiency. However, it may be more efficient to work to fixed but realistic deadlines than for the court to wait until everyone is ready.

(v) Should there be any other principles?

Are the child's interests the only interests which can be taken into account? The other consideration which has featured prominently in the past is the parents' own conduct towards one another. The way in which they have behaved towards their *children* is a vital factor in judging the children's welfare; sometimes their behaviour towards *one another* is relevant to their suitability as parents, particularly in the case of violence. The parties often want the law to take their "innocence" or the other person's "guilt" into account for its own sake. It is only natural for an "unimpeachable" father whose wife has left him for another man to resent her claim to the children.

The law used to agree with him. As late as 1962, the Court of Appeal declined to give the care of two little girls aged four and six to their mother, although they clearly thought that she could look after them better, because the "claims of justice" could not be over-looked and she had wantonly broken up the home to go and live near her "paramour" (*Re L. (Infants)* [1962] 1 W.L.R. 886, C.A.). This suggested that the claims of justice might be balanced against the welfare of the children, and even that such a wife should not be given all that she wanted, because then she would have no inducement to return. Both ideas have since been firmly rejected by the Court of Appeal (*Re K. (Minors) (Children: Care and Control)* [1977] Fam.179, C.A.; *S. (B.D.)* v. *S. (D.J.) (Children: Care and Control)* [1977] Fam.109, C.A.).

Re K. is a good general illustration. It concerned a boy aged five and a girl aged two. Their father was an Anglican clergyman; their mother had been a teacher of religion; but the marriage was not happy and the mother fell in love with another man. She eventually decided to set up home with him, although they would not be able to marry for many years. She did not want to leave without the children and so applied for permission to take them with her. The father strongly opposed this, arguing that the children would suffer harm by being brought up by their mother and a man living together in blatant defiance of all that their father believed in, and also that as the "unimpeachable" parent his wishes were entitled to consideration.

Nevertheless, the court held that the children should go with their mother. No modern judge could easily contemplate removing a two-year-old girl from a good mother who intended to live with a man whom the children knew well and liked, or separating the children from one another. The harm which they might suffer from knowing of their mother's immorality would happen whether they stayed or went, for they were bound to see a lot of her and to ask why they were not together. There was no such thing as an "unimpeachable" parent and his wishes could not be taken into account against the welfare of the children.

This approach is attractive to anyone who shares the view of the Court of Appeal in *Re K.*, that the courts are not competent to decide upon the rights and wrongs of a marital breakdown and that children should not be regarded as prizes for good matrimonial behaviour, any more than losing them should be regarded as a punishment for bad. But it is still worthwhile asking whether the interests of one child should invariably be regarded as paramount over the interests of everyone else.

For a start, there is no reason to elevate the interests of the child involved in the litigation above the interests of any other child who may be affected by the decision (see Law Commission, 1988). The court have recognised this in a decision giving equal weight to the welfare of a teenage mother in seeing her baby at least until a long term placement was found and to the welfare of the baby who would derive no positive benefit from it (*Re H. (A Minor)*, *The Times*, February 23, 1993). But are not the wishes and feelings of all parents entitled to consideration in their own right and not just for light they throw upon the children's welfare? Should a marginal benefit for the child be bought at the cost of devastating the life and happiness of one of the parents? And is there not a case for saying that parents have claims which are based, not on their respective behaviour towards one another, but on their respective commitment to and behaviour towards the child? Should there perhaps be some sort of presumption in favour of the person who has carried out the bulk of the work of looking after the child in the past (Smart and Sevenhuijsen, 1989)? This is not to suggest a presumption in favour of mothers, although it will usually have that effect, for it may be that the father has done the bulk of the work for a particular child. But although both parents make an important contribution to a child's life, especially when looked at in retrospect when he has grown up, if disputes arise when he is a child, is it right or realistic to ascribe equal weight to the very different contributions which each of them commonly makes? Perhaps, as Bainham (1993) has suggested, we need a more sophisticated approach to weighing the competing interests of everyone involved in family decisions; the child's interest in a new pair of trainers may not be as important as the whole family's interest in a trip to the seaside.

4. INDEPENDENT AND EXPERT EVIDENCE

It is often said that children's cases are not like other kinds of litigation (Mnookin, 1975). The court is not asked simply to decide what has happened in the past and then to apply straightforward rules of law to those facts in order to arrive at a result. There are no rules of law; instead there is a discretion in which a number of factors have to be taken into account; but the underlying values, other than the primacy of the child's welfare, have not been articulated. In assessing this the court is less concerned with what has happened in the past than with what is likely to happen in the future and with the interaction of the characters and personalities of everyone involved. This is all very alarming. It is only natural that courts should recognise the difficulties of their task and look for help from others whom they believe to be experts in making these judgments. There are two possibilities open to them.

(i) Welfare officers' reports

English law recognised in the 1950s that it is a mistake to assume that adults who are themselves under emotional strain will present all the relevant material to the court or even be aware of it. Their lawyers' first duty is to the adult client, although many urge parents to consider their children's welfare carefully. The comparative rarity of disputes may result partly from legal advice as to the prospects of success (particularly for fathers) and partly from the parents' own appreciation of the damage which a dispute could do.

Any court considering any question about a child under the Children Act 1989 has power to call for a welfare officer's report on "such matters relating to the child's welfare as are required to be dealt with in the report" (1989 Act, s.7(1)). It is a great help to the welfare officer if the court makes plain the purpose of the report (residence, contact, or some specific issue) and the matters about which it particularly needs to be informed. The Lord Chancellor also has power to make regulations specifying what has to be dealt with in a report unless the court orders otherwise (1989 Act, s.7(2)).

The report may be required either from a probation officer or from a local authority which may ask either a social worker or any other appropriate person to provide it (1989 Act, s.7(1)). Unless the local arrangements are different, welfare officers' reports are provided by the probation service. This is somewhat outside their normal responsibilities relating to offenders, but many services have specialist civil sections. Even so, their professional context and organisation is very different from that of the local authority social workers who make up the panels of guardians *ad litem* in care proceedings (see Chapter 10). Nor do they have the right to seek expert evidence on behalf of the child. Their role is not to represent the child as such, but to help the court. Many have also seen it as their role to try to get the parties to agree; originally they would do this themselves, and the court may ask them to do so; increasingly, however, referrals are made to an independent mediation service.

Promoting reconciliation was the original reason for the involvement of probation officers in matrimonial cases. Nowadays, there is more emphasis on conciliation (or mediation as it is now usually known), working with the parties to improve communication between them, to help them to come to terms with the separation, and to co-operate rather than to fight about its practical consequences, especially the future of their children (Parkinson, 1986; Fisher, 1990). But while a report-writer may adopt a conciliatory approach, the courts have emphasised that the two functions should be kept quite separate (*Re H. (Conciliation: Welfare Reports)* [1986] 1 F.L.R. 476; *Scott* v. *Scott* [1982] 2 F.L.R. 320). Mediation must be carried on in circumstances where each party is able to speak freely, not only about what has happened in the past but also about his or her plans and proposals for the future (statements made are therefore privileged from disclosure in legal proceedings; see *Re D. (Minors) (Conciliation: Disclosure of Information)* [1993] 2 W.L.R. 721, C.A.). An officer who is charged with investigation and reporting back to the court cannot give the necessary guarantee of confidentiality. Also, the method chosen may be quite different—a series of family meetings in which feelings, relationships and options are explored with a view to reaching an acceptable solutions may be the right way of conducting mediation; it may be quite the wrong way of finding out what the court needs to know from an independent source before it can decide the case.

Welfare officers' reports are confidential in the sense that they should not be disclosed beyond the parties to the case. They must, however, be disclosed to the parties so that they can have a proper opportunity of challenging or rebutting anything contentious (Family Proceedings Rules 1991, r. 4.13). This is a simple aspect of the rules of natural justice, but has not always been clearly understood in the past (Murch, 1980).

If the court calls for a report, it will want some straightforward information about the family and each of the homes offered, but also an assessment of the quality and stability of relationships within them and with the child and the quality of care which each may offer. It is highly desirable that the same officer should visit each home, although if they are far apart this may not be possible. The court will also want to know how the child is getting on at school, something of his own character and relationships, and what he feels about the situation. The report should differentiate quite clearly between matters of which the officer has first hand knowledge and matters which are merely hearsay, and also between statements of fact and expressions of opinion (*Thompson* v. *Thompson* (1975) [1986] 1 F.L.R. 212). The court may take account of any relevant statement in a report, and any evidence given in respect of matters contained in it, even if these contravene the ordinary rules of evidence (1989 Act, s.7(4)). A parent who wishes to challenge unverified statements is placed in an unjustifiable dilemma, for he may have to choose between antagonising the court and allowing a false picture to emerge. If a definite recommendation is made, it carries a great deal of weight, so much so that the court should always give reasons for rejecting it (*Stephenson* v. *Stephenson*, page 78, above; *Re T.* (1980) 1 F.L.R. 59).

(ii) Expert evidence

The courts' attitude to expert medical evidence is said to be entirely different. They cannot call for independent medical reports and so the evidence is presented on behalf of one or both of the parties. Thus, in both wardship and family proceedings the court's leave is required for any medical or psychiatric examination or other assessment for the purpose of preparing expert evidence for the proceedings (Family Proceedings Rules 1991, r. 4.18). When medical evidence is offered, the courts affect to treat it with great caution. If the child is suffering from some physical or mental disorder, his doctor's evidence obviously has an important bearing on who is best suited to care for him, but as Lord Upjohn said in *J.* v. *C.* [1970] A.C. 668 at 726:

"you have the case of a happy and normal infant in no need of medical care . . . who is sent to a psychiatrist or other medical practitioner for the sole purpose of calling the practitioner to give quite general evidence upon the dangers of taking this, that or the other course . . . [This] evidence may be valuable if accepted but . . . only as an element to support the general knowledge and experience of the judge in infancy matters . . . "

The courts do not want to abandon their discretion to doctors, who do rely heavily on retrospective studies of self-selected groups in offering this evidence. But there is no doubt that the judges have been greatly educated and helped by the expert evidence they have heard and they now give the evidence of child psychiatrists a great deal of weight. Indeed, the view is sometimes expressed that they may be inclined to give it more weight than the true state of scientific development in this area warrants (see Mnookin, 1975; King 1981). This is an especial danger if experts can only be called by the adult parties.

The courts have recently realised that in this respect the guardian *ad litem* system in public law proceedings has advantages (see Chapter 10) over the welfare officer's report system in private law proceedings. The guardian *ad litem* has the task of investigating and presenting the case for the child who is a party to the proceedings. If necessary she can instruct independent experts to examine and report on the child's behalf; as a social worker she may also have access to a wider range of services to assess and assist the family. There is a case for making the guardian *ad litem* system available in some particularly difficult private law cases.

5. MAINTENANCE AND PROPERTY

There are now two separate systems of ordering provision for a child whose parents are living apart, the child support system introduced by the Child Support Act 1991 and the residual powers of the courts under the matrimonial legislation and the Children Act 1989. The child support system is being phased in between 1993 and 1997; it will handle all new cases (whether or not the recipient is on benefit) from April 1993, and take over existing benefit cases by stages from 1993 to 1996 and existing non-benefit cases from 1996 to 1997. This means that existing settlements can be partially unpicked, by increasing the amount of child support payable, but the capital element cannot be varied unless power to do this was built in at the beginning.

(i) The Child Support Act 1991

The impetus for the 1991 Act came from the massive increase in the numbers of lone parent families living on income support, from 330,000 in 1980 to 770,000 in 1989, and the decrease in the proportion of these who were receiving any maintenance from the other parent, from 50 per cent. in 1981/

82 to 23 per cent. in 1988/89. Court orders had become inadequate, inconsistent and ineffective in enforcing parental liabilities. One reason is that courts are largely in the hands of the parties, particularly when they have agreed. A combination of the courts' own philosophy of the "clean break" and the parties' own "welfare benefit planning" led to settlements where the carer parent got the house in exchange for nominal maintenance for herself and sometimes even for the children. The temptation to do this is obvious when the paying parent cannot afford enough to keep them above the means-tested benefit levels and anything he pays reduces the benefit they get pound for pound. Both the courts and the D.S.S. recognised that in practice he would give priority to his new family, including children of his new partner. Maintenance plays a larger part in the incomes of lone parents who go out to work and some might find that it makes all the difference to their ability to do so.

(a) Who is liable?

Under the 1991 Act, each parent of a "qualifying child" is responsible for maintaining him (1991 Act, s.1(1)). A qualifying child is one who has at least one "absent parent" (1991 Act, s.3(1)); an "absent parent" is one who does not live in the same household as the child, provided that the child does have his home with a "person with care" (1991 Act, s.3(2)); a "person with care" is a parent, guardian, person with the benefit of a residence order, or anyone else with whom the child lives and who looks after him day to day (unless in an excepted category) (1991 Act, s.3(3),(4)). Thus, while the recipient carer need not be a parent, the liability to pay falls only on the child's natural or adoptive parents. The idea is that parents should be identified and made to honour their liabilities throughout the child's life and that one's own children should always take precedence over anyone else's. Step-children are not taken into account on either side of the calculation.

If someone disputes parenthood, the child support officer (C.S.O.) cannot go ahead with assessing maintenance unless the case is cast iron, *i.e.* he is an adoptive parent, or has been declared or found to be the child's parent in other proceedings (1991 Act, s.26). For this purpose there is no presumption that a child born to a married woman is her husband's child. The D.S.S. or the applicant can then apply to any family court for a declaration of parentage for the purpose of this Act (1991 Act, s.27). Whether the presumption will be applied in those proceedings remains to be seen.

(b) Applying for an assessment

Either the carer or the absent parent can apply for an assessment (1991 Act, s.4(1)). There is nothing to prevent them making a maintenance agreement instead (1991 Act, s.9(2)) but this cannot prevent either of them, or anyone else, applying for an assessment and a contractual provision trying to prevent this is void (1991 Act, s.9(3),(4)).

However, any carer parent who claims income support, family credit or

disability working allowance will normally be obliged to have an assessment, whether or not she claims benefit for the child (1991 Act, s.6(1)). This
can be waived if there is a risk that she, or any child living with her, will suffer
"harm or undue distress" as a result (1991 Act, s.6(2)). A waiver may be
granted if the child is the result of rape, sexual abuse or incest, or where there
is a real risk or fear of violence, but not just because mother and father have
never lived together or want nothing more to do with one another. However,
the intention is to believe what she says "unless it is implausible" and not to
require corroboration of her fears (D.S.S., 1992). If she refuses to cooperate
in naming the father or giving particulars which will help to trace him, and
the C.S.O. does not think she has a good reason, her benefit will be reduced
by 20 per cent. for the first six months and by 10 per cent. for the next 12
months (disregarding any periods when she comes off benefit) (Child Support
(Maintenance and Assessment Procedures) Regulations 1992, reg. 36). She
can appeal.

(c) *The formula*

Maintenance is assessed according to a strict arithmetical formula. This
begins with the "maintenance requirement", which is supposed to be the
amount needed to support the child. But it is fixed by adding up the income
support rate for each child, the income support family premium, the income
support rate for a person of 25 or more (provided that at least one child is
under 16), and the income support lone parent premium, and deducting the
amount of child benefit payable for each child. It therefore covers some of the
adult carer's needs as well, but contains no extra element for housing costs.
    The formula then calculates the "assessable income" of each parent. This
means their total incomes from all sources (except for most means-tested
benefits), net of tax, national insurance contributions, and half any pension
contributions, and less the "exempt income" required for their own living
expenses (including the needs of their own children living with them but not
those of a partner or any other children). The exempt income is worked out in
a very similar way to the maintenance requirement but includes an element
for housing costs.
    Each parent is then notionally expected to meet half the maintenance
requirement. This means that a "deduction rate" of 50 per cent. is applied to
the assessable income of each parent until the maintenance requirement is
met. This seems to place the same burden on the carer parent who goes out to
work as is placed on the absent parent, but there is some compensation in the
carer element in the maintenance bill. Most absent parents, even if the
calculation would mean that they paid nothing at all, will be required to pay
a little something *pour le principe.*
    So far, the only real complexities in the formula are the treatment of the
different kinds of benefit in assessing income, and the treatment of housing
costs in assessing what is exempt. However, it can be adjusted upwards if the
assessable income is more than the maintenance requirement; then an
"additional element" will be calculated at a deduction rate of 25 per cent.,

up to a maximum additional maintenance requirement (calculated by reference to three times income support rates for the children in question). On the other hand, the amount deducted under the assessment can be adjusted downwards, to ensure that the absent parent does not fall below a "protected level of income". This is designed to preserve his work incentive by ensuring that he is left with what he would be getting for himself and the whole of his family were he on income support, with a margin on top. It takes into account more of his costs than does the exempt income calculation and includes an allowance for any step-children. The shortfall from what he should otherwise pay can, however, be made up later.

There are also adjustments for special cases, for example where both parents are absent parents, or where they share care between them. Adjustments will be made where the child spends an average of two nights or more a week with the other parent. The incentive which this will give to parents to play a greater part in looking after their children might be thought a good thing by some. The incentive which it will give to battle over this will not.

(c) *Payment, collection and enforcement*

Once assessed, paying and collecting the money will be a private matter between the parties. However, the agency may provide a collection service in any benefit case or where either party asks (1991 Act, ss.4(2), 6(1), 29(1)). The agency will then try to arrange payment by the safest method appropriate to the parties' circumstances, whether directly to the recipient, or into a bank account opened for her, or via the agency, but avoiding further involvement of the agency if possible.

The Secretary of State has power to make a "deduction from earnings order" against a liable person in respect of either arrears or future amounts due or both (1991 Act, s.31). The order operates in much the same way as attachment of earnings orders made to enforce debts in the ordinary courts. It is addressed to the person's employer, instructing him to make deductions from the person's earnings and pay these (less an administration charge) to the agency. The order specifies the normal deduction rate but also the protected earnings rate (which is equivalent to the exempt income in the formula) below which his net earnings must not fall. If the normal deduction cannot be made, because the earnings are not enough, the deficit is carried forward to be made up as soon as possible (but if his income falls below the protected earnings rate, that deficit is added to his next protected earnings, so as to make an average). It is a crime, though punishable only with a (level 2) fine, to fail to comply with the requirements of a deduction order (1991 Act, s.32(8)).

If arrears start to build up, and the liable person fails to make or keep an agreement to discharge them, he can be charged interest from the first payment missed. If this does not work, payment can be enforced by the agency applying to a magistrates' court for a liability order (which can only relate to arrears, not to anything falling due after the application) (1991 Act, s.33). Once made, the Secretary of State can enforce the order direct by levying distress (seizure and sale of goods by bailiffs contracted to the agency) (1991 Act, s.35); or by applying to a county court for a garnishee order (against a bank account) or charging order (against property) (1991 Act, s.36); or if all else fails, and there is "wilful refusal or culpable neglect", by applying to a magistrates' court for a warrant committing the person to prison for up to six weeks (which can be suspended to give time to pay) (1991 Act, s.40).

(d) Reviews and appeals

Unlike court orders, assessments can be automatically reviewed each year as benefit rates change. Also, either party can apply for the assessment to be reviewed on the ground that there has been a change of circumstances which would result in a significant change in the amount payable (1991 Act, s.17(1),(2)). It is also possible to ask for a review of a refusal to make an assessment or to review the amount, or for a review of the assessment itself, or of the cancellation of or refusal to cancel an assessment (1991 Act, s.18(1),(2),(3),(4)). Then anyone aggrieved by the result can appeal to a child support appeal tribunal (C.S.A.T.) (1991 Act, s.20). Anyone aggrieved by a reduction of benefit because of refusal to cooperate in naming or tracing the other parent can appeal direct (1991 Act, s.46(7)). If the appeal is allowed it has to be sent back to a C.S.O., but the tribunal can give directions as to what he is to do. C.S.A.T.s are modelled on social security appeal tribunals, with an appeal on a point of law from them to child support commissioners (but only with leave) and then to the Court of Appeal.

(ii) The courts' powers

Once the child support agency has jurisdiction to make a maintenance assessment, then whether or not it has been asked to do so, and whether or not it would do so if asked, the courts no longer have power to make, vary or revive any maintenance order against the absent parent concerned in relation to the child concerned (1991 Act, s.8(1),(2),(3)). Thus all new cases, whether or not they involve the payment of benefit, have been taken away from the courts and existing cases will be transferred between 1993 and 1997 (see above).

There are a few exceptions. Just as parents can make their own agreements, they can still have those agreements embodied in a consent order during the transitional period (1991 Act, s.8(5)). More importantly, the courts still have jurisdiction to make orders for the payment of school fees (1991 Act, s.8(7)), or for "top up" maintenance where the parental income is so high that it is appropriate to order more than the additional element (1991 Act, s.8(6)), or where the child is disabled and the object is to provide for the expenses attributable to that disability (1991 Act, s.8(8)). The courts also retain their powers to make orders for property and capital settlements and spousal maintenance, which cannot be made under the Child Support Act 1991.

By far the most comprehensive powers are those of the divorce courts, for they are usually regulating the total break-up of the family. In effect, they can take into account all the assets of husband and wife from any source and then share them out in whatever way seems fair and reasonable, in order to provide for the family's needs and to recognise the spouses' respective contributions to its assets and its welfare. Subject to the Child Support Agency's jurisdiction over periodical payments for children, they may order either party to make periodical payments, with or without security, or to provide lump sums for the other party or for the children (Matrimonial Causes Act 1973, s.23(1)). These may be ordered even though the proceedings for divorce, nullity or judicial separation are unsuccessful (1973 Act, s.23(2)). If a decree is granted, the court also has power to order the transfer or settlement of any property owned by either spouse to or for the benefit of the other spouse or the children (1973 Act, s.24(1)) and to transfer a protected, statutory, assured or secure tenancy from one spouse to the other or from joint names to one alone (Matrimonial Homes Act 1983, s.7 and Sched. 1).

In deciding how to exercise its powers under the 1973 Act, the court must give first (but not paramount) consideration to the welfare of the children of the family while they are under 18 (1973 Act, s.25(1)). It must also take into account the relative financial needs and resources of both spouses and the children, the standard of living enjoyed by the family before the breakdown, and any physical or mental disability of either spouse or the children. For the spouses, it must also consider their ages, the duration of the marriage, the contribution made by each to the welfare of the family (including looking after the home and caring for the family), and the potential loss of benefits such as pensions (1973 Act, s.25(2)), but must also explore the possibilities of a "clean break" bringing their mutual financial obligations to an end (1973 Act, s.25A). The way in which the spouses have behaved towards one another is irrelevant unless the behaviour of one was so much worse than that of the other that it would be inequitable to disregard it (1973 Act, s.25(2)(g)). For the children, the court must also consider their actual or expected education and training (1973 Act, s.25(3)).

In practice one of the most important objectives in divorce cases has been to preserve a home for the children. There are many different ways of doing this. One possibility is to re-settle the matrimonial home so that it cannot be sold without the agreement of both parties until the children have finished their education (*Allen* v. *Allen* [1974] 1 W.L.R. 1171, C.A.); another is to transfer it outright to the parent with whom they are to live, perhaps in return for a lump sum or a reduction in periodical payments which would otherwise be ordered (*Hanlon* v. *Hanlon* [1978] 1 W.L.R. 592, C.A.). Thus the decision about the children's upbringing might easily dictate what was to happen to the home.

Magistrates' family proceedings courts have much more limited powers to order one spouse to make periodical payments or to pay lump sums of up to £1,000 to the other spouse or, again subject to the Child Support Act 1991, to or for the benefit of any child of the family (Domestic Proceedings and Magistrates' Courts Act 1978, ss.2(1), 6(2), 7(2)). These are governed by the same sort of considerations as govern divorce courts, but there is no power to order the settlement or transfer of any kind of property. In practice, although they will keep their power to award maintenance for the spouse, the child support scheme is likely to supplant them almost completely.

Outside matrimonial proceedings, the courts' powers to order provision for children were brought together in the Children Act 1989 (1989 Act, s.15 and Sched. 1). This allows the High Court and county courts to order parents to make secured or unsecured periodical payments (but only until the Child Support Act takes over) or make lump sum payments, either directly to the child or to another person for the benefit of the child, or to settle property for the benefit of the child, or to transfer property to or for the benefit of the child (1989 Act, Sched. 1, para. 1 (2)). Magistrates' courts' powers are limited in the same way as they are between adults (1989 Act, Sched. 1, para. 1(1)(b)).

These powers can be exercised at any time; but whereas periodical payment orders can be varied or discharged (during the transition to the Child Support Act) and new lump sum payment orders can be made, only one property adjustment order can ever be made against the same person in respect of the same child (1989 Act, Sched. 1, para. 1(3),(4),(5)). This is to mirror the "one bite at the cherry" which is involved in property adjustment orders under the Matrimonial Causes Act 1973, which only take place when there is a divorce and cannot later be varied or improved upon unless power to do so is built into the order at the outset (1973 Act, s.31). The considerations which the court must take into account also mirror those in the matrimonial legislation, apart from those which are only relevant to provision between the adults (1989 Act, Sched. 1, para. 4). It will generally be better for the child to make an order even if the parties are agreed (*K.* v. *H.*, *The Times*, December 31, 1992).

Orders cannot be made for children who have reached 18, unless they are, will be, or would be if maintenance were ordered, still undergoing education or training (even if combined with a job) or there are other special circumstances. Such a child may apply himself if there are divorce proceedings (*Downing* v. *Downing* (*Downing intervening*), [1976] Fam.288) or under the 1989 Act if his parents are living apart (1989 Act, Sched. 1, para. 2; "parent" does not for this purpose include a non-parent who has treated him as a child of the family; *ibid.* para. 16(2)). These applications will not usually be excluded by the Child Support Act 1991, which in effect only covers children for whom child benefit can be paid (1991 Act, s.55).

(iii) Commentary

What role will then be left for the courts once the Child Support Act 1991 has been extended to everyone? They have some powers which are not available under the 1991 Act: (a) to make lump sum and property adjustment orders for the benefit of children; (b) to order financial provision for some children over 18; (c) to order anyone other than a natural parent to provide for a "child of the family" (see further in Chapter 6); and (d) to make orders for the benefit of adults. They will also be able to order periodical payments to "top up" the sums derived from the child support formula (a) for school fees, or (b) if the family income is high, or (c) if the child is disabled. It is far too early to say whether the formula will result in rich as well as poor parents paying more in total than they otherwise would have done, although it may well result in more of what they already pay being attributed to their children rather than to their former spouse. The children themselves will only benefit if more comes into their household, and this is unlikely for either rich or poor; but for those in the middle a truly "portable" maintenance assessment could be a passport from benefit to employment. The main fear, however, is that the 1991 Act will reduce the numbers of settlements in which the children are assured of their home even if they have to subsist at income support levels for the rest of their childhood. The way out for many of their mothers used to be remarriage (see Chapter 6) but the Act will also have an effect on that.

Chapter 5

DEATH

The death of one or both parents is a tragedy for a child, but it usually has fewer unfavourable consequences for him than almost any of the other events discussed in this book. It is also much rarer. In 1989, of all families with dependent children just one per cent. were headed by widows (compared with nine per cent. headed by separated or divorced mothers and five per cent. headed by single mothers). There are almost always material disadvantages associated with growing up in a one-parent family, but the financial and housing situation of the bereaved is markedly better than that of the others (Finer, 1974; Ferri, 1976). Nor do children who have lost a parent show a significantly increased rate of delinquency (Rutter, 1971), or educational problems (Ferri, 1976), although some may be at greater risk of depressive illness in adult life (Bowlby, 1980; cf. Kuh and Maclean, 1990). Bereavement is a quite different experience from other types of separation or loss (Richards, 1987). It is rarely accompanied by prolonged hostilities and bitterness between the parents, or by legal disputes about the children's future. The family's resources may be much reduced, but they do not have to shared between two households. Their lot attracts only sympathy and compassion from society and none of the condemnation which is still sometimes attached to marital breakdown and unmarried parenthood.

1. PARENTS AND GUARDIANS

If a parent dies, the law rarely has to decide a dispute about where his children are to live; but it does regulate who is to have parental responsibility for them. This used to be determined by the law of guardianship, which recognised three main types of guardian: natural, testamentary and court-appointed. This has all been changed by the Children Act 1989.

(i) The surviving parent

Under the old law, the child's parents were his "natural guardians", either at common law or by statute (but the unmarried father did not automatically become guardian after the mother's death unless at that time there was a court order giving him custody). The Children Act 1989 has adopted an entirely different approach. Parental guardianship has been replaced by the concepts of parenthood and parental responsibility. The old rule that the father was sole guardian of his legitimate child was expressly abolished (1989 Act, s.2(4)). Married parents each have parental responsibility (1989 Act, s.2(1)), which continues automatically if one of them dies. An unmarried mother always has parental responsibility (1989 Act, s.2(2)), which continues automatically if the father dies. An unmarried father may also have parental responsibility because of a court order or agreement (1989 Act, s.4(1)), and this too continues automatically if the mother dies. If he does not have responsibility when she dies, he may apply to the court, either for a parental responsibility order (1989 Act, s.4(1)(a)) or to be appointed guardian (1989 Act, s.5(1)). The difference between these two has already been discussed in Chapter 2.

The 1989 Act also provides that parental responsibility includes all the rights, powers and duties which a guardian of the child's estate (if appointed before the Act) would have had in relation to the child and his property (1989 Act, s.3(2)); and that this includes the right to receive and recover in his own name, for the benefit of the child, property of any description, situated anywhere, which the child is entitled to receive or recover (1989 Act, s.3(3)). This removed the doubt which there used to be about whether parents had the same powers as other guardians had in relation to their children's property.

Where both parents have parental responsibility, the 1989 Act made a radical change to the position of the one who survives. Under the previous law, she would act jointly with any guardian appointed by the one who had died; and if he had not appointed a guardian, the court had power to do so. The idea that one parent could continue to rule the other from the grave, by choosing a guardian who could veto her decisions, or even try to have her ousted, was a relic of the old common law dominance of the father; its time had come. Normally, now, any guardian appointed by the parent who dies first cannot take office until after the other parent has died; nor can the court appoint a guardian for him. Generally speaking, the courts were reluctant to do this anyway. Thus in one case where the mother had died, the child's grown-up sister applied to be appointed guardian jointly with the father; the High Court said that joint guardianship was unlikely to be in the child's best interests, especially where the potential joint guardians were at loggerheads with one another (*Re H. (An Infant)* [1959] 1 W.L.R. 1163). Problems can arise, however, when the parents are separated or divorced and so an exception is made if the parent who has died had a residence order in her favour at the time (see (ii) and (iii) below).

(ii) Testamentary guardians

Testamentary guardians are those appointed by the child's parents to take their place in the event of their death. Any parent with parental responsibility may appoint another individual to be the child's guardian in the event of his death (1989 Act, s.5(3)); a father without parental responsibility cannot do so. On the other hand, the Children Act 1989 now provides that a guardian may also appoint another individual to take his place as the child's guardian in the event of his death (1989 Act, s.5(4)); the Act does not say, but must presumably intend, that such appointments can only be made and take effect if the guardian's own appointment has taken effect. An appointment under either of these provisions can be made by two or more persons acting jointly (1989 Act, s.5(10)); so parents can together decide who is to act when they are both dead.

Only an "individual" can be appointed guardian. An "individual" is a human being, whereas a "person" includes non-human legal persons, such as local authorities and other corporate bodies, and even unincorporated associations (Interpretation Act 1978, s.5 and Sched. 1). This reflects the Act's philosophy that guardianship should be as much like ordinary parenthood as possible; the guardian stands in the shoes of a parent and should have the same sort of human responsibility for and relationship with the child.

The Act also tries to encourage parents to appoint guardians by providing a rather simpler method of doing so, which can be used by people who do not want to make a will. This is part of the philosophy of respecting the parents' own decisions. In the past, appointments could only be made by deed or, more commonly, by will, hence the term "testamentary" guardian. Most appointments are probably still made by will. However, many people, especially the young, are reluctant to make wills. They may be superstitious about anticipating their own deaths, or suspicious of lawyers and reluctant to do it themselves, or they may not see the need to provide for what is to happen to their property when they die (perhaps because they do not have any property or assume that the law of intestacy will provide a satisfactory solution for what they do have). All parents should, however, be encouraged to think about who should become responsible for their children, particularly if they are single, separated or divorced (and many solicitors do see this as part of the package for their divorcing clients). So the formalities should be as simple and non-deterrent as possible.

The 1989 Act, therefore, only insists that the appointment is made in writing, dated and signed by the person making it; alternatively, (a) if it is contained in a will which is not signed by the testator, it may be signed at the testator's direction in accordance with section 9 of the Wills Act 1839, or (b) if it is not in a will it may be signed at the direction of the person making the appointment, in his presence and in the presence of two witnesses who each attest the signature (1989 Act, s.5(5)). This is to cater for people who are unable to sign themselves, either because they cannot write at all or are too ill to do so. Any appointment contained in a properly executed will is automatically valid; so is an appointment contained in a will which has some formal defect, provided that it is properly signed and dated.

It is also easier to change an appointment than it is to change a will. Any later appointment revokes an earlier one made by the same person in respect of the same child, even if the earlier one is contained in a will or codicil which is otherwise unrevoked, unless it is clear (either expressly or by necessary implication) that the later appointment is intended to be in addition to 'the earlier one (1989 Act, s.6(1)). Otherwise, an appointment (again including an appointment in a will or codicil which is otherwise unrevoked) can simply be revoked without a replacement, if the person who made it does so in writing, dated and either signed by him or at his direction in his presence and in the presence of two witnesses who each attest the signature (1989 Act, s.6(2)). An appointment made in a will or a codicil is, of course, revoked if the will or codicil is validly revoked (1989 Act, s.6(4)). An appointment not made in a will or codicil can similarly be revoked if the person who made it either destroys, or has some other person destroy in his presence, the document making the appointment, provided that he did so intending the appointment to be revoked (1989 Act, s.6(3)).

Obviously, no sensible parent or guardian would appoint someone as guardian without first getting that person to agree to take it on; and any sensible person who knows that he has been named as a guardian will let the parent or guardian know if he changes his mind. But sometimes people are not sensible, or their circumstances change, or they may even forget about something which they agreed to do many years ago, knowing that it was extremely unlikely that the appointment would ever take effect. Hence, a person appointed guardian by a parent or guardian can disclaim his appointment, provided that he does so within a reasonable time of his first knowing that it has taken effect, by a written document signed by him (the Lord Chancellor has power to make regulations prescribing the way in which such disclaimers are to be recorded; if and when he does so, the disclaimer will be of no effect unless it is recorded in the prescribed way; 1989 Act, s.6(5),(6)).

The earliest time at which an appointment can take effect is on the death of the parent or guardian who made it. But even then it only takes immediate effect if either (a) there is then no surviving parent with parental responsibility for the child (because both parents are dead or the other parent does not have parental responsibility), or (b) immediately before the death of the person making the appointment, there was a residence order in force providing that the child should live with that person (and not also with the parent who has died) (1989 Act, s.5(7),(9)). The same applies if there was in force a custody order made under the old law. If, on the other hand, the child still has a parent with parental responsibility and there was no residence (or custody) order in favour of the deceased, then the appointment only takes effect when the child no longer has a parent with parental responsibility for him (1989 Act, s.5(8)).

This means that a lone parent who carries all or most of the legal responsibility for the child's care and upbringing can make an appointment which takes effect immediately when she dies. This could be a good reason for the court to make a residence order despite the so-called "no order" principle (1989 Act, s.1(5); see page 80, above). The problems which can arise when parents are separated or divorced are amply illustrated by two reported cases, both involving little girls who were aged eight or nine when their mothers died, having been divorced from their fathers when they were four or five.

In *Re F.* (*A Minor*) (*Wardship: Appeal*) [1976] Fam.238, C.A., there had been a stormy marriage, including some violence by the father which had been witnessed by the child; the father had eventually forced his wife and child out of the house and installed another woman. The mother was granted custody at the divorce. The father sent presents and some money for the child, but saw little of her, mainly because of the hostility of the mother and her family. The mother became ill and the grandmother and aunts looked after the child. The mother died when the child was nearly eight and eleven days later the father came and took her away to live with him and his new family. The grandmother made the child a ward of court, but by the time the case was heard, a year later, the little girl was settled with her new family and the Court of Appeal decided that she should stay. The grandparents were very close to the child, but extremely hostile to her father; however, he had turned over a new leaf and was also ready to recognise the child's fondness for her maternal relatives.

In *Re H.* (*A Minor*) (*Custody: Interim Care and Control*) [1991] 2 F.L.R. 109, on the other hand, the mother had re-married after the divorce and appointed the grandmother and step-father guardians in her will. The child was again made a ward after the mother's death, but although the first judge ordered her immediate return to her father (relying on *Re K.* (*A Minor*) (*Ward: Care and Control*) [1990] 1 W.L.R. 431, C.A., see page 125, below), the Court of Appeal overturned that and later upheld a decision that she should stay with the grandmother for the time being, while the welfare officer made a full investigation of the case. The need for her to stay with people who were close to her mother was of great importance during the early stages of her bereavement, whatever might be best for her in the long run.

It is difficult to say how much difference it made that the step-father and grand-mother had been appointed guardians; but it must have made it harder for the father simply to take the child away; and it gave them all equal standing to go to the court to resolve their dispute; they could now do this under the Children Act, instead of making the child a ward of court, if they preferred.

A guardian has exactly the same parental responsibility for the child concerned as a parent does (1989 Act, s.5(6); see Chapter 1). It is no longer possible to appoint a guardian for a limited purpose or simply to look after the child's property or "estate". In the past, it was not uncommon for the child to be looked after by relatives or friends, while a more remote figure took charge of his property. Nowadays, a guardian is expected to assume full responsibility for the child's upbringing, even if he delegates some of this responsibility to others. If there is substantial property which needs to be safeguarded and managed, this is usually better done by appointing trustees, who become legal owners of the property and whose powers and duties are clearly laid down, than by guardians whose powers and duties over property owned by the child have never been properly defined.

Guardians therefore have more responsibility than do people who simply have the benefit of a residence order; their agreement to the child's adoption is necessary unless it can be dispensed with and they themselves have the power to appoint testamentary guardians. They are treated like parents for child welfare and protection purposes; an unrelated guardian who is looking after the child in his own home is not subject to the controls over private foster parents (see Chapter 9).The only difference between guardians and parents (whether natural or adoptive) is that guardians have no *financial* liability to other people or to the state for the child's maintenance. Their criminal liability for neglect, ill-treatment or failure to educate is, however, the same as that of a parent.

If guardians share parental responsibility, either with other guardians or with a surviving parent, then the position is just the same as it is between parents. They have the same power of independent action (1989 Act, s.2(7), (8); see page 9, above) and the same access to the courts to resolve any disputes about the child's care and upbringing (1989 Act, s.10(4)(a); see page 62, above).

Unlike most parents, however, a guardian can be removed from office; his appointment can be brought to an end at any time by order of the court, either (a) on the application of any person who has parental responsibility for the child, which would include the guardian himself, as well as a surviving parent, or another person in whose favour a residence order is made, or a local authority having the child in their care; or (b) on the application of the child himself, if the court gives leave; or (c) of the court's own motion in the course of any family proceedings, if the court considers that it should be brought to an end even though no application has been made (1989 Act, s.6(7)); this means that if the court decides that it will be better for the child to live with someone else, or even to go into care, the court can end the guardian's appointment without requiring a fresh application and yet more paperwork and costs.

(iii) Court-appointed guardians

The court has power to appoint an individual (again not a non-human person) guardian for a child, provided that either (a) the child has no parent with parental responsibility for him or (b) a residence order has been made with respect to the child in favour of a parent or guardian (but not also the surviving parent) who has died while the order was in force (1989 Act, s.5(1),(9)). Once again, therefore, the courts do not have power to make appointments if there is a surviving parent who was equally responsible for the child when the one parent died.

The appointment can be made either in free-standing proceedings on the application of the person who wants to be appointed (1989 Act, s.5(1)) or of the court's own motion in any family proceedings in which the court considers that the appointment should be made even though there is no application for it (1989 Act, s.5(2)). Obviously, the court is not going to appoint someone who does not want to be appointed. But the desirability of making an appointment might emerge during the course of some other case.

One example might be where there is been a dispute between relatives about who is to look after an orphaned child and the court thinks that the residence order should be supplemented with the further responsibilities (including the power to appoint a guardian) of a guardian. Another example might be where the child has to go into care but there is a responsible member of the family who wishes to play the part that the deceased parent would have played; as with an unmarried father, the court may think it desirable that a member (or members) of the family should have some legal standing in relation to the child's future, even if the local authority is in the driving seat for the time being.

Guardians appointed by the court under these powers are in exactly the same position as guardians appointed by a parent or guardian (see (ii) above). However, the 1989 Act has preserved the common law power of the High Court to appoint a guardian of the child's estate, but only if this is provided for by rules of court, which has not yet been done (1989 Act, s.5(11)); the rules could prescribe the circumstances in which, and the conditions subject to which, such appointments can be made (1989 Act, s.5(12)). This is to allow for those very rare situations in which it may be necessary to provide for someone other than the person with parental responsibility to receive and safeguard a child's property. This is usually done by the Official Solicitor, for example with criminal injuries compensation for abuse which has taken place within the family or payments due from abroad for which a parental receipt is not sufficient. All court-appointed guardians can be removed in the same way as those appointed by a parent or guardian (1989 Act, s.6(7); see (ii) above).

(iv) Appointments under the old law

Any appointment under the old law which has already taken effect is deemed to be an appointment under section 5 of the 1989 Act (1989 Act, Sched. 14, para. 12(1)). This has the rather odd effect of converting guardians who have been appointed for a limited purpose, for example as guardians of the estate, into guardians with full parental responsibility. However, if this is inappropriate the court can always bring the appointment to an end (1989 Act, s.6(7)). Testamentary appointments contained in wills executed before the 1989 Act came into force which have not yet taken effect will in due course take effect under section 5 of the 1989 Act (1989 Act, Sched. 14, para. 13). Old-fashioned wills sometimes disposed of the "custody and tuition" of a child and such a disposition made before the 1989 Act came into force is taken to be the appointment of a guardian (1989 Act, Sched. 14, para. 14). Nothing sums up the new philosophy of the 1989 Act better than the difference between "disposing of the custody and tuition" of one's child and appointing someone to undertake parental responsibility for him.

(v) Other kinds of guardian

The 1989 Act expressly provides that a guardian of a child may now only be appointed in accordance with the provisions of section 5 (1989 Act, s.5(13)).

References to a child's "guardian" in other legislation will therefore usually mean someone whose appointment is made or takes effect under the 1989 Act. However, it is always advisable to check the definition in the particular statute concerned, as some of them give a specially extended meaning to the terms "guardian" (as in the Children and Young Persons Acts or in the Education Acts) or "guardianship" (as in the Mental Health Act 1983). It should also be borne in mind that the court itself becomes the guardian of a child who is made a ward of court and this is now more often done when the parents are still alive than when they have died (see Chapter 4).

(vi) Informal guardians

No doubt a great many orphaned children are cared for by relatives or friends without any formal appointment as guardians. There is no need to be appointed a legal guardian in order to claim social security "guardian's allowance" (see 2. (ii) below). Non-relatives who undertake the care of orphaned children without being appointed guardians are, however, subject to the controls over private foster parents (see Chapter 9). All people with actual care of a child may incur criminal liability for neglect, ill-treatment or failure to educate him properly; but they do not have the non-delegable responsibility of parents or legal guardians (see page 13, above); and they do not have any parental responsibility, for example over such matters as marriage, which could be to the child's disadvantage.

2. MAINTENANCE AND PROPERTY

Widows' families, though worse off than those with two parents or a sole male parent, tend to be better off than other fatherless families for two main reasons.

(i) Succession to property

A parent who loses a partner through death can normally expect that whatever capital assets they had, including their home, will remain intact, whereas after divorce these will usually have to be shared in some way between two households. If a person dies leaving children (whether or not they have grown up) but no will, his surviving spouse is entitled to personal chattels and the first £75,000 (soon to be raised to £125,000) of the estate absolutely, and also to a life interest in half of the rest (Administration of Estates Act 1925, s.46). If the couple owned their home as joint tenants, the dead partner's half goes automatically to the survivor. If they owned it as tenants in common, or the dead partner was sole owner, the survivor is entitled to ask for his interest in it to be transferred to her as part of the £75,000; if it is worth more and she can afford it, she may make up the difference. If the home is rented under a protected or local authority secure tenancy, the survivor is normally be entitled to take it over whether the landlord likes it or not. These provisions only apply if the survivor was living there at the death; nor does a building society have to agree to transfer any mortgage; but provided that the income can be found to keep up the outgoings, the bereaved family should not lose their home.

The children (including the children of a child who has died before his parent) are entitled to one half of the residue immediately and to succeed to the other half after the surviving spouse's life interest. If they are still under 18, the property is held on trust until they reach 18 or marry, but the income may be used for their maintenance and education before then. If there is no surviving spouse, the whole estate goes to them. (In turn, parents succeed to the estates of their children who die before them without leaving a spouse or children of their own.)

These rules only apply if the deceased left no will. If he did make a will, this is usually in order to make proper provision for his family. Sometimes, however, a will or the rules of intestacy can produce unjust results. A man may leave a substantial legacy outside his family, perhaps not realising how small the residue will be; or a wife may abandon the family, but her husband never obtain a divorce or judicial separation (which prevents the usual rules operating) or think to make a will; or children who are self-supporting may have shares which will leave dependent children without proper support.

Under the Inheritance (Provision for Family and Dependants) Act 1975, therefore, a variety of people may apply to the court for reasonable financial provision from the estate. These are the surviving spouse; any former spouse who has not remarried (unless at the divorce it was ordered that she should not be able to apply because their affairs were settled then); any child of the deceased, of whatever age; any other child, again of any age, who was treated as a "child of the family" in relation to any marriage to which the deceased was ever a party (that is, any child, apart from a child fostered with them by a local authority or voluntary organisation, who was treated by both spouses as a member of their family, whatever his parentage); and any other person who was being maintained by the deceased immediately before his death (1975 Act, s.1(1)).

The court has power to award periodical payments, or lump sums, or order that property be transferred or settled upon them, or that property be bought out of the estate and transferred to or settled upon them (1975 Act, s.2). It has a wide discretion to take into account the needs and resources of all claimants and the beneficiaries under any will, and many other factors such as the education which was planned for the children and the conduct of the claimants towards the deceased (1975 Act, s.3). Provision for the surviving spouse should be full financial provision, at least as good as she might expect on divorce (as the other principal claimant to the family's assets is now dead, it might be thought that it ought to be better, but the courts have not always taken this view). Provision for children is not confined to those who are under 18, or dependent or destitute, but it should only be what is reasonable for their maintenance (which could include a house) and in general adult children are expected to look after themselves. For other adult claimants, there must have been financial dependence on the deceased, and probably some indication that he accepted responsibility for them; the most successful claimants so far have been mothers of the deceased's children.

(ii) Income

The family may have lost a breadwinner, but the various ways of compensating for this tend to be more reliable than periodical payments on divorce or separation. If the death was caused by wrongdoing to the deceased, a claim can be brought against the wrongdoer under the Fatal Accidents Act 1976, by the surviving spouse, a cohabitant of two years' standing and any dependent children. There may be an occupational pension or private life assurance; and provided that her husband has paid the requisite contributions, a widow is usually entitled to widowed mother's allowance if she has with her or is maintaining a child of the family under the age of 19; if she is aged between 40 and 65 when her husband dies or she ceases to be entitled to widowed mother's allowance, there is a widow's pension; and widows under pensionable age are usually entitled to a lump sum widow's payment (Social Security (Contributions and Benefits) Act 1992, ss.36 to 39). These benefits are not, or course, available to divorced women, who do not become widows when their former husbands die, or to widowed or divorced men. These benefits have the great advantage that they are not means-tested. Although, surprisingly perhaps, they are suspended during co-habitation, they are not lost or reduced because of private pensions, annuities or earnings. They are, however, taxable, which can be a very sore point.

The state also gives special help for true orphans. Social security "guardian's allowance" is payable, without contribution conditions, to anyone who is caring for or maintaining a child if either (a) both parents are dead (or, usually, only the mother if the parents were not married to one another); or (b) only one parent is dead, but all reasonable efforts have been made but failed to trace the other, or he is in prison (Social Security (Contributions and Benefits) Act 1992, s.77). The allowance is not lost by adopting the child. It is not means-tested, nor is it taken into account in calculating means-tested benefits apart from income support. So the state is noticeably kinder to widows and orphans than it is to other victims of family breakdown.

3. COMMENTARY

Very little is known about the practice of guardianship and so few children are now orphaned that there must be much less need for it. It could either be seen as an anomaly, because it allows parents to confer their parental status on others without any court appointment or outside scrutiny, or as a sensible means of enabling responsible parents to provide for their children's care. The Children Act 1989, in implementing the recommendations of the Law Commission (1985 and 1988), has come down firmly in favour of the latter view.

Chapter 6

STEP-FAMILIES

Step-families are becoming more and more common. In 1991, 18 per cent. of all families with dependent children in Britain were headed by lone parents and most of these will probably find a new partner. In 1985, of all children who were not living with both natural parents, about one half (one in two) were living with a non-cohabiting lone mother, one in three with a mother who had remarried, one in twelve with a mother who was cohabiting and the rest with their father or with neither parent; remarriage was more common amongst divorced than amongst spinster mothers (see Haskey, 1990). Remarriage is most common amongst lone fathers (who seem to attract almost universal sympathy; Marsden, 1969) and least common amongst widows, but these are the two least common forms of lone parenthood.

Step-families come in many forms. The birth family may have been broken by death, separation or divorce or never have set up a household together at all. The children may then have lived mainly with their mother or mainly with their father. Either parent may then re-partner, either by marriage or by cohabitation. We tend to think of a step-parent as someone who has married the parent with whom the children are living, but someone who has married the other parent may well feel that they are also part of her family. It is not clear how far the law recognises this, but it is clear that the law has not so far given much recognition to non-marital step-relationships (a cohabitant step-father cannot be made to provide for the children as a married step-father can: *J. v. J. (Property Transfer Application)* [1993] 1 F.L.R. 471.

The social, psychological and financial implications are even more complex. Remarriage can be the quickest way out of poverty for a mother on her own (Maclean, 1991), although if her new partner also has children, the Child Support Act 1991 will make it more difficult for him to support them all (see Chapter 4). Even if remarriage helps financially, the psychological and social disruption caused to the children seems to be even worse than if their mother had not remarried (Kiernan, 1992). And the step-relationship is even harder than parenthood for the step-parent to get right (Maddox, 1980).

---

1. THE LEGAL STATUS OF STEP-PARENTS

A step-parent who is married to (or living with) the parent looking after the children is in the same position as anyone else with actual care (Children Act 1989, s.3(5): see page 10, above) but he does not automatically have parental responsibility (*Re N. (Minors) (Parental Rights)* [1974] Fam.40) or any family relationship with them. Some step-families feel the need to appear "normal" more acutely than others (Burgoyne and Clark, 1984). They are perhaps most likely to do so when the natural parents' relationship has ended by divorce and in this case the practical problems are also less easy for them to resolve.

The most immediate is likely to be the children's surname. A widowed or unmarried mother with sole parental responsibility may change it to that of her new partner whenever she wants. However, if a divorced or unmarried father has parental responsibility, the mother cannot change the children's name without his written consent or the leave of the court, even if there is a residence order in her favour (1989 Act, s.13(1)(a)). The decision probably relates to the children's "upbringing", so the court must regard their welfare as the paramount consideration (1989 Act, s.1(1)). But there have been differences of opinion in the Court of Appeal about the importance of this issue and where the true welfare of the children lies. Some cases (see *R. v. R. (Child: Surname)* [1977] 1 W.L.R. 1256, C.A.; *D. v. B. (otherwise D.) (Surname: Birth Registration)* [1979] Fam.38, C.A.) suggested that it was "no big deal"; as long as the children retain a knowledge of their true identity, a change of name can spare them embarrassment and promote the security of their new home. More recent cases (see, for example, *W. v. A.* [1981] Fam.14, C.A.) have rejected the idea that it is a minor matter or that it could ever be justified by the administrative convenience of mother or school; nor did they show much sympathy for the children's own feelings about being singled out as having a different name from the family in which they lived. The courts must now take account of a child's wishes and feelings (1989 Act, s.1(3)(a)), but they are still likely to regard this symbolic link with the other side of the family as having psychological and material benefits for the child as well as the absent parent.

The surname question is part of the wider debate about how far children should maintain their links with both sides of their genetic inheritance. Unlike contact, however, it is much harder to see how the children rather than the parent benefit from keeping this badge of belonging. (It is not, of course, available to children who are living with their fathers rather than their mothers.) Knowing and keeping in touch with one's origins is not the same as being publicly labelled with them and must be set against feeling comfortable and secure in the new arrangements. Some children will hate to feel disloyal to their absent parent but also hate to stand out in the crowd. Although the courts talk of the rights of the child, it sometimes seems that they act more in the interests of the absent parent.

The other legal difficulties of step-families tend to arise on the death of either the step-parent or natural parent. They can in theory be solved by each of them making appropriate wills. If the step-parent dies without making a will, his step-children have no right to share in his estate; but as "children of the family", they can apply to the court for reasonable financial provision from it (see Chapter 5). The court will take into account the extent to which he assumed any financial responsibility for them and the liability of anyone else (such as a divorced or unmarried father) to maintain them (Inheritance (Provision for Family and Dependants) Act 1975, s.3(3)). Grown-up children who have become self-supporting have little chance of success. These powers are not as favourable as automatic inheritance rights. Step-children have no legal relationship with other members of the step-parent's family and no claim upon their property unless it is expressly given to them.

If the parent to whom the step-parent is married dies, the step-parent does not have parental responsibility, unless he has been appointed guardian (see Chapter 5) or the court makes a residence order in his favour (see Chapter 4) either before or after the death. A surviving parent with parental respons-ibility can reclaim the children unless immediate steps are taken to prevent this. However, the Children Act 1989 has made it much easier for a step-parent to apply for court orders about his step-children.

2. ADOPTION

Although most of the practical problems can be solved by the parent and step-parent making appropriate wills, step-families often want more. They want to present a "normal" front to the world and to have some legal recognition and security (Burgoyne and Clark, 1984). Adoption is the most popular solution, because it solves all their practical difficulties and creates a secure legal relationship, not only with the step-parent but with his whole family. It may also be popular with the other parent, as it ends his financial liability for the children. This is all very natural, but if there is any insecurity in the relationships within the new family, it is doubtful how far the law should go in satisfying it. A striking example was the case of *Re M. (Minors)* [1990] F.C.R. 993, where the court allowed a birth father to appeal out of time against an adoption order (to which he had reluctantly agreed) when the mother died shortly afterwards and the step-father could not cope. Remar-riages have an even higher chance of breaking down than do first marriages, and the presence of step-children increases this. The children may need to retain their links, not only with the other parent (if they have one) but also with their grand-parents and other members of his family. Now that step-families are becoming so common, we may all have to adjust our ideas of what is "normal": the step-relationship is not usually the same and we should not pretend that it is. Both the Houghton Committee (1972) and the Adoption Law Review (1992) have expressed grave reservations about step-parent adoptions, especially after divorce.

There is least legal obstacle to the adoption of step-children where one parent has died (even if he has appointed a guardian, that appointment does not take effect while the surviving parent is alive, and so the guardian cannot prevent the adoption: see Chapter 5). However, the local authority's report to the court should mention any relative of a deceased parent who in the authority's opinion ought to be made a respondent (see Chapter 12). It is very questionable whether these adoptions are of any benefit to the child. There are no disadvantages of birth outside marriage to be removed; he will lose all relationship with the family of his dead parent; and this may be deeply distressing to him and add to the trauma and loss that he has already sustained.

There may also be little legal obstacle to adopting a step-child whose parents were not married to one another, for the father's agreement is not required unless he has parental responsibility. If he opposes it, the courts' attitude has traditionally been sympathetic to adoption; but if the parents have lived together for some time and the father has established a firm relationship with his child, their approach may now be different (see Chapter 2). He is now more likely to have parental responsibility, in which case his agreement is required and the courts' approach to dispensing with it is likely to be just the same as if he had been married to the mother.

The courts have been very reluctant to allow a step-father to adopt his step-children against the wishes of a natural father who has been divorced. The applicants may argue that his agreement should be dispensed with because he has persistently failed, without reasonable cause, to discharge his parental obligations. But in *Re D. (Minors) (Adoption by Parent)* [1973] Fam. 209, the court declared that some estrangement was only to be expected during the upset of a divorce; any failure must be so grave that the children will derive no benefit from maintaining the relationship. Alternatively, it may be argued that he is withholding his agreement unreasonably. A "reasonable parent" places great weight on what will be best for his children, so the court must first ask itself whether the adoption would be best (*Re B. (A Minor) (Adoption by Parent)* [1975] Fam. 127). That is no easy question. However, if the parents' marriage broke up when the child was very young, contact between father and child has since been minimal, and the child thinks of the step-father as his "real" father, it is possible that the court will conclude that the parent is being unreasonable (*Re D. (An Infant) (Adoption: Parent's Consent)* [1977] A.C. 602; but beware because this father was homosexual).

The trouble is that adoption is no more likely to be in the child's interests (or even what he wants) whether the other parent agrees to it or not. There are objections, not only to cutting the child's links with the other side of his family, but also to the artificial nature of the links created in the new one. The natural parent becomes an adoptive one, which may not matter much in law but is psychologically unsatisfactory for them both. The step-parent becomes a parent and his family becomes the child's family. But the step-family is itself quite likely to break down and is much more likely to do so if there are young children because their presence adds so much to the tensions in the relationship. There is then no way in which the child can revert to his family of birth, other than by his natural parent re-adopting him. This can only happen while he is a child and if his parents remarry or if his natural adoptive parent agrees to a sole application by the other natural parent.

For these reasons, the Children Act 1975 tried to discourage all adoptions by step-parents, even if there was no-one with the legal right to oppose them, by requiring the court to consider the alternative of joint custody or custodianship instead. However, the provisions were difficult to interpret and did not give the court a free choice between adoption and the alternatives. They have therefore been repealed by the Children Act 1989; instead, because adoption proceedings are "family proceedings", the court always has power, of its own motion, to make a residence or other section 8 order rather than an adoption order.

The question is still a difficult one, and it is not surprising that the courts differed widely in their approach to the 1975 Act—some granting virtually no post-divorce adoptions and some continuing much as before (Masson, Norbury and Chatterton, 1983). The complete severance of the child's natural relationships, and their replacement with those which he knows to be artificial, may damage him both legally and emotionally (Houghton, 1972), but so might a life of uncertainty and insecurity which he perceives as abnormal. There are other ways of satisfying a child's need to know his origins apart from maintaining a legal link which is of no other benefit to him. It all depends upon his age and understanding, and upon the quality of his relationships, not only with the absent parent but also with the absent parent's whole family.

The Adoption Law Review (1992) has once again considered whether step-parent adoptions should be prohibited or at least discouraged by the law. Its conclusion was that step-parent adoptions might sometimes be justified but that they did deserve special treatment. First, instead of parent and step-parent both becoming adoptive parents, it should be possible for the step-parent to adopt, taking over from the other birth parent, but leaving the parent to whom he is married still a birth parent. Secondly, it should be possible to revoke such adoptions if the step-parent's marriage breaks down, whether or not the birth parents have remarried. This recognises that adoption is not just a way of providing for a child's upbringing: it affects his status and family relationships throughout his life. Some people would therefore prefer adoption to be banned or severely discouraged; the alternatives will usually be better in the long run, whatever the children's views at the time.

3. ORDERS UNDER THE CHILDREN ACT 1989

A step-parent who is (or has been) married to a parent with whom a child is living is usually a "party to a marriage (whether or not subsisting) in relation to whom the child is a child of the family" (Children Act 1989, s.10(5)(a)). A "child of the family" means "any other child, not being a child who is placed with those parties as foster parents by a local authority or voluntary organisation, who has been treated by both of those parties as a child of their family" (1989 Act, s.105(1)). This is not limited to step-children, but they are the most obvious example. It is irrelevant that the mother's husband thought that he was the child's real father (A. v. A. (Family: Unborn Child) [1974] Fam.6). Yet marriage to a parent is not, without more, enough to turn a child into a child of the family; both parent and step-parent must behave towards him as if he were a member of their common family. Not a great deal is required. This raises the interesting question of whether a child who is living with, say, his mother can become a "child of the family" in relation, not only to the mother and the step-father to whom she is married, but also in relation to the natural father and the step-mother to whom he is married. Ideally both families will regard the child as part of their own family. The more time the child spends in each household, the more likely this is to be so (and what you would think if the child were living with his father and step-mother but spending plenty of time with his mother and her new partner?).

If the child is a child of the family, the step-parent may apply without leave for a residence or a contact order (1989 Act, s.10(5)), but has to seek leave to apply for a specific issue or prohibited steps order. This is an improvement on the previous law, under which the step-parent could generally only apply for orders about the children once his own marriage to the parent had broken down, although he might sometimes be granted custody or care and control (jointly with the parent to whom he was married) in the parents' divorce proceedings. It is not clear, however, why he cannot automatically apply for any kind of section 8 order. In practice, disputes are most likely to arise with the absent parent (perhaps after the parent whom he has married has died or disappeared leaving him with the child) or with his own spouse after their marriage has broken down. Some step-parents, particularly those who married single mothers while their children were very young, are to all intents and purposes natural parents of their step-children. They may have very intense feelings for their step-children; in a dispute about contact the courts will have to weigh very carefully what the step-father can bring to the child against the child's difficulties and confusion in coping with several different father figures (Re C. (A Minor) (Access) [1992] 1 F.L.R. 309, C.A.). Others have quite tenuous links with their step-children, so generalisation is difficult.

If a residence order is made in favour of a step-parent, whether alone or together with the parent to whom he is married, then (like any other non-parent in that situation) he has parental responsibility for as long as the residence order is in force (1989 Act, s.12(2)). However, this does not give him the right (a) to consent or refuse to consent to an application to free the child for adoption, or (b) to agree or refuse to agree to an adoption order, or (c) to appoint a guardian for the child (1989 Act, s.12(3)).

4. MAINTENANCE AND PROPERTY

If he has parental responsibility either as guardian or under a residence order in force in his favour, a step-parent can apply under Schedule 1 to the Children Act 1989 for financial provision or property adjustment against either parent for the benefit of the child (1989 Act, Sched. 1, para. 1(1)). New applications for periodical payments will, however, be covered by the Child Support Act 1991 (see Chapter 4).

On the other hand, a step-parent can himself be ordered to make financial provision or even a property settlement for a child who has been treated as a child of the family in relation to any marriage to which he has been a party. He counts as a "parent" against whom a parent, guardian or indeed anyone with the benefit of a residence order can make an application under paragraph 1 of Schedule 1 to the 1989 Act (1989 Act, Sched. 1, para. 16(2); he does not, however, count as a parent against whom a child who has reached 18 can make an application under paragraph 2 of that Schedule). The same orders can be made against him in divorce, nullity or judicial separation proceedings between himself and the parent to whom he is married (Matrimonial Causes Act 1973, ss.23 and 24).

Step-parents (and others who have treated a child as a child of the family) are the only non-parents who can be ordered to provide for the child in this way. In deciding whether and how to exercise these powers, the court has to take into account whether, to what extent, on what basis, and for how long a spouse has assumed any responsibility for the maintenance of a child who is not his own; whether he did so knowing that the child was not his; and the liability of anyone else to maintain the child (1973 Act, s.25(3); 1989 Act, Sched. 1, para. 4(2)). If the court makes an order under the 1989 Act against a person who is not the child's father, it must record that it did so on the basis that he was not (1989 Act, Sched. 1, para. 4(3)); although these powers are equally available against a step-mother who has treated a child as a child of her family, the court is not then required to record that it does so on the basis that she is not the child's mother. Motherhood is thought more obvious than fatherhood.

However, no matter how long and how deep his involvement with the child, a step-parent is not liable to contribute towards the child's maintenance under the Child Support Act 1991. Nor can his legal or moral obligations towards his step-children be taken into account in assessing his liability towards his own children, although they are taken into account in fixing the level below which his earnings should not be allowed to fall (see Chapter 4). The 1991 Act is premised on the duty of both natural parents to support their children throughout childhood no matter what the circumstances. Given the prevalence of formal and informal step-relationships these days, this may cause difficulties. A step-father who has assumed sole responsibility for his wife and her children (perhaps because their father has died or disappeared many years ago) will find that this is not taken into account in calculating his liability towards his own children (even if their mother has married a much richer man). Equally he will not be liable under the Act should the step-family break up, but the courts still have power to order him to make provision under the ordinary law.

5. COMMENTARY

Step-families throw into sharp relief one of the basic dilemmas of family law: should priority be given to preserving a child's ties with his family of birth or to cementing the new ones? It is better for the child if he can integrate all parents and step-parents into "his" family (Wallerstein and Kelly, 1980). However, what is the law to do if this is not felt to be enough by the step-families themselves? The present flexible approach may be good enough, but it can easily lead to inconsistencies where like families are not treated alike.

The Adoption Law Review (1992) has taken up earlier suggestions (Masson, 1984; Law Commission, 1985) that step-families need a new procedure, whereby parent and step-parent can agree to share parental responsibility without having to go to court and without depriving the other parent of whatever status he has. This would be along similar lines to parental responsibility agreements between unmarried mothers and fathers (see Chapter 2) but would require the agreement of any parent with parental responsibility. All of these suggestions are limited to step-families formed by marriage. A man who has never been married to the child's mother is not yet regarded as a step-parent by the law.

Chapter 7

RELATIVES, FOSTER PARENTS AND OTHERS

Children are often looked after by someone other than their natural parents or legal guardians. There is a wide variety of arrangements, with relatives or with non-relatives, for short or long periods, with or without payment, and with or without the intervention of a child care agency. Nowadays, there is an increasing recognition of the importance of the wider family, not only as a source of help for children and parents in need, but also as a significant component in the child's upbringing and sense of himself and his place in the world.

This raises two questions for the law. The first is how far it can or should impose some control over the arrangements parents make for their children to be looked after outside the immediate family: most of these are operated by local social services authorities and will form the subject-matter of Chapter 9. The second question is how far the law gives relatives, friends and other people who have been looking after or are concerned about a child some standing to raise questions about his care or upbringing.

1. INSECURITY

One of the main justifications for social work involvement in arrangements for the care of children away from home is the extreme difficulty of the foster parent's task. She must be able to supply both the physical and psychological needs of a child who has experienced the stress, either of separation from his most-loved adult, or of previous negative relationships with the adults around him. She must try to do this, not as total substitute for the parents, but in partnership with them and with the agency (if there is one). Except where the placement breaks down at her own request, it is the agency or the parents who decide how long the child may stay.

But agency foster parents are different from others; relatives or private foster parents usually have some connection with the child apart from the simple fact of care; they may be acting out of kindness or family feeling; and they may receive little or no payment. Agency foster parents form part of the

113

agency's child care service; they are professionally chosen and advised; they may be relatives, and increasingly this is encouraged, but usually they have no previous connection with the child; they often have the child for quite short periods; and they are paid. Until recently, the fostering allowance was expected to do no more than cover the costs of keeping the child, and sometimes not even that; foster parents who would only act for profit, however small, were regarded with suspicion. The truly professional foster parent, who receives intensive training and social work support, in return for taking particularly difficult children at a realistic fee, is a relatively recent development.

The official approach to fostering has changed over the years. When children came into public care because they had been orphaned, abandoned or removed from extremely damaging homes, it was easier to see foster care as a completely "fresh start." When the service was extended to children who needed substitute care because of illness or other misfortunes and often for a very short time, the emphasis changed (Packman, 1981). Parents had to feel that they did not run the risk of losing their children forever if they used the service. This coincided with a growing understanding of the dangers of separating children from their most-loved parent-figures and of the confusion and self-doubt experienced by many children who are brought up away from their natural families. The aim became to reunite the family if at all possible. The emphasis was upon an "inclusive" model of fostering, in which links with the family were maintained and encouraged, and both families and agency worked together towards a common end (Holman, 1975).

In practice, this was extremely difficult. Research studies show a considerable gap between social workers' theories and foster parents' experiences (Rowe et al., 1984; see Triseliotis, 1989). There are many short term placements where the child soon goes home or leaves for something more permanent. There are many long term placements which break down. But there are also a good many which start temporary but gradually develop into something more permanent. Only a few of these appear to fit the preferred "inclusive" model, although the favourable results of many placements with relatives suggests that this would indeed be the best if it could be achieved (Rowe et al., 1984; Berridge and Cleaver, 1987; see Triseliotis, 1989). As time goes on the child puts down roots, yet both he and his foster family must experience all the ambiguities and insecurities of the fostering relationship (see Triseliotis, 1980 and 1983).

This inevitably led to debates about whether permanence and security can only be achieved by expanding the use of adoption or whether there is a need for a "half-way" house, in which the child cannot readily be moved but remains a member of his natural family and can retain his links with them (see, e.g. Tizard, 1977). These debates are often coloured by the knowledge that much more could and should be done to preserve and foster those links at the outset (Triseliotis, 1980; Rowe et al., 1984; Millham et al., 1986; Thoburn et al., 1986). It seems that children can find foster child status acceptable provided that it is seen as permanent (Thoburn, 1990).

The legal position, however, is simple. The relatives or foster parents with whom the child is living have actual care of him but not parental responsibility; they can do whatever is reasonable in the circumstances to safeguard or promote his welfare (Children Act 1989, s.3(5); see page 10, above). However, unless the child is in the compulsory care of a local authority, any parent with parental responsibility may remove him at will. This is so whatever may have been agreed between them, for it is not possible to surrender or transfer parental responsibility by agreement (1989 Act, s.2(9)). It is also so when the child is simply being accommodated by a local authority (1989 Act, s.20(8)). And whenever the child is being looked after by a local authority (or voluntary organisation), whether compulsorily or by arrangement with the parents, the foster parents must agree to surrender him to the agency when asked (see Chapter 8).

2. ACCESS TO THE COURTS

Relatives and other people may want to take their concerns about the upbringing of a child to court even though they are not looking after him and do not wish to do so. For example, grandparents or other members of the family may want to remain in contact with a child, perhaps after the parents' relationship has ended by death, divorce or separation (grandparents were given the right to apply for access in very limited circumstances in 1978). A professional person involved in a child's health or education, may want to challenge a decision made by the parents which he thinks will be prejudicial to the child's longer-term welfare (such as the educational psychologist who challenged the decision to sterilise an 11-year-old handicapped girl in *Re D. (A Minor) (Wardship: Sterilisation)* [1976] Fam.185; page 17, above).

Few people, however, would want to resolve such problems by going to court. They are much more likely to go to court if they want to offer a home to the child. Until December 1985, virtually the only ways of establishing a legal relationship with someone else's child were by adopting him (which is rarely possible or desirable) or by making him a ward of the High Court and seeking care and control (which is expensive and until recently little known). This limited choice was thought to lead, on the one hand, to unsuitable adoption applications which would distort rather than replace the child's natural family, and on the other hand, to difficulties in establishing the child in a secure and committed substitute home (Houghton, 1972).

The solution might have been to allow anyone to apply to the ordinary courts for what was then called legal custody and to trust the courts to make orders only where this was genuinely best for the child. But in agency cases this would have given the courts unprecedented powers to review the merits of social workers' decisions. It would also have had serious implications for the nature of fostering and the confidence of parents in the child care service. The result was the compromise of "custodianship", introduced by the Children Act 1975 but only brought into force in 1985. Certain people could apply (although of course they might not succeed) for an order giving them legal custody, but only if they had been looking after the child for some time; these periods differed as between relatives and other applicants and according to whether the application was made with or without parental consent. The procedures also reflected its origin as an alternative to adoption.

Perhaps because of these restrictions, or because it took so long to bring into force, or because it was a difficult concept to grasp, custodianship was not much used. Its main use seems to have been by grandparents who had looked after their teenage daughters' children since birth (Bullard and Malos, 1990). It has now been replaced by the scheme of section 8 orders under the Children Act 1989.

(i) The Children Act 1989

(a) *Section 8 orders*

Section 8 orders (described in Chapter 4) consist of a "residence order", a "contact order", a "specific issue order", or a "prohibited steps order" and orders to vary or discharge such orders.

A residence order in favour of someone who does not already have parental responsibility for the child is a little different from a residence order in favour of one of the child's parents. Between the parents, it simply settles the arrangements to be made as to the person (or persons) with whom the child is to live but otherwise leaves their existing responsibilities intact. In other cases, the person in whose favour the residence order is made acquires parental responsibility for the child for as long as the order remains in force (1989 Act, s.12(2)). The added responsibility and security which this brings may well make it better for the child to make a residence order, rather than no order at all (see 1989 Act, s.1(5), page 80, above), even though there is no risk that the arrangements will change (*B*. v. *B*. (*A Minor*) (*Residence Order*) [1992] 2 F.L.R. 327).

This does not mean that the parents lose their own parental responsibility (1989 Act, s.2(6)). Each person with parental responsibility can, as usual, act alone and independently in meeting that responsibility, to the extent that this is not incompatible with any court order under the 1989 Act (1989 Act, s.2(7),(8)). If there are any difficulties, a prohibited steps order can prevent the parents from interfering; they could also be prohibited from applying for the order to be changed without leave of the court (1989 Act, s.91(14)). In practice, however, most of these responsibilities can only be met by the people who are looking after the child; they are in full control of his upbringing and it is for the parents to challenge any decision they do not like.

Parental responsibility is a larger concept than legal custody, so that people with the benefit of residence orders are in a stronger position than custodians used to be, but there are some limitations. First, unlike parents or guardians, they do not have the right to give or withhold consent to an application to free the child for adoption, or to give or withhold agreement to the child's adoption, or to appoint a testamentary guardian for the child (1989 Act, s.12(3)). The restrictions relating to adoption are logical: these people might have preferred to adopt the child and in any case the parents' rights in adoption cases are there to reflect the special status and importance of the child's family of birth. The restriction relating to guardians is also logical; guardians have virtually all the rights of parents because they stand in the shoes of parents who have died and are their surrogates—usually chosen by them—in safeguarding the special standing of the family of birth. Nevertheless, the wish to appoint a testamentary guardian is one of the main factors leading grandparents to want to adopt their grandchildren (particularly when the parents were not married to one another).

Secondly, whenever there is a residence order in force, no-one may change the child's surname or remove him from the United Kingdom, without either the written consent of everyone with parental responsibility for him or the leave of the court (1989 Act, s.13(1)). Unless the court specifically forbids it, this does not prevent the person with the benefit of the residence order taking the child abroad for less than one month (1989 Act, s.13(2)). The foster parents can go away on ordinary holidays or for other short trips without having to get the parents' consent or go back to court. They cannot, however, do anything which will result in the child being known by a different surname unless they get consent. The same applies, of course, if a child in compulsory care is living with a foster family; in that case, the local authority cannot change the child's surname without consent; and if the whole purpose of fostering rather than adoption is to keep alive the child's links (however tenuous) with the birth family, it would rarely be right to change his name; but occasionally permission may be given, even without notifying the parents (but see *Re J. (A Minor) (Change of Name)* [1993] 1 F.L.R. 699).

These rules are logical, not only because a residence order is meant to be something different from an adoption order, but also because of the many different situations in which they may be made. Sometimes the placement is intended to last throughout the child's childhood, but sometimes it may be changed as the child's own circumstances and those of his family change. Where it is intended to last, the Adoption Law Review (1992; see Chapter 12) has suggested various minor ways in which a residence order could be strengthened, so that its attractions as an alternative to adoption would be increased. The foster parents would be appointed *inter vivos* guardians of the child, having parental responsibility until he reached 18 (instead of the usual 16) and all the powers of a post mortem guardian (see Chapter 5) apart from the right to agree or refuse to agree to adoption or to change the child's surname. In reality, the most important change would be the right to call oneself "guardian".

People with the benefit of a residence order can apply for a lump sum or property adjustment order (1989 Act, Sched. 1, para. 1(1)) against either or both of the child's parents and people with care can apply for a maintenance assessment under the Child Support Act 1991 against them both (see Chapter 4). However, the local authority also have power to contribute towards the cost of the child's maintenance (1989 Act, Sched. 1, para. 15), as a residence order may well be an alternative to continued local authority fostering.

(b) *When can section 8 orders be made?*

The court can make a section 8 order either when a person with the right (see (c) below) or with leave (see (d) below) to do so has applied for it or of the court's "own motion" (*i.e.* without any application having been made) in the course of any "family proceedings" (see page 63, above). This means that section 8 orders, and in particular residence orders, can always be made instead of the order applied for, including an adoption order. The law does not require adoption agencies, or courts hearing adoption applications, to consider whether any alternative order might be better for the child. But it does allow the court to make a residence order instead of an adoption order, whether or not the prospective adopters would have been entitled to apply for it in the first place.

(c) *The right to apply*

The following people are entitled to apply for some or all section 8 orders (these categories are modelled on, but simpler than, the people who had a right to apply for custodianship):

(1) anyone *who already has a residence order* in their favour can apply for any section 8 order (1989 Act, s.10(4)); anyone who has applied for and *obtained any other order*, or is named in a contact order, can apply for it to be varied or discharged (1989 Act, s.10(6));

(2) anyone *with whom the child has lived for at least three years* can apply for a residence or contact order (1989 Act, s.10(5)(*b*)); the three years need not be continuous or still continuing when the application is made, but it must have begun not more than five years before and ended not more than three months before the making of the application (1989 Act, s.10(10));

(3) anyone *who has the consent of each person who would otherwise have the right to decide where the child is to live* can apply for a residence or contact order; where there is no residence or care order already in force, this means the consent of each person (if any) who has parental responsibility for the child; where there is a residence order in force, it means the consent of each person in whose favour the order was made; and where there is a care order in force, it means the consent of the local authority (1989 Act, s.10(5)(*c*));

(4) rules of court may prescribe additional categories of people who are entitled to apply for prescribed types of order (1989 Act, s.11(7)); the object of this is to do away with the need for leave if it turns out that certain kinds of people are almost invariably being given it if they ask— one possibility might be grandparents or other close relatives applying for contact, particularly in the sorts of case where grandparents used to have the right to apply (for example, where the parent

who was their own child has died); but at present no additional categories have been prescribed.

(d) *Leave to apply*

People who are not entitled to apply for a section 8 order can still do so if the court gives them leave (1989 Act, s.10(1)(a)(ii), (2)(b)). Leave can be granted *ex parte* and without a hearing; it can only be refused after a hearing, but the court can choose who should be informed (Family Proceedings Rules 1991, r. 4.3(2)); in hopeless cases, it may be less disruptive to the child and his family if they do not know. The decision whether or not to grant leave (to someone other than the child concerned) is not "a question with respect to the upbringing of the child" so the court does not have to regard the welfare of the child as its paramount consideration (*Re A. and Others (Minors) (Residence Orders: Leave to Apply)* [1992] Fam.182, C.A.; see page 121, below).

The Act requires the court to have particular regard to:

(1) the nature of the proposed application for the section 8 order;

(2) the applicant's connection with the child;

(3) any risk there might be of the proposed application disrupting the child's life to such an extent that he would be harmed by it; and

(4) where the child is being looked after by a local authority, the authority's plans for the child's future and the wishes and feelings of the child's parents (1989 Act, s.10(9)).

The court may also take account of the child's wishes (*Re A. (A Minor) (Residence Order: Leave to Apply)* [1993] 1 F.L.R. 425; and see *Re A. and Others*, page 121, below) and whether the application has a chance of success (*G. v. Kirklees Metropolitan Borough Council* [1992] F.L. 561; and see *Re A. and Others*, page 121, below).

The fourth criterion was meant to discourage the courts from allowing local authority foster parents to make applications which would undermine the authority's longer-term plans for the child, and the parents' confidence in them, without a very good reason indeed. However, the Act imposes yet another restriction on local authority foster parents if they need leave before they can apply for a section 8 order: a person who is, or was at any time within the last six months, a local authority foster parent of a child cannot apply for leave unless she is either a relative of the child or has the consent of the local authority or the child has lived with her for at least three years before the application, not necessarily continuously but beginning not more than five years beforehand (but in that case she will usually not require leave) (1989 Act, s.9(3),(4)). A "relative" is a grandparent, brother, sister, uncle or aunt (including half-relationships and relationships by marriage) and a step-parent (1989 Act, s.105(1)). The effect of this is so complicated that it is worthwhile summarising the position of local authority foster parents separately.

(e) *Local authority foster parents*

As a result of all the rules set out above, the position of local authority foster parents is as follows:

(1) A foster parent with whom the child has lived for a total of *three years* (beginning not more than five years ago and ending, if it has ended, not more than three months ago) can apply *as of right* for a residence or contact order, whether the child is in compulsory care, or simply being accommodated, or is no longer being looked after by the authority at all.

(2) If the child is in compulsory care, a foster parent who has the *consent of the local authority* can apply *as of right* for a residence or contact order, irrespective of how long the child has lived with her and whether or not he is still doing so.

(3) If the child is simply being accommodated, or is no longer being looked after by the authority at all, a foster parent who has the *consent of each person with the benefit of a residence order or (if there is no order) each person with parental responsibility* can apply as of right for a residence or contact order, irrespective of how long the child has lived with her and whether or not he is still doing so.

(4) A foster parent who is a *relative* of the child can apply *for leave to apply* for any section 8 order, irrespective of how long the child has lived with her and whether or not he is still doing so, whether or not the child is still being looked after by the local authority, and whether the child is or was in care or simply being accommodated.

(5) A foster parent who *stopped being a foster parent of this child more than six months ago* can also apply *for leave to apply* for any section 8 order, in just the same way as a foster parent relative can do so.

(6) However, an *unrelated foster parent who is still fostering the child or who stopped doing so less than six months ago, cannot even apply for leave* to apply for a section 8 order unless he has the consent of the authority, whether or not the child is still being looked after by the authority and irrespective of whether the child is or was in compulsory care or simply being accommodated. This does not apply to foster parents with whom the child has lived for a total of at least three years out of the previous five, but those people would usually be entitled to apply for a residence or contact order anyway (see (1) above); the only difference between this three year rule and that one is that these three years may end more than three months before the application.

It is difficult to see why the position of a local authority foster parent has been made quite so complicated. It is most unlikely that she would be given leave to apply for an order against the wishes of a local authority who are still looking after the child unless the circumstances were very unusual. This is amply demonstrated by the case of *Re A. and Others (Minors) (Residence Orders: Leave to Apply)* [1992] Fam.182, C.A. Six very disturbed children had been taken into compulsory care and placed with a dedicated, experienced and strong-minded "super-mum" foster mother. At first things went well; then the two oldest ran away. The local authority's concerns grew and they decided to remove the four younger children for an assessment. After a period in a children's home they were now placed with other foster parents. Allegations were made, hotly contested by the foster mother, which certainly deserved proper investigation and clarification. The children had only been with her two years and so she was not entitled to apply for residence orders. She applied for leave to do so. The Court of Appeal refused it: the welfare of the children was not paramount; both the local authority and the mother were opposed to the application; although the court could now interfere with authority's plans (a change from the old law) it should approach matters on the basis that their plans were designed to safeguard and promote the child's welfare (see 1989 Act, s.22(3); page 144, below) so that departing from them might well cause a harmful disruption in his life; in this case the children (aged between 9 and 13) did not want to go back, so that a lengthy and bitter battle in court would serve no useful purpose.

For the sake of simplicity, everyone agreed to assume that the foster mother had applied for leave more than six months after the children had left her; it does seem odd to require this wait, although it makes her chances of success even slimmer. Perhaps a more useful purpose of the rule is to safeguard the child's current placement after the local authority has recently stopped looking after him.

(ii) Wardship

The wardship jurisdiction of the High Court can be invoked by anyone with a proper interest in the child's welfare. Although local authorities can no longer use it as an alternative to the statutory care system (see Chapter 10), no such restrictions have been placed upon its use by private individuals. Anyone involved in the sorts of "tug of love" with which we are concerned here, whether relatives, foster parents or the child's own parents, might try to resolve matters by making the child a ward of court. Before the 1989 Act, relatives were the largest category of plaintiffs in wardship cases, after local authorities and natural parents (Law Commission, 1987b). Now that they can apply, or seek leave to apply, under the 1989 Act they may be less likely to use wardship. It is much more expensive and time-consuming, legal aid may be difficult if not impossible to obtain, and a residence order gives them more than care and control in wardship and without the continuing supervision of the court.

It is also unlikely that the High Court will allow wardship to be used to get round the restrictions on the making of Children Act applications by local authority foster parents. Before the 1989 Act, it was clearly established that wardship should not be used to interfere in the statutory responsibilities of local social services authorities (*A. v. Liverpool City Council* [1982] A.C. 363; see also page 134, below). This principle was first developed in cases where the court refused to allow foster parents to challenge the local authority's decision to take away a child who was in their compulsory care (*Re M.* [1961] Ch. 328, C.A.; *Re T. (A.J.J.) (An Infant)* [1970] Ch. 688, C.A.). Where children were simply being accommodated (in what was then known as voluntary care) the same principle would apply if the authority just wanted to change the placement, for this was clearly within their statutory child care responsibilities. Where the parents had asked for the child be returned to them, so that the local authority had largely dropped out of the picture, the case might be allowed to proceed. It was, however, always open to the authority to "waive the jurisdictional point" —in other words not to oppose the application on this ground.

It is not yet clear whether the court will allow wardship to be used where it could not have been used under the old law. In *Re W. (A Minor) (Wardship: Jurisdiction)* [1985] A.C. 791, it was decided that relatives could not use wardship in order to try and obtain the child's discharge from compulsory care. The parents had rejected their four year old daughter and consented to care proceedings with a view to freeing her for adoption. Her uncle and aunt and grandparents knew nothing of this and wanted her to remain in the family, looked after by uncle and aunt. The House of Lords held that it was for the local authority to choose between the advantages of bringing her up in her natural family and the dangers of doing so when that family included the parents who had rejected her. The decision clearly lay within the authority's statutory powers and the court should not interfere.

Nowadays, the family would have a much better chance of being heard in the care proceedings, where the court can and should consider all the alternatives, so there may be less need for them to fall back on wardship. Once a care order has been made and the local authority have made permanent plans for the child, leave to apply for a residence order will only rarely be given (see *Re A. and Others*, page 121, above). It is also likely that the High Court will still take the view that wardship is not to be used to circumvent the details of the statutory scheme. The court and the authority should, however, have canvassed all the options, including those involving the family, before the order was made.

Thus, despite its apparently broad scope, wardship is not an ideal method for a concerned relative or foster parent to seek some legal security for the child.

(iii) Adoption

Adoption is the ultimate solution, for it involves a complete and irrevocable transfer of the child from one family to another. The outcome for the child is usually far more favourable than in any other form of substitute care-giving

(Seglow, Kellmer Pringle and Wedge, 1972; but see also Thoburn, 1990). One reason for this may be the high degree of security and commitment which it involves. Another reason could be that it tries to reproduce, as closely as possible, the "normal" family. The Children Act 1975 introduced changes (now in the Adoption Act 1976; see Chapter 12) designed to make it rather easier for local authorities to plan for children in their care to be adopted. These included the procedure for freeing for adoption, so that issues of parental agreement and other claims could be dealt with between the authority and the family, without involving the potential adopters at all; an additional ground for dispensing with parental agreement in child abuse cases; and the introduction of adoption allowances to make it easier for "hard to place" children to be adopted. The 1975 Act also tried to make it easier for long term foster parents to adopt, even if the local authority did not want them to do so, by providing that a child who had lived with them for more than five years could not be removed against their will once they had given notice that they wanted to adopt him.

On the other hand, because adoption is supposed to replace the original family, it is not always the right solution, particularly where the child ought to remain in touch with his parents or other members of his family. Still less is it usually thought right for relatives to adopt the child, because this will distort the family structure and introduce all sorts of confusion and potential for later conflict (Houghton, 1972). However, provisions in the Children Act 1975 which required the courts to consider alternatives to adoptions by step-parents and relatives were badly drafted and proved largely ineffective. The courts have been prepared to allow an unmarried mother's parents to adopt her child. In *Re S. (A Minor) (Adoption or Custodianship)* [1987] Fam.98, C.A., the court took the view that the security of becoming the grandparents' child would reduce rather than increase the risk of emotional confusion when he was eventually told the true facts about his parentage. The balance might tip even further in favour of an unmarried father's parents, who may be less likely to feel that the child will otherwise be a full member of their family, whatever the law may say (see *Re O. (A Minor) (Adoption by Grandparents)* [1985] F.L.R. 546). These grandparents had the support of the children's parents and the position might have been different if they had withheld their agreement. Whether the Children Act alternatives will be any more popular with relatives or with the courts remains to be seen.

3. THE PRINCIPLES

Both the Children Act and wardship jurisdictions are governed by the familiar principle in section 1(1) of the 1989 Act:

"When a court determines any question with respect to—(a) the upbring-ing of a child; or (b) the administration of a child's property or the application of any income arising from it, the child's welfare shall be the court's paramount consideration."

Children Act proceedings are also governed by the "checklist" of factors in section 1(3) (see page 75, above) and it is quite likely that the court hearing wardship proceedings will also consult it. But how do the courts interpret the child's welfare in disputes between parents and others? And what is the weight to be given to the wishes and claims of the natural parents if these conflict with the welfare of the child? These questions were discussed at length by the House of Lords in the leading case of *J. v. C.* [1970] A.C. 668.

In 1958 a little boy was born to Spanish parents who were working in England. The mother was ill, so he was looked after by an English couple for some 10 months, until she was better. The parents took him back to Spain, but the family lived in very poor circumstances in Madrid, the climate did not suit him and his health deteriorated. In 1961, it was arranged that he would come back to the English couple. Nobody contemplated that this would be permanent, but no time limit was agreed. The local authority agreed to accommodate him and fostered him with the couple (who could then claim the boarding-out allowance). He settled down well and his health improved. In 1963 he started school, and the foster mother wrote a "tactless" letter to the mother, remarking how English he was becoming. The mother became worried, and after a request for him to spend a holiday in Spain had been refused, formally asked the local authority for his return. The foster parents countered with notice of intention to apply to adopt. In December 1963, the local authority made him a ward of court. It took until July 1965 for the case to be heard and the parents, having been assured that the authority would look after their interests, were not there. The judge decided that he should stay with the foster parents, but be brought up a Roman Catholic and with knowledge of his Spanish origins and the Spanish language. In 1967, the foster parents applied to change his religion so that he could be sent to an Anglican choir school; the parents countered with another application for his return. By this time their material circumstances and the mother's health were very much better, but the boy was now nine, had been with the foster family since he was three, was very close to his foster brother, had learned to play cricket and spoke only "pidgin" Spanish. The case was heard by the judge in 1967, then by the Court of Appeal, and finally by the House of Lords in 1968. All decided that he should stay where he was but remain a Roman Catholic.

If it was the law that the natural parents had claims which could only be overridden if the child's welfare was clearly in danger, these parents might have succeeded. They had never ill-treated their son, could hardly be criticised for letting him go to England and now had a satisfactory home to offer. If, on the other hand, his welfare was paramount, he should surely remain where he was happy and settled, whatever the rights and wrongs between the parents and foster parents. As Lord MacDermott said ([1970] A.C. 668 at 710-711), the welfare principle connotes:

"a process whereby, when all the relevant facts, relationships, claims and wishes of parents, risks, choices and other circumstances are taken into account and weighed, the course to be followed will be that which is most in the interests of the child's welfare. . . . it is the paramount consideration because it rules on or determines the course to be followed."

This suggests that the claims of natural parenthood are only relevant in so far as they indicate what will be best for the child. But does that mean that, in all disputes between parents and other people about where a child is to live (or how he is to be brought up), the court simply tots up the advantages and disadvantages of each household (or solution) from the child's point of view?

In *Re K.* (*A Minor*) (*Ward: Care and Control*) [1990] 1 W.L.R. 431, the Court of Appeal was quite clear that this was not the right approach. The dispute was between the unmarried father of a little boy of four, whose parents had lived together until his mother had committed suicide when he was three, and the maternal aunt and uncle who had looked after him since then. They had obviously done a good job and could offer him an excellent home. The father was also a stable and hardworking man who could offer a reasonable home with the help of his own parents. Both the welfare officer and the mother's psychiatric social worker thought that he would be a satisfactory parent and rise to the occasion. Lord Justice Fox said that "the question was not where [the boy] would get a better home. The question was: was it demonstrated that the welfare of the child positively demanded the displacement of the parental right".

This might have heralded a return to the days before *J.* v. *C.*. Luckily, Mr. Justice Waite also said:

"The principle is that the court in wardship will not act in opposition to a natural parent unless judicially satisfied that the child's welfare requires that the parental right should be suspended or superseded. . . . the term 'parental right' is not there used in any proprietary sense, but rather as describing the right of every child, as part of its general welfare, to have the ties of nature maintained wherever possible with the parents who gave it life."

In other words, as the Court of Appeal emphasised in *Re H.* (*A Minor*) (*Custody: Interim Care and Control*) [1991] 2 F.L.R. 109 (see page 99, above), it is the welfare test which is being applied, but it is generally the child's right to be brought up by his own parents. If there is any discrepancy between what was said in *Re K.* and in *Re H.*, the welfare principle in *Re H.* is now to be preferred (*Re W.* (*Residence Order*), *The Times*, April 16, 1993, C.A.). The child's right not to be separated from his family unless it is necessary for his own best interests is also guaranteed by Article 9 of the United Nations Convention on the Rights of the Child (1989).

The facts in *J.* v. *C.* and *Re K.* were very different and the decisions would probably have been just the same whatever language the courts had used. In disputes between parents and "strangers" there is often a conflict between two important welfare factors. One is the danger of disturbing a situation which has been working well for a long time. The other is the possible risk to the child's sense of identity and personal worth if he is brought up by people who are not his "own," particularly if he is cut off from other links with his family and background or given a negative picture to them. In 1926, a judge was able to discount the dangers of disruption:

" . . . at her tender age [six] one knows from experience how mercifully transient are the effects of partings and other sorrows, and how soon the novelty of fresh surroundings and new associations effaces the recollection of former days and kind friends . . . " (*Re Thain* [1926] Ch. 676).

A modern judge would certainly not dismiss as "transient" the effects of "partings and other sorrows", but he would also be more alive, not to the rights of the natural parents, but to the reasons why it is usually better for children to be brought up by them. Truly "natural" parents love their children and feel responsible for them, and the child will benefit both from this and from the sense of normality and identity which it will bring. If other people have developed the same love and commitment towards the child, so that the child feels normal and secure with them, their equally natural relationship cannot lightly be put at risk for the sake of more dubious advantages to the child's later sense of his place in the world.

4. COMMENTARY

We have gone beyond seeing these cases as a conflict between the "rights of parents" and the "welfare of the child". The one is now an important component of the other. Procedurally parents are in a much better position than other people, because they begin with parental responsibility and others have such limited rights of access to the courts to challenge it. Given this, is there any case for giving the same preference to natural parents in disputes with individuals as they have in their disputes with local authorities? (See Chapter 10). The Law Commission (1986) thought that to do so might put the welfare of some children seriously at risk. Also, if a child has made his home with another family for some time, and especially from an early age, it is impossible to say whether his "birth" or his "psychological" parents should have the preference. As Lord Templeman said in *Re K.D.* (*A Minor*) (*Access: Principles*) [1988] A.C. 806 at 812:

"The best person to bring up a child is the natural parent. It matters not whether the parent is wise or foolish, rich or poor, educated or illiterate, provided that the child's moral and physical health are not endangered. Public authorities cannot improve upon nature."

It is not a question of choosing between the family and the institutions of the state but between two families, both of which could well be called "natural".

PART III: INTERVENTION—
THE PUBLIC LAW

Chapter 8

LOCAL AUTHORITY SOCIAL SERVICES

Local social services authorities have three main roles in helping children and their families. The most important, which is the subject of this chapter, is to provide a wide range of social services for "children in need" and their families. A second, which is the subject of the next chapter, is to monitor the private arrangements made by parents for other people to look after their children, whether for part of the day or for longer periods away from home. The third, which is covered in Chapter 10, is taking compulsory steps to protect children from harm.

All of these have been brought together in the Children Act 1989. This was meant to make things simpler and clearer for practitioners and families and to lay down a common set of guiding principles (R.C.C.L., 1985). These begin with the idea that parents are responsible for bringing up their own children and that it is better for their children if parents are allowed to do this with the minimum of interference from the state. But the state has an important role in providing special services for families who need them. This should not entitle the state to interfere against their will—people who need help are just as entitled to respect for their privacy and the integrity of their family lives as are people who can do everything for themselves. Only when a child is at risk of significant harm, more so than might reasonably be expected of a child in his circumstances, should compulsory measures be taken.

Before looking at the present law, it may be worth sketching a history of how child care law has developed since the second world war (see Heywood, 1978; Packman, 1981). It was during the war that concern about how badly the state was looking after the children for whom it was responsible first surfaced (Monckton, 1945; Curtis, 1946). Steps to remedy matters were taken as part of the package of legislation setting up the welfare state in the post-war period.

1. CHILD CARE LAW SINCE WORLD WAR TWO

By 1946, local authorities had acquired two main types of responsibility to care for children. One was the duty to act as a "fit person" for children whom the courts had removed from home because they were delinquent, troublesome or being neglected or ill-treated. The other was the duty of the old Poor Law authorities to take care of orphaned, abandoned and destitute children. They were often not very good at either. The answer was to set up specialist children's departments, with trained child care officers under the direction of a motherly Children's Officer, who would look after these children properly (Curtis, 1946). This was done by the Children Act 1948, which also obliged local authorities to provide a service for all children whose parents were, for whatever reason, temporarily or permanently unable or unwilling to look after them. Even so, apart from a small and decreasing number of orphaned and abandoned children, those coming into care were usually from the poorest families, who could not look after them because of homelessness, single parenthood, relationship breakdown, short or longer term illness.

The child care service was, in theory at least, a voluntary service giving no right to remove children against their parents' will. However, the 1948 Act retained the power of the old Poor Law authorities to pass a resolution assuming the rights of a parent of a child in their care if, for a variety of reasons, that parent was unfit to resume care of the child. Also, "fit person" orders were, by their very nature, compulsory against both the child and his parents. Beginning in 1958 (as we have seen in Chapter 4) divorce and other courts hearing disputes between parents acquired the power to insist that the child be admitted to care instead. The number of legal routes into care grew and grew.

Originally, it was expected that many children would stay in care for a long time. During the 1950s, however, the focus changed towards shorter term admissions with the aim of reuniting the child with his family as soon as possible. This in turn led to the aim of preventing the admission in the first place, first enshrined in section 1 of the Children and Young Persons Act 1963. The best local authorities began to develop a wider range of services aimed at helping families to stay together.

An enormous upheaval in local authority social services took place in 1971. The Local Authority Social Services Act 1970 brought together the services provided by their children's departments with those provided by their health and welfare departments for old, handicapped, disabled or mentally disordered people; the Chronically Sick and Disabled Persons Act 1970 increased their responsibilities towards disabled people; and the Children and Young Persons Act 1969 transferred to them the main responsibility for dealing with young offenders, bringing them into the same system as children in need of care and protection. Children coming into care (as Packman, 1986, was later to observe) could be divided into the "victims", the "villains", and the "volunteered", although the legal and factual categories might not always coincide.

These changes were all part of the philosophy that the immediate reason for a child's presence in care was less important than the proper assessment of his needs and how they might best be met. It was still assumed that most children would eventually go home and preferably as soon as possible. This assumption received a heavy blow with the publication of a research study (Rowe and Lambert, 1973) revealing that most children who had been in care for six months or more could expect to remain there for a very long time (there was no magic in the six months, which was simply the minimum period chosen for the research sample; later studies suggested that the critical period was much less than that). Many of these children would have benefitted from more positive attempts to reunite them with their families or to find them permanent alternative homes. Even so the study found large numbers of children in care who had been assessed as needing a permanent substitute home but who were still waiting for this to be arranged. Parental opposition was seen as one of the reasons for this.

Those findings coincided with two other important documents. The Report of the Inter-departmental Committee on the Law of Adoption (Houghton, 1972) proposed the creation of a comprehensive professional adoption service, in which social services departments would take the lead role, and the emphasis would be upon finding homes for children who needed them rather than upon finding children for parents who wanted them. The Report of the Committee of Inquiry into the death of Maria Colwell (Field-Fisher, 1973) was the first in a long line of inquiries into the apparent failures of local authorities to protect children from being killed or seriously harmed in their own homes (see D.H.S.S., 1982; D.H., 1991). The feature of that case which stood out most strongly at the time was that as a young baby Maria had been compulsorily removed from her mother, who was unable to cope with her, and had spent most her life living apparently happily with an uncle and aunt. At the age of six she was sent back to her mother, who had recently remarried, and was killed by her step-father 15 months later.

Not surprisingly, this all led to a reassessment of the balance between the parents' rights and the longer term welfare of their children. The trend of the law was at that time moving strongly in favour of the children (see *J.* v. *C.* [1970] A.C. 668, page 124, above). Greater emphasis was placed on planning for the future of children in care instead of assuming that they would eventually return home. Permanent life in care was, and still is, generally thought to be a bad thing. If a child could not be returned home within a reasonable time, therefore, it was better to find him a secure and permanent substitute home whether his parents liked it or not. On the whole, adoption was thought preferable to long term fostering, because of the security and commitment involved in adoption and the known insecurity of many long term fostering placements.

This approach was reflected in a number of legal changes introduced by the Children Act 1975, which allowed a breathing space before returning children who had been in voluntary care for six months or more and expanded the grounds for keeping them there; it also implemented the recommendations of the Houghton report on the law of adoption, some of which were designed to make it easier to find permanent new homes for children in care (see Chapters 7 and 12). Some changes were introduced quite quickly; but others, notably the half-way house of custodianship, had to wait for several years. Inevitably, in the new atmosphere of permanency planning, adoption expanded to fill much of the gap. Attention turned to how and when to bring contact between parents and child to an end (see Adcock and White, 1980).

Local authorities were also turning to the wardship jurisdiction of the High Court, to give them the flexibility to plan for the children in their care and to make up for the deficiencies and complexities of the legal system which had grown so rapidly. The courts showed themselves more than willing to help. If a local authority felt that their statutory powers were insufficient or inappropriate, there was nothing to prevent them making the child a ward of court. This could be because the grounds for acquiring compulsory powers were thought too narrow (see, for example, *Re C.B. (A Minor)* [1981] 1 W.L.R. 379, C.A.); or because the authority had failed in a lower court and wanted to appeal (see *Re D. (A Minor) (Justices' Decision: Review)* [1977] Fam.158, C.A.); or because a high status court with open-ended powers and procedures was preferred to a lay bench with more limited powers and more rigid rules of evidence and procedure; or because the authority preferred to have the guidance of the High Court in solving a particularly complex or delicate case (for example, a proposed abortion, *Re P. (A Minor)* [1986] 1 F.L.R. 272 or sterilisation, *Re B. (A Minor) (Wardship: Sterilisation)* [1988] A.C. 199). Social workers found that parents also preferred being told that their child was to be placed in the guardianship of the High Court to being told that the authority wanted to take away their rights because they were unfit.

But while local authorities were encouraged to invoke the wardship jurisdiction in these cases, the family were not allowed to use it for the same sort of purposes. A mother could not use wardship to seek access to a child removed under a care order (*A. v. Liverpool City Council* [1982] A.C. 363) or even to forestall care proceedings which had not yet been started (*W. v. Shropshire County Council* [1986] 1 F.L.R. 359; *W. v. Nottinghamshire County Council* [1986] 1 F.L.R. 565). At first, she might be allowed to use it in effect to appeal against an unfavourable result in care proceedings but it was later decided that she could not even do this. Relatives or foster parents who had no claims under the statutory schemes could not fill the gap with wardship instead (*Re W. (A Minor) (Wardship: Jurisdiction)* [1985] A.C. 791, page 122, above).

The legal reason for this apparent discrepancy lay in the sovereignty of Parliament. The courts must not use a jurisdiction which stems from the royal prerogative to interfere or conflict with the decision of Parliament, enshrined in statute, that certain matters are within the province of local authorities. If the authority had power to decide the matter (whether it was access or placement with relatives or anything else) the court could not interfere unless the authority either agreed or asked it to do so. If, however, Parliament had left gaps in the authority's powers, there was no conflict and the court could use its own powers to help. The High Court also has power to quash the decisions of local authorities who have broken their statutory duties, abused their powers or taken a decision which no reasonable authority could have taken, but the normal process of judicial review and not wardship should be used to do this (*Re D.M. (A Minor) (Wardship: Jurisdiction)* [1986] 2 F.L.R. 122, C.A.).

The end result was widely felt to be unjust. If the court could fill the gaps left by Parliament in the authority's powers to protect children, why could it not fill the gaps left in the courts' powers to hear claims by parents or relatives? The underlying reason was that it would then become virtually impossible to prevent parents and others from invoking wardship whenever they felt unhappy or aggrieved by an authority's decision about anything important. It was feared that this would "open the floodgates" to huge numbers of cases which would swamp the courts (see *A.* v. *Liverpool City Council*, page 134, above). There was also a view that local authorities should be allowed to concentrate their resources on doing the best job they could for children and families alike and that the courts are not the right places to reviewing the details of how they go about it (House of Commons, 1984; R.C.C.L., 1985). Others (see, for example, Family Rights Group, 1982 and 1986) felt that if the gaps left by Parliament in the family's rights were thought to be deliberate, why were not the gaps left in the authority's powers also deliberate?

In two respects, the law was found to be so unjust to children in care and their families that it had to be changed in order to conform to the European Convention on Human Rights. Children in care could be locked up in secure accommodation without any right to challenge their detention (contrary to Article 5(4), which guarantees the right to a speedy judicial review of the merits of any detention); parents could be deprived of care, or even of all contact with their children without any right of appeal (contrary to Article 8, which guarantees respect for family life). Limited new procedures were introduced in 1983 to deal with each of these.

But there were many other ways in which the law was unsatisfactory. It was excessively complicated and obscure, having grown piece-meal as each new crisis arose. It differentiated too sharply between "prevention" and "care", regarding care as a last resort to be avoided at all costs, rather than as part of a continuum of services which might be needed for different children at different times. If a child was admitted to care, however, the procedures and practice did not differentiate sharply enough between voluntary arrangements, intended to help children and their families, and compulsory intervention, designed to protect children from their neglectful or abusive families or to protect society from unruly children. The compulsory procedures themselves were mostly modelled on what was appropriate for unruly or offending children rather than what was appropriate and fair for children who might need to be protected from their families.

Another complication brought to light at this time was that the child care service first established under the Children Act 1948 was legally distinct from the same authorities' powers (under the National Assistance Act 1948 and what became the National Health Service Act 1977) to provide accommodation and other services for physically or mentally handicapped or disordered people, including children. These children were not usually received into care, unless there were also difficulties in their families. This may have avoided the potential stigma involved, but it also deprived the children of the benefit of the authorities' duties to safeguard and promote their short and long term welfare.

The Review of Child Care Law (R.C.C.L., 1985) was set up in response to the recommendations of the House of Commons' Social Services Committee (1984), to review the whole of child care law apart from the law relating to juvenile offenders. The Review recommended that all the social services for children and their families should be brought under one umbrella. The children would all receive the same attention, through the regulations about visiting them, reviewing their care and planning for their future. Equally, their families would all be expected to be involved in and consulted about the care provided for their children, in partnership with the local authority. Families whose need for help stemmed from their own rather than the child's difficulties would be accorded the same respect and consideration as the parents whose need for help stemmed from their children's handicaps or disabilities. The aim would be to help them to help themselves rather than to take over from them.

The voluntary child care service would therefore be shorn of all the elements, such as the power to assume parental rights by resolution or to delay the removal of children from voluntary care, which made them seem compulsory or coercive. Compulsory procedures would be quite separate. These should be unified and simplified, based on coherent principles, and with procedures which were fair to all three parties, the child, his family and the local authority. Once this had happened, it no longer seemed right to allow the authorities to use the wardship procedure to circumvent or supplement the statutory scheme.

2. CHILDREN IN NEED

Under section 17(1) of the Children Act 1989:

"It shall be the general duty of every local authority . .

(a) to safeguard and promote the welfare of children within their area who are in need; and

(b) so far as is consistent with that duty, to promote the upbringing of such children by their families,

by providing a range and level of services appropriate to those children's needs."

For this purpose, there are three different kinds of children "in need" (1989 Act, s.17(10),(11)):

(a) children who are unlikely to achieve or maintain, or to have the opportunity of achieving or maintaining, a reasonable standard of health (physical or mental) or development (physical, intellectual, emotional, social or behavioural) without the provision of social services for them;

(b) children whose health or development (defined as before) is likely to be significantly impaired, or further impaired, without the provision of social services for them; and

(c) disabled children (who are included whether or not their health or development will be affected); a child is disabled if he is blind, deaf or dumb or suffers from mental disorder of any kind or is substantially or permanently handicapped by illness, injury or congenital deformity (or any other disability which may be prescribed).

As long as a service is provided for the sake of safeguarding or promoting the child's welfare, it may be provided for his family or any member of his family (1989 Act, s.17(3)). The "family" of a child in need means anyone with parental responsibility for him and anyone else with whom he has been living (1989 Act, s.17(10)). It does not include relatives or friends who may be very important to him unless he has at some time lived with them.

Authorities are not expected to meet every need in their area but they should identify the extent of local need and decide their priorities in the light of this and all the circumstances, including their own resources (D.H. and W.O., 1993). They are allowed, indeed expected, to "facilitate" the provision of these services by others, particularly voluntary organisations and may contract any services out as they see fit (1989 Act, s.17(5)). They can also give assistance in kind or, in exceptional circumstances, in cash; this can be unconditional or on terms, including repayment or reimbursement of its value; but the authority must have regard to the means of the child and each of his parents and cannot require repayment from someone who is on income support, family credit or disability working allowance (1989 Act, s.17(6),(7),(8)). This does not mean that social services should take over the responsibilities of housing departments and the D.S.S.; but they may think that helping out, perhaps with furniture or big bills, is a better way of discharging their general duty under section 17(1) than providing accommodation for the child under section 20 (see 4. below).

The general duty in section 17(1) is fleshed out by the further responsibilities set out in Schedule 2 to the 1989 Act. Some of these are in deliberately general terms and others are more specific. There is a general duty to take reasonable steps to discover the numbers of children in need in the area, to publish information about the services which they (and others, particularly voluntary organisations) provide, and to try to see that those who might benefit from their services know about them (1989 Act, Sched. 2, para. 1).

There is a much more specific duty to keep a register of individual disabled children (1989 Act, Sched. 2, para. 2). There are also specific duties to assess the needs of individual children under other legislation. Thus the needs of disabled children must be assessed under the Chronically Sick and Disabled Persons Act 1970 and the Disabled Persons (Services, Consultation and Representation) Act 1986 and children with special educational needs must be assessed under the Education Act 1981 (to be replaced by the 1993 Bill, Pt.III). When doing this, the authority may also assess the child's needs for services under the 1989 Act (1989 Act, Sched. 2, para. 3). Otherwise there is no obligation to assess the needs of each individual child who may be in need (although if a child is involved in legal proceedings, the courts may be able to order this; see Chapter 10).

Schedule 2 also contains a mixture of (1) specific services which should be provided for any purpose (within the general obligation in section 17(1)); (2) specific purposes for which any kind of service may be provided; and (3) specific duties towards particular kinds of children. All are carefully phrased with a view to ensuring that no individual child can bring proceedings claiming to be entitled to anything in particular (*cf. A.G. ex rel. Tilley* v. *Wandsworth Borough Council* [1981] 1 W.L.R. 854, C.A.).

In the first category is the duty to "make such provision as they consider appropriate for the following services to be available" for children in need in their area who are living with their families:

(a) advice, guidance and counselling;

(b) occupational, social, cultural or recreational activities;

(c) home help (including laundry services);

(d) facilities or assistance for travelling to services;

(e) help with holidays for the child and his family (1989 Act, Sched. 2, para. 8).

Similarly, they must "provide such family centres as they consider appropriate" for the children in their area. Family centres are places where a child, his parents or any other person who has parental responsibility or is looking after him, may come for occupational, social, cultural or recreational activities, or for advice, guidance or counselling; if for the latter, accommodation may also be provided (1989 Act, Sched. 2, para. 9). Family centres now play an important part in assessment and in helping parents learn to look after their children properly.

In the second category, every local authority must take reasonable steps to prevent children in their area suffering ill-treatment or neglect. (This is backed up by a range of duties to investigate suspected abuse which are discussed in Chapter 10.) There is also a specific duty, when they think a child in their area is likely to suffer harm, and lives or is going to live in another area, to inform the other local authority, specifying the harm they think he is going to suffer and (if they can) where he is going to live (1989 Act, Sched. 2, para. 4). In the same category, every local authority has to take reasonable steps designed to reduce the need to bring care, family or any sort of proceedings in respect of children in their area, including criminal proceedings, to encourage children in their area not to commit crimes, and to avoid the need for children to be locked up in secure accommodation (1989 Act, Sched. 2, para. 7).

In the third category is the duty to take such steps as are reasonably practicable to help a child in need who is living apart from his family, but not with the local authority, either to return to his family or to keep in touch with them, if in their opinion this is necessary in order to safeguard or promote his welfare (1989 Act, Sched. 2, para. 10). Many of these children will be living in private foster homes or other places where the local authority already have responsibilities for safeguarding and promoting their welfare (see further in Chapter 9). Also in this category is the obligation to provide services designed to minimise the effect of their disabilities on disabled children in their area and to give these children the opportunity to lead lives which are as normal as possible (1989 Act, Sched. 2, para. 6).

3. DAY CARE

Most of what might be called ordinary day care is provided by day nurseries and child-minders through private arrangements made by parents (see further in Chapter 9). Social services authorities tend only to provide day care for priority groups of children in need. Under section 18(1) of the 1989 Act, they have a duty to provide such day care "as is appropriate" for children in need in their area who are aged five or under and who are not yet attending school, and a power to do this for such children even if they are not "in need" (1989 Act, s.18(2)). They also have a duty to provide school children in need in their area with care or supervised activities outside school hours or during school holidays, again "as appropriate", and a power to do this for such children who are not in need (1989 Act, s.18(5),(6)).

They must also help, promote and regulate the provision of day care by others. They may provide facilities (including training, advice, guidance and counselling) to people caring for children in day care (meaning any form of care or supervised activity for children during the day) (1989 Act, s.18(4)). They must, with the local education authority, review the provision which they themselves make under section 18 and the availability of child-minding and other private day care facilities for children under eight in their area, taking other local facilities and any relevant representations into account (1989 Act, s.19(1),(2),(4),(7)). This must be done within the first year after the

Act came into force and then every three years after that (1989 Act, s.19(5)). The results must then be published (1989 Act, s.19(6)).

4. ACCOMMODATION

The Children Act emphasises that providing accommodation is only one of the services which should be available for children in need. The numbers of children for whom local authorities provide temporary or permanent homes have steadily diminished in recent years. The snapshot is traditionally taken on March 31 each year; in 1979, there were more than 100,000 children "in care" in England and Wales; this figure included all those admitted to voluntary or compulsory care, but not disabled and handicapped children accommodated under other legislation. By 1984, the number had fallen to just below 79,000 (D.H.S.S., 1986). By 1991, the last year of the old system, the figure for England was 59,800, of whom 17,615 were in voluntary care. In 1992, despite the inclusion of handicapped and disabled children, the estimated figure for England has fallen to 55,000, but the figure for those "accommodated" under voluntary arrangements rather than "in care" or some other form of compulsion had risen to 18,000 (D.H. and W.O., 1993).

Under the 1989 Act, children who are provided with accommodation as a service for them and their families are not "in care"—that term is reserved for children for whom the local authority has parental responsibility under a care order or its equivalents under the old law, which are now deemed to be care orders. The umbrella term covering all these children, whether in care or accommodated (and others admitted in under emergency protection orders or remanded or detained in local authority accommodation), is that they are being "looked after". When looking up any provision in the Act, Regulations or Guidance, therefore, it is important to notice whether it refers to a child who is "accommodated" (voluntary), "in care" (compulsory), or "looked after" (both).

(i) Powers and duties to provide accommodation

The 1989 Act significantly expanded the powers and duties of local authorities to provide an accommodation service for children. There are now two different duties and two powers.

(a) Section 20(1)

Under section 20(1), every local social services authority has a duty to provide accommodation for any "child in need" (see 2. above) within their area who appears to them to require accommodation because:

(a) there is no-one who has parental responsibility for him;

(b) he is lost or has been abandoned; or

(c) the person who has been caring for him is prevented (whether or not permanently, and for whatever reason) from providing him with suitable accommodation or care.

This provision is the direct successor to section 1 of the Children Act 1948 (which became section 2 of the Child Care Act 1980). The main differences are that it extends to all children in need up to the age of 18 and that it clearly covers disabled and similar children in need where it is the child's needs rather than the parents' problems which are preventing them from looking after him suitably.

Like the provisions it replaced (and unlike those about family centres and other preventive services) section 20(1) is framed in terms of a positive duty to the individual child, although it obviously leaves a great deal of discretion to the local authority "gate-keepers" in deciding whether the degree of need is sufficient. The duty is owed to any child in the area, irrespective of where he comes from. But if accommodation is provided for a child who ordinarily lives in another local authority's area, that authority have to pay for it (1989 Act, s.29(7)) and may take over within three months of being notified that the child is being accommodated (1989 Act, s.20(2)).

(b) *Section 20(3)*

This introduced a brand new duty upon social services authorities to provide accommodation for any child in need in their area who has reached the age of 16 and whose welfare the authority consider "is likely to be seriously prejudiced if they do not provide him with accommodation". Potentially this should have a profound effect upon the responsibilities of social services (as opposed to housing) authorities to cater for the needs of homeless young people but the early indications are that they have not yet grasped the full extent of this (Centrepoint, 1993).

(c) *Section 20(4)*

This gives a new power, but not a duty, to social services authorities to provide accommodation for any child in their area (even though there is a person with parental responsibility who can do so) if they consider that this would safeguard or promote the child's welfare. This extends to children who are not "in need" or who for some other reason do not fall within the duty in section 20(1) but who will benefit from being accommodated by the local authority for a while.

(d) *Section 20(5)*

This repeats a provision in the previous law. It allows a local social services authority to provide accommodation for anyone who has reached 16 but is under 21, but only in a community home which takes people of that age, again if they consider that to do so would safeguard or promote his welfare. This again is not limited to children in need, or indeed to children at all, but it is limited to a particular type of accommodation.

(ii) Consultation and agreement

It is a fundamental principle that the accommodation service is provided voluntarily; parents or children who have reached 16 can choose whether or not to use it. The Act does not require the parents' consent before a child can be accommodated, because there may not be a parent available to give it. However it does insist that accommodation cannot be provided if anyone who has parental responsibility for the child and who is willing and able to arrange accommodation for him objects (1989 Act, s.20(7)). This means that, if both parents have parental responsibility, one of them can arrange for the child to be accommodated and the other cannot prevent this unless he has an alternative to offer. However, anyone with parental responsibility can remove the child from local authority accommodation at any time (1989 Act, s.20(8)).

There are two exceptions. The first is where there is a residence order under the 1989 Act or an order giving care of the child to a particular person in wardship proceedings. If the person with the benefit of such an order (or all the people if there is more than one) agree to the child being accommodated, then no-one else who has parental responsibility can either object or remove the child (1989 Act, s.20(9),(10)). This repeats the old law; where the parents are separated or divorced and there is an order saying that the child is to live with one of them, then that one can arrange for the child to be accommodated by the local authority irrespective of the other's views. The same applies to relatives or foster parents who have obtained an order that the child is to live with them. There may be all sorts of reasons why it would be wrong to give the other parent an absolute right to remove the child. However, the authority might agree to his doing so if this seemed right for the child. It would then be a matter for the individuals involved to sort out whether they wanted to enforce, vary or disregard the court order. The second exception is that the parents' rights to object or to remove the child do not apply if he has reached the age of 16 and wants to be in local authority accommodation (1989 Act, s.20(11)). This is consistent with the Act's general approach to children who have reached 16; by and large it is for them, rather than their parents, to choose whether or not to accept an offer of accommodation.

Whatever the child's age, he must, if possible, be consulted before he is placed in social services accommodation. A new provision in the 1989 Act requires the local authority, so far as is reasonably practicable and consistent with the child's welfare, to ascertain the child's wishes about the provision of accommodation and give due consideration to these, having regard to his age and understanding (1989 Act, s.20(6)).

The Act does not require any written agreement between the authority and the parents or child. However, the regulations insist that if possible the arrangements to be made for accommodating any child who is not in compulsory care should be agreed with a person with parental responsibility (or if there is no such person with whoever is caring for the child), preferably in advance or failing this as soon as soon as possible after the placement. If a child aged 16 or more is accommodated the agreement should be with him. This should cover the sort of placement, its address, the services to be provided for the child, the respective responsibilities of the authority, the child and the people with parental responsibility, including any delegation of day to day care, how they are to be involved in decision making and notified of changes, the contact there is to be between the child and his family, friends and anyone else connected with him, how long the placement is expected to last and what arrangements there will be for getting the child back home. The agreement should be set down in writing (Arrangements for Placement of Children (General) Regulations 1991, reg. 3, Sched. 4).

In principle, this is a splendid way of involving parents in the care of their child. In practice, how much choice will they have? And will they see the agreement as binding upon them even though it is not? It may, for example, quite properly record why it would not be practicable or right for the child if a parent has contact with him; or provide for a period of notice to prepare the child for returning home after a long period away; or limit the parents' involvement in the child's day to day life; and it may even warn them that the authority may apply for an emergency protection order if the parents take action which the authority think harmful (D.H. Guidance, vol. 3, paras. 2.63 to 2.67). Are these sensible precautions, which will protect the child from thoughtless or damaging actions by his parents and warn the parents of the possible consequences, or are they threats? Do they reinforce the whole idea of a voluntary partnership in looking after the child or do they undermine it?

(iii) Compulsory accommodation

Where a child is subject to a care order, or the former equivalents now deemed to be care orders under the Act, the local authority obviously have a duty to arrange accommodation for him (1989 Act, s.23(1)(a); see further in Chapter 10). They also have a duty to look after children who are removed or kept away from home under child assessment or emergency protection orders or (if asked to do so) children taken into police protection or detained after arrest (1989 Act, s.21(1), (2)(a), (b); see Chapters 10 and 11); these children could be accommodated in other places, but if this is anywhere other than local authority accommodation or an N.H.S. hospital the local authority has to pay (1989 Act, s.21(3)). Local authorities must also receive and accommodate children who have been remanded to local authority care in criminal proceedings or are subject to supervision orders with a residence requirement under section 12AA of the Children and Young Persons Act 1969 (see Chapter 11).

5. LOOKING AFTER THE CHILDREN

The children "being looked after" by a local authority are all those in compulsory care, whether or not they are currently in local authority accommodation, and all those who are actually being provided with accommodation, for a continuous period of more than 24 hours, under any of the statutory functions which are referred to their social services department under the Local Authority Social Services Act 1970 (1989 Act, s.22(1),(2)). Mainly, of course, this means the duties to provide voluntary or short term compulsory accommodation that are described above.

(i) General duties

In looking after any child, the local authority must "safeguard and promote his welfare" (1989 Act, s. 22(3)). The two are different: safeguarding a child's welfare means keeping him free from harm; promoting it means taking positive steps to secure that he is properly looked after and brought up. The previous reference to the need to safeguard and promote the child's welfare "throughout his childhood" (see Child Care Act 1980, s.18(1)) has gone, but the authority must still look ahead and make positive plans for the child's future, rather than allowing the situation to "drift".

The authority must also make such use of the services available for children living with their own parents as seems reasonable in his case (1989 Act, s.22(3)). The aim should be to provide their children with as normal and ordinary life as possible rather than setting them apart from others. They should, for example, go to the local schools whenever possible, join in local activities such as cubs and brownies, go to the local sports grounds, swimming pools and libraries, and so on.

The authority must always try to consult the child and his family and pay attention to their views. Before making any decision about a child they are already looking after, or even proposing to look after, they must as far as is reasonably practicable, discover the "wishes and feelings" of the child, his parents, any other person who has parental responsibility for him, and anyone else whose views they consider relevant (1989 Act, s.22(4)). This is all part of the partnership concept, which emphasises cooperation and agreement with the family wherever possible, even if the child has been compulsorily removed from home. They must then give "due consideration" to whatever views they have been able to discover, depending in the child's case upon his "age and understanding" (1989 Act, s.22(5)(a),(b)).

They must also take into account the child's "religious persuasion, racial origin and cultural and linguistic background" (1989 Act, s.22(5)(c)). The importance of this cannot be over-emphasised, given the large proportions of children from certain ethnic minority backgrounds who are looked after by local authorities. It does not mean that they should slavishly follow some particular policy which ignores, rather than caters for, the needs and wishes of the individual child.

However, the authorities are allowed to behave in a way which may be inconsistent with these general duties, if this appears to them necessary for the purpose of protecting members of the public from serious injury (1989 Act, s.22(6)). If the Secretary of State considers it necessary, for the same purpose, he may give directions to a local authority about how they should deal with a particular child they are looking after, and the authority must comply (1989 Act, s.22(7),(8)). These powers to put the protection of the public above the child's welfare, or respect for his or his family's views or his background, apply to all children but were first introduced to take account of children who came into care because of their criminal behaviour; nowadays, care orders cannot be made in criminal cases, but local authorities are still responsible for most children who are refused bail and for those who are required to live in local authority accommodation for up to six months as part of a supervision order (see Chapter 11).

(ii) Planning the placement

The advantages of social services accommodation, at least in an ideal world, are that there are a wide range of facilities available and expert staff to select the one which is most appropriate for each individual child; to handle it with sensitivity to the needs and feelings of all involved; and to make constructive long-term plans based on regular reviews. The placement options are set out in section 23(2). These can be summarised as:

(a) home placement with the child's own family;

(b) family placement, with relatives or unrelated foster parents;

(c) residential placement in a community, voluntary or registered children's home or youth treatment centre; and

(d) other arrangements.

Each of these is subject to its own regulations and guidance which will be dealt with below, but there are some general principles which apply to them all. The first is that preference must be given to placement at home or with relatives. Subject to other requirements the authority have a positive duty to make arrangements to enable any child they are looking after to live with a parent or other person with parental responsibility for him (or if the child is in compulsory care a person who had the benefit of a residence order immediately before the care order was made) or with a relative, friend or other person connected with him, unless this would not be reasonably practicable or consistent with his welfare (1989 Act, s.23(6)). Although the Act never says in so many words that parents or, failing them, relatives are normally the best people to bring up any child, this is one of the many provisions in the Act which is designed to reflect and reinforce that approach. Secondly, the authority must try to find accommodation near the child's home and to keep siblings together, as far as reasonably practicable and consistent with the child's welfare (1989 Act, s.23(7)). Also, so far as reasonably practicable, accommodation for a disabled child must be "not unsuitable" to his particular needs (1989 Act, s.23(8)).

The authority must draw up a written care plan, preferably before making any placement and if not, as soon as possible afterwards (Arrangements for

Placement of Children (General) Regulations 1991, reg. 3(1),(2)). A series of short-term placements in the same place can be treated as one if they total no more than 90 days in a year and none is longer than four weeks (reg. 13). The authority must think about their immediate and long term arrangements for the child; what has happened to him before and whether any change is needed; whether there should be a change in the child's legal status; the plans for contact and whether to appoint an independent visitor; what preparations need to be made for when the child leaves; and whether plans should be made to find a permanent substitute family for him; they also have to consider the child's health care needs and what should be done about them; how to achieve continuity in his education and to discover and meet his educational needs generally (regs. 3–4, Scheds. 1–3).

(iii) The placement options

(a) *Home placement*

Section 23(2)(*a*) allows the authority to place any child they are looking after with a family, relative or other suitable person. Normally, this will be with foster parents (see (b) below). However, it also covers placements at home, whether "on leave" from where the child normally lives or "on trial" with a view to reuniting the child with his family. These placements accounted for 12 per cent. of children being looked after by local authorities in England on March 31, in 1991 and in 1992 (D.H. and W.O., 1993).

Placement at home for this purpose means placement with a parent, anyone else with parental responsibility, or (if the child is in care) anyone else who had a residence order in their favour immediately before the care order was made (1989 Act, s.23(4)). Normally, if a child is simply using the accommodation service, he will no longer be accommodated if he goes home to someone with parental responsibility for him. Possibly, however, a child accommodated under an arrangement agreed with one parent might be placed with the other parent, perhaps for a short while on an experimental basis, while the local authority remain responsible for his accommodation.

However, if a child is subject to a care order (but not any other compulsory arrangement), any arrangements for him to go home for more than 24 hours at a time are governed by regulations (1989 Act, s.23(5),(5A)). This is because of the death of Jasmine Beckford at the hands of her father after she had been taken into compulsory care but returned home in questionable circumstances and allowed to live there virtually unsupervised (see Blom–Cooper, 1985). A care order can only be made when the child is at risk of significant harm if he stays or goes home (see Chapter 10) so taking good care before letting him do so makes obvious sense.

The main precautions required are to make proper inquiries about the suitability of the home and the adults in it (beforehand if possible but immediate placements can be sanctioned as long as the proposed carer is interviewed first and the inquiries are all made as soon as possible) (Placement of Children with Parents etc. Regulations 1991, regs. 3, 4, 6, Sched. 1);

to obtain the prior sanction of the Director or his delegate (reg. 5); to make a proper agreement with the proposed carer clarifying who is responsible for what (reg. 7, Sched. 2); to notify everyone who has to be consulted (see (i) above) and also the health and education authorities and the G.P. (reg. 8); to supervise the placement properly the child must be visited (and if possible seen alone) within the first week, then at intervals of not more than six weeks during the first year and three months after that (reg. 9); and the authority must remove the child immediately if the child's welfare or safety is at risk (reg. 11).

A series of short term placements (defined as in (ii) above) is treated as one and need only be visited during the first month and once after that (reg. 13). These short term placements are more in the nature of contact or respite than "home on trial". The regulations do not apply when they are inconsistent with any order or directions about contact given by the court (under the 1989 Act, s.34; see Chapter 10). If the child is spending a long time at home, however, does he really have to stay in compulsory care? If compulsion is still thought necessary because a successful partnership with the parents has not developed, then should he really be at home?

(b) *Family placement*

Anyone else with whom a child is placed under section 23(2)(*a*) (see (a) above) is called a local authority foster parent, whether or not they are related to the child (1989 Act, s.23(3)). Local authority fostering used to be known as "boarding-out", a term which dates back to the old Poor Law. Before the 1969 Act, local authorities had a positive duty to foster all children in their care, unless this was impracticable or undesirable. This was repealed, partly because the initial enthusiasm faded when it became clear how many long-term placements broke down (Dinnage and Kellmer Pringle, 1967), and partly because it was not suitable for many of the juvenile offenders then coming into care. Family placement is still better (and cheaper) than residential placement for most children. On March 31, in both 1991 and 1992, 58 per cent. of the children being looked after by local authorities in England were in foster placements (although the actual numbers had gone down) (D.H. and W.O., 1993).

The regulations require foster parents to be properly approved before any children are placed with them (Foster Placement (Children) Regulations 1991, reg. 3). This involves making very thorough inquiries about them and their household, taking up at least two references, checking their health and police records, and generally assessing whether they are suitable people to look after other people's children (reg. 3(4), Sched. 1). This will involve looking at the suitability of the prospective foster parents' home, the attitudes of everyone in it (including their own children), their general "life-style" and approach to parenting, including their attitudes to contact with the foster child's family, education, and discipline, the place of religion in their lives and their race, culture and linguistic background and any special knowledge or experience they may have in this area (D.H. Guidance, vol. 3, paras. 3 and 3.15 to 3.31).

If they are approved, the authority must make a written foster care agreement with them (reg. 3(6), Sched. 2). This should cover the support and training to be given by the authority on the one hand, and the general promises made by the foster parents on the other; these include looking after the children as if they were members of the family and never using corporal punishment upon them (Sched. 2). Approval can be in general or in relation to particular children or types of children or particular types of placement and must be reviewed annually (regs. 3(5), 4). Emergency placements can, however, be made for up to 24 hours with any approved foster parent (reg. 11(1),(2)); and if necessary an immediate placement can be made for up to six weeks with a "relative or friend" who has not been approved at all, provided that proper inquiries have been made and a basic agreement reached (reg. 11(3)–(5)). After that, they could be approved just for this child. It has at last been realised that even if the local authority has to provide a child with accommodation, doing so with a relative or family friend often provides the best way of "promoting and maintaining family links in a familiar setting" (D.H. Guidance, vol. 3, para. 3.33).

Each placement must in theory be properly chosen as the most suitable for the child and (except in emergency or immediate placements) a written placement agreement must be made; this covers such things as the information which the authority must give the foster parents about the child and their plans for him, delegation of medical treatment decisions, arrangements for contact with the family and visits by the authority, cooperating with the authority's plans, and the financial arrangements (reg. 5(1),(5), Sched. 3). Visits have to be arranged within one week, then every six weeks in the first year and every three months after that; emergency and immediate placements must be visited each week; the child should be seen alone when appropriate and a written report made after each visit (reg. 6). A series of short placements (see (ii) above) is treated as one, and should be visited during the first and again six months after that began (reg. 9). Any placement should be ended if it is no longer the most suitable way of looking after the child (reg. 7).

Foster parents obviously have to look after the child as a prudent parent would and the child could claim damages if he was injured as a result of their failure to do this; but the courts will consider this in the light of the daily domestic routine and should beware of expecting too much of them (*Surtees* v. *Kingston upon Thames Royal Borough Council*; *Same* v. *Hughes and another*, [1991] F.L.R. 559, C.A.). Foster parents are not employees of the local authority and so the authority are not vicariously responsible for their negligence as opposed to that of their own officers in choosing or supervising the placement (*S.* v. *Walsall Metropolitan Borough Council* [1986] 1 F.L.R. 397).

(c) *Residential placements*

The authority may provide for any child they are looking after by maintaining him in a community home, voluntary home, registered children's home, or youth treatment centre provided by the Secretary of State (1989 Act, s.23(2)(*b*),(*c*),(*d*),(*e*)). Apart from the tiny numbers in youth treatment centres, residential placements accounted for 18 per cent. of those in 1991 but had gone down to 16 per cent. in 1992; the difference, however, is accounted for by a rise in "other arrangements" (see (d) below) which may be no good thing (D.H. and W.O., 1993).

Local authorities must arrange for community homes to be available for children they are looking after, or for "purposes connected with the welfare of children" whether or not they are being looked after (1989 Act, s.53(1)). There should be a suitable variety of homes, whether residential nurseries, ordinary children's homes, or those which approximate to the old remand homes and approved schools (1989 Act, s.53(2)). Some are provided by local authorities (1989 Act, s.53(3)(*a*)); some, called "controlled" community homes, are provided by voluntary organisations but a local authority takes on the responsibility for managing, equipping and maintaining them (1989 Act, s.53(3)(*b*)(i), (4)); some, called "assisted" community homes, are provided, managed, equipped and maintained by the voluntary organisation (1989 Act, s.53(3)(*b*)(ii), (5)). Local authorities can also accommodate children in voluntary homes and in registered private children's homes (1989 Act, s.22(2)(*c*),(*d*); see Chapter 9).

These homes are all subject to the Children's Homes Regulations 1991. These give each child the right to his own space (reg. 6), to practise and observe his own religion as far as practicable (reg. 11), to a choice of food (reg. 12), to buy his own clothes (reg. 13). His parents have the right to be told of his death, serious harm, accident or illness and the outbreak of any notifiable disease (reg. 19). Facilities must be provided for children to meet family, friends and official visitors privately (reg. 7(3)).

Most important of all in the light of recent scandals (see Levy and Kahan, 1991; Warner, 1992) are the controls over the use of discipline. Disciplinary measures have to be those approved by the authority. The following sanctions are not allowed: any form of corporal punishment, deprivation of food or drink, or sleep, restriction of visiting or other outside contacts (unless necessary in order to protect or promote the child's welfare), requiring the child to wear distinctive or inappropriate clothes (apart from school and other uniforms), fines, using or withholding medication or medical or dental treatment, and intimate physical examination. Exceptions are made for action authorised by a doctor or dentist which is necessary to protect the child's health and any action necessary to prevent injury to anyone or serious damage to property, and for directions given by the Secretary of State (reg. 8). The Department of Health (Circular LAC (93) 13) has since given guidance on permissible forms of control in residential care. This points out that physical restraint is allowed to prevent *detained or remanded* children from escaping or where immediate action is needed to prevent injury to the person or serious damage to property; that talking to a child who is misbehaving or threatening to leave may be reinforced by standing in his way, placing a hand on his arm, or holding a highly distressed child, if these are intended to be persuasive rather than coercive; but that any intervention should be tailored to the particular child and the incident which gave rise to it; and that staff should "convey a strong sense of wanting to form constructive relationships with resident children" and "create a positive ethos", involving the children both individually and in groups in defining unacceptable behaviour and examining its consequences. It recognises that the testing or destructive behaviour of some children can be very difficult for staff but cannot justify low standards of care or a poor living environment.

The Department of Health itself provides and manages two homes, known as youth treatment centres, for children who are in need of the particular facilities and services which are provided in them and which are unlikely to be readily available in community homes (1989 Act, s.82(5)). In some respects these are the children's equivalent of the special hospitals for particularly disturbed psychiatric patients, being the responsibility of the Department rather than the mainstream services and mainly designed for the most disturbed young offenders. They are not, however, hospitals, so that the children in them cannot be treated as if they were compulsory psychiatric patients.

(d) *Other arrangements*

There is a residuary power to make "such other arrangements" for a child "as seem appropriate" to the authority, although this is now subject to any regulations made by the Secretary of State (1989 Act, s.23(2)(f)). Obvious examples are hostels, residential employment, boarding schools, and bed and breakfast houses. The authority may "volunteer" a child in compulsory care for assessment or treatment in a psychiatric hospital (*R.* v. *Kirklees Metropolitan Council, ex p. C. (A Minor)*, *The Times*, March 23, 1993) and must visit him while he is there (Mental Health Act 1983, s.116). This might also be within the range of "other arrangements" for accommodated children, but subject to the parents' or the child's views on any medical treatment offered.

(iv) Keeping the plans under review

Authorities must make plans for the future of any child they are looking after. Children who need permanent homes should not be kept waiting, but neither should children who need to be reunited with their families as soon as possible. The evidence was that statutory reviews played little part in positive planning for children in care (Sinclair, 1984), and indeed that purposeful forward planning was still all too rare, despite more than a decade of consciousness of the "children who wait" (see *e.g.* Vernon and Fruin, 1986).

The Review of Children's Cases Regulations 1991 require the first review to take place within four weeks of the child coming into local authority accommodation, the next within three months of that and after that not more than six months from the previous review (reg. 3). The views of the child and his parents must be obtained and taken into account and they must if possible be involved in the review and told of the outcome (reg. 7). If they become more purposeful, reviews may make decisions which can vitally affect the interests of the whole family, yet it is difficult to see how far they can or should go in trying to observe the rules of natural justice.

As with the initial plan (see (ii) above), the object is to collect information about what is going on, and to consider the child's legal status, the arrangements for contact, the immediate and long-term plans for his accommodation, his educational progress and needs, what is to be done when he is no longer looked after by the authority, and whether plans need to be made to find a permanent substitute family for him (Scheds. 1, 2). Touchingly, the regulations insist that the authority make arrangements to implement the outcome (reg. 8).

(v) Keeping in touch with family, friends and the outside world

There is a positive and a negative side to maintaining family links. On the positive side, the authority have a statutory duty to try to promote contact between the child and his parents, anyone else who has parental responsibility for him, and any relative, friend or other person connected with him (1989 Act, s.23(9), Sched. 2, para. 15(1)). This is backed up by a new duty for the authority to take reasonable steps to keep the child's parents, and anyone else with parental responsibility for him, informed of where he is living (para. 15(2)(a)); if a child is transferred from one authority area to another, both have this duty (para. 15(3)). An exception is made if the authority have reasonable cause to believe that telling a particular person about the whereabouts of a child in compulsory care would prejudice the child's welfare (para. 15(4)); other people must still be told.

In return, both parents, and anyone else with parental responsibility for the child, must keep the authority informed of their addresses (para. 15(2)(b)). It is a crime, triable only in a magistrates' court and punishable only with a level 2 fine, not to do this without a reasonable excuse (para. 15(5)); but one (usually a parent) who is living with another (usually the other parent) and can prove that he reasonably believed that the other had told the authority where they were both living has a defence (para. 15(6)). The original purpose of these rules, which have a long history, was no doubt to enable the authority to discharge the child as soon as possible and, if they could not do that, to collect their accommodation charges. Perhaps today they can play a more positive part in keeping family and child in touch.

The authority have power to pay travelling expenses, either to a parent, anyone else with parental responsibility, a relative, friend, or anyone else connected with the child, who is visiting him, or to or for a child who is visiting any of these people, but only if the visit cannot otherwise be made without "undue hardship" and the circumstances warrant it (1989 Act, Sched. 2, para. 16).

One of the most depressing findings of recent research into children looked after by local authorities has been the lack of positive effort to keep family and child in touch, particularly in the early days after an admission, even though the chances of leaving care depend so much upon what happens to the family in the meantime (Millham *et al*, 1986; 1989). Some people think that a period of settling in is important for the child and that visiting too soon may disturb him. In some placements, particularly with foster families, relations with the family in general and visiting in particular may be difficult. That is one reason why some parents prefer residential placements. There are also some parents who are unreliable, abusive or even violent. For all these reasons, maintaining family links requires hard work, just as it does when family relationships break down, and it is understandable if not excusable that it has been given a relatively low priority in the past. For a while professional attention may also have been diverted by the equally important work needed in deciding how and when to sever links with the family with a view to planning a permanent substitute home (see Adcock and White, 1980). Perhaps a more balanced picture will now emerge, given that the great majority of children looked after by local authorities do eventually go back to their parents (Millham *et al*, 1986; 1989).

On the negative side, no-one is entitled to deprive a child of contact with his family or indeed with the outside world generally. There are, now, specific procedures for the courts to resolve disputes about contact with children compulsorily removed from home (see Chapter 10). In theory, no such procedures are necessary for children who are simply using the accommodation service, because their parents can always remove them. This may not always be possible and even if it is it may not be good for the child. The care plan agreed with the parents should cover the contact arrangements (see (ii) above). If the authority or the placement do not respect these, or the parent no longer thinks them reasonable, the parent could seek a section 8 contact order (see Chapter 4) against the person with whom the child is living, rather than the authority as such. With leave, the child could also do so. If the parents do not keep up the contact, there is nothing the authority or the placement can do to force them, but they can offer practical help and encouragement.

If contact between any child and his parents (or anyone else with parental responsibility) is "infrequent" or the child has not been visited by or visited them for a year, the authority must appoint another person to visit him, if they think this would be in his best interests (1989 Act, Sched. 2, para. 17). This is no longer limited to children in certain kinds of community home. A child who is old enough to make an informed decision can object to a visitor being appointed or continuing. The visitor must be independent of the members or officers of the authority (Definition of Independent Visitors (Children) Regulations 1991) and has the job of visiting, advising and befriending the child. Her expenses must be paid, but otherwise she is a lay volunteer, who is not expected to become a substitute parent, carer, social worker or even an advocate for the child (D.H. Guidance, vol. 3, paras. 7.33–7.35 and 7.47–7.48).

(vi) Secure accommodation

Secure accommodation means any place provided for restricting the liberty of children who are being looked after by a local authority, whether in a community home, youth treatment centre, behaviour modification unit in a psychiatric hospital (see *R. v. Northampton Juvenile Court, ex p. London*

Borough of Hammersmith and Fulham [1985] F.L.R. 193), or anywhere else. "Restricting liberty" usually means locking someone up, but there could be wider interpretations. Safeguards against the unjustified imprisonment of children in this way were first introduced in 1983 in order to conform to Article 5 (4) of the European Convention on Human Rights, which requires a speedy judicial review of the merits of any deprivation of liberty. They apply to all kinds of children being looked after by local authorities, apart from those who are detained under the Mental Health Act 1983 (who have the safeguards provided by that Act) or section 53 of the Children and Young Person Act 1933 (see Chapter 11); they also apply to children accommodated by health authorities, N.H.S. trusts, or Local Education Authorities, or in adult residential care homes, nursing homes and mental nursing homes (Children (Secure Accommodation) Regulations 1991, regs. 5(1), 7). Children kept away from home under child assessment orders and children of 16 to 21 who are living in community homes cannot be locked up at all (reg. 5(2)) nor can children in voluntary or registered children's homes (reg. 18). There are special rules about children who are detained, remanded or committed to local authority accommodation pending criminal proceedings (see further in Chapter 11).

The point about these provisions is that they are a safeguard for the child rather than for his parents. Children who are simply being accommodated may be locked up if the criteria and procedures are followed, but their parents can still remove them if they wish (1989 Act, s.25(9)).

Children can only be locked up in two situations: either where they have a history of absconding and are likely to abscond from any other accommodation and if they abscond, are likely to suffer significant harm; or where they are likely to injure themselves or other people if kept anywhere else (1989 Act, s.25(1)). It should be regarded as a last resort and never as a form of punishment (D.H. Guidance, Vol. 4, para. 8.5). Local authorities must try to avoid having to put children in secure accommodation (1989 Act, Sched. 2, para. 7(c)) and so should have alternative ways of solving these problems if they can.

Even if the criteria exist, the required procedures must be followed. Children under 13 cannot be locked up in a community home without prior approval from the Department of Health's Social Services Inspectorate (reg. 4). No child can be locked up for a total of more than 72 hours in any 28 day period without the authority of a court (reg. 10(1); there is leeway for children detained during weekends and public holidays, see reg. 10(3)). The court may authorise up to three months more (reg. 11) and then further periods of up to six months at a time (reg. 12). The court will as usual be bound by the welfare and "no order" principles but these are not "family proceedings" for the purpose of making section 8 orders instead (although they are family proceedings for the purpose of the rules allowing the admission of hearsay evidence; see *Oxford City Council* v. *R.* [1992] 1 F.L.R. 648).

The court is usually the family proceedings court, unless the case is already before a county court or the High Court. The child must be given an opportunity of legal representation (1989 Act, s.25(6)) and a guardian *ad litem* will be appointed unless the court thinks this unnecessary. The local authority must first inform him, his parent and any other person who has parental responsibility for him, any independent visitor (see (v) above) and anyone else they think should be involved, of their intention to apply (reg. 14).

In addition, local authorities must appoint panels of at least three people (with at least one independent member) to review each secure placement in a community home, a month after it has begun and then at least every three months (reg. 15). They have to consider the views of all concerned and take into account the child's welfare in deciding whether the criteria still apply and the placement is still necessary (reg. 16). Other residential institutions providing secure accommodation are recommended to make similar arrangements.

(vii) Running away

Unless they are placed in secure accommodation (see (vi) above), children being looked after by local authorities are not and should not be regarded as prisoners. If a child who is in care, or subject to emergency or police protection, absconds or is abducted or goes missing in any way, there is a procedure for recovering him. The person responsible for him can apply for a recovery order which requires anyone who can to reveal the child's whereabouts if asked, directs anyone who can to produce the child if asked, allows the child to be removed, and allows a police officer to enter specified premises where there are reasonable grounds for believing the child to be and search for him there (1989 Act, s.50(1)–(6)). Intentionally obstructing the power of removal is a crime (1989 Act, s.50(9)).

Abducting or harbouring these children or encouraging them to abscond are also crimes, punishable with imprisonment or a level 5 fine or both: it is an offence knowingly and without lawful authority or reasonable excuse to take or keep the child away or to induce, assist or incite him to run or stay away (1989 Act, s.49).

The trouble is that many children in care have or feel that they have good reasons for running away. It is not necessarily a good idea to force them to go into hiding or to return to the situation which they found intolerable. Voluntary organisations in particular have begun to provide refuges for children who run away either from home or from anywhere else. They might then be committing an offence, either under section 49 of the Children Act 1989 or under section 2 of the Child Abduction Act 1984 (see Chapter 1). The Secretary of State can therefore grant an exemption certificate to a refuge provided in a voluntary home or registered children's home or by a foster parent by arrangement with a local authority or voluntary organisation (1989 Act, s.51).

A child can only be accepted into a refuge if it appears that he is at risk of harm. The police must be notified as soon as possible, at the latest within 24 hours, so that they can tell his parents or whoever else is responsible for him that he is in a refuge and give them a telephone number to contact it (but not the address). The object of providing the refuge is to rescue the child and reunite him with his family or carers, if this is consistent with his welfare, so children must not be kept there for more than 14 days or for more than 21 days in any three month period (Refuges (Children's Homes and Foster Placements) Regulations 1991, reg. 3). Certificates will not be given lightly and will be withdrawn if these conditions are not complied with (D.H. Guidance, vol. 4, paras. 9.13, 9.11).

This is a delicate matter; it is difficult enough for the authrities to admit that children who run away from home may need their help; but where children who are being looked after by local authorities run away it may be better to admit that sometimes they have a case and that the alternative of locking them up in secure accommodation is unlikely to be an improvement.

6. CHARGES

If a child is being accommodated under section 20 or a care order (but not an interim order or other short term compulsory powers), the local authority may require him (if he is 16 or over) or his parents (if he is younger) to contribute towards his maintenance (1989 Act, Sched. 2, Pt. III). They can only do this where they think it reasonable to do so and not for periods when the child is placed at home or after notice has been given of intention to adopt him (see Adoption Act 1976, s.31(3)). Parents are not liable while they are on income support or family credit.

If a charge is made, the amount should be "agreed" between the authority and contributor. The authority propose an amount, which can be a standard fee, but cannot be more than their ordinary fostering allowance or more than they think it reasonably practicable for this person to pay. If they do not reach an agreement within a month, or the person later withdraws his agreement, the authority can go to court for a contribution order. The amount ordered cannot be more than the sum proposed but may be less. It can be enforced like any other magistrates' court maintenance order but it can also be replaced by a fresh agreement between the authority and the contributor.

Authorities also have power to charge the parents of a child under 16, or a 16-year-old himself, or any family member provided with a service, for any of their other services, apart from advice, guidance and counselling; but they cannot charge more than it would be reasonable for the customer to pay or when he is receiving income support, family credit or disability working allowance (1989 Act, s.29(1),(2),(3),(4)). They can also charge other authorities whose children they are looking after or providing with after care (1989 Act, s.29(7),(8),(9)).

7. AFTER CARE

Local authorities have a general duty to "advise, assist and befriend" all the children they are looking after so as to prepare them for the time when they leave (1989 Act, s.24(1)). This means making plans for the future, in partnership with the child and his family if possible, and generally giving him the opportunities, support and encouragement that a good parent would give. Preparation for independence should start well before he leaves, building up his practical survival skills, self-esteem and ability to make relationships with others (D.H. Guidance, vol. 4, paras. 7.18, 7.45).

Children who are looked after by local authorities (and in other residential settings) until they grow up are an especially vulnerable group; they are over-represented among homeless young people, young offenders, single parents and other indicators of social risk and deprivation. They often do not have a family to fall back on; nor, as single childless people have they automatically any priority for local authority housing unless they are "vulnerable as a result of . . . mental illness or handicap or physical disability or other special reason" (Housing Act 1985, s.59(1)(c)). The primary responsibility lies with the housing department, and they have been urged to give careful consideration to the vulnerability of homeless young people who have left care, particularly those who are disabled or at risk of sexual or financial exploitation (D.H. Guidance, vol. 4, para. 7.82). Similarly, the D.S.S. is primarily responsible for income support and other benefits.

However, social services authorities have some responsibilities towards their children after they leave. If a child who has left them at or after 16 and is still under 21 asks for help, they must "advise and befriend" him if they think that he needs it (1989 Act, s.24(2),(4),(5)). They may also give him more practical help, which may be in kind or in exceptional circumstances in cash (1989 Act, s.24(6),(7)). Whether or not the circumstances are exceptional, they can make grants towards his expenses in living near his place of work, education or training, or towards his education or training (which can go on beyond 21) (1989 Act, s.24(8),(9)). Financial assistance can be by way of a loan, but the child's means must be taken into account and he cannot be made to repay anything while he is on income support or family credit (1989 Act, ss.24(10), 17(7)–(9)). This sort of help is designed to recognise the special needs of these young people; they do not have to qualify for income support to get it; and any financial help is in addition to whatever means-tested benefits or educational grants they may be getting. They may well not have the sort of family backing which it is now assumed that young people have and local authorities are urged to be as generous as possible in helping them establish themselves in life (D.H. Guidance, vol. 4, paras. 7.72, 7.73).

Local authorities have power to provide similar after-care (but not grants) for children who leave accommodation provided by voluntary organisations, registered children's homes, other private homes and hospitals, health and education authorities, and private fostering, but their only duty is to advise and befriend children leaving voluntary organisations which cannot provide this themselves (1989 Act, s.24(2)(b)–(e), (3),(4)). Voluntary organisations and registered children's homes have to provide preparation for leaving (1989 Act, ss.61(1)(c), 64(1)(c)), but not after care as such.

Aftercare was one of the most contentious areas when the Children Bill was debated in Parliament. There was real concern about the fate of so many of

these young people and the problems which could recur in future generations if they did not have the right kind of help. Social services departments
have been told to have a clear policy on leaving care, developed in
consultation with the young people themselves, and to provide an easy to use
guide to the services available from them and from other agencies (D.H.
Guidance, vol. 4, paras. 7.19–7.27).

8. HOW TO COMPLAIN

The remedies available to aggrieved children and their families depend a
good deal on the nature of the complaint. Of course, a local authority owe a
duty of care towards all the children they are looking after or providing with
other services. If a child is injured as a result of their failure to take reasonable
care of him, he may sue them for damages; the authority will also be
vicariously responsible for injuries wrongfully caused by their officers or
employees in the course of their employment. Difficult questions can arise
when psychological rather than physical damage has been suffered but no
damage has to be proved if a child is wrongly deprived of his liberty.

Usually, however, the complaint is about a decision rather than an injury.
Decisions which interfere with the rights of the child or his parents, to remove
or keep a child away from home against his parents' will, or to deprive the
child of his liberty, or to refuse the child or his family reasonable contact with
one another, have to go to court. Other big decisions, such as where to place
a child and whether to find a permanent substitute family for him, do not. If
the authorities have acted in breach or disregard of their statutory responsibilities, or in a way which no reasonable authority could have acted, the
decision may be challenged by judicial review. Under the previous law, for
example, the duty to consider the welfare and wishes of each individual child
was applied to the decision to close a children's home (*Liddle* v. *Sunderland
Borough Council* (1983) 13 Fam.Law 250) or at least to its timing (*R.* v.
Solihull Metropolitan Borough Council, ex p. C. [1984] F.L.R. 363). There is
scope for similar challenges if these duties are disregarded under the 1989
Act. These cases may be decided by a Family Division judge but he will have
no power to make an alternative decision about what should happen to the
child.

These days, a more likely complaint may be that the child has not been
offered accommodation or some other service when he should have been.
Judicial review may be available to challenge a policy decision, for example
not to provide a particular service at all, or only to provide it on unreasonable
terms; but most of the service-providing powers have been carefully drafted
to avoid giving any individual child a right to any particular service (thus
getting round the decision in *A.G. ex rel. Tilley* v. *Wandsworth Borough
Council* [1981] 1 W.L.R. 854, C.A.). This is not quite so obvious of the duties
to provide accommodation in section 20(1) and (3), although they do depend
upon how things appear to the authority. Generally, however, the courts are

reluctant to hold that a statutory duty gives rise to an individual right of action for damages if the statute also provides for other avenues of complaint.

One avenue, of course, is through the political accountability of the authority members; the child or his family could go to their local councillor for help. Another is the procedure which every authority must now have to handle complaints, from children who are being looked after or are in need, their parents and others with parental responsibility for them, local authority foster parents, and anyone else with a sufficient interest in the child's welfare; people who qualify for aftercare must also have access to it (1989 Act, ss.24(15), 26(3)–(8)). The authority have to consider the complaint with the help of an independent person and formulate a response within 28 days; the complainant must be notified of this; if he is dissatisfied with the proposed result, he can insist that the complaint is referred to a panel of at least three people, at least one of whom must be independent; they must consider it within 28 days of the referral, giving the complainant and the authority an opportunity to make written or oral submissions, before formulating their recommendations; the authority must then decide what to do and the independent panel member has to take part in that decision; the complainant and child must be told the outcome and the reasons for it within 28 days (Representations Procedure (Children) Regulations 1991, regs. 5, 6, 8, 9).

If the complainant is still dissatisfied with how the authority has handled things, he could complain of maladministration to the local government ombudsman. As a last resort, he might ask the Secretary of State to find that the authority have failed without reasonable excuse to comply with their duties under the 1989 Act. If the Secretary of State finds them in default, he can direct them to comply within a stated time, and seek an order of *mandamus* against them if they do not (1989 Act, s.84). It is unlikely, however, that the Secretary of State will regard this procedure as an avenue for complaints about how individual cases have been handled. But if he does not, how will the courts regard it?

Chapter 9

CONTROLLING PRIVATE ARRANGEMENTS

Parents often arrange substitute care for their children, whether because they are working, or ill, or having another baby or simply going out, or because the child wants to go and stay with friends for the holidays. Some child care experts have given the impression that it is damaging for any young child to be deprived of the almost continuous care of his mother, at least until the age of about three (see discussion in Kellmer Pringle, 1974). Others have pointed to the lack of evidence that this is so (Rutter, 1971, 1981; Morgan, 1975), provided that the substitute care is good and reasonably stable (Schaffer, 1990). It is now thought beneficial for young children to spend some time with peers or adults who are not part of the immediate family (D.H. Guidance, vol. 2, para. 5.3).

How far should parents be free to do what they like when making arrangements for their children? Do we begin by trusting them to do their best? Until recently, most of the arrangements traditionally made by middle-class families have escaped control altogether. Historically, however, some poorer families, particularly unmarried mothers, were driven to use baby-farmers and other highly unsatisfactory arrangements which led to the first child protection legislation in the late nineteenth century. Now, the same concern to "safeguard and promote" the welfare of all children has led to the introduction of some sort of control over almost every type of arrangement for children to be looked after outside their families.

1. UNCONTROLLED ARRANGEMENTS

Many parents prefer to provide care in their own homes if they can. It is certainly the conventional middle-class solution. Whether for that reason, or because the risks to the child are indeed much less, or because we recognise that there are limits to official interference in family life, there is usually no control when a child is looked after by someone employed to do so in a place where either of his parents (whether or not they have parental responsibility) lives; parents can employ whomever they want to do this (see 2. (i) below).

The only control operates after the event, either through prosecution for child cruelty (see Chapter 1) or through the removal of children who are suffering, or likely to suffer, significant harm (see Chapter 10). There are no precise standards about when, at what age and for how long, children may be left alone, or about the age and qualifications of the people with whom they should be left. Sixteen is the dividing line drawn for both purposes by the offence of child cruelty, but it will sometimes be safe to leave children below that age, either alone or in the care of someone who is also below that age.

Although legal controls normally begin to operate once a child is cared for outside his own home, there are two more exceptions. The first is where the child is looked after by a non-parent who has parental responsibility for him: this could only be a legally-appointed guardian (see Chapter 5) or a person in whose favour there is a residence order in force (see Chapter 7), whether or not he is related to the child. Thus, parents have an almost unfettered right to choose someone to take over completely after their deaths, but not to arrange for a child to be minded or fostered during their lives. Perhaps this has something to do with the fact that the rich have traditionally used nannies and appointed guardians and the poor have turned to private fostering and child-minding.

The second exception is where a child is looked after in the home of a relative who has assumed responsibility for his care. "Relative" means a grandparent, brother, sister, uncle or aunt, whether of the full or half blood, and irrespective of whether the blood relationship is traced through marriage or not, and including those so related by adoption or marriage, or a step-parent (1989 Act, s.105(1)).

2. DAY CARE

To many, day care outside the home is the next best thing. With a good child-minder or nursery, the child can build and retain a close relationship with his parents and family, while receiving the care, company and stimulation he needs. It can also be a valuable way of relieving stress in the home, or redressing material or social disadvantage. However, because demand always seems to exceed supply and usually relates to very young children, and also because the parents can rarely afford high fees, there is a consider-able risk that the people or places which agree to take children in will neither appreciate their needs nor be able to cater properly for these.

The legal mechanism for trying to secure acceptable standards of child-minding and day care is registration. Every local authority must keep a register of "persons" who either act as child-minders on domestic premises or provide day care for children on non-domestic premises (1989 Act, s.71(1)). The register has a dual function. It gives information and reassurance to parents about the facilities which exist in their area, so it must be open to inspection by members of the public at all reasonable times (1989 Act, s.71(15)(a)). It also allows the local authority to impose minimum standards.

From the point of view of parents, children and responsible providers of day care, the more properly monitored facilities there are, the better. The dilemma for the regulators, however, is that if they try to impose standards which are too rigorous, they will reduce the supply. If they reduce the supply while demand remains high, this increases the risk that parents will turn to even less satisfactory illegal arrangements, which are much more difficult to police (Elfer and Beasley, 1991). Local authorities have some responsibilities to provide day care services themselves (see Chapter 8), but inevitably these are limited to priority or "deserving" groups. The official line is that the same standards should be applied to all kinds of day care, whoever is providing it (D.H. Guidance, vol. 2, para. 6.1), but some providers have complained that the authorities were requiring too much, more than they would of their own facilities. They have since been told not to be too rigid and to strike the right balance between ensuring standards and encouraging development (D.H. and W.O., 1993).

(i) Child-minders

A child-minder for this purpose is someone (other than a parent, person with parental responsibility, relative or foster parent of the child) who looks after one or more children under the age of eight for reward for a total of more than two hours in any day (1989 Act, s.71(2)(a),(4)). There is no express exemption for people looking after children in their own homes, so that a baby-sitter might be covered. However, a person who is employed as a "nanny" for a child by a parent, person with parental responsibility, or by a relative who has assumed responsibility for the child's care, does not act as a child-minder when looking after the child wholly or mainly in her employer's home (1989 Act, s.71(5),(13)). The same applies to nannies who are shared by not more than two employers (1989 Act, s.71(6)). There is no definition of "nanny", so the exception applies to an au pair, baby-sitter or anyone else who is employed in this way.

A good nanny or child-minder may provide the warmth, continuity and domestic environment most suited to a very young child. She also provides the cheapest service, not only because there are no capital costs, but also because of her low status in the child care hierarchy. But an unsubsidised minder can only charge what the market will bear and her inadequacies are particularly difficult to detect and prevent (Jackson and Jackson, 1979).

(ii) Nurseries and playgroups

Nurseries are sometimes regarded as more satisfactory than child-minders. It is not necessarily preferable to have very young children cared for with others in an institutional setting but places are much easier to control than are people operating in private homes. Day care for this purpose means day care for children under eight which is provided for a total of more than two hours in any day, but whether or not there is any reward (1989 Act, s.71(1)(b), (2)(b)). Whereas it is not easy to imagine a non-human "person" as a child-minder, bodies of people might be registered for this purpose. If a person provides day care in a number of different premises, he must be registered in respect of each of them (1989 Act, s.71(3)).

There is an exemption for "occasional facilities" which provide day care for less than six days in any year, as long as the person providing them notifies the local authority in writing before the first time each year that the premises are used for this purpose (1989 Act, Sched. 9, para. 5). Most schools are exempt, as are registered children's homes, voluntary and community homes, residential care homes, nursing homes, mental nursing homes, health service hospitals, and homes provided by the Secretary of State, provided that the day care is being provided as part of that establishment's activities (rather than as a side-line on the same premises) (1989 Act, Sched. 9, paras. 3–4).

(iii) Registration

Child-minders need only make a single application but day care providers must apply separately in respect of each facility. The particulars and fees required (which distinguish between child-minding, sessional day care —such as playgroups held for part of the day on premises also used for other purposes and full day care—usually in purpose-built nurseries or nursery schools) are prescribed by regulations. Registration must be granted and a certificate issued if the application is properly made, unless the local authority is entitled to refuse registration (1989 Act, Sched. 9, paras. 1 and 6; see Child Minding and Day Care (Applications for Registration) Regulations 1991; Child Minding and Day Care (Registration and Inspection Fees) Regulations 1991; and Child Minding and Day Care (Applications for Registration and Registration and Inspection Fees) (Amendment) Regulations 1991). Local authorities are supposed to handle applications "promptly and sympathetically" and to use the whole process in "an enabling and facilitating way," to encourage rather than discourage the development of provision (D.H. Guidance, vol. 2, paras. 4.9, 4.10; D.H. and W.O., 1993).

Even so, some applications must or can be refused. Certain people are disqualified from being registered or involved in child-minding or day care provision, unless the facts are first disclosed to the authority and written permission obtained (see 6. below). An application for registration as a child-minder or day care provider can also be refused if the local authority are satisfied:

(1) that she or anyone looking after children on the same premises, or likely to do so, is "not fit" to look after children under eight (1989 Act, s.71(7),(9)); this means looking at their previous experience or training in looking after young children, their ability to provide warm and consistent care, their ability to treat all children as individuals and with equal concern, their knowledge of and attitude to multi-cultural issues, as well as their physical and mental health and any known involvement

with criminal cases involving child abuse (D.H. Guidance, vol. 2, para. 7.32); or

(2) that anyone living or employed on the premises, or likely to be so, is not fit to be near children under eight (1989 Act, s.71(8),(10)); this means looking at their criminal records or known involvement with child abuse cases (D.H. Guidance, para. 7.32); or

(3) that the premises are not fit for looking after such children, because of their condition or equipment, or for any reason connected with their situation, construction or size (1989 Act, s.71(11)); this means looking at their outside space and access to the road, general safety and hygiene, washing and toilet facilities, cooking facilities, facilities for the children to rest and sleep, and fire precautions, as well as the safety and suitability of the furniture, toys and other equipment (D.H. Guidance, vol. 2, paras. 7.33, 7.34).

Refusals of consent or registration must follow the prescribed procedure (see (vii) below).

(iv) Requirements

The authority must impose requirements on any registered child-minder or day care provider. These have to be reasonable and appropriate to the particular case (1989 Act, ss.72(1), 73(1)). But they must impose limits on the number of children, or the number of children in particular age-groups, who may be minded or provided with day care, taking into account the number of other children who may at any time be on the same premises (1989 Act, ss.72(2), (4), 73(3), (6)). All registered persons must be required to ensure that the premises and any equipment are adequately maintained and safe, and to keep records of the children, anyone who helps look after them and anyone living or likely to live on the premises, and to notify changes in the last two (1989 Act, ss. 72(2), 73(3)). Day care providers must also be required to notify any changes in the facilities provided or the period for which they are provided; and the authority must specify the number of people required to help look after the children (1989 Act, s.73(3)). Requirements must be imposed separately for each set of premises for which a day care provider is registered (1989, s.73(2)). Local authorities can impose additional require-ments but they must not be incompatible with any of the compulsory requirements (1989 Act, ss.72(5), 73(7)). Requirements can be added, varied or removed at any time (1989 Act, ss.72(6), 73(8)). The Department of Health (D.H. Guidance, vol. 2, Chap. 6) lays down recommended standards for the amount of space, staff/child ratios, size of groups, furnishing and equipment and record-keeping and there are also various practice guidelines (National Children's Bureau, 1991; Pre-School Playgroups Association, 1989; Kids Clubs Network, 1989; National Childminding Association, 1991).

(v) Inspection

The local authority must inspect child-minders and day care facilities regularly. An authorised officer may, at any reasonable time and on production of his written authorisation if asked, enter any premises in the area on which child-minding is being carried on or day care provided (1989 Act, s.76(1), (6)). This must be done at least once every year (1989 Act, s.76(4)). The authority have to give notice of their intention to inspect registered premises and a fee is payable (1989 Act, Sched. 9, para. 7). This can be a sore point. There is an equivalent power to enter premises where the local authority have reasonable cause to believe that a child is being looked after in breach of the registration and other requirements of this Part of the Act (1989 Act, s.76(2)). The officer gaining entry may then inspect the premises, any children being looked after there and the arrangements for their welfare, and the records kept about them under the Act; this includes computer records, for which he may require help (1989 Act, s.76(3),(5)).

(vi) Cancellation

The authority may cancel a person's registration if:

(1) circumstances exist which would justify a refusal to register that person in the first place (and if this is so for any one day care facility, all a person's other day care registrations can also be cancelled); or

(2) the care provided by that person is "seriously inadequate having regard to the needs" of a particular child being minded or the children being provided with day care (and in considering these needs, the authority must in particular have regard to the child's religion, race and cultural and linguistic background); this is aimed at the way individual children are being looked after, rather than at the general fitness or suitability of the people or the place; there should be evidence of neglect or other serious short-comings in care (D.H. Guidance, vol. 2, para. 7.52); or

(3) the person has failed to comply with a requirement or to pay the annual fee in time; but if someone has been required to do repairs or alterations to the premises, his registration cannot be cancelled on the basis that the premises are unsuitable unless the time limit for doing them has expired (1989 Act, s.74(1), (2), (3), (4), (6)).

It is obviously more serious to cancel an existing registration and so close someone down than to refuse to register in the first place. Before the 1989 Act, some authorities were apparently finding it difficult to be clear, consistent and tough enough (Elfer and Beasley, 1991). Legal advice should always be sought, because the evidence should be good enough to stand up in court (D.H. Guidance, vol. 2, para. 7.52), but the standard of proof should not be that required for a criminal conviction. Cancellation should be in writing and follow the prescribed procedure.

(vii) Procedure and appeals

The authority has to give written notice, not less than 14 days before refusing or cancelling registration, refusing consent in disqualification cases, imposing, varying or removing a requirement, or refusing an application to vary or remove a requirement (1989 Act, s.77(1)). This must give the authority's reasons and inform the person concerned of her rights of appeal (1989 Act, s.77(2)). The person then has a right to have her objections heard by the authority, either in person or through a representative (1989 Act, s.77(3),(4)); this is in effect a right of appeal from the officers to the social services committee members. If having given this opportunity to object, the authority still wants to take the proposed step, they must give her written notice of their decision (1989 Act, s.77(5)).

Any "person aggrieved" by taking the step in question (who might not necessarily be the applicant or registered person) can then appeal to the magistrates' court (1989 Act, s.77(6)). The court may refuse or allow the appeal; but if it allows an appeal against refusal or cancellation, it may impose requirements; and it may allow an appeal against a requirement by varying rather than cancelling it (1989 Act, s.77(7),(8),(9)).

There is also an emergency procedure for protecting children if all this is going to take too long. The local authority can apply to the court for an order cancelling registration, or varying or removing or imposing any requirement (1989 Act, s.75(1)(a)). The application can be made *ex parte* but must be supported by a written statement of the authority's reasons (1989 Act, s.75(3)). The court can make the order if it appears that a child being looked after by, or in a day care facility provided by, the registered person is suffering or likely to suffer "significant harm" (1989 Act, s.75(1)(b); for "significant harm" see Chapter 10). The order takes immediate effect (1989 Act, s.75(2),(5)). However, as soon as reasonably practicable, the authority must serve notice of the order, with a copy of the statement of reasons, on the registered person (1989 Act, s.75(4)).

(viii) Enforcement

It is a crime, punishable with a level 4 fine, to contravene or fail to comply with a registration requirement without reasonable excuse (1989 Act, s.78(8), (12(a)); it is also a crime, punishable with a level 3 fine, intentionally to obstruct an inspection (1989 Act, s.76(7)). However, the sanctions for providing unregistered day care are slightly different from those for unregistered child minding. It is a crime, punishable with a level 5 fine, for anyone without reasonable excuse to provide day care for children under eight on any premises without being registered in respect of those premises (1989 Act, s.78(1),(2),(12)(c)).

If a person acts as a child-minder without being registered, the local authority first have to decide whether to serve an enforcement notice on her, which will last for a year (1989 Act, s.78(3),(4),(5)). It will then be a crime, again punishable only with a level 5 fine, for her, without reasonable excuse, to act as a child-minder anywhere in the country without being properly registered (1989 Act, s.78(6),(7),(12)(c)). Thus the local authority can decide whether or not to convert "unregistered" into "illegal" child-minding and the unregistered minder does not commit a criminal offence unless she has first been warned not to do it. There are no doubt many arrangements made which are technically child-minding but none of the people involved realise this. A mature and sensible person who occasionally takes in her neighbours' children while they go out for the evening is probably less likely to harm the children than a teenage baby-sitter who is employed in the children's home. But the former should technically be registered while the latter need not.

Nevertheless, unregistered minding which is by no stretch of the imagination a technicality is known to be common. In 1976, some 900,000 mothers of pre-school children were at work, some 200,000 for more than 30 hours a week; but there were only about 61,200 nursery places available, and 34,000 minders registered to care for a maximum of 83,000 children. Even allowing for the small proportion of mothers who can afford help in the home, and the much greater number who rely on relatives, there was a large gap which must have been met by illegal minding (Central Policy Review Staff, 1978). Nowadays, some 41 per cent. of women with children under school age work outside the home and 66 per cent. of those with primary school children do so (D.H. Guidance, vol. 2, para. 5.8). These figures take no account of parents who need to arrange day care for other reasons than their work. Registration is very difficult to enforce, as the "victims" are too young to complain, their hard-pressed parents do not want to, and social workers cannot make regular house-to-house checks. Many social workers would prefer to see more incentives to registration, in the shape of training, advice, equipment and even cash subsidies (Terry, 1979). Local authorities now have power to provide facilities, including training, advice, guidance and counselling, for all day care providers (1989 Act, s.18(3)) and this is the direction in which many of them are moving.

3. PRIVATE FOSTERING

Some parents' reasons for wanting alternative care do not bring them within the priority groups for whom local authority accommodation is usually available, a prime example being Commonwealth couples who have come here to study. Others, and middle-class unmarried or working mothers may be an example, prefer to make their own arrangements. Here again, demand exceeds supply and appears to be largely confined to the very young. The horrors of the Victorian baby-farming cases led quite early to the imposition of legal controls. These are still based, not on general registration, but on notifying the local authority of the individual placement, so that they may supervise and remove the child if necessary, or even prohibit it in advance.

(i) A "privately fostered child"

The Act protects any child under 16 (or a disabled child up to the age of 18) who is cared for and accommodated by someone who is not a parent, other person with parental responsibility, or a relative (1989 Act, s.66(1),(4)), unless he is being cared for in premises where a parent, other person with parental responsibility, or a relative who has assumed responsibility for his care is also living (1989 Act, s.66(5), Sched. 8, para. 2 (1)(a)).

Any arrangement which actually lasts for less than 28 days is excluded unless the foster parent intends it to last for longer (1989 Act, s.66(2)). Sending children to stay with friends for holidays is not covered, but any longer term arrangement outside the immediate family is included, however informal. There is no need for any payment to be agreed or made.

The Act specifically excludes several types of children who are thought to be adequately protected in other ways. These are any child being looked after by a local authority (1989 Act, Sched. 8, para. 1); or in a children's home, or accommodation provided by or on behalf of a voluntary organisation, or in a school where he is receiving full time education (but there are special rules covering children who live in school during the school holidays; see 5. below), or in a health service hospital, or in a residential care home, nursing home or mental nursing home, or in any other home or institution provided by the Secretary of State, unless in each case the person caring for the child is doing so in a personal capacity rather than as part of his duties in the establishment concerned (1989 Act, Sched. 8, para. 2(1)(b)–(g), (2)); children who are in the care of any person in compliance with a supervision order made in connection with criminal proceedings against the child (1989 Act, Sched. 8, para. 3); children who are liable to be detained in hospital or are subject to guardianship under the Mental Health Act 1983 (1989 Act, Sched. 8, para. 4); and children who have been placed for adoption by an adoption agency under the relevant legislation in England and Wales, Scotland or Northern Ireland, or who are "protected" under the adoption legislation (1989 Act, Sched. 8, para. 5).

The 1989 Act draws a clear boundary between fostering and running a private children's home. Generally, if accommodation is, or is usually provided, or is intended to be provided for more than three children at a time, then it is a children's home (1989 Act, s.63(3)(a)). Correspondingly, the usual rule is that a foster parent (public or private) may not foster more than three children at a time; the only exceptions are for sibling groups, where all the children fostered are siblings of one another; and for "super-mums" to whom the local authority have granted special written permission to foster named children. The Act lays down how the local authority are to consider these exemptions and any conditions they may want to impose and requires the authority to have a representations and complaints procedure for people wanting this permission (1989 Act, s.63(12), Sched. 7, paras. 1–4 and 6). People who exceed the Act's fostering limits are automatically treated as carrying on a children's home (1989 Act, Sched. 7, para. 5).

(ii) Advertising

No advertisement indicating that a person will undertake or arrange for a child to be privately fostered can be published, unless it discloses that person's name and address (1989 Act, Sched. 8, para. 10).

(iii) Notification

The foster parent is primarily responsible for notifying the local authority. She must give written notice (which can be sent by post) between 13 and 6 weeks before the placement, unless the child was received in an emergency or became a "foster child" while already in her care, in which case she must notify within 48 hours after the event (1989 Act, Sched. 8, para. 7 and Children (Private Arrangements for Fostering) Regulations 1991, regs. 4(1), (2), 7). The details which must be given are specified in the regulations (reg. 4(3),(4)). The foster parent must also notify a change of address, new arrivals or departures from the household, and new convictions, disqualifications and prohibitions, beforehand if practicable and otherwise within 48 hours of the event (reg. 4(5)). The child's departure and the person to whom he has gone should be notified within 48 hours, unless the child is due to return within the next 27 days, in which case notification is only necessary if he does not do so or there is a change of plan (reg. 5(1),(3)). The child's death must be notified "forthwith" to the local authority and to the person from whom the foster parent received the child (reg. 5 (2)).

The 1991 regulations break new ground by requiring any person who is or who proposes to be involved in arranging for a child to be fostered privately, and any parent or other person with parental responsibility who knows that it is proposed to foster a child privately, to notify the local authority within the same time limits as apply to foster parents (reg. 6(1), (2)). The required particulars are also specified (reg. 6(3)). Any parent and other person with parental responsibility must also notify the ending of the fostering arrangement or any change of address (reg. 6(4)).

But there is still every reason to believe that many placements never come to the notice of the authorities at all. As with child-minding, many people are probably ignorant of the law, and there is no positive incentive to comply with something which could have unwelcome consequences for the parents and the foster parent.

(iv) Prohibitions, disqualifications and requirements

Whenever a person either proposes to foster a child privately or is doing so, the local authority may prohibit her, either from fostering any child anywhere in the authority's area, or from fostering any child in a particular home, or from fostering this particular child, if they think that she or her premises are not "suitable" or that it would be "prejudicial to the welfare" of the particular child to be accommodated there by her (1989 Act, s.69(1),(2),(3)). Their inquiries may take place before or after the placement, but they should be looking at the same sorts of things as they look at when assessing their own foster parents—police records, household relationships, parenting capacity, religion, ethnicity and attitude to parents' visiting, standard of living and general life-style, and attitudes to education and discipline (D.H. Guidance, vol. 8, part 1.5; see Chapter 8). In practice, they may find it harder to prohibit a placement after it has begun than to impose a general or specific prohibition in advance. They can always cancel the prohibition at any time if satisfied that it is no longer justified (1989 Act, s.69(4)).

The same people are automatically disqualified from being involved in private fostering as from child-minding, day care and running children' homes, unless the facts are disclosed to the local authority and their consent obtained (see 6. below). The authority can also impose "requirements" upon foster parents, as to the number, age and sex of any foster children, the standard of accommodation and equipment provided, the arrangements for their health and safety, and any particular arrangements required in caring for them; these may be general or specific to a particular child or type of child and apply only when more than a certain number are fostered; they may be varied, imposed or removed at any time (1989 Act, Sched. 8, para. 6(1)–(3),(5)). The authority can also impose a prohibition which will operate if the requirement is not complied with within the time given for doing so (1989 Act, s.69(5),(6)).

Prohibitions, requirements and refusals of consent must always be notified in writing, giving the reason, and informing the person concerned of their right to appeal within 14 days of the notification (1989 Act, ss.69(7), 68(4), Sched. 8, para. 6(4)). Any "person aggrieved" (who may be the foster parent or employee, or possibly even a parent or the child himself) by the authority's decision may appeal to a magistrates' court (Sched. 8, para. 8) and the court can then do whatever the local authority might have done.

The official guidance (D.H. Guidance, vol. 3, para. 1.11.1) points out that from the child's point of view the experience of fostering is much the same whether it is arranged privately or through a local authority. But the authority do not select or approve private foster parents. Parents have the freedom to place their children with almost anyone they like, but the reality of supply and demand gives them very little choice, and many placements are made with people whom the local authority would not approve (Holman, 1973). Nor is there any social worker to take care over the actual transfer of the child; some are simply "dumped" without prior warning after a casual arrangement between the adults.

(v) Enforcement

It is a crime, punishable by a fine, knowingly to publish, or cause to be published, an unlawful fostering advertisement; or to fail to notify a placement within the required time, without a reasonable excuse; or to fail to give any required information within a reasonable time, without a reasonable excuse; or to provide, or cause someone else to provide, a notice or information which is false or misleading in some material particular; or to fail to comply with a requirement, without a reasonable excuse (1989 Act, s.70(1)(a),(c),(g), (3),(4),(6)). It is a more serious crime, punishable with up to six months' imprisonment, or a fine, or both, to foster in breach of a prohibition or disqualification (1989 Act, s.70(1)(d),(f), (5); see also 6. below). It is also a crime, again punishable only with a fine, to refuse to allow a privately fostered child to be visited or intentionally to obstruct the inspection of the premises (1989 Act, s. 70(1)(b),(c), (4); see (vi) below).

(vi) Protecting the children's welfare

Whether or not they have been properly notified of the placement, the local authority have to satisfy themselves that the welfare of any privately fostered child in their area is being satisfactorily safeguarded and promoted; they must also ensure that the people caring for these children are given any advice which the authority think they need (1989 Act, s.67(1)). The regulations now spell out in detail all the things which the social workers involved must think about, so far as relevant to the particular case (Children (Private Arrangements for Fostering Regulations) 1991, reg. 2):

(a)   the purpose and intended duration of the fostering arrangements;

(b)   the child's physical, intellectual, emotional, social and behavioural development;

(c)   whether the child's needs arising from his religious persuasion, racial origin and cultural and linguistic background are being met;

(d)   the financial arrangements for the care and maintenance of the child;

(e)   the suitability of the accommodation;

(f)   the arrangements for the child's medical and dental care and treatment and, in particular, whether the child is on an N.H.S. G.P.'s list;

(g)   the arrangements for the child's education and, in particular, that the L.E.A. have been informed of the fostering arrangement;

(h)   the standard of care which the child is being given;

(i)   the suitability of the foster parent to look after the child and the suitability of the foster parent's household;

(j)   whether the foster parent is being given any necessary advice;

(k)   whether the contact between the child and his parents, or any other person with whom contact has been arranged, is satisfactory;

(l)   whether the child's parents, or any other person, are exercising parental responsibility for the child; and

(m)   the ascertainable wishes and feelings of the child regarding the fostering arrangements.

Private foster placements now have to be visited with the same frequency as agency placements. An officer must visit "from time to time" as the authority considers necessary, or when reasonably requested either by the child or the foster parent, and in any event within one week of the placement and then at regular intervals, of not more than six weeks during the first year and not more than three months after that; if appropriate, the officer should arrange to see the child alone; and must make a written report after each visit

(1989 Act, s.67(2); Children (Private Arrangements for Fostering) Regulations 1991, reg. 3).

These duties are backed up by the power of the visiting social worker, at any reasonable time and producing his written authorisation if asked, to inspect any premises in the area where he has reasonable cause to believe that a privately fostered child is being or is to be accommodated (1989 Act, s.67(3), (4); this does not give social workers the right to gain entry by force).

If the local authority are not satisfied that the welfare of any privately fostered child in their area is being properly safeguarded or promoted, they must do what they reasonable can to find a parent, or other person with parental responsibility, or a relative who will take over his care, unless they consider that this would not be in the child's best interests. They must also consider whether to exercise any of their own functions under the 1989 Act (1989 Act, s.67(5)). These include providing services for the foster family under Part III of the Act, taking steps to gain entry, assess, and perhaps remove the child under Part V, or taking longer term compulsory measures under Part IV (see Chapters 8 and 10). These compulsory powers are designed to cover all the cases in which children may need this sort of protection, so there are no longer specific provisions for removing children from unsuitable foster parents. It is therefore more difficult to remove children from an unsatisfactory private foster home than it is to change a local authority placement. If local authority places are in short supply, a social worker may well hesitate to suggest removal of a child who will then have to go into care, particularly as it is likely that he would not have been eligible in the first place.

That may be why it was more important to reinforce the authority's responsibility to visit and help these children and their foster families. Although most of the children are under five, and the foster parents have not been professionally chosen, visits used to be much less frequent than they are to local authority foster children (Holman, 1973). Nowadays neglect and cruelty are probably not the major problem. The real difficulty is that these foster parents are having to cope with all the problems of the fostering relationship, but without professional selection, preparation or support. As, traditionally at least, many of the children have come from the ethnic minorities, there may be particularly difficult and sensitive cultural issues. The child's family may be much more accustomed to the idea of arranging for a child to be looked after by someone else for a very long period than are the foster family.

Their relationship with the child is in practice less secure than that of a local authority foster parent and child, for although there may be less risk of a social worker deciding to change the placement, there is more risk that the parent will remove the child suddenly and without warning. Yet the foster parents may have received little advice about this aspect of their role as temporary substitutes for the child's own family. Holman (1973) identified "role uncertainty" as a major and potentially harmful characteristic of private fostering. There are certainly numerous examples in the law reports of a "tug of love" developing as a result (see Chapter 7).

4. CHILDREN'S HOMES

While 70 per cent. of residential care placements are provided by local authorities, 16 per cent. are provided by voluntary organisations and 14 per cent. by the private sector. A voluntary organisation is a body other than a public or local authority whose activities are not carried on for profit (1989 Act, s.105(1)). The major children's charities were the pioneers in providing for orphaned, homeless and destitute children. Their role has been recognised by the law for a long time. Private children's homes, on the other hand, have only recently been distinguished from large-scale professional private fostering. Provision for their registration was first made in the Children's Homes Act 1982 which was never brought into force. The equivalent provisions in the 1989 Act are, however, now in force.

(i) Voluntary organisations

Voluntary organisations may accommodate children in much the same ways as local authorities do. The law is also much the same, except that they cannot acquire compulsory powers (unless given leave to apply for a section 8 order, which is perhaps unlikely). They can accommodate a child by placing him with a family, relative or any other suitable person (in which case the regulations applicable to family placements by local authorities apply); or by keeping him in a voluntary home, community home, registered children's home, or youth treatment centre; or by making any other arrangements which they think appropriate (but again subject to the same regulations as apply to local authorities doing this). Regulations can also require them to review cases and consider representations and complaints (1989 Act, s.59).

(ii) Voluntary and private children's homes

A voluntary home is any "home or institution providing care and accommodation for children which is carried on by a voluntary organisation" (1989 Act, s.60(3)). A private "children's home" is a home providing (or usually or intending providing) accommodation for more than three children (subject to the sibling group and "super-mum" exceptions; see 3. (i) above) (1989 Act, s.63(3)). Obviously for this purpose a voluntary home is not a children's home; also excluded from both definitions are community homes, schools (but see 5. below), health service hospitals, nursing homes, mental nursing homes and residential care homes, homes provided by the Secretary of State, and any other homes excepted by regulations (1989 Act, ss.60(3), 63(5)). Also, children are not regarded as being in a children's home if they are being cared for by or living in the same place as a parent, person with parental responsibility or relative, or by someone in a personal capacity rather than as part of her duties in the home (1989 Act, s.63(4),(7)).

Voluntary homes have to be registered with the Secretary of State (1989 Act, s.60(1); for the details of the registration scheme see Sched. 5, Pt. I).

People carrying on private children's homes have to be registered with their local social services authority (1989 Act, s. 63(1)(11); for the details see Sched. 6, Part I). Otherwise they commit a criminal offence, although punishable only with a fine (1989 Act, s.63(10)). People who are disqualified from day care or private fostering (see 6. below) cannot carry on, or be concerned in the management of, or have a financial interest in, a children's home, nor must anyone employ such a person in a children's home, without in either case disclosing this to the local authority and getting their written consent (1989 Act, s.65(1)(2)). As usual, a refusal must also be in writing, giving the reason and informing the applicant of the right of appeal, in this case to a registered homes tribunal rather than the court (1989 Act, s.65(3)).

Like community homes, these homes are covered by the Children's Homes Regulations 1991 (1989 Act, s.60(4), Sched. 5, Part II; s.63(11), Sched. 6, Part II; see Chapter 8 and D.H. Guidance, vol. 4). The regulations also flesh out the details of the registration scheme, which is outside the scope of this book.

(iii) Duties towards the child

Voluntary organisations and private children's homes each have the same duties, which are closely modelled upon those of local authorities, towards any child they are looking after. They must safeguard and promote his welfare; use the services and facilities available to children living with their parents if they reasonably can; and advise, assist and befriend him so as to promote his welfare when he leaves (1989 Act, ss.61(1), 64(1)). Before making any decision about him, they must, if reasonably practicable, discover not only his wishes and feelings about it, but also those of his parents, any other person with parental responsibility for him, and any other person whose wishes and feelings they think relevant (1989 Act, ss.61(2), 64(2)). They must give due consideration to the child's views, having regard to his age and understanding; to the views of the others which they have been able to discover; and to the child's religion, race and cultural and linguistic background (1989 Act, ss. 61(3), 64(3)).

(iv) Duties of the local authority

The local authority's duties towards children accommodated by voluntary organisations and in private children's homes are virtually identical to their duties towards private foster children. They must satisfy themselves that the organisation or home is satisfactorily safeguarding and promoting the children's welfare (1989 Act, ss.62(1), 64(4)). They must arrange for the children (except those in community homes, who are covered elsewhere) to be visited from time to time (1989 Act, ss.62(2),(3),(4), 64(4); the details are covered in regulations). The visiting officer has power to enter the premises at any reasonable time, on production of his official authorisation if asked, to inspect the premises and the children there, to require the production of the required records (including help in accessing any records held on computer) and to inspect these (1989 Act, ss.62(6),(7),(8), 64(4)). Intentional obstruction is a crime punishable with a fine (1989 Act, ss.62(9), 64(4)). And if the authority are not satisfied that the welfare of any child is being properly safeguarded or promoted, they must do what they reasonably can to secure that a parent, other person with parental responsibility, or a relative takes over the child's care, unless this would not be in his best interests; and in any event they must consider whether there is anything which they should be doing for the child themselves (1989 Act, ss.62(5), 64(4)).

5. HOSPITALS AND SCHOOLS

Hospitals (including private hospitals, which are technically known as nursing homes) and schools are mainly outside the usual rules about day care, fostering and children's homes. Generally, it is for the health and education services to safeguard the interests of the children there. But there are concerns about the general welfare, as opposed to the education, of children who spend much of their time living in school. So local social services authorities do have responsibilities towards some of them.

(i) Children in health or local education authority accommodation or adult nursing or care homes

If a child is provided with accommodation by any health authority or local education authority, or in any residential care home, nursing home or mental nursing home, for a consecutive period of at least three months, or with the intention of accommodating him for that period, then the accommodating authority or home must notify the relevant local social services authority (1989 Act, ss.85(1), 86(1)). A health or education authority must notify the social services authority for the area where the child lived before being accommodated or (if the child did not live in a local authority area before then) for the area where the accommodation is (1989 Act, s.85(3)). A residential care or nursing home must notify their own local social services department (1989 Act, s.86(1)). Each must also notify the child's departure (1989 Act, ss.85(2), 86(2)). It is a crime, punishable by a fine, for the person carrying on a home (but not for a health or education authority) to fail to comply with this without reasonable excuse (1989 Act, s.86(4),(8)).

The social services authority then has to do what it reasonably can to discover whether the child's welfare is being adequately (not satisfactorily) safeguarded and promoted where he is and consider whether they should do anything for him themselves (1989 Act, ss.85(4), 86(3)). An authorised person, on production of his written authorisation if asked, but not necessarily only at a reasonable time, may enter any residential or nursing home in their area to discover whether the section is being complied with (1989 Act, s.86(4),(7)). It is a crime, again punishable with a fine, for any person intentionally to obstruct this (1989 Act, s.86(6),(8)).

(ii) Independent schools

There is no general duty on independent boarding schools (within the meaning of the Education Act 1944) to notify individual pupils, but there are three ways in which local social services authorities may have responsibilities towards them. Children who stay during the school holidays may become private foster children; some schools may be private children's homes; and some schools have duties towards their pupils which social services authorities must try to monitor.

If a pupil at a school which is not maintained by a local education authority lives in school for more than two weeks during the school holidays he is treated as if he were a privately fostered child (1989 Act, Sched. 8, para. 9). If the school proposes to have one or more pupils staying for more than two weeks during any particular school holiday, it must notify the local authority at least two weeks before the first child does this (which in practice means before the end of term) stating the estimated number of children involved. The authority is the one where the first child is ordinarily resident. However, a local authority can exempt a school from this duty for a specified period or indefinitely and can revoke the exemption at any time. It seems odd that this general duty of notification is not to the local authority for the area where the school is situated. However, the school and the parents are not exempt from the usual duty to notify all fostering placements to the local authority where the fostering takes place and it is that authority which will have all the usual responsibilities (apart from the power to impose requirements) towards the children involved.

An independent school (as defined by the Education Act 1944) is a private children's home if it provides accommodation for not more than 50 children and is not approved by the Secretary of State for Education for the placement of children with special educational needs (1989 Act, s.63(6)). This means that it must be registered with and inspected by the local social services authority in the usual way.

Finally, the proprietor and anyone responsible for running an independent boarding school (unless it is a children's home or required to register as a residential care home for disabled or mentally disordered children), has a duty to safeguard and promote the children's welfare while they are accommodated in the school (1989 Act, s.87(1)(2)). The local social services authority for the area must do what they can to discover whether this is being adequately done (1989 Act, s.87(3)). An authorised officer has the usual power to enter and inspect the premises, children and records (1989 Act, s.87(5),(6),(7),(8); Inspection of Premises, Children and Records (Independent Schools) Regulations 1991). Obstruction is an offence (1989 Act, s.87(9). Authorities were advised to visit each school in their area once within the first year of the 1989 Act coming into force, once in the next year to follow up, and then annually or more often if necessary. Eton has protested that this could be a waste of scarce social services resources.

If the authority form the view that the school is not adequately safeguarding or promoting the welfare of any child accommodated there, they must notify the Secretary of State for Education (1989 Act, s.87(4); see D.H. Guidance, vol. 5, para. 4.3.2.). There is no express duty to consider what they themselves should be doing about it, but they will have their usual duty to investigate if child abuse is alleged or suspected (see Chapter 10). Apart from this, the official guidance (D.H. Guidance, vol. 5) tries hard to suggest that boarding schools should be aiming for standards of accommodation, staffing, safety and health care, contact with the outside world, personal relations and discipline similar to those expected of children's homes; but it also recognises that there are "differences in outlook" between social services and the independent education sector and that the parents have usually chosen (and are paying for) the school themselves. To some of these, it will be a startling idea that the social services should be in any way concerned about the arrangements they have made for their children.

6. DISQUALIFICATIONS

Some people are disqualified from registering as child-minders or day care providers, or from carrying on or running or having a financial interest in a day care facility or private children's home, or from private fostering, unless they first disclose the facts to the local authority and obtain their written consent. Similarly, no-one can register as a child-minder or day care provider or foster a child privately if he lives in a household where a disqualified person lives or works, or employ a disqualified person in connection with the provision of day care or in a private children's home, without first disclosing the facts and obtaining consent (1989 Act, ss.65(1),(2), 68(1),(3), Sched. 9, para. 2(1),(3),(4),(5)). There are the same rights of appeal against refusals of consent as there are against other refusals or prohibitions under the Act (see 2. (i), 3. (iv), 4. (ii) above).

The disqualified people are these: parents of any child who has at any time been made the subject of a care order; people who have been prevented from having a child live with them by a care order (under the 1989 Act or the Children and Young Persons Act 1969) or any order deemed to be such under the transitional provisions in the 1989 Act (which includes a parental rights resolution), a supervision order with a residence requirement under the 1969 Act or the equivalent in Scotland, a parental rights resolution in Scotland, an approved school order or fit person order under the Children and Young Persons Act 1933 or the equivalent in Scotland or Northern Ireland, under the adoption legislation in England and Wales, Scotland or Northern Ireland, or under the previous private fostering legislation here or the equivalent in Scotland or Northern Ireland; people prohibited from private fostering here or in Scotland or Northern Ireland; people refused (or who have had cancelled) registration for a nursery, day care or child-minding or a private or voluntary children's home; and people who have been convicted of any of the offences listed in the Schedule to the regulations (these include all the offences against children listed in Schedule 1 to the Children and Young

Persons Act 1933, any offence involving injury or the threat of injury to any person, and a variety of offences under the adoption and child protection legislation itself) (Disqualification for Caring for Children Regulations 1991). The arrangements for checking police records of people who apply to work with children cover prospective foster parents and child-minders and their households (see Home Office Circular No. 102/1988).

It is a crime, punishable with imprisonment for up to six months, or a fine, or both, to contravene any of these rules (1989 Act, ss.65(4), 70(1)(*d*),(5), 78(9),(12)(*b*)); but where a person is prosecuted because someone in the same household or in her employment is disqualified, it is a defence to prove that she did not know and had no reasonable grounds for believing that to be so (1989 Act, ss.65(5), 70(2), 78(10),(11)).

Chapter 10

CHILD ABUSE AND NEGLECT

The law has known for a long time that people are capable of treating children badly, although its notions of what is bad for children have varied with those of society at large. Its first response was simply to punish the wrongdoer, and the special vulnerability of children made it necessary to devise special offences to protect them (the principal offence of child cruelty is discussed in Chapter 1). Its second response was to provide ways of rescuing them from the harmful environment. The third response was to try to improve that environment, to prevent the harm and preserve what was good.

Prosecution is a matter for the police and Crown Prosecution Service. Some child abuse is evil and sadistic and prosecution is richly deserved. Some is the result of poverty, ignorance and other environmental pressures which may be powerful mitigation even if the evidence for a conviction can be obtained. It is clearly necessary to retain the notion that child abuse is a crime, not only to deter the rational but also to define the limits of acceptable behaviour towards children. But a humane and discriminating prosecution policy can be justified in the interests of the victims themselves. Young children in particular will not be helped if their parents are deterred from confessing their difficulties by a fear of punishment, nor if that punishment destroys the hope of maintaining a viable family unit.

Protecting the child is a matter for the social services. The Children Act 1989 emphasises that they must try to promote the upbringing of children within their own families, as long as it is safe to do so (1989 Act, s.17(1)). This means that they must try to work in partnership with parents, only seeking court orders where this is better for the child than making voluntary arrangements (*Working Together*, 1991). Unless the child is already involved in some family proceedings in another court, these public law cases have to begin in a magistrates' family proceedings court, although they can then be transferred to a county court or the High Court in certain circumstances.

1. SIGNIFICANT HARM

The problem in principle is to find a sufficient justification for intervening at all when the family do not want this. It is easy enough to say that children have a right to be protected from harm, but they also have a right to a family life. Everyone, parents and children alike, is entitled to respect for their private and family life (European Convention on Human Rights, Art. 8(1)). Children have the right not to be separated from their parents, unless this is necessary in their own best interests (United Nations Convention on the Rights of the Child, Art. 9). It cannot be "necessary" to separate parent and child just because in an ideal world somebody else might provide him with a better home or upbringing. And who is to say what is better? In a free society, "it is important to maintain the rich diversity of lifestyles which is secured by permitting families a large measure of autonomy in the way in which they bring up their children. This is so even, or perhaps particularly, in those families who through force of circumstances are in need of help from social services or other agencies" (R.C.C.L., 1985, para. 2.13).

We already intervene a good deal in that autonomy, not to provide the best possible outcome for the child, but to safeguard his basic welfare and give him a reasonable opportunity of growing up into a healthy adult who can make his own way in the world. We insist that children of compulsory school age are properly educated, whether their parents like it or not; we also prevent children from earning their own living and limit the extent to which they can do any work outside the home; and we give the authorities a range of powers to protect children from "significant harm".

The risk or actuality of "significant harm" lies at the heart of all the compulsory powers of intervention discussed in this chapter. Its suspicion triggers the social services' duty to investigate (1989 Act, s.47(1); see 2. (ii) below); a possible child assessment order if the family refuse to co-operate with the investigation (1989 Act, s.43(1); see 2. (iv) below); and a possible emergency protection order (E.P.O.) (1989 Act, s.44(2); see 3. (i) below), perhaps coupled with an entry warrant (1989 Act, s.48(9); see 3. (iv) below), if they frustrate those inquiries by refusing access to the child. Belief in the likelihood of harm also justifies an E.P.O. or taking a child into police protection (1989 Act, ss.44(1), 46(1); see 3. (i), 4. below). A finding that the child is suffering, or likely to suffer, significant harm forms the first link in the chain of reasoning which can lead to a care or supervision order to give longer term protection to the child (1989 Act, s.31(2); see 5. (iv) below).

For all these purposes "harm" means "ill-treatment or the impairment of health or development" (1989 Act, s.31(9)). These do not equate simply with positive "abuse" and negative "neglect" although they certainly cover all the ground. "Ill-treatment" carries an implication of abuse rather than neglect, of conduct towards the child which is in some way hurtful or damaging. The Act provides that it includes "sexual abuse and forms of ill-treatment which are not physical" (1989 Act, s.31(9)), although obviously it covers physical ill-treatment as well. Ill-treatment usually impairs the child's health or development in some way, but it is included in its own right in case actual damage of this sort cannot be shown. "Impairment of health or development" involves some sort of damage or deficit in what might normally be expected of the child. This could arise either from positive abuse or from neglect. "Impairment" is not defined in the Act but should carry its ordinary meaning of damage or weakening. "Health" means "physical or mental health" and "development" means "physical, intellectual, emotional, social or behavioural development" (1989 Act, s.31(9)). A child who is not receiving a proper education, or who is not learning to control his behaviour as others do, may well be suffering significant harm, just as much as a child who is not meeting his physical or developmental milestones. In deciding whether this impairment is "significant" this child's health or development is to be compared with "that which could reasonably be expected of a similar child" (1989 Act, s.31(10)).

Thus, while all ill-treatment is a bad thing, and the only question is whether it is sufficiently "significant" to justify intervention, impairment has to be judged by looking at what might reasonably be expected of a child with similar characteristics. Children with handicaps or disabilities may be impaired in their development, but it is only if this child falls below what would be expected for a child like him that he can be said to be suffering harm, let alone significant harm. And his development does not have to be the best that can be expected, merely what is reasonable. Conversely, a child with exceptional abilities may be falling below what could reasonably be expected of him. The focus is meant to be on this child: how well would we expect him to be doing?

That is not, however, quite what the Act says. In talking about a "similar child" rather than "this particular child", what characteristics does it mean us to consider? Is it only the child's own characteristics or are his social, economic and cultural background and circumstances to be included (as the *D.H. Guidance*, vol. 1, seems to suggest)? This is delicate ground. All the children in his neighbourhood may be noticeably disadvantaged, in terms of their physical health and educational development, when compared with children of the same innate characteristics from another neighbourhood with better schools which is further away from the local chemical works. Interfering in the lives of all these children would involve social engineering on a huge scale. Yet is it any better if only one child in the neighbourhood is suffering in this way, for this is to discriminate against poor or disadvantaged families whose children suffer in comparison with their richer neighbours? In principle, therefore, a "similar" child ought to be one with the same innate characteristics rather than one from the same social, economic or cultural background. In practice, however, it may be difficult to tell the difference.

The Act does not offer a definition of "significant". The Review of Child Care Law (R.C.C.L., 1985, para. 15.15) considered that, having once decided what standard of upbringing might reasonably be expected for the particular child, it should be necessary to show a "substantial" deficit. "Significant" is no doubt less than "substantial" but obviously more than "minimal". The Concise Oxford Dictionary gives the following definition:

"noteworthy, of considerable amount or effect or importance, not insignificant or negligible".

Usually the Act requires either that the child "is suffering" or "is likely to suffer" significant harm. "Is suffering" was deliberately chosen rather than "has suffered", to emphasise the need for a current rather than a past cause for concern. However, it cannot be taken too literally—by the time the court comes to decide the question in care proceedings, for example, the child has usually been removed from home in the hope of preventing or arresting the harm which he was suffering there. It has been held to refer to the situation as it was before the process of protecting the child began (*Northamptonshire County Council* v. *S.* [1993] Fam. 136). But how far back should that go? In that case, the child had been voluntarily admitted and the care proceedings began six months later.

The past is also the best guide to the future. Most cases have a long history, which may begin with some obvious and significant harm; once the authorities become involved, it can be very hard to shake them off, even though the evidence of present or likely harm is extremely slim; there is an understandable tendency for all concerned to want to monitor the situation and keep it under observation "just in case".

Nor does the Act define "likely". An event is "probable" if it is more likely to happen than not: otherwise it is merely possible. But an event can be "likely" without being "probable". It is enough that there is a real risk of the harm occurring (*Newham London Borough Council* v. *A.G.* [1993] 1 F.L.R. 281). If the harm which is feared is not very great, it may seem unduly oppressive to allow the authorities to intervene when it is not even probable that it will happen, but in this case it is unlikely to be in the child's interests to make an order. On the other hand, if the harm will be catastrophic if it occurs, it may be right to intervene even though it is not very likely to happen.

2. INVESTIGATION AND ASSESSMENT

The official guidance (*Working Together*, 1991, para. 5.10) identifies six stages in handling individual cases: referral and recognition, immediate protection and planning the investigation, investigation and initial assessment, the child protection conference and possible registration, comprehensive assessment and planning, and finally implementation, review and possible de-registration.

(i) Referral and recognition

Referrals in cases of suspected child abuse or neglect come from many sources, professionals and members of the public. By the time a case gets to court, there is usually a substantial file detailing the various minor and major ways in which the child or his family has already come to the notice of the social services. Most of the notorious cases in which child protection procedures have failed have, regrettably, already been well known to the social services and other agencies (D.H.S.S., 1982; D.H., 1991).

Some countries make it a crime, at least for members of certain professions, not to report their suspicions to the authorities. There are many reasons why people may be reluctant to do so. Neighbours, family, and other members of the public may well fear the consequences whether or not their suspicions are well-founded. However, the public interest in encouraging them to make a report is so great that they can be guaranteed confidentiality by the agency (*D.* v. *N.S.P.C.C.* [1978] A.C. 171). Professionals may fear a conflict of interest between their responsibility towards the child and their professional duty to preserve the confidentiality of information they receive from patients or clients. The professional guidance given to doctors is now quite clear that "if a doctor has reason for believing that a child is being physically or sexually abused, not only is it permissible for the doctor to disclose information to the third party but it is the duty of the doctor to do so" (G.M.C., 1987). Guidance for both nurses and social workers is not quite so clear, but it certainly contemplates that confidential information may be disclosed in order to protect other people from harm (see *Working Together*, 1991, paras 3.13, 3.14). The official view (R.C.C.L., 1985) was that this was enough—in a country where most health services are provided publicly rather than privately, professionals can be trusted to share their information properly without the need for mandatory reporting laws.

The starting point, therefore, is that "any person who has knowledge of, or a suspicion that a child is suffering significant harm, should refer their concern" to one of the agencies with the power to do something about it—the social services department, the police or the N.S.P.C.C. (*Working Together*, 1991, para. 5.11.1). Of course, it helps if some of the people involved have specialist skills in recognising and interpreting the signs of child abuse and in knowing how serious they may be. These days, we are all aware of the phenomenon known as "secondary child abuse", in which the harm done by unnecessary investigation and intervention may be as great if not greater than the harm done by leaving things alone.

Where there is a risk to the life of the child or a likelihood of serious injury, the first priority must be to secure the immediate safety of the child. A decision must urgently be made whether to remove the child to another place, either under an E.P.O. (see 3. below) or voluntarily, while the investigation proceeds (*Working Together*, 1991, para. 5.12). If a court order is used, then the investigation will have to proceed within the statutory timetable. There ought to be a strategy discussion, particularly if the police are contemplating prosecution and the child may have to be called as a witness. There is often a conflict between the actions needed to protect the child from immediate harm and what will best promote his welfare in the longer term, and an even greater conflict between these and the actions needed if there is to be a successful prosecution of the abuser.

(ii) The duty to investigate

While the police have the duty to investigate crime, the duty to investigate and decide how best to protect a child from harm is squarely placed upon social services authorities. Whenever they:

183

(a) have themselves obtained an E.P.O.; or

(b) are told that a child living or found in their area is already the subject of an E.P.O. or is in police protection; or

(c) have reasonable cause to believe that a child living or found in their area is suffering or likely to suffer significant harm,

they must make whatever enquiries they think necessary to enable them to decide what action they should take to safeguard or promote the child's welfare (1989 Act, s.47(1),(2)). The object is to decide whether they should bring any sort of proceedings, or exercise any of their other powers under the Act, and also whether they should take over responsibility for children in category (b) above (1989 Act, s.47(3)).

Unless they already have enough information, they must take whatever steps are reasonably practicable to gain access to a child they do not already have under their own protection; and if access is refused they must apply for an order, unless they are satisfied that his welfare can be satisfactorily safeguarded without it (1989 Act, s.47(4),(6)).

They are also entitled to ask other authorities to help. Any other local authority, any local education or housing authority, any health authority or N.H.S. trust, and anyone else authorised by the Secretary of State for this purpose, has a duty to co-operate with these enquiries if asked to do so, unless it would be unreasonable in the circumstances of the particular case (1989 Act, s.47(9),(10),(11)). If the child normally lives in another local authority area, they must consult that authority, which can take over the enquiries instead (1989 Act, s.47(12)). If there seem to be matters about the child's education which need investigation, they must consult the L.E.A. (1989 Act, s.47(6)).

If the authority decide that they should action to protect the child, then they have a statutory duty to do so as far as they can (1989 Act, s.47(8)). If they decide not to take proceedings, they must decide whether, and if so when, to review the case again (1989 Act, s.47(7)). So it is not enough to do what they can to find out what is going on; they must also do enough to enable them to reach some sort of conclusion and then act upon it.

(iii) Interviewing children

During the investigation, it is essential to interview the child himself (*Working Together*, 1991, para. 5.14.6). This is an extremely skilled and difficult task. The interviewer has to know how to talk to children and to gain their confidence without putting them under any sort of pressure. Adult opinion tends to swing from excessive scepticism about whether a child is to be believed to excessive acceptance of everything that he says. The important thing is to keep an open mind, to listen carefully to what the child is saying, and to take everything he says seriously. There is now a great deal of evidence about the capacity of children to give accurate accounts of what has happened, about the pressures they may be under either to deny or to misrepresent what has taken place, and about when they may be more than usually susceptible to the suggestions made by others.

It is necessary to keep very clearly in mind the different purposes for which the child may be being interviewed. Some interviews may be designed simply to get at the facts and some for therapeutic purposes. An interview which uses hypothetical or leading questions or other ways of overcoming the child's reluctance to "tell" may be of little or no evidential value in any later proceedings, however helpful it may be to the child. Where prosecution is contemplated, it is only sensible to obtain the evidence (and a video-recording may now be admitted in place of the child's evidence-in-chief, although there is still a right to oral cross-examination) before embarking upon therapy.

The Cleveland Report (Butler-Sloss, 1988) laid down the following guide-lines for conducting interviews in cases of suspected sexual abuse, and anyone who ignores them is likely to get short shrift in care proceedings (see, for example, *Re A. and Others (Minors)* (*Child Abuse: Guidelines*) [1992] 1 F.L.R. 439): it is undesirable to call them "disclosure" interviews (thus projudging the issue of whether or not abuse had taken place); those undertaking them must have training, experience and aptitude; they must approach each interview with an open mind; the style should be open-ended questions to support and encourage the child in free recall; there should be where possible only one and not more than two interviews for the purpose of evaluation and the interview should not be too long; it should go at the pace of the child and not the adult; the setting must be suitable and sympathetic; it must be accepted that the result may be inconclusive; it should be carefully recorded, whether or not it is videoed; facilitative techniques may cause difficulties in any later court proceedings; these may be appropriate in some circumstances, but only as a second stage, with an interviewer, who has special skills and specific training, and is conscious of the limitations and strengths of the techniques used. In particular, "anatomically correct" dolls should only be used by people who really know how to interpret the results (see *Re K.S. and G.S.* (*A Minor: Sexual Abuse*) [1992] 2 F.L.R. 361).

(iv) Child assessment orders

Child assessment orders were introduced at a late stage in the passage of the Children Bill through Parliament. Some felt that there should be a half-way house between relying entirely on what the parents would let the authorities do and an order which allowed for the sudden and complete removal of the child from home. However, under an E.P.O., the child does not have to be removed from home; in fact, it is now unlawful to remove him if it turns out to be unnecessary to do so. But any order which allows for the child to be removed if necessary must be based on grounds which are sufficient to justify such a drastic step. There must therefore be some solid evidence that he is at risk or at least an unreasonable denial of reasonable requests to see him. There may be cases where there is sufficient concern to justify making a proper assessment of the child and his situation, but not such as to justify his immediate removal from home.

Hence a local authority or an "authorised person" (the N.S.P.C.C.; see page 197, below) may apply for a child assessment order. The court must be satisfied that the *applicant* has reasonable cause to suspect that the child is suffering or likely to suffer significant harm; that an assessment of the child's health or development or of the way in which he is being treated is necessary to enable the applicant to make up their minds whether this is in fact so; and that without an order it is unlikely that an assessment or at least a satisfactory assessment can be carried out (1989 Act, s.43(1)).

These orders are not intended for emergencies. The applicant should be in the throes of a section 47 investigation which is being frustrated by the parents. The guidance sternly warns that there is no excuse for the investigation to be merely superficial; the court will expect to be given details of the investigation and how it arose and to be satisfied that all reasonable efforts have been made to get the family to co-operate (*Working Together*, 1991, para. 5.14.5). The order cannot be made *ex parte*. The applicant must always take such steps as are reasonably practicable to ensure that notice is given to the child, his parents, anyone else with parental responsibility, anyone else caring for him, and anyone with the benefit of a contact order (1989 Act, s.43(11)).

The court will need details of exactly what the assessment is to consist of and why. The order authorises the carrying out of an assessment in the terms specified in the order (1989 Act, s.43(7)). This is likely to involve receiving visits from certain professionals and taking the child to see others or for observation at a family centre or clinic. While the order is in force it is the duty of anyone who is in a position to produce the child to produce him to the person(s) named in the order and to comply with the directions for the child's assessment which are specified in the order (1989 Act, s.43(6)). The directions can provide for the child to be kept away from home for specified period(s) but he should only be kept away if it is necessary for the purposes of the assessment (1989 Act, s.43(9)). If he can be kept away, the order should also give directions about the contact he is to have with other people while he is away (1989 Act, s.43(10)). The child can always refuse to submit to a medical or psychiatric examination or some other assessment if he is of sufficient understanding to make an informed decision (1989 Act, s.43(8)). This was meant to reflect the House of Lords' decision in *Gillick* v. *West Norfolk and Wisbech Area Health Authority* [1986] A.C. 112; it ought not to have been affected by the decision in *Re W.* (*A Minor*) (*Medical Treatment: Court's Jurisdiction*) [1993] Fam.64, C.A. (see page 16, above); but the courts will be reluctant to hold that a child has the understanding required to refuse and examination or assessment when he so clearly needs it (see *Re H.* (*A Minor*) (*Care Proceedings: Child's Wishes*) [1993] 1 F.L.R. 440; page 209, below); ultimately, however, it must be for a doctor or assessor to decide whether the child's refusal is valid. The order must specify the date on which the assessment is to begin and its duration, which cannot be more than seven days (1989 Act, s.43(5)).

However, the court may always treat an application for a child assessment order as if it had been an application for an E.P.O. and if it is satisfied that the grounds exist and that this is a case for an E.P.O. rather than the more leisurely child assessment it cannot make the child assessment order (1989 Act, s.43(3),(4)).

In practice, child assessment orders are rare events (see Dickens, 1993). If the level of concern is such as to justify taking the case to a court at all, it is likely to justify some more substantial effort to protect the child. But the very existence of the possibility may sometimes be a useful tool in persuading parents to co-operate with medical examinations, clinic appointments, child guidance assessments and day centre attendances. While preserving what was thought to be the child's right to refuse to refuse to co-operate, it removes any right of the parents to veto such an examination or assessment of their child.

(v) Child protection conferences and registers

The guidance says that an initial case conference must be called within eight days of a referral, unless there are good reasons for a delay (*Working Together*, 1991, para. 5.15.3). Officially, the object of any case conference is not to decide whether or not abuse has taken place (*Working Together*, 1991, paras. 5.15.2, 6.1). It is to bring together all the interested professionals and the family, so that they can pool information and plan the future together.

All the agencies with specific responsibilities for child protection should be invited, including the social services and N.S.P.C.C., the police, education, health, the G.P., health visitors, probation, and any appropriate voluntary organisations. Involving the police used to be controversial, because of their very different professional views and objectives. Similarly, social workers and health care professionals were not always comfortable when lawyers were involved, but the guidance now says that the chair must have access to legal advice, particularly when legal proceedings are contemplated. There is some tension between the need to collect and assess evidence and the need to pool and evaluate information, opinions, impressions and plans.

As if that were not hard enough, the guidance stresses the need for "as much openness and honesty as possible between families and professionals" (*Working Together*, 1991, para. 6.11). The child himself should be encouraged to come to the conference, unless he does not want to or this would not be right in view of his age or understanding (*Working Together*, 1991, para. 6.13). The parents should also be invited; excluding either or both of them should be kept to a minimum and always needs special justification (such as a risk of violence to others attending) (*Working Together*, 1991, para. 6.15).

It is not the function of the conference to decide what to do. It will discuss and record a proposed plan of action. But it is for the agency representatives to decide whether or not to accept the part which it is recommended should be played by their agency in implementing the plan (*Working Together*, 1991, para. 6.8). The only decisions which the conference can take are whether or not the child should be placed on or removed from the child protection register and to appoint a key worker for those who are registered. For this, however, the conference does need to decide whether there is, or is a likelihood of, significant harm leading to a need for a child protection plan. The initial conference will also decide if and when to hold a review; if the child is placed on the register, this must be reviewed every six months.

Every local authority area has to have a child protection register. This is not a list of children who are known to have been abused. Nor is the register itself any guarantee of protection. It is simply a list of all the local children "for whom there are unresolved child protection issues and for whom there is an inter-agency protection plan" (*Working Together*, 1991, para. 6.36).

There are four categories of abuse defined for the purposes of registration (*Working Together*, 1991, para. 6.40). These are not legal categories, for the law depends on the concept of "significant harm" (see 1. above). But they provide an indication of the sort of circumstances in which the authorities will consider that the risk of harm is such that some protective action ought to be taken:

(a) "*Neglect*: The persistent or severe neglect of a child, or the failure to protect a child from exposure to any kind of danger, including cold or starvation, or extreme failure to carry out important aspects of care, resulting in the significant impairment of the child's health or development, including non-organic failure to thrive."

(b) "*Physical Injury*: Actual or likely physical injury to a child, or failure to prevent physical injury (or suffering) to a child including deliberate poisoning, suffocation and Munchausen's syndrome by proxy" (submitting the child to medical examination or treatment for ailments or injuries caused or invented by the carer);

(c) "*Sexual Abuse*: Actual or likely sexual exploitation of a child or adolescent. The child may be dependent and/or developmentally immature."

(d) "*Emotional Abuse*: Actual or likely severe adverse effect on the emotional and behavioural development of a child caused by persistent or severe emotional ill-treatment or rejection." (This category should only be used when it is the sole form of abuse, because all abuse involves some emotional ill-treatment.)

Children should not be placed on the register unless there is good reason to suspect them to be at risk of harm. The guidance says that there must either be (a) one or more identifiable (and identified) incidents which have adversely affected the child, with a professional judgement that further incidents are likely, or (c) a professional judgement that significant harm is expected based on the findings in this case or on research evidence (*Working Together*, 1991, para. 6.39).

All of these instructions may seem very formal and elaborate, when what is at stake is making sure that children do not suffer because the people who should be protecting them are not properly informed. But however limited the official function of a case conference, in practice the decisions taken there are likely to be at least as important as any decisions taken later by a court. The conference will establish a level of concern and set in motion a train of events which can easily have a momentum of its own. Being on the register adds to those events and can certainly be stigmatising for all concerned. As Lord Justice Butler-Sloss herself has said, "In coming to its decision, the local authority is exercising a most important public function which can have serious consequences for the child and the alleged abuser" (*R.* v. *Harrow London Borough, ex p. D.* [1990] Fam. 133).

In that case, the court upheld a decision to state on the register that abuse of a child by the mother was "substantiated". Although the mother had not been invited to the case conference, she did know what had been alleged against her and had been given an opportunity to explain the child's injuries to the consultant paediatrician (although not to the social worker) and to make written representations to the case conference. In *R.* v. *Norfolk County Council, ex p. X.* [1989] 2 F.L.R. 120, however, a teenage girl made allegations of sexual abuse against a plumber; after a case conference he was recorded on the register as an abuser and his employers were informed; they suspended him pending an internal inquiry; the first he heard of the allegation was a letter telling him of the decision to place his name on the register. Not surprisingly, the court held that the authority had acted as no reasonable local authority could have acted and that the decision to place his name on the register was therefore invalid. Although resort to judicial review to challenge case conference decisions should be very rare, they ought at least to follow minimal standards of fairness and reasonableness.

(vi) Comprehensive assessment and planning

In many cases where a child has suffered or may be suffering harm, there is no need for the authorities to take any further action. Once a child is registered, however, there should be a comprehensive assessment, in order to "acquire a full understanding of the child and family situation" (and see D.H., *Protecting Children—A Guide for Social Workers Undertaking a Comprehensive Assessment,* 1988). This should lead to a written plan which will make clear the contributions and expectations of everyone involved, including the family and each of the agencies concerned. Children and parents should be given copies of the plan. Every effort should be made to ensure that they understand, accept and are willing to work with it. If their wishes are not respected, they should be told why, and of their rights to complain (see Chapter 8). In some cases, a plan may have to involve compulsory intervention through the courts, but every effort is made to avoid this.

Many social workers prefer to make voluntary arrangements for services to be provided, even when these involve the child leaving home for a while, rather than to risk the hostile step of care proceedings. The temptation is obvious, particularly if only a short break seems needed, but there are disadvantages. The parent may feel under as much pressure to agree as does a juvenile offender faced with the choice between a caution and prosecution. The authority may find themselves in difficulties if the parent wishes the child to come home too soon. Long-term planning in the child's best interests may be impeded. Little may be gained by pretending that what is essentially an authoritarian intervention is in fact quite voluntary.

3. EMERGENCY PROTECTION ORDERS

Sometimes, there may be no alternative to compulsory intervention, particularly it is impossible to gain access to a child about whom there is serious concern (as happened in the Kimberley Carlile case; see Blom-Cooper, 1987). Social workers, health visitors and other professionals concerned with the welfare of children have no general power to enter other people's property without their consent, still less to force their way in and remove the children. There is no equivalent in the child protection field to the power of an approved social worker under the Mental Health Act 1983 to enter and inspect any place where a mentally disordered patient is living if there is reason to believe that the patient is not under proper care (1983 Act, s.115).

Before the Children Act 1989, there was power to apply to a single magistrate, without giving notice to the parents or anyone else, for a "place of safety" order; this allowed the child to be removed from home for anything up to 28 days with no right of appeal; there was no need to prove anything or even swear an oath; all the social worker had to do was satisfy the magistrate that he had reasonable cause to believe that any of the primary conditions for care proceedings were made out. Not surprisingly, many authorities found this a convenient way of beginning care proceedings, because a place of safety order could then lead to an interim care order, and the authority appeared to be firmly in charge of the child throughout the time up to the hearing. In cases of suspected sexual abuse, many professionals also believed that it was essential to remove the child and cut him off completely from the abusive environment, so that he could begin to feel that it was safe to disclose what had been happening.

Equally unsurprisingly, this state of affairs was widely thought to be unjust, even before the dramatic events which took place in Cleveland in 1987 (R.C.C.L., 1985; Norris and Parton, 1987; Butler-Sloss, 1988). Emergency protection orders under the Children Act 1989 are intended, not as the standard way of beginning care proceedings, but as a genuinely emergency measure to protect a child from immediate harm or to gain access to a child who may be at risk. They are much shorter than their predecessor, the procedure is tighter, and the interference with the child and his family is less.

(i) Grounds

A court may make an E.P.O. in two rather different circumstances. The order should name the child whenever it is reasonably practicable to do so, but obviously there are times when the child's name is not known, and the order must then describe him as clearly as possible (1989 Act, s.44(14)).

(1) The first ground can be invoked by any applicant, not just a local authority or the N.S.P.C.C.. The court may make the order if it is satisfied that there are reasonable grounds to believe that the child is likely to suffer significant harm if he is not removed from or not kept in the place where he is currently being accommodated (1989 Act, s.44(1)(a)). This ground concentrates on the risk, rather than the presence of, significant harm; the object is prevention and protection rather than reaction to what has already happened. Further, although the Act does not state that the risk must be immediate, it does require there to be a link between preventing the harm and removing or retaining the child. Therefore, unless the risk is such that it can only be prevented by the immediate short-term removal or retention of the child, the order should not be made. As with all Children Act orders, it should not be made at all unless doing so will be better for the child than not making it (1989 Act, s.1(5); see page 80, above).

(2) The second ground can only be invoked by a local authority or "authorised person" (the N.S.P.C.C.; see page 197, below), where they are making enquiries either under section 47 (1) (see 2. (ii) above) or because the N.S.P.C.C. has reasonable cause to suspect that a child is suffering or likely to suffer significant harm. The court can make an order if those enquiries are being frustrated because an authorised officer is being unreasonably refused access to the child and the applicant has reasonable cause to believe that access to the child is urgently required (1989 Act, s.44(1)(b),(c)). Under this ground, the applicant does not have to satisfy the court that there is good reason to believe the child to be at risk; it is enough that the applicant is conducting enquiries and has good reason to believe that someone needs to see the child urgently. The person seeking access for this purpose must produce written authorisation if asked to do so (1989 Act, s.44(3)).

(ii) Procedure and evidence

An E.P.O. was always intended as an emergency measure where more leisurely steps to protect the child could not be risked. It can be granted without giving notice to the child or his parents. It can also be granted by a single magistrate out of hours if need be, although in general it is better if it is done more formally at court.

The court can take account of any statement contained in a report made to the court, and any evidence given during the hearing, provided this is relevant, even if the ordinary law of evidence would normally prevent it doing so (1989 Act, s.45(7)). This allows the court to take account of "hearsay" evidence. Put simply, it is "hearsay" when a person giving evidence puts forward a statement (whether spoken or written) made to him by someone else in order to prove the truth of something in that statement. The obvious example is a social worker or police officer telling the court that a child has told them that she has been abused. Under the ordinary law of evidence, this would not be admissible to prove that the child had indeed been abused, although it might be admissible to prove something about the child's state of mind. Hearsay evidence is not as reliable as direct evidence, for two reasons. First, the witness may not give an accurate account of what the other person said (although if there is a direct written statement or video-recording, that problem can be overcome); and secondly, the other person was not giving evidence under oath at the time and is not available for cross-examination in court so that the evidence can be tested in the traditional way.

The Civil Evidence Act 1968 allowed the use of hearsay evidence in civil, but not criminal, proceedings in certain circumstances. But this was never extended to magistrates' courts. This did not matter when magistrates were granting warrants and place of safety orders; they had only to be satisfied about what the applicant thought, rather than that what he thought was right. Once the 1989 Act required the court to form its own view, it had to make provision for them to rely on hearsay where necessary. Shortly afterwards, however, it was decided that in any family proceedings, evidence given in connection with the upbringing, maintenance or welfare of a child should be admissible despite the hearsay rule (1989 Act, s.96(3); Children (Admissibility of Hearsay Evidence) Order 1991, 1993). This is helpful, not only for what the child has said, but also for the mass of documentary records which are normally involved in child abuse cases. It is still necessary for the court to exercise a great deal of care in deciding how reliable the evidence is.

(iii) Effect

The main effect of an E.P.O. is to authorise the applicant either to remove the child at any time to accommodation provided by the applicant and to keep him there, or to prevent the child being removed from any hospital or other place where he was just before the order was made (1989 Act, s.44(4)(b)). Anyone who intentionally obstructs the removal or retention of the child is guilty of a criminal offence, punishable by a level 3 fine (1989 Act, s.44(15),(16)). However, the applicant can only remove or retain the child in order to "safeguard" his welfare (1989 Act, s.44(5)(a)), so if it turns out on gaining entry to the premises that the child will be safe there, he must be left where he is.

Although anyone can apply for an E.P.O. on the first ground, and the accommodation for the child has to be provided by the applicant, every local authority have to make arrangements for the reception and accommodation of children removed or kept away from home under an E.P.O. (or a child assessment order) (1989 Act, s.21(1)). And if the child is kept anywhere other than local authority accommodation or a hospital, the local authority have to pay (1989 Act, s.21(3)). When the authority are making their enquiries (see 2(ii) above), therefore, they must consider whether the child ought to be in their own accommodation (1989 Act, s.47(3)(b)). It is not clear, however, that they have power to insist.

Furthermore, the child must normally be allowed home the moment it appears to the applicant that it is safe to do so, either to the care of the person from whom he was removed, or if this is not practicable, to a parent or other person with parental responsibility or "such other person as the applicant (with the agreement of the court) considers appropriate" (1989 Act, s.44(10),(11)). However, the applicant can take the child back again for as long as the order remains in force, if it appears to him that a change in the circumstances makes this necessary (1989 Act, s.44(12)).

An E.P.O. also gives parental responsibility to the applicant for the duration of the order (1989 Act, s.44(4)(c)). This is to emphasise the personal responsibility which the applicant has taken on, but obviously there are limits to what the applicant can do. He is only allowed to take whatever action is reasonably required to safeguard or promote the child's welfare (having regard to the length of the order) (1989 Act, s.44(5)(b)). Taking any irrevocable step in the child's upbringing would certainly not be right.

Also, the court has power to give directions about the medical or psychiatric examination or other assessment of the child (1989 Act, s.44(6)(b)). This can include a direction that there is to be no such examination or assessment or only if the court agrees (1989 Act, s.44(8)). Even if the court directs that there should be an examination or assessment, the child has the right to refuse to submit to it, if he is of sufficient understanding to make an informed decision (1989 Act, s.44(7); but see page 186, above). Obviously, the court should not give directions for medical examination or assessment if it thinks that the child is old enough to understand and is likely to object. Often, however, the court will not know and it will be for the practitioner conducting the examination or assessment to judge whether or not the child's objection is valid.

The applicant must allow the child reasonable contact with his parents, anyone else who has parental responsibility for him (and an E.P.O. does not bring a residence or care order to an end), anyone with whom he was living when the order was made, anyone who already has a contact order in his favour, and anyone acting on behalf of any of these people (1989 Act, s.44(13)). The assumption is that children will not be held incommunicado from their parents while they are under emergency protection. Perhaps just as importantly, the parents can instruct their own doctor or another person to visit the child. However, this duty is subject to the court's power to give directions about the contact which is, or is not, to be allowed between the child and any named person (1989 Act, s.44(6)). During an E.P.O., therefore, the court has power to ban contact altogether.

These directions can be given at any time during an E.P.O. and they can also be varied (1989 Act, s.44(9)). These powers are clearly the product of the Cleveland experience. They reflect a sense of the injustice done to the children as well as to their parents by whisking them away from home, holding them incommunicado, and subjecting them to several medical examinations and interviews, even though these actions were all done with the best of intentions and in the belief that this was the right way to get at the truth.

(iv) Finding the child

An E.P.O. automatically operates as a direction to anyone who is in a position to do so to produce the child to the applicant (1989 Act, s.44(4)(a)).

Sometimes, however, the child may have disappeared. If the applicant does not know where the child is, but someone else does, the court can include in the E.P.O. an order requiring that person to disclose what he knows about the child's whereabouts to the applicant (1989 Act, s.48(1)). It is no excuse that the answer might incriminate that person (usually of kidnapping or some offence under the Child Abduction Act 1984; see Chapter 1); but the answer cannot be used in any criminal proceedings (1989 Act, s.48(2)).

An E.P.O. may (but does not automatically) authorise the applicant to enter specified premises and search for the child (1989 Act, s.48(3)). Also, if the court is satisfied that there is reasonable cause to believe that there may be another child on the same premises with respect to whom an E.P.O. ought to be made, it may authorise the applicant to search for that child there too (1989 Act, s.48(4)). It may well be difficult for the authorities to know how many children there are in a particular place, even though they have very good reason to believe that any child on those premises will be in some way at risk (for example, in cases of organised sexual abuse). This order operates like an E.P.O. if when the applicant gets in and finds the child it turns out that the grounds exist for making an E.P.O. in respect of that child (1989 Act, s.48(5); the applicant must tell the court if so; s.44(6)). It is a crime, punishable by a level 3 fine, intentionally to obstruct these powers of entry and search (1989 Act, s.48(7),(8)).

These powers do not give the applicant, who is usually a social worker, any power to batter down the door and gain entry by force. That is a job for the police, who need a warrant unless there is an immediate risk to life or limb (Police and Criminal Evidence Act 1984, s.17(1)(e)). If someone acting under an E.P.O. has been refused entry to the premises concerned or has been refused access to the child, or it appears likely that this will happen, anyone can apply to the court for a warrant authorising any constable to help gain entry or access to the child, by force if need be (1989 Act, s.48(9)). The person who applied for the warrant can go with the police officer if he wants, unless the court directs otherwise (1989 Act, s.48(10)). The court can also direct that a doctor, nurse or health visitor may go with the police officer if he wants this (1989 Act, s.48(11).

These warrants and orders should also name the child if they can, and if not should describe him as clearly as possible (1989 Act, s.48(13)).

(v) Duration and challenge

In deciding how long an E.P.O. should last, a difficult balance had to be struck (R.C.C.L., 1985). Taking a child away from his home, particularly when this has not been carefully planned and agreed in advance, is a serious interference with the child and his family which may have traumatic and damaging consequences for the child. On the other hand, it may sometimes be the only way of rescuing the child from serious risk, or of gaining access to the child in order to find out how serious the risk is. In civil liberties terms, the intervention should always be on notice if at all possible and should last for the shortest time possible. In human terms, however, a longer period might give the authorities time to make a proper assessment and to negotiate a voluntary protection plan with the family. Too short an order might propel them into taking care proceedings simply in order to be able to complete their inquiries and assessment. By and large, civil liberties prevailed.

An E.P.O. can last for a maximum of eight days (or if the eight days would expire on a public holiday, up to noon on the following day) (1989 Act, s.45(1),(2)). There can be one extension, for up to seven days, but only if a local authority or the N.S.P.C.C. applies and the court has reasonable cause to believe that the child is likely to suffer significant harm if it is not extended (1989 Act, s.45(4),(5),(6)).

There is no right of appeal against an E.P.O., because the time is so short (1989 Act, s.45(10)). But there is a right to challenge those which were made without an opportunity of arguing against it at the outset. The child himself, any parent or other person with parental responsibility, or anyone with whom he was living just before the order, can apply for the order to be discharged (1989 Act, s.45(8)), unless that person was given notice of, and was present at, the hearing at which the order was made (1989 Act, s.45(11)). These applications can be made straightaway, but will not be heard by the court until 72 hours after the order was made (1989 Act, s.45(9)).

4. POLICE PROTECTION

The police are often the first people to learn that a child is at risk. Neighbours may call them when children are abandoned or left alone in their homes, although they could then usually contact the social services department before taking action. They also come across young runaways on the streets or in other public places, and may want to take such children in without arresting them, even if an offence might have been committed. It seems that this was quite a frequent occurrence before the 1989 Act, even though it might not have been formally recorded as a use of their power to take children to a place of safety (R.C.C.L., 1985). The 1989 Act preserves that power, but only for long enough to enable them to contact the social services department and make other arrangements for the child.

Where a police officer has reasonable cause to believe that a child would otherwise be likely to suffer significant harm, he may remove the child to suitable accommodation and keep him there, or take reasonable steps to prevent the child's removal from hospital or anywhere else (1989 Act, s.46(1)). He must then inform:

(a) the local social services authority (for the place where the child was found) of what has been done and why;

(b) the local social services authority (for the place where the child normally lives) where the child is;

(c) the child himself (if he appears capable of understanding) what has been done, why and what may happen next; and

(d) the child's parents and anyone else who has parental responsibility for him or with whom he was living just before being taken into police protection, of what has been done, why and what may happen next (1989 Act, s.46(3)(*a*),(*b*),(*c*), (4)).

The police officer concerned must also try to discover the child's own wishes and feelings. He must ensure that the case is enquired into by the officer designated for the purpose. And he must get the child moved into local authority accommodation or a refuge as soon as possible (1989 Act, s.46(3)(*d*),(*e*),(*f*)), although the child will still be under police protection while there. Neither the police officer who took him in nor the designated inquiry officer have parental responsibility for him, but the designated officer must do what is reasonable in all the circumstances for the purpose of safeguarding or promoting the child's welfare (having regard to the length of time for which the child will be under police protection) (1989 Act, s.46(9)). No doubt the idea of individual police officers having parental responsibility for the children they take in was a startling one, although scarcely less startling than with individual applicants for E.P.O.s. In practice, it is difficult to see what difference it would make—they both have to do their best for the child while they have him and cannot do more than is reasonable given the short time available.

The designated officer, or the local authority if the child is now in local authority accommodation, must allow whatever contact (if any) is both reasonable and in the child's best interests between the child and his parents, anyone else with parental responsibility for him or with whom he was living just before being taken into police protection or who has the benefit of an existing contact order, and anyone acting on their behalf (1989 Act, s.46(10),(11)).

As soon as he has made his inquiries, the designated officer must release the child from police protection unless he thinks that there is still cause to believe that the child would suffer significant harm if released (1989 Act, s.46(5)). The child cannot be kept in police protection for more than 72 hours (1989 Act, s.46(6)); so wherever he is being kept he must be allowed to leave after 72 hours if he wants to, unless some other order is obtained which forces him to stay.

While the child is in police protection, the designated officer can apply for an E.P.O. on behalf of the local social services authority whether or not the authority either knows or agrees (1989 Act, s.46(7),(8)). If the order is made, the maximum period of eight days dates from the day on which the child was first taken into police protection (1989 Act, s.45(3)).

5. CARE PROCEEDINGS

"Care proceedings" is no longer a technical term. It is simply a convenient way of referring to an application for a care order or a supervision order. A care order is the only way in which a local authority can assume long term responsibility for a child's care and upbringing. Local authorities are not allowed to apply for residence or contact orders or courts to make such orders in their favour (1989 Act, s.9(2)); they could seek leave to apply for a prohibited steps or specific issue order on the same terms as anyone else (see Chapter 7), but not if the child is in care (1989 Act, s.9(1)). Care proceedings are therefore the main machinery, not only for protecting children living at home or in the community, but also for securing the long-term future of children living in local authority accommodation.

(i) Applications

Applications can only be made by a local social services authority or an "authorised person" (1989 Act, s.31(1)). This means the N.S.P.C.C. and any of its officers. The Secretary of State has power to authorise others for this purpose but has not done so (1989 Act, s.31(9)). The court cannot make either a care order or a supervision order "of its own motion". The application can, however, be made either in the course of other family proceedings or on its own (1989 Act, s.31(4)); and the court can make a supervision order on an application for a care order and a care order on an application for a supervision order (1989 Act, s.31(5)).

No doubt other agencies and professionals, including the courts, sometimes wish that they had power to force the social services to take action. Insisting on proper applications, however, is a protection for the child and his family—the court cannot commit a child to care without proper investigations being undertaken by the local authority and by a guardian *ad litem* appointed to represent the child's particular interests. Insisting that proceedings are only brought by local authorities and the N.S.P.C.C. emphasises where the primary responsibility lies. It is also, for the most part, the local authority which will have to implement the order. They are far more likely to see the case in proportion and in the context of all the other social problems facing families in their area than are agencies such as the police, health and education services, or even the courts.

The role of the N.S.P.C.C. in bringing proceedings is a recognition of their historical importance in rescuing children from harm. Before making an application, however, they must if practicable consult the local authority for the area where the child usually lives (1989 Act, s.31(6)). This authority will be the one to assume responsibility if a care order is made, unless the child does not live in any local authority area, in which case it will be the authority where the circumstances leading to the care order arose (1989 Act, s.31(8)). The court cannot deal with an application by the N.S.P.C.C. if there is already a pending application for a care or supervision order, or the child is already subject to a care order or a supervision order made either in care proceedings or in criminal proceedings or the equivalent in Scotland (1989 Act, s.31(7)). It would not be very sensible for the N.S.P.C.C to make an application at all in such circumstances, or indeed where the child was already being accommodated by a local authority on a voluntary basis, but they might not always know before the proceedings were launched.

(ii) Grounds

No care order or supervision order can be made in respect of a child who has reached the age of 17 (or 16 if the child is married) (1989 Act, s.31(3)). The tidy-minded would no doubt find it easier if the rule were the same in both private and public law, whether it was an absolute cut-off at the age of 16 or of 18, or the present private law compromise of allowing orders in respect of 16 and 17 year olds only if there are exceptional circumstances (see page 70, above). When deciding whether or not to make a care order or a supervision order, the court has to go through a multi-layered thought process, although the evidence can all be heard at once. Hearsay evidence is admissible if it relates to the upbringing, maintenance or welfare of a child (see page 192, above) .

(a) *The threshold criteria*

The first stage is to decide whether the so-called "threshold criteria" are made out. These are not "grounds", because there is still a long way to go even if they are established; but they are the necessary first step along the road. The court must be satisfied (1989 Act, s.31(2)):

"(a) that the child concerned is suffering, or is likely to suffer, significant harm; and

(b) that the harm, or likelihood of harm, is attributable to—

(i)   the care given to the child, or likely to be given to him if the order were not made, not being what it would be reasonable to expect a parent to give to him; or

(ii) the child's being beyond parental control".

The meaning of (a) has already been discussed (see 1. above). Requirement (b) does not arise in the short term procedures, where the focus has to be on immediate protection and assessment. The cause or source of the harm which the child is suffering, or is likely to suffer, is not so important at that stage. But when the court is faced with an application to remove, or keep, the child from his family for what might be the rest of his childhood it becomes crucial. As the Review of Child Care Law (R.C.C.L., 1985, para. 15.23) put it, "the court should be expressly required to find that the care available to the child is not merely wanting, but falls below an objectively acceptable level or that he is beyond parental control so that he cannot benefit from the care on offer".

The criteria have to cater for two rather different situations. The first is where the child is (or was until the proceedings were set in train) living at home. It must first be shown, either that he already is suffering or that he is likely to suffer "significant harm"; as we have already seen, where the harm is a deficit in his health or development, rather than ill-treatment, this must be judged according to what might reasonably be expected of a child like him, with all his particular characteristics. It must next be shown that the harm, or the likelihood of harm, is caused by his not being given (or being likely to be given) the care which a reasonable parent would give him (or by his being beyond parental control). His actual parents or carers may be doing the best they can, but if this is not what could reasonably be expected, then the condition is satisfied. The child must be protected even if his parents are doing their best.

The other situation is where the child has been living away from home for some time in accommodation provided or arranged by the local authority under voluntary arrangements and the local authority wish to prevent the parents taking him away. If this has not been going on for long, it might be possible for the authority to argue that he "is suffering" significant harm, attributable to the care which he was given before he came into local authority accommodation (see *Northamptonshire County Council* v. *S.* [1993] Fam. 136, page 182, above). This is a dangerous approach, however, because it might mean that the threshold criteria could always be satisfied if the local authority thought better of the voluntary arrangements which had been agreed at the outset. Then the parents would only be able to resist an order on the basis of the other requirements (see below), which might be very difficult for them to do.

If, on the other hand, the authority cannot rely on the harm which the child has suffered in the past, they will have to rely on the likelihood of harm in the future if he goes home. They will also have to show that this likelihood of harm is attributable to the care which the parents are likely to give him. This may present difficulties. Parents have often gone through great changes in their lives since parting with their children. A young mother who was quite unable to cope with a small baby along with a great many other pressures and problems may have formed a stable relationship and sorted out her life completely. She may now be able to give exactly the sort of care that it would be reasonable to expect any parent to give to this child. The fear may be, however, that the child will suffer harm because of the disruption in his settled life in his current placement with his foster parents or elsewhere. On a pure test of what would be better for him, at least for the time being, he would stay where he was. Applying the threshold criteria, however, he would have to go home, unless it could be argued that removing him from a settled home where he is doing well is not giving him the "care" that a reasonable parent would give. "Care" is not defined in the Act and this would certainly stretch its meaning a very long way.

There may be less difficulty with the "yo-yo" children who are taken in and out of local authority accommodation against the authority's advice and probably contrary to the care agreement made between the parents and the authority (see Chapter 8). This sort of failure to offer consistent care seems to fit the criteria more easily.

(b) *The welfare test and checklist*

Having decided that the threshold criteria are met, the court has to decide what will be best for the child and in doing so it must take into account the "checklist" of factors relevant to the child's welfare, which have already been discussed in Chapter 4. The last item in that checklist is, of course, the "range of powers available to the court under this Act in the proceedings in question" (1989 Act, s.1(3)(*g*)).

(c) *The options and no order principle*

The court has a wide range of powers available in care proceedings. It can always choose between making a care order or a supervision order (1989 Act, s.31(5)). It can always make a residence order, contact order, specific issue order or prohibited steps order (see Chapter 4) instead of a care order or in combination with a supervision order, and whether or not anyone has applied for one. And it must always consider the "do nothing" option; the court must not make the order, or any of the orders, unless it considers that doing so would be better for the child than no order at all (1989 Act, s.1(5); see page 80, above).

This means that there are two sorts of options for the court to consider. The first is whether there is a better alternative plan for the child than the one put forward by the applicant. Should the child be staying at home under supervision rather than going into local authority accommodation? Or should the child be going to live for a while with relatives or with the other parent? Would either of these solutions be helped by restricting the extent to which either of the parents can meet their parental responsibilities towards the child? These options should be thoroughly explored before the court makes a care order, especially where there is an alternative application before the court (*Hounslow London Borough Council* v. *A.* [1993] 1 W.L.R. 291).

Once the court has decided what is the best plan for the child's future, the second question is whether a care or supervision order is the best way of achieving it. Even if the child should be living in local authority accommodation for a while, does this have to be done by way of a care order or can it be achieved by voluntary arrangements? Even if the child will be spending time at home as well as in local authority accommodation, is this a case in which it is essential for the local authority to have parental responsibility and be placed in effective control of the situation? If the child should be staying within the family for the time being, what combination of orders will offer the best protection? Are there issues relating to his upbringing, such as where he is to go to school or how he is to receive the medical treatment he needs, which could be resolved effectively by way of a specific issue order rather than by a care or supervision order?

Although a different combination of orders may be useful, especially in the interim period (*C.* v. *Solihull Metropolitan Borough Council* [1993] 1 F.L.R. 290), the court should not be using them for purposes for which they were not designed or where the local authority ought to have parental responsibility for the child. For example, a prohibited steps order cannot be used to keep parents apart, or as a substitute for a residence order, or to oust one parent from the home (*Croydon* v. *London Borough Council* v. *A.* [1992] 3 W.L.R. 267; *Nottinghamshire County Council* v. *P., The Times,* April 8, 1993, C.A.).

(iii) Interim orders, timetables and procedures

As with private law proceedings, the court must also have regard to the general principle that any delay in determining the question is likely to prejudice the child's welfare (1989 Act, s.1(2)). It must therefore draw up a timetable with a view to disposing of the proceedings without delay and give directions designed to ensure that so far as practicable the timetable is met (1989 Act, s.32(1)). The evidence of the length of time taken in care proceedings before the 1989 Act was extremely gloomy. It seemed that delay was most likely in just those cases, involving the abuse or neglect of young children, in which it was most likely to be harmful to the child and prejudicial to the family. Tackling the "culture of delay" built into a system which depends upon co-ordinating many different professionals each with their own timetables and agendas is no easy task (Murch *et al.*, 1987, 1992). The evidence is, however, that timetabling can be made to work (Plotnikoff, 1992; see also Booth, 1992).

Although waiting a while before making final decisions can be constructive, there are all sorts of reasons why delay is likely to be harmful to the child, and one of them is that in most care cases he will be separated from his family for the interim period. But one object of the 1989 Act was to get away from the assumption that this would always happen.

Whenever a care case is adjourned, the court has several options. It may make no order at all, in which case the child will remain in whatever legal situation he was before the proceedings started, but he may already be in local authority accommodation, or in hospital, or in some other placement away from home. If the court is satisfied that there are reasonable grounds for believing that the threshold criteria (see (ii) (a) above) are met, it may make either an interim care order or an interim supervision order (1989 Act, s.38(1)(a), (2)). Alternatively, the court could make any or any combination of section 8 orders. However, if it is satisfied in this way and nevertheless decides instead to make a residence order, for example that the child is to live with one of the parents (but not the other) or with another member of the family or with the foster parents, it must make an interim supervision order unless satisfied that the child's welfare will be satisfactorily safeguarded without it (1989 Act, s.38(3)).

There are complicated rules about the duration of interim orders. The court can specify how long the order is to last, within the maximum periods laid down in the Act (1989 Act, s.38(4)). The idea was to reduce the number of court appearances needed before the full hearing by giving a reasonably long initial period and then tightening up on the renewals. The initial period is therefore eight weeks from the date of the first order. That order can last for the full eight weeks (1989 Act, s.38(4)(a)) unless of course the proceedings are disposed of during that time (1989 Act, s.38(4)(c),(d)). Alternatively, the court could make any combination of orders up to the end of the first eight weeks (1989 Act, s.38(4)(b), (5)(b)). In deciding how long the order is to last, the court has to consider whether the opposition (principally of course the parents) were in a position to argue their case in full on the first occasion (1989 Act, s.38(10). If the first interim hearing has followed very quickly upon an *ex parte* E.P.O., for example, the parents may have got their case together at all. An initial order of one week or two weeks, followed by a hearing at which the court might decide to make a second order of seven or six weeks, could be fairer to them. The maximum length of any order which is to expire after the initial period, however, is four weeks (1989 Act, s.38(4)(b), (5)(a)).

As with an E.P.O., the court can take charge of how the various investigations are to be conducted. At any time while an interim care order or an interim supervision order is in force, it can give directions about the medical or psychiatric examination or other assessment of the child; this can include a direction that there is to be no such examination or assessment or only if the court says so; a child of sufficient understanding to make an informed decision can refuse to submit (1989 Act, s. 38(6),(7),(8); but see page 186, above). It seems that at this stage the court can oblige the authority to carry out an assessment, even if they do not want to do so (*Berkshire County Council* v. *C.* [1993] 2 W.L.R. 475; see also *Re B.* (*Minors*) (*Care: Contact: Local Authority's Plans*) [1993] 1 F.L.R. 543 C.A.).

Otherwise, an interim care order or an interim supervision order has the same effects as a full order (1989 Act, s.31(11)), except that the court cannot include requirements for medical and psychiatric examination and treatment in an interim supervision order (1989 Act, s.38(9)).

(iv) Care orders

Once a child has gone into care, the court does not generally have any power to direct the local authority how he is to be looked after or brought up. The authority are in the driving seat. This was controversial, particularly amongst those with experience of the wardship system, under which the court could give directions about what was to be done and any important step in the child's life had to be referred to the court. Many people felt that some steps, such as a move into long term fostering with a view to adoption, were so important that the parents should have the right to challenge them directly. Others felt that although courts could decide disputes between people who were putting forward alternative proposals, they could not oblige anyone to look after a child in a particular way. They could not conjure up the right kind of placement for every child or decide upon the delicate questions of resource management involved (R.C.C.L., 1985). The compromise was to give the courts considerable control over the contact which was to be allowed between the child and his family, which would obviously have important consequences for the type of placement which would be feasible, without giving them control over the placement as such.

(a) *Parental responsibilities*

A care order places the child in the care of a designated local authority (1989 Act, s.31(1)), who then have parental responsibility for him (1989 Act, s.31(3)(*a*)). This is important: the Report of the Inquiry into the Death of Tyra Henry (Sedley, 1987) illustrated how easy it was for an authority to forget that they were responsible for the care and maintenance of a child who was subject to a care order even if they allowed that child to live at home. This is emphasised by the authority's duties to receive the child into their care and keep him there for as long as the order is in force (1989 Act, s.33(1)) and to provide him with accommodation (1989 Act, s.22(1)(*a*)). This does not mean that the authority cannot allow the child to go home from time to time, provided that they observe the right procedures (see page 146, above).

Although the local authority have parental responsibility, the parents do not lose theirs. They still have a part to play, in partnership with the local authority, in bringing up their child, who is quite likely to come home to them, not only while he is in care, but in the long term. The local authority may, if satisfied that it is necessary in order to safeguard or promote the child's welfare, determine how far each parent (or guardian) may meet his or her responsibilities (1989 Act, s.33(3)(*b*),(4)). This may be particularly appropriate while the child is at home. The authority may feel, for example, that the parents should be told that they cannot change the child's school. But this does not stop a parent (or guardian) who has care of the child for the time being doing whatever is reasonable in all the circumstances in order to safeguard or promote the child's welfare (1989 Act, s.33(5)); nor does it affect any rights the parent may have under other legislation, for example to withhold consent to the child's marriage (1989 Act, s.33(9)).

The local authority are added to the list of those whose consent is required to the child's marriage, but they cannot bring the child up in a different religion from the one he would otherwise have had; or give or refuse consent to the child's adoption or freeing for adoption; or appoint a guardian for him (1989 Act, s.33(6)). No-one can change the child's surname or take him out of the United Kingdom without getting the written consent of everyone with parental responsibility or the court's leave or going through the emigration procedure (see Chapter 1), except that the authority can allow a trip abroad of no more than one month (1989 Act, s.33(7), (8)).

Apart from these special rules, the authority do of course have all the usual responsibilities for the children they are looking after (see Chapter 8). These include their duty to consult the child and his parents about any decision they are taking about his future, to promote the upbringing of children by their own families, and to promote contact between them.

(b) *Family contacts*

The local authority must allow the child to have reasonable contact with his parents, any guardian, and anyone who had the benefit of a residence order (or care and control in wardship proceedings) just before the care order was made (1989 Act, s.34(1)). This is not the same as saying that contact is in the discretion of the local authority; they must allow these people to have some contact with the child and that contact must in all the circumstances be reasonable. It is as if the court had made an order for reasonable contact.

However, before the court makes a care order at all, it must consider the contact arrangements proposed by the local authority and invite the parties to comment upon them (1989 Act, s.34(11)). If it considers these reasonable, it could leave matters as they stand. Alternatively, it could make an order dealing with contact. These orders can be made either at the same time as the care order or later (1989 Act, s.34(10)). They can also be made of the court's own motion, either when the care order is made or in any family proceedings relating to a child in care, even though no-one has applied for one (1989 Act, s.34(5)).

The court may make two kinds of order under the section: either:

(1) "such order as it considers appropriate with respect to the contact which is to be allowed between the child" and a particular person; applications can be made by the local authority, the child, anyone entitled to reasonable contact, and anyone else who has obtained the court's leave; (1989 Act, s.34(2),(3)); or

(2) "an order authorising the authority to refuse to allow contact between the child" and a particular person who would otherwise be entitled to reasonable contact; applications can only be made by the authority or the child (1989 Act, s.34(4)).

Either order can impose conditions (1989 Act, s.34(7)). Any order can be varied or discharged on the application of the authority, the child or the person named in it (1989 Act, s.34(9)).

The intention was that the court would either deal with the quantity and quality of the contact which was to be allowed or would permit the authority to suspend or terminate all contact, but not that the court would forbid the authority to allow any contact at all. Although the local authority have the principal responsibility for bringing up the child, they nevertheless share that responsibility with the child's parents unless and until the child is adopted into another family (or freed for adoption). The presumption is that the child should remain in touch with his parents (and other significant members of his family) although it may be necessary to define or control this. If the authority want to plan a permanent substitute home, they may want to bring all contact to an end; but if the authority change their mind, or the family circumstances change, it should surely be open to them to allow contact to continue or be resumed.

The court, especially if it has been used to the old wardship system, may have different ideas from the authority about what the long terms plans for the child should be. If the court thinks that a permanent substitute home for the child is the right solution, it may want to prohibit a rehabilitation plan which inevitably involves contact. In *Kent County Council v. C. and Another* [1993]

Fam. 57, it was said that an order of type (1) above could include an order that there be no contact, although this would usually be unwise as the parties could always depart from this by agreement. More importantly, if the court thinks that the authority are wrong to be planning a permanent substitute home and cutting off contact with the family, it can now order that contact is to continue and may even order the authority to carry out a further assess-ment (*Re B.* (*Minors*) (*Care: Contact: Local Authority's Plans*) [1993] 1 F.L.R. 543 C.A.). The child's welfare is the paramount consideration in contact cases.

There may be emergencies when it is necessary to refuse contact to someone who would otherwise be entitled to it, either under the general rule or under a court order. The authority can do this if satisfied that it is necessary to safeguard or promote the child's welfare, it is decided upon as a matter of urgency, and lasts for no more than seven days (1989 Act, s.34(6)). Written notice must be given to all concerned (see the Contact with Children Regulations 1991). The parties can also agree alterations to what has been ordered by the court (1989 Act, s.34(8)).

(c) *Duration, discharge and effect on other orders*

A care order of any sort kills all previous orders about the child; it discharges any section 8 order, including any residence order, any supervision order, and any school attendance order and if the child is a ward of court it brings the wardship to an end (1989 Act, s.91(2),(3),(4),(5)). A full care order lasts until the child is 18 unless it is brought to an end earlier (1989 Act, s.91(12)). It will be brought to an end either by being discharged (1989 Act, s.39(1)) or by the court making a residence order (1989 Act, s.91(1)). A residence order is the only sort of section 8 order which can be made while a care order is in force (1989 Act, s.9(1)).

An application to discharge a care order can be made by anyone who has parental responsibility for the child, or by the child himself, or by the designated local authority (1989 Act, s.39(1)). The same people can also apply for a supervision order to be substituted for the care order (1989 Act, s.39(4)) and the court can do this without having the threshold criteria proved again (1989 Act, s.39(5)).

Anyone else who wants the order discharged should apply for a residence order and most people will first need the court's leave to do this (see further in Chapter 7). An unmarried father who does not have parental responsibility does not need the court's leave to apply for a residence order. If he does not want the child to live with him but does want the order discharged he could instead apply simply for a parental responsibility order which would then give him the right to apply for discharge. The reported cases suggest that the courts might be sympathetic to an application for parental responsibility, even if the child is going to stay in care, so it would always be wise to apply (see Chapter 2).

Theoretically, if the court makes a residence order which brings a care order to an end, it cannot make a supervision order without having the threshold criteria proved—there is logic in this, as the child is unlikely to be returning to the same home which gave rise to the care order in the first place. However, if the local authority want to have a supervision order, it may be simpler for them to apply for the substitution while the others apply for the residence order.

(v) Supervision orders

Supervision orders used to be generally despised by social workers. If the child could be adequately protected by leaving him at home this was because the family were cooperating with the child protection plan. So there was no need for the hostility, uncertainty and aggravation involved in going to court. If the family were not cooperating, this would be made worse by the proceedings, and a supervision order was unlikely to be strong enough. It remains to be seen whether the changes made by the 1989 Act will affect this.

A supervision order places the child under the supervision of a designated local authority or a probation officer (1989 Act, s.31(1)(*b*)). The authority are that for the area where the child lives or will live unless another authority agree to act. A probation officer will only act if the local authority ask and there is already a probation officer working with another member of the household (1989 Act, s.35(2), Sched. 3, para. 9). The supervisor has to "advise, assist and befriend" the supervised child and to take such steps as are reasonably necessary to give effect to the order (1989 Act, s.35(1)(*a*),(*b*)).

The order can include all sorts of directions aimed either at the child or at the "responsible person", which means anyone with parental responsibility or with whom the child is living (1989 Act, s.35(2), Sched. 3, para. 1).

The order can require the child to comply with the supervisor's directions to do any or all of the following:

(a) to live at a specified place for specified period(s);

(b) to present himself to specified person(s) at place(s) on specified day(s);

(c) to participate in specified activities on specified day(s).

The precise content of the directions is for the supervisor to decide (para. 2(1),(2)). The total number of days which can be involved is 90 or any lesser amount specified in the order (para. 7).

The court can also require the child to submit to medical or psychiatric examination or treatment (paras. 4–5). This may be by a particular doctor, or as an out-patient at a particular place, or as an in-patient in a hospital (or in psychiatric cases a mental nursing home). To require an in-patient examination, or treatment of any kind, the court must have medical evidence (from a doctor approved under the Mental Health Act 1983 in the case of psychiatric treatment) of a condition which requires and may be susceptible to treatment (but in the case of psychiatric treatment is not such as to warrant compulsory admission under the 1983 Act) and, for an inpatient examination, that it cannot be done properly without. Satisfactory arrangements must already have been made for the proposed examination or treatment. If the child has sufficient understanding to make an informed decision, the requirement cannot be made without his consent. The period of any treatment requirement must be specified in the order, but no maximum is laid down. When a treatment requirement has been made, the doctor may decide that he does not want to go on or that the requirements should be varied in some way—if so he should report to the supervisor who should report to the court.

A "responsible person" can be required to take all reasonable steps to ensure that the child complies with the supervisor's directions (under para. 2) or the required medical or psychiatric examination or treatment (under paras. 4 or 5). He can also be required to comply with any directions given by the supervisor that he attend personally at a specified place for the purpose of taking part in specified activities, at a specified time and with or without the child (para. 3(1),(2)). These requirements can only be imposed upon a responsible person if he consents.

The order can require the child to keep the supervisor informed of any change in his address and to allow the supervisor to visit him at home. A responsible person must always inform the supervisor of the child's address if asked (and if he knows it), and may be required by the order to keep the supervisor informed of his own address if this is different from the child's. If a responsible person is living with the child, he must always allow the supervisor reasonable contact with the child (paras. 3(3), 8).

A supervision order lasts initially for one year; the supervisor can apply for it to be extended for specified period(s) totalling up to three years from the date when it was made (para. 6). The supervisor, the child himself, and anyone with parental responsibility can apply for it to be varied or discharged (1989 Act, s.39(3)); a "person responsible" who does not have parental responsibility can only apply for variation of the order as it affects him (1989 Act, s.39(4)). The supervisor must consider whether or not to apply for the order to be varied or discharged if it is not being complied with or he considers that it may no longer be necessary (1989 Act, s.35(1)(c)).

The Act does not provide any specific sanction for failing to comply with a supervision order, but of course all courts have general powers to punish disobedience to their orders. Nor does the Act provide specifically for a care order to be substituted for a supervision order. This means that if the order proves ineffective it will be necessary to prove the case for a care order all over again. In emergencies, of course, an E.P.O. can be obtained. The requirements which can now be imposed upon the child's family are quite tough, and may improve the attractions of the order, but some authorities may still be deterred by the lack of obvious inducements to comply.

(vi) Orders pending appeal

When care proceedings were modelled on criminal prosecutions, an unsuccessful applicant had no right of appeal on the merits, but could make the child a ward of court instead. Now that applications for care and supervision orders are modelled on other family proceedings, an unsuccessful applicant can appeal. If the court refuses an application for a care or supervision order, and at the time the child is the subject of an interim care or supervision order, or if it discharges a care or supervision order, the court can order that the care or supervision respectively is to continue until the time for appealing has gone by or an appeal has been determined (1989 Act, s.40). The appeal court cannot do this but, if the circumstances are right, it could make an interim order pending the determination of the appeal. Either way, the appeal should be heard quickly.

6. GUARDIANS *AD LITEM*

Under the previous law, care proceedings covered children who had committed crimes, children who had committed the so-called "status offences" of childhood, truancy or unruly or immoral behaviour falling short of crimes, and as something of an afterthought, children suffering abuse or neglect. Procedurally they were modelled on criminal proceedings against the child. The applicant and the child were the parties and originally the parents were not parties to the proceedings at all. In practice, however, the parents would usually be allowed to represent the child although there would often be a conflict of interest; this was clearly illustrated in the Maria Colwell story (Field-Fisher, 1973), where there was no-one to represent Maria's point of view when the local authority decided not to oppose her mother's application to discharge the care order, despite very clear indications from Maria that she did not want this. However, if legal aid was granted, the lawyer's duty was to the child and he could not take his instructions from the parents if these conflicted with his client's best interests; this might be good for the child but made things difficult for the parents. Some solicitors began to commission reports from independent social workers to advise them on this.

The Children Act 1975 first provided for panels of social workers to act as the guardians of the child's interests in care proceedings, in partnership with any lawyer engaged to represent him. The system was fully implemented in 1984 and extended under the 1989 Act. At the same time, it has been recognised that the parents' interests are also vitally affected and that they too should be full parties to the proceedings.

Guardians must be appointed in all public law proceedings, unless the court is satisfied that it is not necessary to do so in order to safeguard the child's interests (1989 Act, s.41(1)). The proceedings covered are applications to make, discharge, vary or extend a care order or supervision order, including applications for residence orders to replace a care order; referrals in family proceedings where the court has made or is thinking of making an interim care order; cases about contact, change of name, emigration or leaving the country relating to a child in care; secure accommodation cases (see Chapter 8); proceedings relating to child assessment and emergency protection orders; and appeals in all these proceedings (1989 Act, s.41(6); Family Proceedings Rules 1991 and Family Proceedings Courts (Children Act 1989) Rules 1991, r. 2(2)).

A guardian should therefore be appointed right at the beginning of the proceedings and can see them through to the end, but should not have any further role in the child's career (*Kent County Council* v. *C. and Another* [1993] Fam. 57). Her function is to safeguard the interests of the child in the proceedings (1989 Act, s.41(2)(*b*)), having regard to the checklist of factors in section 1(3) and to the principle that delay is likely to be prejudicial to the child's welfare (1991 Rules, r. 11(1)). She should sit in an directions hearings and advise the court about the child's maturity (for example to refuse medical examinations or assessment), his wishes (for example about coming to court), the timing and forum for the proceedings, the options available and the suitability of each. She should also advise other people whom she thinks it would be in the child's interests to be joined as a party (1991 Rules, r. 9(4), (6)).

Her main task is to investigate the case thoroughly and to prepare a report for the court, advising on the child's interests and the options available, and to provide the court with any other help it needs (1991 Rules, r. 11(9)(*a*), (10)). She has a right to inspect and copy all the local authority's records about the child, whether or not they were compiled for the purpose of the proceedings; anything she copies and refers to in her report is admissible in evidence, even if the authority could otherwise claim public interest immunity for it (1989 Act, s.42); she must therefore tell the court about anything she find which will help in its decision (1991 Rules, r. 11(9)(*b*)); she also has the right to inspect the records of voluntary organisations and registered children's homes (Children's Homes Regulations 1991, reg. 16). Finally, she may obtain whatever professional help she thinks appropriate or the court directs. This means that in an especially difficult case she can instruct a child psychiatrist and other relevant experts to give evidence on behalf of the child (1991 Rules, r. 11(9)(*c*)).

The child is a party and automatically entitled to legal aid. It is no longer assumed that he must attend, although the court can order him to do so (1989 Act, s.95). Magistrates' courts are used to him being there, while the High Court is probably more comfortable if he is not and guardians have been advised to think carefully before arranging for the child to attend even if he wants to do so (*Re G. (A Minor: Care Order, The Times,* November 19, 1992). The guardian must appoint a solicitor unless the court has already done so (1991 Rules, r. 11(2)(*a*)). Normally, the solicitor will act on the guardian's instructions; however, if the child wants to give different instructions and the solicitor considers that he is able to do so, he must act on the child's instructions; the guardian must still try to represent the child's best interests and may seek leave to have separate legal representation for herself. If there is no guardian *ad litem*, and the child is able and willing to give instructions, the solicitor must act upon them; otherwise he must further the child's best interests (1991 Rules, r. 12(1)).

Hence the guardian's role is unambiguous: she must further the child's best interests, even if her view of these conflicts with the child's own wishes. If the child has "sufficient understanding", however, he is entitled to have his solicitor advocate those wishes before the court. He is not entitled to change his guardian, but he is entitled to ask for a different solicitor (1991 Rules, r. 12(3)). It was wrong for a solicitor to continue to act for both when it was clear that the views of the guardian differed from those of an intelligent though emotionally disturbed boy of 15 (*Re H. (A Minor) (Care Proceedings: Child's Wishes)* [1993] 1 F.L.R. 440).

Each local authority must set up a panel from which guardians must be chosen (1991 Act, s.41(7),(9); Guardians *ad litem* and Reporting Officers (Panels) Regulations 1991). The panel administrator is appointed and employed by the authority but must be independent of their social services department; similarly, the panel members are appointed and paid by the authority; in care proceedings they are always social workers, either self-employed, or working for a local authority or voluntary organisation (probation officers can act in adoptions but not care proceedings); but the guardian in any particular case must be independent of the local authority, N.S.P.C.C. or any voluntary organisation concerned in the case and must not have been professionally involved as a social worker with the child at any time during the past five years (1991 Rules, r. 10(7)).

Should guardians be social workers, probation officers or some-one quite different? It is vital that the child and his family feel that the guardian is genuinely independent of the authority who are trying to take the child away. It is also vital that the guardian is able both to communicate with everyone, but particularly the child, and to conduct a proper review of the quality of the work which has been done. Unfortunately, people who are good at talking to children and their parents are not always so good at talking to courts and judges, who tend to feel more comfortable with a rather different style.

7. THE INHERENT JURISDICTION

Wardship and local authority care are no longer compatible. The High Court's inherent jurisdiction (see Chapter 4) cannot be used to put a child in care or in local authority accommodation or under local authority supervision or to make a care order child a ward of court or to give a local authority power to exercise parental responsibility over the child (1989 Act, s.100(2)). These things can only be done by way of orders under the Act and if a care order is made in respect of a ward of court, the child ceases to be a ward (1989 Act, s.91(4)).

In theory, the 1989 Act should have provided for all eventualities; just in case it has not, however, local authorities can still seek leave to invoke the inherent jurisdiction (1989 Act, s.100(3)); but they can only get leave if they want to do something which cannot be done by any other order for which they could apply (such as a care, supervision, specific issue or prohibited steps order under the Act) and there is reason to believe that child is likely to suffer significant harm if the court does not intervene (1989 Act, s.100(4),(5)). The case law about when this inherent jurisdiction can or should be used is in some confusion.

If a care or supervision order is not appropriate, the authority should be able to get leave to apply for a specific issue or prohibited steps order. The High Court has recently given leave to invoke the inherent jurisdiction in order to allow a child to be given a blood transfusion to which his parents objected (*Re S. (A Minor) (Medical Treatment)* [1993] 1 F.L.R. 376; *Re O. (A Minor)*, *The Times*, March 19, 1993). A later case has held that specific issue orders should be used in preference to the inherent jurisdiction (*Re R. (A Minor) (Blood Transfusion)*, *The Independent*, June 9, 1993). However, specific issue and prohibited steps orders are not available if the child is in care (1989 Act, s.9(1)); the authority are supposed to decide for themselves how to meet their parental responsibilities. They may therefore have to take issues such as sterilisation (see p. 17, above) to court in this way. There may also be times when the child needs the extra protection, particularly against harmful publicity, which only the High Court can give and sometimes it may be a last resort when all else fails (*South Glamorgan County Council* v. *W. and B.* [1993] 1 F.L.R. 574).

8. A CONCLUDING CASE HISTORY

Child abuse cases are always difficult even when the complexities of sexual abuse are not involved. Imagine a young woman with a serious personality disorder who becomes pregnant by a man she meets in a therapeutic community. This is her first baby but she has previously been convicted of assaults upon a disabled man who died as a result. A careful assessment is carried out by social workers who decide that because of her history and continued personality disorder her new-born baby will be at serious risk. They therefore obtain an interim care order shortly after the baby is born. However, it seems unduly harsh, to the mother and to the child, to deprive them of the opportunity of making a life together. The baby is placed with short-term foster parents, where he thrives, but he sees his mother several times a week while the proceedings are pending. After initial concerns that she is seeing him more like a possession or extension of herself, she begins to make some progress in understanding and responding to his needs. The case comes to court when the child is nearly six months old. Evidence is given by one adult psychiatrist and two child psychiatrists. All agree that the mother is not mentally ill but has a severe personality disorder of a type for which there is no conventional treatment other than the slow processes of maturation. They also agree that the parallels between the demands of a growing child and those of an emotionally dependent disabled man are sufficiently close to give serious cause for concern about the child's safety. The mother wants to go to a residential mother and baby placement where she can learn under close supervision to live with others and look after her child on a full-time basis. The guardian fears that the mother will learn to cope with a relatively young baby in the protective environment of the residential placement, but that it will never be possible to be confident about his safety during the difficult and demanding days of toddlerhood, when mother and child will be trying to live independently for the very first time and that no package of protection which the local authority can devise will give sufficient guarantees. She therefore wants the child to be placed for adoption as soon as possible, before he has reached the age when he will be damaged by interrupting the attachment processes. One child psychiatrist agrees; the other thinks that, on balance, it is worthwhile trying out the residential placement; the adult psychiatrist is very pessimistic about the prognosis for the mother but uncertain of what will be best for the child.

Are the threshold criteria satisfied? What are the options? Which of these, in the light of the checklist, will be best for the child? Will an order be better than no order? If an order, should it be a supervision order with a requirements for mother and child? Or should it be a care order with extensive contact between mother and child? Or should it be a care order with permission to refuse contact so that a permanent substitute home can be found? If so, does it make sense in this case to provide for continued contact between mother and child or is a clean break the only sensible solution?

What difference would it make if the mother and father had developed a relationship which might be lasting? Or if the father had shown an interest in developing a relationship with his son? Or change the facts rather more drastically and imagine that it is the father who has the history of violence towards others, and probably towards the mother too, although he has never been prosecuted for this; he may have a personality disorder but this has never been diagnosed because his offences were not seen as pathological in the way they would be if committed by a woman; but the mother is immature and inexperienced and completely dominated by the father. Would there have been enough reason to take the child away at birth? What should then happen if he is brought to casualty with quite serious bruising, for which at first the parents give unconvincing explanations and then refuse to give any explanation at all?

In such a case a good deal will depend upon the subsequent assessment of the most likely cause of the injuries, the child's general health and development, and what can be learned about his relationship with his mother and her ability to look after and protect him. The authority might prefer to assess this while the child stays at home, if the father can be persuaded to leave for a while; the authority have power to help him find somewhere to go, but at present the court has no power to require this while the assessment is going on (Law Commission, 1992).

Chapter 11

JUVENILE OFFENDING

When an adult is thought to have behaved in a way which the law defines as criminal, he will usually be prosecuted. He will be brought before a magistrates' court, which will either try him or, if the offence is serious, commit him to be tried by a judge and, if he pleads not guilty, a jury in the Crown Court. The normal adult is presumed to know the law, to know what he was doing, and to have chosen freely to do it. He may properly suffer his just desserts, provided always that his guilt has been admitted, or proved beyond reasonable doubt in a trial which bristles with procedural and evidential safeguards. These are not just for the benefit of the individual accused. They are there to reassure the rest of us that no-one is unjustly punished. If we keep to the rules, nothing can be done to us. The case will be heard in open court, before the press and public, and if he pleads or is found guilty he will be sentenced.

The sentence is designed to protect society by removing, reforming or deterring him, and by deterring others, but it is also a punishment intended to reflect the extent of society's disapproval of his conduct. As such it should be related in gravity and length to the gravity of the offence, on a so-called "tariff". This sounds and is punitive, but it also limits the sentences of those who have committed relatively minor offences, even if they are virtually certain to do it again when released. The tariff sentence may be reduced if there are mitigating factors suggesting that a more lenient course would do more good for the offender and thus for society. In a few cases, notably of mental disorder, the court may make an order which is intended to do good rather than to punish. But the price which the offender must pay is that those who are doing him good are allowed as long as they need to complete the cure. The tariff no longer applies.

If the offender is a juvenile, it is harder to ascribe his offences to free will and much easier to put them down to the normal naughtiness of growing up or to poor family and environmental influences. It seems foolish to invoke the majesty of the law to deal with the first, while the second might merit not punishment but an attempt to mend matters before it is too late. Our juvenile justice system tends to swing uneasily between the "justice" and "welfare" models (Parsloe, 1978; *cf.* Priestley, Fears and Fuller, 1977; Taylor, Lacey

---

213

and Bracken, 1979; Morris, Giller, Szwed and Geach, 1980).

Up until the Children and Young Persons Act 1969 it was a modified version of the adult system, more approachable in its procedures and more humane in its disposals, but operating on basically the same principles. The philosophy behind the 1969 Act (Home Office, 1965 and 1968) was that each case should be looked at in the light of the needs of the individual child. If these could be met in other ways, then prosecution was to be avoided. Indeed, for children under 14, it was to be prohibited altogether, except for homicide; and for young persons, it was to be limited to particular types of case and where nothing else would do. However, an alternative was to be provided, not only for those cases where prosecution was prohibited or restricted, but to allow a less punitive form of proceeding in any case. This was care proceedings, where the applicant had not only to show that the child had committed an offence but also that a court order was required to give him the care or control which he needed. In theory, care proceedings did not involve the stigma of prosecution. The only orders available were designed to help and not to punish. The same orders were also to be the principal disposals in criminal proceedings, although a few more punitive orders were retained as well.

However, these changes were attacked from the beginning for being unfair to children who committed identical offences, perhaps together, but who came from different backgrounds. The restrictions on prosecution were never brought into force, so that the more cumbersome alternative of care proceedings was scarcely ever used. It has now been abolished. The reasons are practical, but the welfare philosophy on which the 1969 Act was based has fallen foul of radical thought on both the left and the right. The Children Act 1989 and the Criminal Justice Act 1991 have together brought about a complete retreat from its principles, at least once a juvenile offender gets to court. Diversion from prosecution is still encouraged, and there are some specialist disposals for younger offenders, but once at court the principles of liability and sentencing are much the same as they are for adults. Criminal cases are now dealt with in a "Youth Court" which is separate from the family proceedings court dealing with care and other civil proceedings. "Juveniles" now include anyone under 18 (Children and Young Persons Act 1933, s.107(1); 1969 Act, s.70(1)), except in police stations where they still become adults at 17. References to a "child" in this chapter will cover all juveniles, unless it is necessary to distinguish between a child under 14 and a young person of 14 to 17.

1. THE CRIMINAL RESPONSIBILITY OF JUVENILES

Should children be expected to learn and obey the same rules as the rest of us? By and large, the criminal law is the same for children as it is for adults, but it is conclusively presumed that no child under 10 can be guilty of any crime (Children and Young Persons Act 1933, s.50). A child of 10 and under

14 can be found guilty of crime, but in theory he is presumed to be incapable of it (*doli incapax*) until the prosecution proves otherwise. To rebut this, in addition to proving the offence, the prosecution must show that the child knew it was seriously wrong (*J.M.* v. *Runeckles* (1984) 79 Cr.App.R. 255); but this seems inept for minor offences and it is probably enough to show that he knew it was a crime (Law Commission, 1989). It is not enough for a boy of nearly 12 to know that his acts amounted to childish mischief (*H. (A Minor)* v. *Chief Constable of South Wales, The Times,* July 5, 1986). It may sometimes be enough to show that the child was of normal intelligence for his age (*J.B.H. and J.H. (Minors)* v. *O'Connell* [1981] Crim.L.R. 632), but it is not necessary. A child of 14 is regarded as just as responsible for his criminal behaviour as is an adult. In all criminal proceedings, of course, it is necessary for the accused either to admit his guilt or for the prosecution to prove it beyond reasonable doubt.

One effect of the Children Act 1989 has been to draw a much sharper distinction between prosecuting a child for a criminal offence and bringing care proceedings in respect of him. They now come before different courts and lead to very different results. Even so, a local authority can apply for a care or supervision order on the basis that the child is suffering or likely to suffer significant harm because he is not being looked after properly or is beyond parental control. The court is not then burdened by the concepts of criminal responsibility, or the stricter standard of proof. The child may find it hard to understand the difference between care proceedings and punishment, particularly for truancy. Some countries solve this problem by giving the same "due process" safeguards to "unmanageable" children as they do to offenders. Here, we have theoretically abolished this category of care case (R.C.C.L., 1985; D.H.S.S., 1987); but while children may thus have been protected from punishment disguised as care, they may also have been exposed to a more punitive approach in criminal proceedings.

2. TAKING JUVENILES TO COURT

(i) Diversion or prosecution?

It is accepted that there should be a presumption against prosecuting juvenile offenders and there are several other ways of dealing with them; these include taking no further action, giving an informal warning, or administering an instant or formal caution. Recently, the Home Office has tried to encourage the greater use of cautions for older offenders, so the present guidance (Home Office, 1990) covers them all.

One possibility is undoubtedly to do nothing. Another is for the police officer to deliver an unofficial "ticking off" on the spot. Either may be thought right if there is serious doubt about whether the child is responsible, or the offence is very trivial, or if the family is known or can be contacted quickly and is willing and able to take any necessary action itself. The incident is not formally recorded and a damaging over-reaction to "normal" naughtiness is avoided. But the police have always to bear in mind that if certain children, particularly those from "good" homes (which are still so often thought associated with social class), appear to be escaping official action altogether, others may feel a grave sense of injustice.

A common course is the official caution. This is a formal warning, delivered by a senior uniformed policeman, to the effect that although the matter will be taken no further on this occasion it would be advisable not to do it again. In more straightforward cases it can be given very soon after the offence without the usual consultation required before a formal caution. Both types are recorded against the child and may later be cited in court. The experience may deter many a child from again incurring official displeasure, and its immediacy and form may make it more effective as well as less damaging than a court appearance. Cautioning has steadily increased; by 1984, it was used for 79 per cent. of children found guilty or cautioned and 50 per cent. of young persons (Home Office, 1986a) and it has continued to increase since then.

Cautioning does give the child a "record" of sorts and there is a risk that official cautions have increased, not only at the expense of court appearances, but also at the expense of informal on-the-spot warnings. Perhaps worse, a caution should not be used unless the child and his parents have admitted his guilt and agreed to be cautioned. The child, therefore, may be faced with a choice between admitting it and being "let off" with a caution, or denying it and being taken to court. Although prosecution is not the inevitable consequence of a refusal to be cautioned, this is often how it will appear, however scrupulous the police. The same problem arises with all official methods of "diverting" children out of court, whether by informal supervision or other voluntary steps. Hence the police should always have enough evidence to launch a prosecution before they decide on an official caution instead.

Whether the public interest requires them to prosecute must also be considered. Many factors may lead to court action. It used to be almost automatic for traffic offences committed by juveniles, however trivial, on the curious ground that these are not "real" crime. If the child does not admit his guilt, the authorities may be reluctant to let the matter go even if a court appearance would not otherwise be indicated. If the offence was committed in the company of others, it may be desirable to treat them all alike to avoid allegations of bias. This may mean that if someone aged 17 or over is involved, the child may not escape prosecution because the adult will not, unless discrimination between them is justified by the circumstances of the offence. The views of any victim of the offence should also be considered, for if the child is prosecuted, the court may order either the child or his parents to pay compensation. Most important of all are the seriousness of the offence, the child's past record of offending, and his attitude to the current offence. While minor and first offenders should normally be cautioned to keep them out of the system as long as possible, and serious or persistent offenders prosecuted, in the middle much will depend on the offender's character and family circumstances.

The police are therefore advised to make more extensive enquiries and to consult other agencies before deciding what to do. Many have specialist juvenile liaison machinery for the purpose. Social services authorities have a duty to provide services to reduce the need to prosecute juveniles. The Crown Prosecution Service is also instructed to regard prosecution as a last resort and to consider the juvenile's welfare as well as the public interest before continuing a prosecution begun by the police. Once proceedings are begun, the local authority (1969 Act, s.5(8),(9)) and, if the child is aged 13 or over, the probation service (1969 Act, s.34(2)) must be notified.

(ii) Procedure before trial

A juvenile may simply be summonsed to appear in court, but if he is arrested (with or without a warrant), he may be detained for inquiries like any other alleged offender, under the Police and Criminal Evidence Act 1984 (PACE) (the maximum without charge is 36 hours, extendable by magistrates for up to 96 hours). Whenever a juvenile is in police detention, his parent or guardian, or the local authority if he is in care for any reason, or anyone else who has assumed responsibility for him, should be found and told as soon as possible; any supervisor under either the 1969 Act or the 1989 Act, and any local authority which is accommodating him under the 1989 Act should also be told as soon as possible (1933 Act, s.34(2)–(11); see also PACE Code of Practice (C)3.7, 3.8, 3.9). Confusingly, a "juvenile" for this purpose, and for the PACE procedures generally, means someone under 17 (S.I. 1992/333, Art. 2(4)).

A detained juvenile should not be interviewed or asked to make a statement without an "appropriate adult" (once again, his parent or guardian, or the care authority, or a social worker, or some other responsible adult who is independent of the police), unless delay would involve immediate risk of harm to people or serious loss of or damage to property (Code of Practice (C) 11.14, 11.15, 11.16). A non-parent is obviously preferable if the parent may himself be involved in the offence. The adult's role is active: to advise the child, to observe the fairness of the interview, and to help the police and child communicate with one another. The police are warned that the child's information may be "unreliable, misleading or self-incriminating" and to check it if they can. The child has all the same rights as anyone else under PACE (for example, to consult a solicitor or phone a friend) as well. Children should not be interviewed at school unless the Head agrees and the circumstances are exceptional and they should only be arrested there if it is unavoidable.

Detained juveniles should not be put in police cells unless there is nowhere else where they can be properly supervised (Code of Practice (C) 8.8). Generally, while juveniles are detained in police stations, or being taken to and from court, or waiting in court, arrangements must be made to prevent their associating with any adult defendant apart from a relative or one jointly charged with the same offence. Girls must be under the care of a woman (1933 Act, s.31(1)).

Once an arrested juvenile is charged, he must normally be given bail, although unlike an adult he may be detained "in his own interests" (1984 Act, s.38(1)). If detained, he must be moved to local authority accommodation, unless (a) this is impracticable, or (b) he is 15 or more, there is no secure accommodation available, and keeping him in other local authority accommodation would not be enough to protect the public from serious harm from him (if he is charged with a sexual or violent offence, this means death or serious personal injury from other such offences) (1984 Act, s.38(6)–(8)). He must normally be brought to court next day (s.46). He then has a right to bail (Bail Act 1976), unless there are good reasons for thinking that he would not appear, or would commit an offence or obstruct the course of justice while on bail, or he requires to be detained for his own protection or welfare.

If he is refused bail, he must be remanded to local authority accommodation (1969 Act, s.23(1),(3)). The court can impose conditions on the child in the same way that it could if he were on bail (1969 Act, s.23(7),(8),(10)); it can also require the local authority's help in securing compliance with these and forbid the authority to place the child with a particular person (1969 Act, s.23(9)). The local authority must be consulted first. However, the child can only be kept in secure accommodation if the local authority apply (to the criminal court) under section 25 of the 1989 Act (see Chapter 8). The criteria are wider than in ordinary cases: (a) the offence charged must be violent sexual or very serious (*i.e.* punishable with 14 or more years in prison) or allegedly committed while on remand by a child who has a recent history of absconding while on remand to local authority accommodation; and (b) the child must be likely to abscond from ordinary accommodation or to injure himself or others if kept there (Secure Accommodation Regulations 1991, reg. 6). However the usual Children Act welfare and "no order" principles apply.

The court can remand some boys (not girls) aged 15 or more to a remand centre or prison instead of to local authority accommodation (1969 Act, s.23(4)). The offence criteria are the same as for secure accommodation and the court must think that sending him to prison is the only thing which will protect the public from serious harm (1969 Act, s.23(5)). The boy must first be given the opportunity of legal representation and the court must give reasons (1969 Act, s.23(4A)(6)). A local authority to which such a boy is remanded can later apply for him to be sent to a remand centre or prison instead (1969 Act, s.23(9A)). Under the Criminal Justice Act 1991, the eventual plan is to phase out remands to prison, but only once there is enough local authority secure accommodation to which the court can remand offenders. Whether remanded to the local authority or to prison, a child has the usual right to apply to a Crown Court judge for bail. The same rules apply to juveniles who are committed for trial or sentence in the Crown Court (see 3.(i) below).

3. YOUTH COURTS

(i) Jurisdiction

A juvenile under 18 who is prosecuted must normally be tried in a youth court, rather than an ordinary magistrates' court or the Crown Court, even if the offence is a serious one for which an adult would have or could choose to be tried by jury. The main exceptions are for homicide, some very serious charges, and cases where adults are also involved:

(a) All "homicide" charges must be tried in the Crown Court; these include murder, manslaughter and other unlawful killings, but not attempts.

(b) Juveniles aged 14 or over who are charged with very serious offences (*i.e.* punishable with 14 or more years' in prison) may be sent for trial in the Crown Court if the magistrates think that it ought to be possible to order them to be detained for a long fixed period (Magistrates' Courts Act 1980, s.24(1)(a)); children under 14 cannot be sent to the Crown Court for this reason, but if they are there for some other reason, the detention order could be made.

(c) Juveniles who are charged jointly with "adults" aged 18 or more must first appear in the ordinary magistrates' court (1933 Act, s.46(1)(a)). If the charge is serious, the court may, but need not, commit the juvenile for trial with the adult in the Crown Court; and if so, the juvenile may also be committed for any other serious charges which are connected with it (Magistrates' Courts Act 1980, s.24(1)(b), (2)). If the juvenile has pleaded not guilty, while the adult has pleaded guilty or been discharged or been committed for trial in the Crown Court, the magistrates' court may send the juvenile for trial in the youth court (Magistrates' Courts Act 1980, s.29). Otherwise, both will remain in the ordinary magistrates' court. A juvenile may also, but need not, be tried there on charges which are not joint, but are in some way connected with an offence with which an adult is charged (1963 Act, s.18(b)) or where an adult is charged with aiding and abetting a juvenile (1933 Act, s.46(1)(b)) or vice versa (1963 Act, s.18(a)).

(d) If a juvenile appears in the adult court by mistake, the magistrates may if they wish go on and decide the result (1933 Act, s.46(1)(a) and note s.46(1A) where juveniles plead guilty to motoring offences by post).

However, even if he is tried (*i.e.* has pleaded or is found guilty) in an adult court, a juvenile must be sent to the youth court to be dealt with, unless the offence is homicide or the trial court thinks this "undesirable" (1933 Act, s.56). The Crown Court may well have more reason to think this than a magistrates' court. In any case, an adult magistrates' court must remit the juvenile to the youth court unless it decides to impose only a discharge, fine or parental recognisances (1969 Act, s.7(8)). Conversely, if a youth or magistrates' court thinks a young offender aged 15 or more ought to receive more than six months' detention (and the offence carries this), it may commit him to the Crown Court for sentence (1980 Act, s.37(1)).

Incidentally, a youth court may continue if a person reaches 18 after proceedings have begun (1963 Act, s.29(1)), but he may also elect jury trial and be given an adult sentence if he reaches that age before the decision is taken (*R. v. Islington North Juvenile Court, ex p. Daley* [1983] A.C. 347).

(ii) Constitution

Special courts for the trial of juvenile offenders were first set up in 1908. The object was and is to provide a tribunal which is separate from the adult courts with all their undesirable associations and better suited to the youngsters' needs. Suggestions during the 1960s for a more radical departure from the ordinary court process, along similar lines to the Children's Hearings in Scotland, were rejected and youth courts remain just specially constituted magistrates' courts.

The aim of keeping juveniles apart from adult courts is probably best realised in very large towns, where the pressure of business is sufficient to justify a specially designed court in a different building, or in much smaller places, where it is possible to hold juvenile courts on different days albeit in the same building. The only legal requirement is that a youth court must not be held in the same room in which an adult court has sat or will sit within an hour (1933 Act, s.47(2)). Arrangements must be made to prevent juveniles waiting at court from associating with adult defendants unless these are relatives or jointly charged (1933 Act, s.31).

The magistrates must have been selected to serve on the youth court panel (1933 Act, s.45 and Sched. 2). In London a specialist panel is chosen by the Lord Chancellor, but in the provinces it is elected by the local magistrates from amongst themselves. No qualifications are laid down but members must be under 65 (Juvenile Courts (Constitution) Rules, 1954). It is suggested that they should be between 30 and 40, and certainly not over 50, when first appointed. They should have practical experience of dealing with young people, through teaching, youth organisations, welfare or similar work, and "a real appreciation of the surroundings and way of life of the children who are likely to come before the courts." No formal commitment to a "welfare" rather than a retributive theory of juvenile justice is required and courts vary considerably in their style and approach.

With the exception of stipendiary magistrates, who are lawyers with considerable practical experience but who usually do not sit in juvenile courts, magistrates are part-time unpaid laymen. They are advised on the law by their clerk, but while the Clerk to the Justices must be a lawyer, the assistant sitting in court may be unqualified. Lay magistrates must sit in twos or threes to try cases, and in youth courts there should be one of each sex. Stipendiaries may sit alone, but only if delay is "inexpedient."

(iii) Trial procedure

The procedure is basically the same as that in an ordinary magistrates' court, with a few modifications. This is thought more suitable for youngsters than the procedure of the Crown Court, because it is quicker, simpler and less formal. These are advantages if the child admits the offence, but summary trial can have drawbacks if he denies his guilt on a serious charge. The prosecution evidence does not have to be written down and given to him or his legal advisors in advance, as it is when someone is committed for trial in the Crown Court. The prosecution may now be required to produce at least a summary of its evidence in some cases (Magistates' Courts (Advance Information) Rules 1985), but the defence task is still more difficult. The magistrates combine the roles of judge and jury. They decide on guilt as well as on disposal, on any legal points as well as on disputed facts, and on the admissibility of evidence. These issues are kept strictly separate in the Crown Court, and with the best will and advice in the world lay magistrates can find this hard to do.

However, youth courts are still courts and conduct themselves in much the same way as others do. Outlawing the terms "conviction" and "sentence" and "promising" rather than "swearing" to tell the truth (1933 Act, ss.28 and 59) is mere window dressing. The main differences relate to the privacy of the hearing and the publicity it may be given. The law tries to diminish the trauma and stigma to the child while preserving the principle of open justice. The only people who may be present are those directly concerned in the case, representatives of the media and anyone else the court allows (1933 Act s.47(2)). Any parent or guardian can be required to attend throughout, and must be so required if the child is under 16, unless the court thinks this unreasonable in the circumstances (1933 Act, s.34A(1)); this applies just as much to a local authority having parental responsibility for the child, but if the child is living at home, they can all be required to come (1933 Act, s.34A(2)). The general public are not admitted. Nevertheless an alarming number of people can take part, and the child and his parents may be confronted with a bewildering row of tables, accommodating at least two magistrates, their clerk (who does most of the talking and is thought by many children to be in charge), the probation officer, the local authority's court liaison officer, a prosecutor and sundry police officers or ushers.

Press reports or other publicity given to youth court hearings must not disclose anything likely to identify the child or any other child concerned in the proceedings (such as a witness); but the court or Secretary of State can lift the ban in relation to a particular child for the purpose of avoiding injustice to him (1933 Act, s.49; 1963 Act, s.57(4)). This also applies to appeals (1963 Act, s.57(2)). Children appearing in other courts do not have the same automatic protection, but the court has power to prohibit identifying publicity (1933 Act, s.39; 1963 Act, s.57(4)). It usually either does so or relies on the restraint of the press itself.

The actual hearing follows the same pattern as in other courts, and this is often confusing to a child or his parents, who are given only limited help by the rules (Magistrates' Courts (Children and Young Persons) Rules 1992). The court has to explain the nature of the proceedings and substance of the charge to the child in simple language and ask whether he pleads guilty or not guilty (1992 Rules, rr. 6 and 7). The High Court has said that:

> "where the defendant is not represented or where the defendant is of tender age or for any other reasons there must necessarily be doubts as to his ability finally to decide whether he is guilty or not, the magistrate ought . . . to defer a final acceptance of the plea until he has a chance to learn a little bit more about the case, and to see whether there is some undisclosed factor which may render the unequivocal plea of guilty a misleading one" (*R.* v. *Blandford Justices, ex p. G.* [1967] 1 Q.B. 82).

The court can allow the child to change his plea, if this seems right, at any time before the final order is made (*S.* v. *Recorder of Manchester* [1971] A.C. 481), and in some cases should itself take the initiative.

If the charge is not admitted, the prosecution opens its case and calls witnesses, who may be cross-examined (1992 Rules, r. 8). If the child is not legally represented, the court must allow his parent to help him, and if the parent cannot be found or required to attend, the court may allow any relative or other responsible person to do so (1992 Rules, r. 5). If the child is neither legally represented nor given assistance, the court is allowed to translate assertions made by the child into questions for the purpose of cross-examining witnesses (1992 Rules, r. 8(3)). This is all very well, but many parents are equally unfamiliar with the concept of cross-examination and may have to be restrained from simply putting forward their child's version of events. The danger then is that they will see no point in doing so at the right time, after the prosecution case is finished (1992 Rules, r. 9). Some courts positively dislike legal representation for children, not only because it tends to impose more formality on the proceedings, but also because a lawyer will fight for what his client regards as the best result, whether or not it is what the court or the professionals think he needs (Anderson, 1978). It has been suggested that legal aid is unnecessary for juveniles, because the court must always "have regard to the welfare of the child" (1933 Act, s.44). Legal aid is however available, subject to his parents' means, at the discretion of the court.

Formality is always much more a matter of personalities and atmosphere than procedural rules. Some magistrates think it right to preserve a stern unbending countenance, in a deliberate attempt to strengthen the deterrent effect of the court appearance. Parents having trouble with a child may build up an appearance as an awe-inspiring experience and be disappointed if the court seems to bend over backwards to be kind. Other magistrates prefer to reject formality in favour of the Scottish model of a general discussion between themselves, the professionals and the family on the best way of helping the child out of his difficulties.

In Scotland, the children's hearing deals only with the treatment of those whose guilt is admitted, or proven elsewhere. This distances the circumstances of the offence from the choice of treatment, but there may be a greater risk of admissions in the hope of a quick and sympathetic disposal. In England, there is no reason why juvenile courts should not adopt a sympathetic appearance, but the central issue of innocence or guilt should not be lost sight of in the general concern for the child's welfare. Otherwise he will not receive that vital reassurance that nothing unpleasant can be done to those who keep the rules.

4. DISPOSAL

If guilt is admitted or proved, the court must allow both the child and his parents to make a statement; and before deciding on an order it must consider all the background information about the child's general conduct, home surroundings, school record and medical history (1992 Rules, r. 10(1)(2)). The police will supply their records, including cautions and the rest may be supplied by a pre-sentence report.

(i) Pre-sentence reports

Anyone prosecuting a juvenile must give notice to the local authority for the area where he lives (or, if he lives nowhere, where the offence was committed). If the child is aged 13 or over, notice must also be given to a probation officer for the court's area. It is then normally the duty of the local authority to make investigations and produce a home surroundings report, unless this seems unnecessary (1969 Act, s.9); but if the child is aged 13 or over, this duty falls instead on the probation service in those areas where arrangements are in force for it to do so (s.34(3)). Either must comply with any request from the court for specific information or investigations (s.9 or Powers of Criminal Courts Act 1973, Sched. 3, para. 8). Courts must now obtain pre-sentence reports before imposing supervision orders with extra requirements, other community sentences, or any custodial penalty (1991 Act, ss.3(1), 7(3)). There is an exception where the court thinks a report unnecessary before imposing a custodial penalty for an offence which is so serious that it can normally only be tried in the Crown Court (1991 Act, s.3(2)), but this should surely never be made in a youth court.

Any written report from a probation officer, local authority, L.E.A., educational establishment or doctor can be received and considered by the court without being read aloud and if necessary for the child's sake the court can ask him or his parents to withdraw (1992 Rules, r. 10(2)(d),(e)). Copies of any written reports must be given to his lawyers, his parents (if there) and the child himself, unless the court thinks this impracticable because of his age or understanding or undesirable because it might do him *serious* harm (1992 Rules, r. 10(3)). If the child does not have a lawyer and has not seen or heard the report, or if he or his parents have been asked to leave, the court must tell the child the substance of anything which bears on his character or conduct and seems relevant to the order, unless this is impracticable having regard to his age and understanding (but should a child be prosecuted at all if he cannot understand the information on which the court's order will be based?); and the parent must be told of any relevant information bearing on his own character or conduct, or the character, conduct, home surroundings or health of his child (1992 Rules, r. 10(4)).

The object of this is to make sure that orders are not made on the basis of factual information contained in reports which the family has had no opportunity of seeing and challenging. This is an essential principle of open justice, however embarrassing it may be to a probation officer or social worker for his client to realise that he has revealed damaging information. Sometimes there may be information about the parents, or the home, or his own health, which ought not to be revealed to the child, and the rules allow some discretion. There is very little which may lawfully be kept from the parents.

It is usual for these reports to include details of the family structure and of the physical and material conditions in the home. There often follows an examination of the parents' characters, their relationships with one another and with this and other children, and their attitude to this offence. The child's own character and personality are covered, including any relevant medical and psychiatric history, his school record and attendance, his work record if he is old enough, his criminal record if he has one, and his attitude to this offence and the circumstances in which it was committed. If he is already in some residential establishment, the report may be made from there. It may well conclude with a recommendation for the disposal which the reporter feels most appropriate to the case.

This can place a social worker in a difficult position. He is there to provide essential objective information to the court, but he is often already involved with the child or his family. He could be reluctant to forfeit their trust by revealing certain things about them or making a "hostile" recommendation, particularly if he has to carry out any order which the court makes. He may feel obliged to be something of an advocate where a child is not represented. Yet he may also have been involved in the decision to bring the child before the court and his professional orientation is likely to be towards meeting the child's needs as he sees them rather than achieving what the child will see as a good result. Nor are recommendations which the court thinks unrealistic the best way of helping either the child or the court.

(ii) The principles

It can be difficult to make realistic recommendations to a youth court because there is so much uncertainty about what the court should be trying to do. Section 44(1) of the 1933 Act requires every court dealing with a juvenile offender to "have regard to the welfare of the child or young person and . . . in a proper case [to] take steps for removing him from undesirable surroundings, and for securing that proper provision is made for his education and training". This stops short of making his welfare the first, let alone the paramount, consideration, because a criminal court must sometimes give priority to the protection of the public. Both the welfare of the child and the protection of the public provide logical justifications for the complete abandonment of any "tariff" related to the seriousness of the offence. They rather suggest that it should be replaced by a "ladder", which the child climbs at each successive court appearance. The less drastic orders have obviously failed to meet either his need for a more constructive upbringing or our need for him to stop committing offences. More drastic intervention is therefore required, however trivial the occasion for invoking it. This approach was particularly seductive in the early days after the 1969 Act, when the principal responsibility for dealing with juvenile offenders was transferred to local social services authorities and the disposals available were almost all therapeutic or welfarist in their intent. The major disposals, apart from discharges and fines, were supervision or care orders, and custody was reserved for the oldest and most serious offenders.

Recent Criminal Justice Acts, together with the Children Act 1989, have brought about a dramatic change, away from welfarist disposals and back towards proportionality and punishment. As a disposal in criminal cases, care orders had two controversial characteristics arising from their therapeutic aims. They could go on for a very long time indeed, usually for as long as the social workers thought it necessary, and the placement of the child during that time was entirely in their discretion. Hence they were attacked from all sides; by magistrates who were sorry that they no longer had power to insist on a definite period of detention in a secure home; by traditional libertarians who disliked the power to decide upon institutional treatment by bureaucratic machinery without due process of law; by more radical theorists who found the notion that care orders can cure either the child or his family of their pathology even more sinister than the old retributive or "tariff" principle; by those retributionists who still felt that a serious offence should receive a commensurate mark of society's disapproval; and by the children themselves, who saw only an indefinite and often uncomfortable period away from home in prospect, whatever might actually happen. The care order might still be defended if there were evidence that the children's needs were being individually and properly assessed and suitable treatment then devised, but such evidence was hard to find. Once the Criminal Justice Act 1982 made more punitive measures available for older juveniles, courts began to use them instead. Care orders more than halved between 1982 and 1984/85, when they accounted for only 4.2 per cent. of disposals of children under 14 for indictable offences and 1.9 per cent. of young persons' (Home Office, 1986a).

The 1989 Act took this to its logical conclusion and abolished the care order altogether in criminal cases (1989 Act, s.90(2)). The Criminal Justice Act 1991 increased the range of community sentences and rationalised the custodial penalties available. More importantly it reintroduced the "tariff" or proportionality principle as the guiding light for dealing with offenders of all ages. It provided that community and custodial penalties could only be imposed if the offence itself was serious enough to justify it and must be proportionate to the offence in their nature and extent. It tried to outlaw the "ladder" by saying that the offence is not made more serious because of the offender's previous record or his failure to respond to previous sentences (1991 Act, s.29(1)). All depended upon the elusive idea of the seriousness of the offence and the court had to take any aggravating or mitigating factors into account (1991 Act, ss.3(3)(a), 7(1)); a previous record could sometimes aggravate the offence (1991 Act, s.29(2)) but nowhere was it stated that youth is a mitigation. However, the Home Secretary announced in May 1993 that some of these new rules were to be dropped. Whether this means that youth courts can go back to their old ways remains to be seen.

5. THE ORDERS AVAILABLE

(i) Binding over and deferring sentence

Juvenile courts, as magistrates, have the ancient common law power to bind over those who disturb the peace not to do so again within a specified period, on pain of committal to custody for up to six months. No finding of guilt need be involved. They also have power to defer making an order for up to six months, with a view to taking an offender's later conduct into account (Powers of Criminal Courts Act 1973, s.1). The idea is not only to discourage further offences, but to encourage even better behaviour, such as making amends to a victim, by the hope of a lesser disposal. Both powers require the offender's consent.

(ii) Absolute and conditional discharge

An absolute discharge means that the offence has no further consequences, a conditional discharge that it has no further consequences provided that the offender does not offend again within a specified period of up to three years (Powers of Criminal Courts Act 1973, s.1A(1)). If he does, he may be sentenced again for the original offence and this must be explained to him in ordinary language when the order is made (1973 Act, ss.1A(3), 1B). Offences for which an offender is discharged are not treated as convictions for any purpose apart from the proceedings themselves, and driving penalties (1973 Act, s.1C; Road Traffic Act 1988, s.46). Discharges are the lowest rungs on the ladder, with minimal deterrent or therapeutic effect. Their continued popularity with youth courts must indicate either that a beneficial effect is attributed to a court appearance alone or that many children are still being needlessly prosecuted.

(iii) Fines, compensation and other payments

Fines can hardly be anything other than punishments, but they have always been remarkably popular in youth courts, perhaps because they are next on the ladder and have a built-in tariff. Magistrates may fine a child under 14 up to £250 and a young person up to £1,000 (Magistrates' Courts Act 1980, s.36), unless a lower maximum is laid down for the offence. Under the 1991 Act, the unit fine system applied to all offences unless they were so serious that an adult could only be tried in the Crown Court. The number of units was fixed according to the seriousness of the offence and then multiplied by the offender's disposable income. If the juvenile was to pay the fine himself, there were special rules for calculating his income (see 1991 Act, s.18). However, the Home Secretary announced in May 1993 that the unit fine system is to be scrapped. The court can also make an order for costs (Costs in Criminal Cases Act 1973, s.2(2)) and for compensation to be paid to the victim of any personal injury, loss or damage caused by the offence (charged or taken into consideration). Compensation can be ordered as well as or instead of any penalty and takes precedence over a fine if the offender cannot afford both (1973 Act, s.35(1),(4A)). The main problem with all these orders is ensuring that they are paid, and paid by the right person, whether the court thinks this is the juvenile himself or his parents.

The court must now order the parent or guardian to pay any fine, compensation or costs imposed upon a juvenile under 16, unless he cannot be found or it would be unreasonable in the circumstances to do so (1933 Act, s.55(1)); the same applies to fines imposed for breach of supervision or community service orders (1933 Act, s.55(1A)). Where the offender is 16 or 17, this is a power rather than a duty (1933 Act, s.55(1B)). If the court does this, the parent's income or means, rather than the child's, are used to assess the amount (1991 Act, s.57(3)). The parent should be given a hearing, unless he was required to attend the trial and did not do so. He can appeal against the order (1933 Act, s.55(2)–(4)). "Parent" presumably carries its pre-Children Act meaning, which excludes unmarried fathers, but "guardian" includes anyone who for the time being has "charge of or control over" the child (1933 Act, s.107(1)).

If a local authority have parental responsibility for a child who is in their care or is being provided with accommodation by them, the authority and not the parent are now responsible for paying the money (1933 Act, s.55(5)). A unit fine was assessed as if the child had the maximum disposable income for his age, but luckily other payments are not assessed according to the authority's means (1991 Act, s.57(4)). Even so, paying fines for their juvenile offenders is becoming a major item.

The 1969 Act abolished all sanctions against juvenile fine defaulters, leaving only the unlikely remedies of attachment of earnings, seizing his goods, or a fine supervision order. In 1977 the possibility of an attendance centre order was restored (see Criminal Justice Act 1982, s.17(1)), and powers to bind over a parent or guardian (with his consent) to see that the defaulter pays, or to order the parent or guardian to pay the remaining sum himself were introduced (see Magistrates' Courts Act 1980, s.81). None of these can be ordered without a personal inquiry into the defaulter's means, and an order against the parents can only be made if the child has actually had the money to pay but failed to use it for that purpose.

(iv) Parental recognisances

Another way of holding parents responsible for their children's misdeeds is to get them to promise, for a specified period of up to three years or until the child reaches 18 if earlier, to take proper care of him and exercise proper control over him (1991 Act, s.58(2)(a), 3(b)). The order may only be made with the parent or guardian's consent, but if this is unreasonably refused he can be fined up to £1,000 (1991 Act, s.58(2)(b), (4)). If the parent consents but he fails to keep his promise, he may forfeit a specified sum of up to £1,000, taking into account his means (1991 Act, s.58(3)(a), (5)). This is all in addition to whatever sentence is imposed on the child; if the child is under 16, the court has to do this if it will help to prevent him offending again, and if it does not do so, it must announce why (1991 Act, s.58(1)).

(v) Hospital and guardianship orders

These may only be imposed for prisonable offences (Mental Health Act 1983, s.37). The child must be suffering from mental illness, psychopathic disorder, significant or severe mental impairment. For a hospital order, psychopathic disorder and significant impairment must be "treatable". For guardianship, the child must be 16 or more. Neither order can be combined with a fine, supervision, or detention (s.37(8)). Each lasts initially for six months but may be renewed by the medical authorities for another six months and then for 12 months at a time. They may therefore last indefinitely, subject to review by a Mental Health Review Tribunal. They are hardly ever imposed upon juveniles.

(vi) Community sentences

The Criminal Justice Act 1991 has introduced the concept of a "community sentence". This means any or all of the following:

(i) a supervision order, available for offenders aged 10 to 17 inclusive;

(ii) an attendance centre order, available for offenders aged 10 to 20 inclusive; and

(iii) a probation order, community service order or combination order, available for offenders aged 16 or more.

A community sentence or sentences can only be imposed if the offence (or the offence and one other associated with it) is serious enough to warrant it (1991 Act, s.6(1)). The actual order or orders made have to be "commensurate with the seriousness of the offence (or the offence and others associated) as well as suitable for the offender (1991 Act, s.6(2)). This applies just as much to juveniles as to adults, although the orders available for children under 16 are very limited. It is not clear whether these provisions are to survive.

(a) *Supervision and intermediate treatment orders*

Under the 1969 Act, supervision orders were the same in criminal and civil cases. Changes made in 1977 and 1982 restored the order made in criminal proceedings to something more like probation and more possible requirements are added all the time. The court may place an offender under the supervision either of the local authority (for the area where he lives or some other authority with their agreement) or of a probation officer for the court's area; an offender under 13 must be supervised by the local authority, unless a probation officer is already working with another member of the household and the authority ask that he should also supervise the child (1969 Act, ss.7(7)(*b*), 11 and 13). Probation officers are specialists in working with offenders but social workers are specialists in working with children.

The supervisor's duty is to "advise, assist and befriend" the child (1969 Act, s.14) so the order can require the child to inform the supervisor immediately of any change of address or employment, to keep in touch with the supervisor as he directs, and to allow the supervisor to visit him at home (1969 Act, s.18(2)(*b*) and 1992 Rules, r. 29(2) and (3)).

The court may also require the child to live with a named individual who agrees to this (1969 Act, s.12(1)). More important are the court's powers to authorise intermediate treatment. This is intended to make a positive contribution towards widening the child's horizons and bringing him into contact with a different environment, interests and experiences, which may be more beneficial to him than a life of crime. In true therapeutic spirit the court simply decides what should be possible and fixes the maximum duration; then the supervisor decides whether, in what way and for how long to make use of that possibility. The child may be required from time to time to do all or any of the following: to live at a specified place or places for a specified period or periods; to present himself to a specified person or persons at a place or places for a specified period or periods; or to participate in specified activities on a specified day or days (1969 Act, s.12(2)). The total time required cannot be more than 90 days or a shorter period laid down by the court; days on which the supervisor's instructions have been disobeyed are ignored (1969 Act, s.12(3)). There is no statutory form for giving instructions, although the Home Office (1970) sensibly recommended writing them down, to avoid any later doubts and arguments.

The original idea was to avoid the impression that the court was ordering the child to do anything. It was hoped that the supervisor would be able to persuade the child that a particular activity was a good idea, as indeed most of them are; examples are outward bound centres, summer camps, sporting activities, scouting, handicrafts, evening classes, youth clubs, voluntary social service and community work. Most of these are only suitable for genuine volunteers. The D.H.S.S (1977) recommended that the whole family should be involved and that schemes should cater not only for children under statutory supervision but also for children who might otherwise come before the courts. This might help to reduce resentment in the families of children who have not committed offences; they may be equally unable to give the children all the opportunities for exciting activities that they would wish. However, although supervisors may be reluctant to emphasise the point, children under supervision orders are legally required to participate, and supervisors should keep records of what has been required and performed and of their clients' progress.

Alternatively, the court may now impose its own requirements on the child. When it does this instead of imposing a custodial sentence, it must explain why the criteria for what would otherwise be a custodial sentence (see page 233, below) are satisfied (1969 Act, s.12D). The requirements may be "positive," requiring him to do any of the things a supervisor may be authorised to require (1969 Act, s. 12A(3)(a)); or "negative," requiring him not to participate in specified activities (such as going to football matches) on a particular day or days or throughout all or part of the order (1969 Act, s.12A(3)(c)). The total number of days cannot exceed 90 (1969 Act, s.12A(4)); The court may also impose a curfew or "night restriction" order (1969 Act, s.12A(3)(b)). This requires the child to stay at a particular place or places, which must include his home, for up to 10 hours between 6.00 p.m. and 6.00 a.m., though he can leave if accompanied by his parent or guardian. The curfew cannot be imposed for more than 30 nights (1969 Act, s.12A(8)–(13)). None of these requirements can be imposed without the consent of the parent or guardian of a child under 14 or of a young person himself; the supervisor must be consulted about their feasibility; and the court must think them necessary to secure good conduct or prevent more offending (1969 Act, s.12A(6)). Anything requiring cooperation from another person needs that person's consent as well (1969 Act, s.12A(7)).

The court may also require an offender of school age to comply with the arrangements made by his parents for his education; his consent is not needed, but the approval of the L.E.A. to the arrangements is required (1969 Act, s.12C).

While abolishing the power to make care orders in criminal cases, the Children Act 1989 introduced power to require a juvenile under supervision to live in local authority accommodation for a specified period of up to six months (1969 Act, s.12AA(1),(5)). This can only be done if the child has previously been subject to a supervision order containing a requirement under section 12A(3) or under this new provision and while that order is in force the child is found guilty of a prisonable offence which the court thinks serious and (unless committed during a residence requirement) due, to a significant extent, "to the circumstances in which he was living" (1969 Act, s.12AA(6)). Although available for children of all ages, this is the closest the law comes to providing a custodial penalty for children under 14 (apart from section 53 of the 1933 Act, see (vii) below). The child must therefore be given the opportunity of legal representation (1969 Act, s.12AA(9)). The court must first consult the local authority involved (the one where the child lives) and can prohibit them placing the child with a particular person (1969 Act, s.12AA(2)–(4)). All the other possible requirements can be included too (1969 Act, s.12(11)).

Last, there is power to require psychiatric treatment. The court must have evidence from an approved specialist in mental disorder that the child's mental condition is "such as requires and may be susceptible to medical treatment" but is not such as to warrant a hospital order. It may then require him for a specified period to submit to in-patient treatment at any hospital other than a special hospital, or out-patient treatment at any specified place, or any treatment by or under the direction of a specified doctor (1969 Act, s.12B(1)). The requirement cannot be made, or inserted later, without the consent of a child who has reached 14 and cannot in any event last beyond the age of 18 (1969 Act, ss.12B(2), 16(7)). If the doctor in charge thinks that a change should be made in an existing requirement, he must report to the supervisor, who must refer it to the court, which can then cancel or vary the requirement (1969 Act, s.15(9), (10)).

Either the supervisor or the supervised person can apply for the court to discharge the order (but if this is refused, no-one can apply again within three months without the court's leave; 1969 Act, s.16(9)), or to add, vary or discharge any requirement which was or could have been made at the outset; except that a new curfew or psychiatric treatment requirement cannot be inserted after three months (1969 Act, s.15(1),(2)). If the supervised person does not comply with any requirement in the order (apart from psychiatric treatment), the supervisor can take him to court; the court can then impose a fine of up to £1,000 or an attendance centre order (1969 Act, s.15(3)(a)). Those aged 18 or more can be punished again (but not with detention) for the original offence (1969 Act, s.15(3)(b)), as can anyone who disobeys the court's order to take part in specified activities (under s.12A(3)(a)) having been warned (under s.12D) that this was imposed instead of custody (1969 Act, s.15(4)(b)).

Supervision orders last for three years or a shorter specified period and do not expire when the offender reaches 18 (1969 Act, s.17), although no new residence requirements can be inserted then (1969 Act, s.12AA(1)). However, probation orders are now available for 16- and 17-year-olds (see (c) below).

(b) *Attendance centre order*

This can be imposed for any offence punishable in the case of an adult by imprisonment, for fine default, and for breach of a supervision order (Criminal Justice Act 1982, s.17(1)). The standard length is 12 hours, but it can be less for a child under 14; and it can be more, up to 24 hours for a 14- or 15-year-old, or up to 36 hours for a 16- or 17-year-old, if 12 would be too little (1982 Act, s.17(4),(5)). There are three sorts of centre: juniors taking boys aged 10 to 17, junior mixed taking boys and girls aged 10 to 17 and seniors taking boys aged 16 to 20. Boys aged 16 and 17 should go to a senior centre if one is available locally (Home Office Circular 72/1992). Attendance centres open on Saturdays, seniors for three hours (which is the maximum in any one day; 1982 Act, s.17(11)), and juniors for two.

The object is to interfere with football matches but not with school or work (see 1982 Act, s.17(8)). Centres are provided by the Home Office, usually by arrangement with local police but sometimes with social services or education authorities. Schools and similar buildings are used. The regime includes physical training, "disciplinary tasks", craftwork and lectures. Registers are kept and the attenders must be orderly and obedient (Attendance Centre Rules 1958). Disobedience or absence may result in return to court to be fixed up to £1,000 or dealt with again for the original offence; in doing so, the court can assume that he has refused to consent to a community sentence (see below) so can impose a custodial penalty if appropriate (1982 Act, s.19(3)–(5A)). But orders may also be varied or discharged; and if made for default in payment, they lapse automatically if payment is made, pro rata for part payment (1982 Act, s.17(13)).

The Home Office considers that centres have three aims: to vindicate the law by loss of leisure; to bring the offender under the influence of representatives of state authority; and to teach the more constructive use of leisure. The child may perceive more of the first two than the last, but will appreciate the defined and limited nature of an order which has all the hallmarks of traditional punishment. As orders can only be made if a place in a reasonably accessible centre is available (1982 Act, s.17(7)), facilities have been expanded for a treatment which is apparently popular with almost everyone.

(c) Probation, community service and combination orders

These are only available for 16- and 17-year-old juveniles. A probation order can be imposed for any offence if it is desirable to rehabilitate the offender or to protect the public from harm or to prevent re-offending. The offender is placed under the supervision of a probation officer (not a social worker) for a specified period of between six months and three years (1973 Act, s.2(1)). He must agree to comply (1973 Act, s.2(3)). The minimum requirement is to keep in touch with the probation officer and notify changes of address (1973 Act, s.2(6)). Other requirements can be added, for residence, participation in activities or attending at a probation centre (for up to 60 days), refraining from certain activities, psychiatric treatment, and treatment for alcohol or drug dependency (1973 Act, Sched. 1A). Probation orders are often discharged early, once active supervision is no longer needed, but they can now be converted into a conditional discharge for the remainder of the term (1973 Act, s.11).

Community service (C.S.O.) can only be imposed for prisonable offences. The offender must perform between 40 and 240 hours unpaid work for the community (1973 Act, s.14(1)), normally to be completed within 12 months of the order (1973 Act, s.15(1)). His consent is required (1973 Act, s.14(2)). The work is organised by the probation service and is definitely intended as a punishment. Conflict with the offender's religious beliefs, work or education should if possible be avoided (1973 Act, s.15(3)). At its best, community service can be remarkably successful, especially for boys with nothing better to do, despite the tendency for courts and offenders to see it as a soft option.

Probation and community service can now be combined in a combination order, requiring between 12 months and three years' supervision and between 40 and 100 hours' work (1991 Act, s.11(11)). The offence must be one punishable with imprisonment and the order must be desirable for the same reasons as a probation order (1991 Act, s.11(2)). The effect of each part is the same as an ordinary probation order or C.S.O. (1991 Act, s.11(3)).

If an offender is in breach of a probation, community service or combination order, the court can either allow the sentence to continue but punish the breach (with a fine of up to £1,000, up to 60 hours' community service, or for breach of probation, an attendance centre order) or revoke the order and deal with him again for the original offence (1991 Act, Sched. 2, para. 3). Committing another offence during the order is no longer a breach as such. All these matters have to be explained to the offender in simple language when the order is bring made.

(vii) Custodial sentences

For a juvenile offender, there are three possible custodial sentences:

(i) detention in a young offender institution, for offenders aged between 15 and 20;

(ii) detention under section 53(2) of the Children and Young Persons Act 1933, for offenders aged between 10 and 17; and

(iii) detention for life under section 53(1) of the 1933 Act, again from the age of 10.

Under the 1991 Act, a custodial sentence can only be imposed in three situations (and except in the first the court must explain why): first, where an offender has refused to consent to a community sentence which requires it (1991 Act, s.1(3)); second, where he has committed a violent or sexual offence and only custody is enough to protect the public from serious harm (1991 Act, s.1(2)(b)); or third, where the offence committed, either on its own or in combination with *one* other associated with it, is "so serious that only such a sentence can be justified" (1991 Act, s.1(2)(a)). The fate of these provisions, and what might take their place, is not yet known.

The courts have been wrestling with the third idea for some time in relation to young adult offenders. Arson, unprovoked street violence causing injuries, and most kinds of domestic burglary have usually qualified on their own. Many youngsters, however, commit large numbers of smaller offences such as thefts from cars, joy-riding, criminal damage or shop-breaking, which by themselves might not be enough but taken together might be thought more serious. The 1991 Act provision that only two can be taken together for this purpose is apparently to be abandoned, but it is not clear what is to happen to the rules that the length of any custodial sentence must be proportionate to the seriousness of the offence, either alone or combined with any of the others associated with it (1991 Act, s.2(2)(a)); for a violent or sexual offence, the court can impose a longer term if this is necessary to protect the public from serious harm (1991 Act, s.2(2)(b)), but if so it must say why.

233

Detention in a young offender institution can only be imposed on offenders aged 15 or more. The minimum term is two months (1982 Act, s.1A(4A)); the maximum is 12 months in all (1982 Act, s.1B(2)(4)); magistrates (including youth) courts are limited to six months for any one offence, but can pass consecutive terms totalling no more than 12 months for two or more serious offences (1980 Act, s.133); of course the maximum for the offence itself always applies (1982 Act, s.1B(2)) but custody is unlikely to be appropriate at all for offences carrying less than 6 or 12 months. Magistrates who think that more than six months is right for the particular offence can commit the juvenile to the Crown Court for sentence (1980 Act, s.37); however, the Crown Court will still be limited to 12 months.

There is power to impose a longer period of detention, under section 53(2) of the Children and Young Persons Act 1933. This applies only to juveniles (of any age) who are actually tried in the Crown Court and found guilty of an offence for which an adult could be sentenced to 14 or more years in prison (or for indecent assault on a woman by a 16- or 17-year-old). Only children aged 14 or more can be committed for trial simply so that this will be possible; thus unless a child under 14 is committed there for some other reason, this power cannot apply. The Home Secretary decides where these offenders are held. Until they reach 19, this can be in a youth treatment centre or community home (1969 Act, s.30); otherwise it may be in a young offender institution or a prison.

The Court of Appeal has said that section 53(2) should not be used simply to get round the 12 month limit (*R.* v. *Horrocks* [1986] Crim.L.R.412; *R.* v. *Fairhurst* [1986] 1 W.L.R. 1374); but equally it is no longer limited to crimes of the utmost gravity for which it was obviously originally intended (*Fairhurst* again); in practice, therefore, it is a way of disregarding the limit, except perhaps for offences which are "worth" between 12 months and two years, when the difference may not merit it (*R.* v. *Dewberry and Stone* [1985] Crim.L.R. 412; *Fairhurst* again); for under 15-year-olds where this is the only custodial sentence available, shorter periods may well be imposed (*Fairhurst*, again).

All this looks like extending the same "tariff" as is applied to young adults (the 18- to 20-year-olds) down to the 15- to 17-year-olds who appear in the Crown Court. Quite what discount, if any, ought to be given for the offender's youth (*R.* v. *Burrows* [1985] Crim.L.R. 606) is not clear.

This trend is emphasised by bringing section 53 into the general scheme of rules about how long the offender actually spends "inside". Time spent on remand in police detention, prison or secure local authority accommodation is automatically deducted (Criminal Justice Act 1967, s.67). Anyone sentenced to no more than 12 months' detention is automatically entitled to be released after serving half (1991 Act, s.33). A young offender is then subject to supervision for three months (and can be fined or sentenced to up to 30 days' detention for breach) (1991 Act, s.65). If he commits another prisonable offence during the unexpired period of the sentence, he can be sent back into detention for the balance of time outstanding when he committed the offence (as well as anything imposed for the new offence)

(1991 Act, s.40(1)). If the sentence is between 12 months and four years, he is still entitled to be released after serving half, this time on licence until three-quarters of the term has gone by (1991 Act, ss.33, 37(1)). Offenders serving four years or more are entitled to release on licence after serving two-thirds (1991 Act, s.33) and are eligible for parole after serving one half (1991 Act, s.35).

Juveniles found guilty of murder are ordered to be detained during Her Majesty's Pleasure (1969 Act, s.53(1)). The effect is the same as a sentence of detention for life under section 53(2). They can be released on licence, but only on the recommendation of the Parole Board after consultation with the trial judge and the Lord Chief Justice.

6. COMMENTARY

Sixteen- and 17-year-olds are now treated very like young adults; 15-year-olds and some 14-year-olds can also be given custodial sentences; but for most offenders under 16 the most severe punishment available is supervision with a variety of requirements, for which the social services rather than the penal system are still responsible. The government has recently announced its intention to create a new Secure Training Order for 12- to 15-year-olds who commit three or more imprisonable offences while on remand or under sentence and who are unable or unwilling to comply with the requirements of supervision. When this happens, the retreat from the welfarist ideals of the 1969 Act will be almost complete; but it also seems that there is to be a retreat from the retribution ideals of the 1991 Act. When both have gone, what will there be left?

PART IV: A NEW START

Chapter 12

ADOPTION

Adoption is the virtually complete and irrevocable transfer of a child from one legal family to another. It was first introduced into English law in 1926; in other legal systems its purpose has been to provide an heir to carry on the family's name and property. In England its principal object is now to provide permanent and secure family care for a child whose natural parents are unable or unwilling to keep him. In the early days, when there was a good supply of healthy white babies for adoption, it may sometimes have seemed more concerned to provide childless couples with replacements for the children they were unable to have. The typical adoption was seen as the placement of a baby by an unmarried mother through an adoption society with a childless couple who were complete strangers to the natural family.

Nowadays, most adoptions are quite different. They involve step-parents adopting after the parents' relationship has ended through death, divorce or separation; or local authorities arranging permanent substitute families for children who have been removed from damaging homes or languished for long periods in local authority accommodation; or most recently of all, would-be parents going abroad, often to third world countries, to find orphaned or abandoned children to adopt. But the stereotype has had an important influence upon the law and its practice; and these are once again under review, to bring them more into line with what is actually going on (Adoption Law Review, 1992).

1. WHO CAN ADOPT AND BE ADOPTED

The qualifications to adopt and be adopted make some attempt to reproduce a normal family structure. A person can only be adopted while still a child under 18, and only then if he has never been married (Adoption Act 1976, ss.72(1) and 12(5)). Every applicant for adoption, whether related to the child or not, must be at least 21 years old (1976 Act, ss.14(1) and 15(1)). The law lays down no maximum age, but many agencies are known to set age limits.

It is reasonable to insist that people adopting a young child have a reasonable chance of remaining healthy, vigorous and financially stable throughout his childhood, and perhaps a little while longer. But different children have different needs and arbitrary rules of eligibility can impede the search. They can also cause great resentment if used as a simple rationing device, particularly for couples who have waited, then tried for a long time to have children, and then had complex but ultimately unsuccessful infertility investigations and treatment.

Applications may be made by one person or by two people together, but joint applicants must be married to one another (1976 Act, s.14(1)) and the stability of their relationship will be an important factor. Unmarried partners, whether heterosexual or homosexual cannot adopt jointly but one might apply to do so alone. Now that the Children Act 1989 allows unmarried parents to share parental responsibility equally, there is less reason to prevent them adopting jointly. However, if they are not prepared to accept a joint responsibility and commitment towards one another, should they be allowed to do so towards a child? The Adoption Law Review (1992) thought not. A sole applicant must either be unmarried (that is, single, widowed or divorced) or, if married, must satisfy the court that his or her spouse cannot be found or is incapable because of physical or mental ill-health of making an application or that they are living apart and the separation is likely to be permanent (1976 Act, s.15(1)). Applicants must attach medical reports to their application, unless one is the child's parent or it is an agency placement, when the agency will do so, for their health is an important factor in safeguarding the welfare of the child throughout his childhood.

The applicant, or one of joint applicants, must be domiciled in part of the United Kingdom, Channel Islands or Isle of Man (1976 Act, ss.14(2)(a) and 15(2)(a)). If this is not the case, it may be possible to obtain a convention adoption order (1976 Act, s.17) or an order allowing the applicant to take the child abroad to be adopted (1976 Act, s.55).

Adoptions by step-parents (Chapter 6), by one natural parent (Chapter 2) and by other relatives such as grandparents (Chapter 7) have already been discussed. They all raise problems because they do not conform to the traditional view (Houghton, 1972) that adoption should replace, rather than distort, the natural family. This emphasis on the clean break has also led to a tradition of secrecy in the adoption process, reflected in the procedure for concealing the applicants' identity under a serial number (Adoption Rules 1984, rr. 14 and 23(3)). This may protect them and the child from the problems which might arise should the mother regret her decision and try to trace them, but the mother does not have a similar privilege.

An important modern trend is towards more openness in adoption, not necessarily more contact between an adopted child and his birth family, but more involvement of the birth parents in the initial process, a greater exchange of information afterwards, and above all the acknowledgment that many adopted people will eventually feel curious about their origins and want to know as much as possible about them, whether or not they want to trace or meet their original parents.

2. ARRANGING ADOPTIONS

The law puts certain general limitations on arranging adoptions and also makes detailed rules about how individual placements are to be carried out.

(i) Prevention of "trafficking"

The first object is to stop children being bought and sold. It is a crime to give or receive any payment or reward either for giving or for receiving a child for adoption or for making the arrangements (1976 Act, s.57). Courts are prohibited from making adoption orders in favour of people who have broken this rule (1976 Act, s.24(2)). Contributions towards the expenses of an adoption agency are excepted, and so are payments specifically permitted by the court (1976 Act, s.57(3)). The court may approve these retrospectively at the time of the hearing (see *Re Adoption Application: Surrogacy* [1987] Fam.81, although there the judge held that payments made to a surrogate mother who had not acted for profit were not in fact "payment or reward" under this section). Adoption agencies can pay fees to one another or to approved voluntary organisations who put them in touch so that they can arrange adoptions for one another (1976 Act, s.57(3A)(b),(c)). This is especially important for specialist adoption services. Agencies can also pay prospective adopters' legal and medical expenses (1976 Act, s.57(3A)(a)) and adoption allowances in accordance with the Adoption Allowance Regulations 1991 (1976 Act, s.57A). The object is to encourage adoptions of whole families, handicapped children or long-term foster children, where applicants might be deterred by the expense or the loss of the fostering allowance.

It is also an offence either for parents or for prospective adopters to advertise their desire for adoption, or for anyone other than an adoption agency to advertise their willingness to make adoption arrangements (1976 Act, s.58). Contravening this, however, does not inevitably mean that the court cannot make an order.

(ii) Agency placement

The law also tries to ensure that the vital placement decisions are handled by qualified and experienced people who are not acting for personal profit. No "body of persons" is allowed to arrange adoptions apart from a local social services authority or approved adoption society (1976 Act, s.11). Adoption societies must be approved by the Secretary of State who may refuse or withdraw his approval, provided that he gives his reasons and an opportunity to make representations beforehand (1976 Act, ss.3, 4, 5, 8 and 9). All local social services authorities have a duty to provide a comprehensive adoption service to meet the needs of children who have been or may be adopted, their natural parents and people who have adopted or may adopt a child. These pre- and post-adoption services can be provided directly or through approved adoption societies (1976 Act, ss.1–2).

All agency placements are subject to the Adoption Agencies Regulations 1983, which should mean that they are superior to placements arranged by private individuals. For example, natural parents should have a clearer idea of what they are doing, because the agency must explain the legal implications and procedures and provide a counselling service for them; this includes unmarried fathers where it is practicable and in the child's interests (1983 Regulations, reg.7(1),(3)). The agency must discover a long list of particulars about them all and obtain a medical report upon the child (reg. 7(2),(3) and Sched.). The prospective adopters should be carefully chosen, for before accepting them as suitable, the agency must provide them with similar information and services, obtain another long list of particulars and a medical report, and also obtain reports on their home and on interviews with two referees, and from their local authority (reg. 8 and Sched.). The risk that placements might turn out badly, whether sooner or later, should be reduced because all the major decisions (that a child should be adopted or freed for adoption; that prospective adopters are suitable to adopt; that particular adopters are suitable for a particular child) can only be taken after considering the view of an expert adoption panel (regs. 11(1), 10, 9 and 5). When proposing the particular placement to the prospective adopters, the agency must give them written information about the child, his health, history and background. If they accept, the agency must follow up the placement with visits, advice and help (reg. 12).

The law requires an agency to give first consideration to the need to safeguard and promote the welfare of the child throughout his childhood (1976 Act, s.6). In recent years, the emphasis of adoption practice has shifted, away from providing the prospective adopters with the perfect babies they wanted to match the ones they were unable to have themselves, towards providing children of all shapes, colours, abilities and sizes with parents whose prime aim is to give a loving and stable home to a child in need. The child, rather than the prospective adopters, must be the first consideration. The agency must also discover, so far as this is practicable, the child's own wishes and feelings in the matter and give them appropriate weight having regard to his age and understanding (1976 Act, s.6; see also reg. 7). Finally, the agency must have regard so far as is practicable to any wishes of the natural parents about the child's religious upbringing (1976 Act, s.7).

After placement, an adoption order cannot be made unless the child is at least 19 weeks old and at all times during the previous 13 weeks has had his home with the applicants or one of them (1976 Act, s.13(1)). The court must also be satisfied that the agency has had sufficient opportunity to see the child with the applicant, or both applicants together, "in the home environment" (1976 Act, s.13(3)). The agency must then make a report to the court (Adoption Rules 1984, r. 22(1) and Sched. 2).

(iii) Private placements

The agency regulations obviously do not apply to private adoption placements, whether by third parties, such as doctors, lawyers or managers of nursing homes, or by the family itself. These placements gave rise to all sorts of concerns (Houghton, 1972). There might be little choice between applicants or children, little opportunity for expert matching or linking, inadequate counselling and supervision, evasion of the rules against payment, adopters who could have been rejected by other agencies, and potentially damaging contact between natural and adoptive families. On the other hand, the National Child Development Study found no evidence that the children did any worse than those who had been placed by supposedly more expert agencies (Seglow, Kellmer Pringle and Wedge, 1972). Nowadays, private placements are more likely to arise in inter-country adoptions, because there is at present no agency in this country to arrange them. All the usual concerns about private placements apply to these adoptions, together with many more—about the scope for child-stealing and deception, the long term risks of trans-racial or trans-cultural placements, and the pressures facing both the natural family and the prospective adopters who may for their different reasons be desperate for the transaction to take place.

Since 1984 it has been an offence for anyone other than an adoption agency to make arrangements or place a child for adoption, except with a relative or under an order of the High Court. It is also an offence to receive a child for adoption in such circumstances (1976 Act, s.11). These offences can be committed if any part of the prohibited conduct takes place in this country. However, the court still has power to make the adoption order and once the child has arrived in this country it may have little alternative but to do so, however great the misgivings (*Re A. (Adoption: Placement)* [1988] 1 W.L.R. 229; *Re An Adoption Application (Adoption of Non-Patrial)* [1992] 1 W.L.R. 596; *Re Adoption Application (Non-Patrial: Breach of Procedures)* [1993] 2 W.L.R. 110). The right way to go about it is to get the local authority to do a home study report, make the arrangements abroad, and then get entry clearance for the child. Instead of ignoring inter-country adoption, or hoping that it would go away, some proper system of regulation obviously has to be devised to meet the growing and understandable demand (Adoption Law Review, 1992).

If a child has not been placed for adoption by an agency, the 13-week probationary period applies if the applicant or one of them is a parent, step-parent or relative of the child, or if the child was placed by order of the High Court (1976 Act, s.13(1)). In any other case, an adoption order cannot be made unless the child is at least 12 months old and has had his home with one or both applicants throughout the preceding 12 months (1976 Act, s.13(2)).

Also, if the child was not placed by an adoption agency, the applicants (whether or not they are parents, step-parents or relatives) must give notice to the local authority for their home area at least three months before the order (1976 Act, s.22(1)). The child then becomes a "protected child" (1976 Act, s.32) and the authority must visit, in order to satisfy themselves about the child's well being and offer any necessary advice to the prospective adopters (1976 Act, s.3(1)). Social workers have power to inspect the premises (1976 Act, s.33(2)); refusal to let them in is a criminal offence (1976 Act, s.36(1)(*b*)).

More importantly, the authority must investigate the proposed adoption and report to the court (1976 Act, ss.22(2) and (3); Adoption Rules 1984, r. 22(2)). The court must be satisfied that the authority have been able to see the child and applicants together "in the home environment" (1976 Act, s.13(3)). The authority must investigate whether the child's placement was illegal. If it was, it has been suggested that only the High Court may grant the adoption order (*Re S. (Arrangements for Adoption)* [1985] F.L.R.579).

3. PARENTAL AGREEMENT

(i) Whose agreement is required?

No adoption order can be made unless the child is "freed" for adoption (see (iii) below) or the court is satisfied that each parent with parental responsibility, and each guardian of the child, freely and with full understanding of what is involved, agrees unconditionally to the making of that order, unless that agreement can be dispensed with (1976 Act, s.16(1)). Agreement is given in writing to a reporting officer appointed by the court, whose task is to witness it and ensure that it is genuine (1976 Act, s.65(1)(*b*) and Adoption Rules 1984, rr. 5 and 17). A mother cannot give effective agreement until she has had at least six weeks to get over the birth, but the child can be placed before then if she has already made up her mind (1976 Act, s.16(4)). The agreement of an unmarried father who does not have parental responsibility is not required (see Chapter 2).

If the mother is married to someone other than the child's father, she may wish to conceal the birth from her husband, but the law presumes that the child is his until it is proved to the contrary. Courts vary in their willingness to accept the mother's word about her child's parentage so that her husband may not have to be approached at all. To keep him in ignorance is to deprive both him and the child of the possible benefit as well as the possible disadvantage of the law's presumption, but if the evidence is clear the court may be prepared to do so.

A parent or "guardian" does not include a local authority or anyone else having parental responsibility under a care order or a residence order, although an agency cannot place a care order child without the authority's consent and they must always be made a respondent to the application (r. 15(2)). The parent's agreement is still required, although in these cases it may sometimes be easier to find grounds for dispensing with it.

(ii) Dispensing with agreement

Most adoptions have parental agreement, but an increasing proportion of them do not, and one of the most difficult legal questions is whether it is proper to deprive parents of their right to decide. Adoption means the complete and final severance of all ties with the child they have brought into the world, yet the child's future well-being, happiness and security may sometimes be much better safe-guarded by adoption than by any other arrangement. The child's welfare is now the first consideration for the court (1976 Act, s.6), but it is not the paramount consideration; if it were, the court might be able to override parental objections simply because the adoption would be better for the child. Given the general evidence of the comparative success rates of children adopted by strangers, children brought up by their mothers alone, and children who are fostered for a long time (see *e.g.* Tizard, 1977), the mother's right to withhold her agreement might virtually disappear once other people had looked after him for any length of time. Instead, the law allows the court to dispense with parental agreement on one or more of six grounds (1976 Act, s.16(2)).

(a) *"That the parent or guardian cannot be found or is incapable of giving agreement"*

"Cannot be found" usually means that all reasonable steps have been taken to find the parent, but without success. In *Re F. (R.) (An Infant)* [1970] 1 Q.B. 385 the applicants wrote to the mother's last known address, advertised in the press, and tried to trace her through the post office, all without success, and so the trial court dispensed with her consent and made the order. When the mother found out about it, she alleged that the applicants knew her father's address and that he was in touch with her, yet never approached him. The Court of Appeal allowed her to appeal, even though five months had now elapsed since the order, because all reasonable steps had not been taken to find her.

Exceptionally, a parent "cannot be found" if there are no practicable means of communicating with him to obtain his agreement, as where the child had illegally escaped to this country from a totalitarian regime and any attempt to communicate with his parents there would be very dangerous for them (*Re R. (Adoption)* [1967] 1 W.L.R. 34). In that case, the parents were also held to be "incapable" of consenting, but this will usually refer to mental incapacity.

(b) *"That the parent or guardian is withholding his consent unreasonably"*

This ground has caused the most difficulty in interpretation, but it is now the most frequently used. Instead of focusing on the parent's capabilities or behaviour towards the child, it asks the court to evaluate the reasonableness of her state of mind; the courts' views on the weight to be given to the child's best interests in making that evaluation have changed a good deal. The early cases suggested that it was always prima facie reasonable for a parent to withhold consent to such a drastic step; and the fact that adoption would be better for the child did not in itself make this unreasonable, although it might be so if the parent had vacillated to an unusual degree or been in some way culpable in her behaviour towards the child.

245

But in the leading case of *Re W. (An Infant)* [1971] A.C. 682 Lord Hailsham rejected the idea that the parent had necessarily to be culpable, callous, indifferent or neglectful of her duties. The court must not simply substitute its own decision for that of the parent; the question is whether a reasonable parent in the circumstances of this particular case could withhold her agreement. A reasonable parent is entitled to take her own feelings into account, but she will also consider very carefully what is best for her child's long term welfare, including the advantages of adoption and the disadvantages of disrupting a young child in a settled home. As Lord Denning said in *Re L. (An Infant)* (1962) 106 Sol.J. 611:

"A reasonable mother surely gives great weight to what is better for the child. Her anguish of mind is quite understandable; but it may still be unreasonable for her to withhold her consent. We must look and see whether it is reasonable or unreasonable according to what a reasonable woman in her place would do in all the circumstances of the case."

The court's duty to give first consideration to the need to safe-guard and promote the welfare of the child throughout his childhood has not affected this test (*Re P. (An Infant) (Adoption: Parental Consent)* [1977] Fam.25, C.A.), but in practice it would have made little difference if it had. The courts have developed a two-part test: first, is adoption in principle the right solution for this child; second, if so, is the parent's objection unreasonable in the sense explained by Lord Hailsham? Not surprisingly, once the court has said "yes" to the first, it is difficult for it to say "no" to the second. Thus the child's welfare may not be the sole or the paramount consideration for the parent, but it certainly plays a great part in the evaluation of her attitude.

The application of this test will vary according to the context. Some cases might better be termed unreasonable "withdrawal" of agreement, because the parents have decided to place their children for adoption and then changed their minds. A mother may have received inadequate counselling from her social worker and been subject to great pressure from family and friends. Her circumstances may now have improved. She can scarcely be blamed for what has happened, but the child may have been with the applicants from an early age and be just at the point where a disruption in the normal process of forming relationships is most dangerous. These were the essential facts in *Re W.* (above); in *O'Connor* v. *A. and B.* [1971] 1 W.L.R. 1227, H.L., the mother had since married the father, but there was some doubt about the stability of their relationship and the child had been with the applicants for two and a half years. In both, the House of Lords dispensed with agreement. In *Re H. (Infants) (Adoption: Parental Consent)* [1977] 1 W.L.R. 471, C.A., Lord Justice Ormrod observed that:

" . . . it ought to be recognised by all concerned with adoption cases that once formal consent has been given or perhaps once the child has been placed with the adopters, time begins to run against the mother and, as time goes on, it gets progressively more and more difficult for her to show that the withdrawal of her consent is reasonable."

Where the parent has never indicated any willingness to have the child adopted, the attitude may be different. This is particularly so with applications by one parent and a step-parent (discussed in Chapter 6) or by long-term foster parents of a child in care, for in each case the court is not usually choosing between the two homes. The child will probably stay where he is, whether or not he is adopted. The question is whether he should become a fully integrated member of the new family or whether he should retain some links with the family of his birth. In judging the reasonableness of the parent's attitude towards that question, the courts have tended to look at the quality of those links and the sincerity of the parent who wishes to keep them, as well as at the benefits of increased security and commitment in the new family.

Most adoptions of children in care, however, took a different course. The authority would first decide that adoption was the best way of providing for the child's needs. If the child was a ward of court, they would then seek the court's leave to place the child with long term foster parents with a view to adoption, usually coupled with the ending of all contact between parent and child. The court's decision would be based on what was best for the child, although no doubt great weight would be given to the importance of family ties. If leave was given, and a suitable placement found, dispensing with parental agreement became a formality. Children in care can no longer be wards of court, so this process is not now available. Understandably, many agencies wish that it were. If the child is not a ward, the authority can first seek to end contact, or to free the child for adoption, or both, before making the placement.

Dispensing with parental agreement to the adoption of a child in care generally turns on whether contact between the child and his natural parents is likely to be beneficial to the child. If it is, then refusing agreement is not unreasonable and a residence order is available as an alternative (*Re M. (Minors) (Adoption: Parental Agreement)* [1985] F.L.R. 921, C.A.; see also *Re H.; Re W. (Adoption: Parental Agreement)* (1983) 4 F.L.R. 614, C.A.). If the child's future security depends upon cementing his ties with the prospective adopters or the possibility of contact is remote, then it may be unreasonable to refuse (*Re F. (A Minor) (Adoption: Parental Consent)* [1982] 1 W.L.R. 102, C.A.; *Re V. (A Minor) (Adoption: Consent)* [1987] Fam.57, C.A.). A great deal will depend upon the age of the child, the circumstances in which he came into care, and the strength of his link not only with his parents but also with other members of his birth family. Contact can be made a condition of an adoption order; alternatively, a contact order under the Children Act 1989 can be made in the adoption proceedings; but this would not normally be done without the agreement of all concerned (*Re C. (A Minor) (Adoption Order: Conditions)* [1989] A.C. 1, see page 257, below). Finding prospective adopters who are able and willing to contemplate contact, particularly after a contested case, may be much harder than finding adopters who are anxious for the more conventional "clean break".

(c) *"That the parent or guardian has persistently failed without reasonable cause to discharge his parental responsibility for the child"*

This is most likely to be alleged in step-parent, foster-parent or possibly freeing applications, for a parent who has placed her child for a conventional adoption has every excuse not to discharge her parental responsibilities. These include the moral obligation to show an affectionate interest in one's children, as well as the legal duty to maintain them financially (*Re P. (Infants)* [1962] 1 W.L.R. 1296). A "persistent" failure must be longstanding and virtually permanent, so that the child will derive no benefit from maintaining the relationship (*Re D. (Minors) (Adoption by Parent)* [1973] Fam.209). This is perhaps more likely to be so where parents have lost touch with their fostered children than it is when the mother and father have been estranged after a divorce (see Chapter 6). But parents should have an excuse if their lack of contact is the result of the local authority's own conduct.

(d) *"That the parent or guardian has abandoned or neglected the child;"* or (e) *"has persistently ill-treated the child;"* or (f) *"has seriously ill-treated the child"* but in this case the rehabilitation of the child within that household must, for whatever reason, be unlikely

These will rarely apply to a conventional placement for adoption, which is not abandonment in the technical sense. Occasionally, they may apply to a divorced parent. More importantly, however, they would justify plans for adoption in serious cases of child abuse. In practice, agencies prefer to rely on "unreasonable withholding" although they may sometimes use these grounds as well.

The Adoption Law Review (1992) has proposed reducing the grounds to two: (a) where the parent cannot be found or is incapable of consenting, and (b) where the benefit to the child from being adopted is so great as to justify overriding the parents' objections to it. Adoption is only one of the ways of securing the child's future in this or any other home and the benefits to him throughout his whole life should be so much greater than any other arrangement if they are to justify granting it against the parents' will. It would help, however, if there were some way of providing for those parents who do not actively object, because they recognise that adoption is best for their child, but cannot bring themselves to sign the form "abandoning" him in this way.

(iii) Freeing for adoption

"Freeing" was designed for two rather different purposes (Houghton, 1972). One was to allow the mother to agree to adoption in principle before any specific application was ready; the object was to spare both her and the prospective adopters the agony of prolonged uncertainty with the ever-present possibility of a change of mind. The other is to enable an agency already having a child in their care to get the parents' agreement dispensed with, either before the child is placed at all, or at least without involving the prospective adopters in a contested hearing. In practice, freeing is now only used for the second purpose. This is rather like the "leave to place" given in wardship cases (see page 247, above); although in theory the court is considering whether to dispense with agreement before looking at the merits of an adoption, it has to consider whether adoption is right in principle before looking at the reasonableness of the parent's attitude (*Re D. (A Minor) (Adoption: Freeing Order)* [1991] 1 F.L.R. 48, C.A.). Agencies vary in their enthusiasm for freeing, which has tended to increase rather than decrease costs and delays (Lowe, 1990; Lowe and Murch, 1991). The Adoption Law Review (1992) has proposed an entirely different approach (see 6. (i) below).

An application to free a child for adoption is made to court by an adoption agency; either one parent must consent to the application, or the child must already be in the agency's care and the agency want the court to dispense with each parent's agreement; after the 1989 Act this means compulsory care, so this type of freeing is only available to local authorities (1976 Act, s.18(2)). The court must be satisfied that the agreement of each parent to an adoption has either been given or can be dispensed with on any of the usual grounds (1976 Act, s.18(1)); but it cannot dispense with any agreement unless the child has already been placed or placement is likely (1976 Act, s.18(3)); parents should not be unwillingly deprived of their child unless an eventual adoption is assured. The court must also be satisfied that an unmarried father either has no intention of applying for parental responsibility or a residence order or would be unlikely to succeed if he did (1976 Act, s.18(7)). If the order is made, the agency will acquire and the parents will lose their parental responsibility (1976 Act, s.18(5)). The Act does not make clear what effect the order has on the child's relationships. It has been held that his parents are no longer automatically entitled as "parents" to apply for section 8 order about him *M. v. C. and Calderdale Metropolitan Borough Council* [1993] 1 F.L.R. 505, C.A.). But what about his relationships for other purposes? Is he still part of the birth family for inheritance, succession and so on, or is he nowhere?

Each parent may declare, either when the child is freed or later (1976 Act, ss.18(6), 19(4)) that she wants no further involvement in the child's future. If a parent does not do this, she must be told after a year whether her child has been adopted or placed (1976 Act, s.19(2)) and if he has not been adopted by then, she must be notified whenever a placement begins or ends or he is eventually adopted (1976 Act, s.19(3)). If he has not been adopted and is not currently placed for adoption, she can apply for the order to be revoked on the ground that she wishes to resume her parental responsibilities (1976 Act, s.20(1); see *R. v. Derbyshire County Council, ex p. T.* [1990] Fam.164, C.A.), but the court must give first consideration to the child's welfare (1976 Act, s.6). If the order is revoked, parental responsibility will return to her (1976 Act, s.20(3)). If her application fails, she will not be able to try again without the court's leave, and the agency will no longer have to keep her informed (1976 Act, s.20(4),(5)).

4. RETURN OR REMOVAL BEFORE THE HEARING

(i) By the prospective adopters

The prospective adopters may decide that they no longer wish to proceed. If the child was placed with them for adoption by an agency they should give written notice of their decision to the agency, and then return the child within seven days of this (1976 Act, s.30(1)(a) and (3)). They should also return the child within seven days of withdrawing an application which is already pending before a court. If the child is being looked after by a local authority, there is no reason why the authority should not foster the child with the same people if they wish; if the child was not originally placed with a view to adoption, the same procedure applies, but it is expressly stated that the child need not be returned unless the authority ask (1976 Act, s.31(1)). In private and family cases, the child may well stay where he is even though an adoption plan is abandoned.

(ii) By the agency or local authority

The agency may decide that they wish to end the placement. Provided that the application has not yet been made to the court, the agency may serve written notice upon the prospective adopters, who must then return the child within seven days (1976 Act, s.30(1)(b) and (3)). Once the application has been made, the agency can only serve such a notice with leave of the court (1976 Act, s.30(2)). If a child being looked after by a local authority was not originally placed with a view to adoption, but the foster parents have given notice of their intention to apply to adopt, the local authority can no longer recover the child by the usual means (1976 Act, s.31(2)). The same procedure as in ordinary agency placements must be used (1976 Act, s.31(1); see (i) above); this requires the court's leave once an application has been made. Thus if one local authority receives notice in respect of a child who is being looked after by another authority, the former must inform the latter (1976 Act, s.22(4)). Parental contributions are no longer payable (1976 Act, s.31(3)).

(iii) By the natural parents

The natural parent may also wish to recover her child. If she still has parental responsibility, she may usually come and take him, but there are three exceptions.

First, if an application is made to free for adoption a child who is in the care of the applying agency, a parent who did not consent to that application cannot remove the child from the person with whom he has his home without the court's leave (1976 Act, s.27(2)). This is scarcely surprising, as these children must be in compulsory care.

Secondly, once an adoption application has been made to the court, a parent who has "agreed to the making of an adoption order" cannot remove the child from the applicants against their will, except with the court's leave (1976 Act, s.27(1)). Once the application is made, therefore, the prospective adopters will usually be able to keep the child if they wish to allege unreasonable "withdrawal" of agreement. Rather surprisingly, it has been held that this provision applies, not only to formal agreements witnessed by the reporting officer, but also to preliminary agreement before placement (*Re T. (A Minor) (Adoption: Validity of Order)* [1986] Fam.160, C.A.).

Thirdly, if the child has had his home with the prospective adopters for a continuous period of five years, the child cannot be removed against their will, except with the court's leave, not only once an actual adoption application has been made (s.28(1)), but also once they have given notice to the local authority of their intention to apply (1976 Act, s.28(2)). In the second case, they cannot "freeze" the situation for ever; the prohibition will lapse after three months unless an application is made before then, and once lapsed it cannot be renewed by giving a fresh notice for the next 28 days, which would give plenty of time to remove the child if this were appropriate. These prohibitions, however, apply not only to the natural parents, but also to anyone else who might otherwise remove the child, the only exceptions being for the child's arrest or some statutory provision. But a local authority can only remove a child who is in their care in accordance with the procedure set out in (i) above.

The purpose of this rule was to make it easier for long-term foster parents to apply to adopt without parental agreement. They still have to persuade the court to dispense with this but at least they can prevent anyone removing the child before they try to do so. Contrary to popular belief, however, it has made no difference to their position with any local authority looking after the child; after the foster parents have given notice, the authority can still serve notice upon them to return the child within seven days, but once they have applied to the court, this can only be done with the court's leave.

It is a crime to contravene any of these prohibitions (1976 Act, ss.27(3) and 28(7)). A court may also prohibit a suspected removal in advance (1976 Act, s.29((2)). Then the High Court or a county court may authorise a court officer, and a single magistrate may authorise a policeman, to search specified premises and return the child (1976 Act, s.29(3) and (4)).

5. REPORTS TO THE COURT

It used to be necessary in every adoption case for the court to appoint a guardian *ad litem* to safeguard the child's interests. This meant that three different social workers might be involved, one from the agency which made the placement, one from the local authority supervising the placement and the guardian chosen by the court. This was thought unnecessary, wasteful and confusing to natural and adoptive parents alike (Houghton, 1972). Since 1984, therefore, their responsibilities have been arranged differently;

essentially the same rules apply to applications both to adopt and to free for adoption.

An agency must now follow up its own placements and report to the court. In non-agency placements, the local authority must supervise, investigate and report to the court. Both reports must give extensive particulars about the child, his parents, the prospective adopters and the actions of the agency or local authority involved. They must indicate whether any respondent is under 18 or mentally disabled and also whether they think that anyone else should be made a respondent, such as an unmarried father, the mother's husband, or a deceased parent's relative. They must conclude with their own views on whether the adoption is in the child's best long-term interests, what effect it will have on the natural parents, whether the child will be fully integrated into adopters' household, family and community, and what effect it is likely to have on them. Where appropriate, the relative merits of adoption and residence orders should be discussed. The report should end with a recommendation for or against adoption and, if against, with alternative proposals. Similar reports are required from an agency which applies to free a child for adoption (Adoption Rules 1984, rr. 22(1),(2), 4(4)(b); report-writers should consult Schedule 2 for the full details).

In addition, parental agreement to adoption must be witnessed and verified by a reporting officer appointed by the court. Reporting officers must be members of the panels (set up under Children Act 1989, s.41(7); see Chapter 10) and independent of any agency which is looking after the child or has been involved in making the adoption arrangements. Thus there is always an independent check upon the reality of parental agreement; in freeing cases, the reporting officer must also investigate whether an unmarried father intends to apply for parental responsibility or would be likely to succeed, and whether the parent has renounced further involvement with the adoption. The officer must report on all this to the court, and also inform the court if any parent or guardian is unwilling to agree (Adoption Rules 1984, rr. 5, 17).

In contested cases, the court must appoint a guardian *ad litem* for the child. In the High Court, the guardian will be the Official Solicitor if he consents and the applicant does not ask for someone else to be appointed. Otherwise, the guardian will again come from the panel and must again be independent of all the agencies involved. There is no objection, however, to the same person acting as reporting officer and guardian.

Thus the independent investigator in adoption cases is now mainly concerned with either verifying or dispensing with parental agreement. The court may, however, appoint a guardian *ad litem* in any other case where there are "special circumstances" and the welfare of the child requires it. Whatever the reason for her appointment, the guardian must investigate (so far as she thinks necessary) the agency or local authority reports and the statement of facts relied upon to dispense with parental agreement. Her object is always to safeguard the interests of the child and she should advise whether the child should attend the hearing. She must make a report to the court and (unless the court excuses her) be present at the hearing (Adoption Rules 1984 rr.6, 18).

All these reports are confidential to the court (Adoption Rules 1984, rr.5(8), 6(11), 17(5), 18(7), 22(5)). The court will send copies of the agency or local authority reports to the guardian *ad litem* or reporting officer, but not the other way about. Individual parties have a right to inspect, for the purposes of the hearing, any part of a report which refers to them personally, but the court may direct that this is not to happen, or that the relevant parts should only be shown to their lawyers, or on the other hand that they may see other information or reports (Adoption Rules 1984, r.53(2)). Anyone obtaining information in the course of adoption proceedings must treat it as confidential (Adoption Rules 1984, r.53(3); there are a few exceptions).

6. THE ROLE OF THE COURT

Adoption cannot take place without a court order. Applications may be made either to the High Court or to the applicants' local county or magistrates' court. The High Court must deal with cases where neither applicant is domiciled in this country, but in practice it deals with only a handful of cases. Under the allocation rules made following the Children Act 1989, adoption applications which will lead to the discharge of another order (such as a care or a residence order) should be made to the court which makes the original order, although they may then be transferred to another court (Children Act (Allocation of Proceedings) Order 1991, Art. 4(1)). Typically, therefore, the adoption of a child in care should begin in a magistrates' court, while a step-parent adoption after the parents' divorce should go to the divorce court. However, the actual role of the court depends on the type of case, contested or uncontested, agency or private placement, and the Adoption Law Review (1992) has prompted a fundamental reconsideration.

(i) The function and timing of court hearings

In what used to be the typical uncontested agency case, the court does two things. First, it acts as a check on the work done by others, ensuring that they get the paperwork in order. In the past, some courts had their own quite decided views on certain types of adoption—the local judge might disapprove of inter-racial or inter-religious adoptions, for example and agencies might have to take these into account. But with the diminishing supply of babies and young children for adoption, and the greater professionalism of the adoption process, should the courts really be substituting their own judgments and values for those of the agencies' expert panels? And if it does have an independent part to play, should this happen earlier, before the placement has become a fait accompli and the court simply a rubber-stamp?

Secondly, the court hearing provides a "rite of passage" for the child and his new family. The applicants must always attend (exceptionally, only one of joint applicants need be there, as long as the other verifies the application) and so must the child unless the court thinks that special circumstances make this unnecessary. In the High Court, the hearing may be in chambers, but in a county court, it is "in camera" (1976 Act, s.64). This means that it is always in private, but in a county court it should be in court rather than in the judge's chambers, and the judge should wear robes. This is probably just what the family want in an uncontested case; where there is any doubt or difficulty, however, they might prefer the more informal atmosphere of a hearing "in chambers" without robes.

Where there is any doubt or difficulty, the court is performing its more traditional adjudicative role, as well as the other two. But does it do so at the right time or on the right principles? Under the ordinary procedure, the child is already placed with the adopters and presumably settling down well; what reasonable mother would disrupt this for the sake of establishing or re-establishing a relationship which may never really have begun? Under the freeing procedure, the court is supposed to consider the case for dispensing with agreement before the child is properly settled in with prospective adopters, but sometimes the child has already been placed; even if he has not, the court will be considering the merits of a hypothetical ideal adoptive family against the all-too-obvious shortcomings of his family of birth; and the courts have to begin by asking whether adoption is best before deciding whether the parent's attitude is "unreasonable" (*Re D. (A Minor) (Adoption: Freeing Order)* [1991] 1 F.L.R. 48, C.A.).

This makes freeing very like the system for adopting wards of court who were in local authority care; the court was first asked to approve adoption in principle and would only be asked to dispense with parental agreement after the child had been placed. This put the parents in the worst of all worlds—the adoption plan would be decided upon simply on the basis of what would be best for the child, without any priority given to their wishes or claims; their failings would be compared with the merits of a hypothetical ideal; contact would usually be ended, partly because a hypothetical ideal who could handle continuing contact (and a potentially contested adoption application) would be harder to find; the child would then be placed and again presumably settle down well; and by the time that the court had to decide whether to dispense with their agreement, the parents might well have given up the struggle.

Understandably, this system was popular with local authorities and agencies, not for any sinister reasons, but because it did indeed enable them to plan the best possible future for the child as they saw it. The Adoption Law Review (1992), however, considered that the special position of the parents was not sufficiently safeguarded under any of the existing systems, that freeing for adoption led to unnecessary duplication of effort and damaging delay, and that the court was not being involved in either contested or uncontested cases at a sufficiently early stage. It has therefore recommended the abolition of freeing. Under the new system, the court would approve the placement before it had become a fait accompli and at the same time resolve any contested issues relating to alternative placements or parental consent. Uncontested cases might be dealt with on the papers, with the court retaining its monitoring role but losing its ceremonial function. Contested cases would require a proper hearing without delay. It would therefore be necessary to identify these at an early stage in order to appoint a guardian and set a time-table. This may well be right in principle but in practice how easy would it be to achieve?

(ii) The welfare and other principles

In reaching any decision relating to the adoption of a child, the court (just like an adoption agency) must have regard to all the circumstances, first consideration being given to the welfare of the child throughout his childhood; it must also, so far as practicable, ascertain the child's own wishes and feelings about the decision and give due consideration to them having regard to his age and understanding (1976 Act, s.6).

This concentrates only on the child's childhood but the crucial difference between adoption and any other order is that it operates for life and there is no going back. It is one thing to ask whether the child needs a permanent family placement and whether this family will give him what he needs. It is another thing to ask what the legal framework for that should be. The Adoption Law Review (1992) has suggested that the court should have to consider its effect throughout his childhood and adult life. A modified version of the Children Act checklist (see Chapter 4) should also be considered. This would mean that the court will also consider the other options available in the proceedings (1989 Act, s.1(3)(g)) and the principle that it should not make any order at all unless to do so would be better for the child than doing nothing (1989 Act, s.1(5)).

(iii) The options available

(a) Granting the adoption

The court can simply grant the adoption, provided that it is satisfied that all the necessary parental agreements have been given or can be dispensed with, or that the child is free for adoption; that the child has been with the applicants for the required length of time; that in a non-agency case proper notice has been given to the local authority; and that the applicants have not made or received any unlawful payment for the adoption.

(b) Interim orders

Provided again that the necessary agreements have been given or dispensed with or the child is free for adoption, and that proper notice has been given to the local authority, a court which is still not sure whether adoption is the right solution can make an interim order. This gives parental responsibility for the child to the applicants for a probationary period, "upon such terms for the maintenance of the child and otherwise as the court sees fit" (1976 Act, s.25(1)). Although it is called an "interim order", other people do not lose their parental responsibility and the child does not change families. The order lasts for a specified period of up to two years (and if originally fixed for less can be extended up to maximum of two years in all) (1976 Act, s.25(2)). The object is to resolve any lingering doubts about the adopters and in agency cases this should be very rare indeed. Even in other cases it will usually be wrong to put off the decision in this way (*Re O. (A Minor) (Adoption by Grandparents)* [1985] F.L.R. 546).

In *S. v. Huddersfield Borough Council* [1975] Fam.113, an interim order was made as a way of leaving the child where he was while the possibility of placing him with his natural father was investigated and tested. Nowadays, there would be better ways of doing this. Adoption proceedings are "family proceedings" for the purpose of section 8 of the Children Act 1989 (see Chapter 4). This means that, either on application or of the court's own motion, it may make any section 8 order either instead of or in conjunction with an adoption order. In the *Huddersfield* case, the court could now make a residence order in favour of the applicants, while providing for the child to have contact with, or even spend longer periods of time with, his natural father. Other placement options could be tested in the same sort of way.

(c) *Section 8 orders*

Section 8 orders can also be used as an alternative legal framework for the existing placement. In an increasing number of adoptions, particularly with older children, the court may be satisfied that the child should remain where he is. But it may be asked to choose between a traditional "clean break" adoption, with no contact between the adoptive and original families; or a more "open" style of adoption with some contact, however limited and consensual, between the two; or a quite different arrangement, making a residence order to confirm the child's security in his new home, but preserving his legal and actual relationship with his family of birth. This means that if the mother refuses her agreement to the adoption, on the basis that a residence order would be more appropriate, and the court considers that she is not being unreasonable in this, the court can make a residence order instead, whether or not the prospective adopters have applied for it.

These choices raise complex issues. When the placement of older and "hard to place" children was being pioneered in the 1970s, there was a very strong view that both the prospective adopters and the child required the commitment, security and permanence of an adoption if it was to be a success. This view may be less prevalent now, when there is a greater understanding of the long term consequences of adoption and of the meaning of the birth family for an adopted person, and alternative ways of securing a permanent family placement do exist. Even so, there is still a feeling that a residence order is not enough. Normally, it only lasts until the child is 16, and can never last beyond 18. It gives the applicants all the responsibilities of a parent, but they still share these with the natural parents, who could apply for a variation at any time. It also means that if the applicants die, neither they nor the court can appoint a guardian to take their place. Above all, perhaps, we have no convenient term to express their relationship with the child. The

Adoption Law Review (1992) has suggested that, where the court makes a residence order in favour of non-parents who will be responsible for the child's upbringing until he grows up, it should also be able to appoint them *inter vivos* "guardians"; they would have parental responsibility until the child is 18 and all the powers of a guardian (see Chapter 5) except the power to give or withhold consent to adoption. The court could also give them special protection against further applications by the parents (1989 Act, s.91(2)).

(d) *Contact*

If the court grants the adoption, there are now two ways in which it might provide for continuing contact with members of the birth family. It may make a contact order under section 8 of the 1989 Act either of its own motion or on application. A "parent" can make such an application as of right, but it has been held that this does not include the natural parents of a child who has been freed for adoption (*Re C. (Minors), (Adoption: Residence Order), The Times*, November 19, 1992, C.A.) still less a child who has actually been adopted (*Re S. (A Minor), The Times*, March 8, 1993). They, and other members of the child's family, would need leave in order to apply. Alternatively, an adoption order may contain "such terms and conditions as the court thinks fit" (1976 Act, s.12(6)). In the past, this has been used to impose access conditions, but the normal approach has been that this should only be done in exceptional circumstances, and even then usually only if the adoptive parents agree (*Re C. (A Minor) (Adoption: Conditions)* [1989] A.C. 1). There may be problems of enforcing, varying or discharging these conditions, so that if they are appropriate at all, a contact order is probably the better way of doing it. But the real question is whether they are appropriate. If regular contact between the child and members of his original family will be good for him, is adoption really the right solution (see *Re M. (A Minor) (Adoption: Parental Agreement)* [1985] F.L.R. 925, C.A.; *Re M. (A Minor) (Adoption Order: Access)* [1986] 1 F.L.R. 51, C.A.; *Re V. (A Minor) (Adoption: Consent)* [1987] Fam.57, C.A.; *Re W. (A Minor) (Adoption: Custodianship: Access)* [1988] 1 F.L.R. 175, C.A.)?

Some courts see the imposition of contact as fundamentally inconsistent with the parenthood of the adoptive parents. Others may be more sympathetic to contact with relatives other than the birth parents, such as siblings (as in *Re C.* above) or grandparents (as in *Re M., The Times*, May 9, 1985), and of course much will depend upon the age of the child. Recently, the Court of Appeal has confirmed that adoptive parents should not be required to provide a photograph every six months, without their consent, unless the circumstances were very exceptional (*Re D. (A Minor) (Adoption Order: Conditions)* [1992] 1 F.C.R. 461).

In the period before custodianship, and later residence orders, became available as an alternative, there may have been a temptation to use contact as a compromise solution, particularly in cases which might otherwise have been contested. It could be seen both as a comfort and as a bargaining tool for parents who might be ready to accept that their children would be better off elsewhere but did not want to abandon them completely. Now that there is an alternative, the choice should become a more balanced one, looking at all the advantages and disadvantages of each potential solution.

On the other hand, the courts have been sympathetic to the occasional need to protect the adoptive family from interference by the birth parents. A non-molestation order should not be made a term of an adoption order, but the child can be protected in wardship proceedings instead (*Re D.* (*A Minor*) [1991] Fam.137, C.A.).

(e) *Refusing the order*

If the court simply refuses the adoption application in an agency case, the child must be returned to the agency within seven days, unless the court extends this up to six weeks (1976 Act, s.30(3),(6)). Any unsuccessful applicant may, of course, appeal against a refusal, but they should not make the child a ward of court as a disguised way of doing so. No court may hear another application by the same adopters for the same child, unless the previous court exempted them from this rule or the second court finds that there has been a change in the circumstances or some other reason for letting them try again (1976 Act, s.24(1)).

7. EFFECTS OF ADOPTION

Adoption is the virtually complete and irrevocable transfer of a child from one family to another, with only a few qualifications and exceptions.

(i) The transfer

There are four aspects to the transfer itself. First, an adoption order gives parental responsibility to the adopters (1976 Act, s.12(1)) as from the time that it is made (1976 Act, s.12(2)). The court has power to impose such terms and conditions as it sees fit (1976 Act, s.12(6)), but these are generally considered to detract from the main purpose of adoption and should only be imposed without the adopters' consent in the most exceptional circumstances (see 6.(iii)(d) above). They will therefore be able to bring the child up as they wish and will have full responsibility for looking after him properly, educating and maintaining him.

The consequences of this are particularly poignant when an adoption breaks down. If an agency finds an adoptive family for an older child who has suffered severe psychological damage as a result of his early life experiences, the family may find it impossible to cope with the behaviour problems which emerge. If they then have to return the child, they are technically responsible to contribute to his maintenance in local authority accommodation (see Chapter 8). They may well resist this on the ground that they were not properly informed of the child's history or supported in their efforts to cope with its effect. Either way, these very sad cases illustrate how difficult it is for us to regard adoption as a complete reproduction of the original.

Secondly, from the time that it is made, an adoption order extinguishes the parental responsibility of anyone who had it before then (1976 Act, s.12(3)(a)). Care orders and any other orders made under the 1989 Act cease (1976 Act, s.12(3)(aa)). The natural parents have no right to keep in touch with the child and no duty to maintain him. Although arrears under a maintenance order or agreement may be recovered, no further liability can accrue (1976 Act, s.12(3)(b); there are two minor exceptions, for maintenance agreements which either constitute a trust or expressly provide for continuing despite adoption, so that a natural parent may deliberately set out to provide for a child who is to be adopted, s.12(4)). No new orders can be made.

However, adoption does more than simply transfer parental responsibility, for this would only be a drastic form of residence order. For almost every legal purpose, adoption removes the child from one family and places him in another. An adopted child is to be treated as if he had been born the child of the adoptive parents' marriage, or as if he had been born in wedlock to a sole adopter (although not to any actual marriage of the adopter) (1976 Act, s.39(1)). He is not to be treated as the child of anyone else (1976 Act, s.39(2)). The Act somewhat unnecessarily declares that this prevents an adopted child from being illegitimate (1976 Act, s.39(4)). The legal effects of adoption therefore last much longer than childhood and once done they can never be undone, except by a fresh adoption while the adopted person is still a child.

Thus, although relationships existing by virtue of adoption can be referred to as adoptive relationships (1976 Act, s.41), the term "parent" and any other reference to a relationship in any statute or legal document will automatically include an adoptive relationship unless the contrary intention is expressed. The adopted family and relatives become the real family and relatives.

This only affects dispositions of property (see 1976 Act, s.46) which took effect on or after January l, 1976 (1976 Act, s.39(6)). Before then, an adopted child could only claim property under a general disposition (for example, "to all my grandchildren") if he had been adopted before it. The person who had died or disposed of his property was presumed only to want to benefit those about whom he had a chance of knowing and whom he could exclude if he wished. Under the new rule, the person who is making such a disposition (which includes dying without making a will, so that the rules of intestacy apply) is presumed to want to benefit any future adopted children just as much as any future natural children; if he wishes to exclude them, he must say so. Dispositions in a will or on intestacy are taken to be made when a person dies, not when the will is executed (1976 Act, s.46(3),(4)). The only difference between adopted and birth relatives now is for dispositions which depend upon the adopted person's date of birth (for example, "to all my grandchildren living at my death"); an adopted child is taken to have been born on the date of the order, so that he is not "living at my death" if the order came later, even if he had in fact already been born. If, on the other hand, the grandfather had left his property to be divided between all his grandchildren when they reached 21, the adopted child will take on his real birthday (1976 Act, s.42(2),(3)).

These rules do not apply where a child is adopted by one natural parent alone, for this does not affect entitlement to property or anything else which depends upon their natural relationship (1976 Act, s.38(3)). If an unmarried mother adopts her own child as sole adopter he is still treated (for example, for the purpose of a disposition to "my oldest grandchild") as if he had been born on his real birthday and not on the date of his adoption (1976 Act, s.43).

Fourthly, when an adoption order is made, it is recorded in the Adopted Children Register and a "birth" certificate based on that entry may be obtained (1976 Act, s.50(1),(2),(3)). The actual birth is marked "adopted" and the Registrar General keeps a register to trace the connection between the two (1976 Act, s.50(4)); but unlike all the other registers, this is not open to public inspection; with two vital exceptions (see (iv) below), information from it cannot be disclosed (1976 Act, s.50(5)).

(ii) Exceptions

The most important exceptions to the general principle relate to marriage, incest, nationality and peerages. There are certain people to whom one is so closely related either by blood (or sometimes by marriage) that one is not allowed to marry them (see Marriage Act 1949, Sched. 1) and sexual intercourse between parents (and grandparents) and their children, and between brothers and sisters, is a crime (Sexual Offences Act 1956, ss.10–11). An adopted child remains in his natural family for this purpose (1976 Act s.47(1)). Thus he cannot marry his natural mother, grandmother, sister, aunt or niece. This raises the problem that an adopted child normally has no way of knowing who his natural relatives are, but he can ask the Registrar General to check his original birth record in order to find out, for this purpose even if he is under 18 (1976 Act, s.51(2). An adopted person is also forbidden to marry his adoptive parent, for this might indeed introduce a damaging ambiguity into the relationship (Marriage Act 1949, Sched. 1), but intercourse between them is not incest. Nor is an adopted person prevented from marrying his other adoptive relatives. There is no eugenic reason why he should be, but the possibility of marriage between adoptive brother and sister might do some damage to normal family relations.

An adopted person is not automatically his adoptive parents' child for the purposes of British nationality, or immigration control (1976 Act, s.47(2)). This is to prevent evasion by adoption abroad, for the general principle applies to all recognised adoptions, wherever they took place (1976 Act, s.38(1)). However, a child who is adopted here either by a married couple either of whom is a British citizen, or by a sole adopter who is a citizen, will automatically gain British nationality if he does not already have it (British Nationality Act 1981, s.1(5)).

Adoption does not affect succession to peerages and other titles, or to any attached property, for these still depend upon the blood line (1976 Act, s.44).

Nor need it affect entitlement to a pension already being paid for a child when he is adopted (1976 Act, s.48), or to an insurance policy against the child's funeral expenses (but nothing more) which is transferred to adoptive parents (1976 Act, s.49).

(iii) Irrevocability

An adoption order cannot be revoked. The only real exceptions relate to adoptions by the child's own parents. If a person has been adopted by his mother or father alone and his parents later marry one another, so that he becomes a "legitimated person" (see Chapter 2), any one of them can apply to the court for the adoption order to be revoked (1976 Act, s.52(1)). The same applies to people who were adopted by both their natural parents before the Legitimacy Act 1959, because until that Act they could not be legitimated if either of their parents had been married to someone else when they were born (1976 Act, s.52(2)).

It is interesting that the law thus regards the natural legitimated relationship as preferable to the adoptive relationship. It is strange that we have not yet provided for a form of step-parent adoption which does not require the natural parent to become an adoptive parent (see Chapter 6). It is perhaps not so strange that, unlike some other countries, we have not yet provided for any adoption by a non-parent to be revoked. The only way round this which has so far been found is to apply for leave to appeal out of time.

An appeal lies from a magistrates' family proceedings court to the Family Division of the High Court, or from a country court or the High Court to the Court of Appeal. Immediate appeals are most likely when an adoption has been refused or when the court has dispensed with parental agreement. There are normally only six weeks in which to appeal, after which an adoption order can be considered final. However, the appeal court can grant leave to appeal out of time and there are at least two reported cases where it has done so. The first was where insufficient effort had been made to trace the child's mother (see page 245, above). The second was where a step-father adopter had been unable to cope with the child when the mother had died quite soon after the adoption (see page 107, above).

These cases were quite exceptional and not long after the event. But some adopted people may want their adoptions revoked when they are grown up and re-establish contact with their original families (there was a recently publicised example of a child of an English mother and a Kuwaiti father who was adopted by an orthodox Jewish couple). Might an appeal be allowed when the court made the order on false or inadequate information? If so, how false or inadequate does it have to be? Or will the courts retreat from opening this particular Pandora's box?

(iv) Discovering origins

The Children Act 1975 gave all adopted people who have reached 18 the right to obtain a copy of their original birth certificate (1976 Act, s.51(1)). A counselling service must be offered to all people who wish to trace their origins in this way, from the Registrar-General's Department itself, or from the local authority for the area where the person is living, from the authority for the area where the adoption order was made, from any other local authority or from the approved adoption society which arranged it (1976 Act, s.51(3),(4),(5)). People who were adopted before the 1975 Act was passed are obliged to take advantage of this offer (1976 Act, s.51(7). The counsellor will usually be able to reveal far more about their origins and the circumstances of their adoption than they will learn from the simple birth certificate to which they have a right. People adopted since the 1975 Act was passed will be reaching 18 from November 1993 onwards. They do not have to accept the offer of counselling but they may still find it useful.

An earlier study of adopted people who traced their origins in Scotland (Triseliotis, 1973) suggested that relatively few adopted people would embark upon a search and even fewer would try to trace and eventually meet their original parents. Many of those who did so were unhappy people, who had learned of their adoption in a distressing or negative way, or whose experiences in their adoptive family had not been entirely satisfactory, and who had a desperate need to discover who they really were. Counselling can help them explore their motivation and discover how their needs can best be met.

Experience since the 1975 Act suggests that the possibility of a meeting which might damage either party causes concern to counsellors in only a tiny proportion of cases. Most inquirers, whatever their own needs, appeared equally considerate towards the feelings of both their original and their adoptive parents (Day and Leeding, 1980; Triseliotis, 1984). In a dramatic case where the adopted person was a Broadmoor patient who had killed his cellmate in the belief that he was killing his adoptive mother, the court held that he did not have an absolute right to his original birth certificate; on grounds of public policy, the Registrar General could refuse to supply it if there was evidence that he would use the information in it to commit a serious crime, in this case to murder his mother (*R. v. Registrar General, ex p. Smith* [1991] 2 Q.B. 393, C.A.).

However, experience since the 1975 Act also suggests that it is natural and normal for adopted people to feel curiosity about their origins, and not simply a reaction to an unhappy adoption experience. Their most desperate need may simply be for more information (Walby and Symons, 1990). This can be supplied by improvements in adoption practice, giving the adoptive parents as much information as possible to pass on to their child, giving them as much help and advice as possible about how and when to do this, and providing a dossier of information which could be available to any adopted person who eventually inquires either of the agencies or of the court (Adoption Law Review, 1992).

Of course, the needs of the more traditional adopted child may be rather different from those of the more recently adopted, particularly older children adopted from care, perhaps after a history of serious abuse or neglect or against their parents' will (Haimes and Timms, 1985). The original families also have needs. The original mother has no right to object to the disclosure of information which could reopen a deeply upsetting experience which she had tried to put out of her mind and which might prejudice her existing relationships. Equally, she has no right to information about the child whom she has given up, often with great reluctance and under severe pressure. Other members of the original family may have similar needs to trace their lost relatives.

The Adoption Contact Register was established to meet some of these needs (1976 Act, s.51A(1)). Original relatives, if they can satisfy the Registrar General that they were related to an adopted person by blood or by marriage and can trace his birth, can register (names and addresses) in one part of the register that they want to make contact with the adopted person (1976 Act, s.51A(2)(b), (5)(6)(13)(a)); adopted people, if they have obtained or are qualified to obtain their original birth certificates, can register (names and addresses) in the other (1976 Act, s.51A(2)(a), (3),(4)). People can cancel their entries (1976 Act, s.51A(7)) but they cannot register that they do *not* want to be contacted. The Registrar General *must* transmit the names and addresses of registered relatives to registered adopted people but not the other way about (1976 Act, s.51A(9)). The register is not open to public inspection (1976 Act, s.51A(11)).

The register is still in its infancy and may not be well-known either to adopted people or to their original relatives. Perhaps its greatest defect is that anyone registering must pay a fee. There are other ways in which people can try to find out more. A long-standing but little known provision allows the High Court, Westminster County Court, or the court which made the original adoption order, to order the Registrar General to disclose the link (1976 Act, s.50(5)); and the original court might be persuaded to give leave to inspect its records (Adoption Rules 1984, r. 53(4)). There are ways in which agencies may be able to help which are quite outside the statutory procedures, for example, by writing to an adult adopted person in very guarded terms asking whether he might be interested in contacting an important person from his past. It is obviously better if these approaches are made in a sensitive and professional way; the depth of the need which is now coming to the surface is such that some people will find other ways of satisfying it if the professionals are unable or unwilling to help.

8. COMMENTARY

We are still rather confused in our approach to adoption, because it calls into question so much of what we believe a "family" to be. Much of the law has developed to fit the picture of the total transfer of a child from one family to another, which seems most appropriate to the stereotype of an unmarried mother giving up her baby to childless strangers. Hence the continuing preoccupation with secrecy, the increasingly wholesale legal effects, and the escalating suspicion of step-parent and intra-family adoptions, despite the continuing public demand for these.

These developments were taking place while the supply of babies for adoption was dramatically decreasing. Adoption came to be considered for the previously "unadoptable"—older or disabled children, children of mixed race, sibling groups, victims of abuse who might be seriously damaged by their early experiences. Adoption of children with their own life stories cannot conform completely to the stereotype. It certainly needs great professionalism, in choosing and preparing both the children and their adopters. It may also need a more flexible approach to family ties. Until the Children Act 1989 made other alternatives available, it began to look as though the courts were developing a more favourable view of "open" adoption in some cases. It is important, however, to unpick the notion of open adoption. It should mean involving the birth parents more closely in the initial process and trying to keep them informed of how the child is getting on if this is what they want. It should mean making sure that the adopted child knows that he is adopted and knows as much as possible about his original family when he is ready. It can also mean that the adopted child and his original family maintain some sort of contact while he is growing up but this is a much more delicate and sensitive issue.

All these issues are made more delicate and sensitive by the changing nature of adoption, which has to come to terms not only with children with special needs, but also with many more contested or at least deeply contentious adoptions, and with the most important recent development of all, the growth in adoptions of children from overseas. The law still needs to be reformed to meet all of these challenges.

REFERENCES AND FURTHER READING

Adcock, M. and White, R. (eds.) (1980b) *Terminating Parental Contact: An Exploration of the Issues relating to Children in Care* (London: Association of British Adoption and Fostering Agencies)

Adcock, M., White, R. and Hollows, A. (1991) *Significant Harm: its management and outcome* (Croydon: Significant Publications)

Adoption Law Review (1992) *Review of Adoption Law: Report to Ministers of an Interdepartmental Working Group: A Consultation Document* (London: Department of Health and Welsh Office)

Adler, R. (1985) *Taking Juvenile Justice Seriously* (Edinburgh: Scottish Academic Press)

Anderson, R. (1978) *Representation in the Juvenile Court* (London: Routledge)

Bagley, C. (1980) "Adjustment, Achievement and Social Circumstances of Adopted Children in a National Survey" (1980) *102 Adoption and Fostering* 47

Bainham, A. (1986) "The Balance of Power in Family Decisions" [1986] *Cambridge Law Journal* 262

Bainham, A. (1993) "Children, Parents and the Law: Non-Intervention and Judicial Paternalism", presented at S.P.T.L. Seminar, *Parents and Children: Rights and Protection*, All Souls College, Oxford

Barker, D. (1975) *Unmarried Fathers* (London: Hutchinson)

Bean, P. (ed.) (1984) *Adoption—Essays in Social Policy, Law and Sociology* (London: Tavistock)

Bean, P. and Melville, J. (1988) *Lost Children of the Empire* (London: Unwin)

Berridge, D. (1985) *Children's Homes* (Oxford: Blackwell)

Berridge, D. and Cleaver, H. (1987) *Foster Home Breakdown* (Oxford: Blackwell)

Blackstone, Sir W. (1765) *Commentaries on the Laws of England* (Oxford: Clarendon Press)

Blom-Cooper, L. (1985) *A Child in Trust—The Report of the Panel of Inquiry into the Circumstances surrounding the Death of Jasmine Beckford* (London: London Borough of Brent)

Blom-Cooper, L. (1987) *A Child in Mind—the Report of the Commission of Inquiry into the Circumstances surrounding the Death of Kimberley Carlile* (London: London Borough of Greenwich)

Blyth, E. (1990) "Assisted reproduction: what's in it for the children?" (1990) 4 *Children and Society* 167

Booth, The Hon. Mrs. Justice (1985) *Report of the Matrimonial Causes Procedure Committee* (London: H.M.S.O.)

Booth, The Hon. Mrs. Justice (1992) *The Children Act Advisory Committee Annual Report 1991/92* (London: Lord Chancellor's Department)

Bowlby, J. (1971) *Attachment and Loss Vol. 1: Attachment* (Harmondsworth: Penguin)

Bowlby, J. (1975) *Attachment and Loss Vol. 2: Separation: Anxiety and Anger* (Harmondsworth: Penguin)

Bowlby, J. (1980) *Attachment and Loss Vol. 3: Loss, sadness and depression* (London: Hogarth Press)

Bradshaw, J. and Millar, J. (1991) *Lone Parent Families in the U.K.* Department of Social Security Research Reporet No. 6 (London: H.M.S.O.)

Brandon, J. and Warner, J. (1977) "A.I.D. and Adoption: Some Comparisons" (1977) 7 *British Journal of Social Work* 235

Bromley, P.M. (1984) "Aided conception: the alternative to adoption" in Bean, P. (ed.), *op. cit.*

Brophy, J. (1985) "Child Care and the Growth of Power: the status of mothers in custody disputes" in Brophy, J. and Smart, C. (eds.) *Women in Law* (London: Routledge)

Bruce, N. (1990) "On the importance of genetic knowledge" (1990) 4 *Children and Society* 183

Bullard, E. and Malos, E. (1990) with Parker, R., *Custodianship—A Report to the Department of Health on the Implementation of Part II of the Children Act 1975 in England and Wales from December 1985 to December 1988* (Bristol: University of Bristol Department of Social Policy and Social Planning)

Burgoyne, J. and Clark, D. (1984) *Making A Go of It: A Study of Step-families in Sheffield* (London: Routledge)

Burgoyne, J., Ormrod, R., and Richards, M. (1987) *Divorce Matters* (harmondsworth: Penguin)

Butler-Sloss, The Hon. Mrs. Justice (1988) *Report of the Inquiry into Child Abuse in Cleveland 1987* Cm. 412 (London: H.M.S.O.)

Central Policy Review Staff (1978) *Services for Young Children with Working Mothers* (London: H.M.S.O.)

Central Statistical Office (1993) *Social Trends 23* (London: H.M.S.O.)

Centrepoint (1993) *Housing our Children* (London: Centrepoint)

Clarke Hall and Morrison *Law relating to Children and Young Persons* 10th (loose-leaf) ed. by Hoggett, B.M., White, R.H., Carr, P. and Lowe, N.V. (London: Butterworths)

Clulow, C. and Vincent, C. (1987), *In the Child's Best Interests? Divorce Court Welfare and the Search for a Settlement* (London: Tavistock)

Council of Europe (1981) *European Convention on the Legal Status of Children born out of Wedlock* (Strasbourg: Council of Europe)

Crellin, E., Kellmer Pringle, M.L. and West, P. (1971) *Born Illegitimate:*

Social and Educational Implications (Windsor: National Foundation for Educational Research)

Crown Prosecution Service (1988) *Code for Crown Prosecutors* Appendix to Annual Report for 1987–88 (London: H.M.S.O.)

Curtis, M. (1946) *Report of the Care of Children Committee* (Chairman: Miss M. Curtis) Cmd. 6922 (London: H.M.S.O.)

Davis, G., Macleod, A., and Murch, M. (1983) "Undefended Divorce: Should Section 41 of the Matrimonial Causes Act 1973 be repealed?" (183) 46 *Modern Law Review* 121

Day, C. and Leeding, A. (1980) *Access to birth records: the impact of section 26 of the Children Act 1975*, A.B.A.F.A. Research Series No. 1 (London: Association of British Adoption and Fostering Agencies)

Deech, R. (1992) "The unmarried father and human rights (1992) 4 *J. Child Law* 3

Derrick, D. (ed.) (1986) *Illegitimate—the experience of people born outside marriage* (London: National Council for One-Parent Families)

D.H. (1988) *Protecting Children—A Guide for Social Workers undertaking a Comprehensive Assessment* (London: H.M.S.O.)

D.H. (1989) *The Care of Children—Principles and Practice in Guidance and Regulations* (London: H.M.S.O.)

D.H. (1991) *Child Abuse—A Study of Inquiry Reports 1980–1989* (London: H.M.S.O.)

D.H. (1991) *Patterns and Outcomes in Child Placement—Messages from current research and their implications* (London: H.M.S.O.)

D.H. Guidance (1991) *The Children Act 1989 Guidance and Regulations*: Volme 1 *Court Orders*; Volume 2 *Family Support, Day Care and Educational Provision for Young Children*; Volme 3 *Family Placements*; Volme 4 *Residential Care*; Volme 5 *Independent Schools*; Volume 6 *Children with Disabilities*; Volume 7 *Guardians ad Litem and other Court Related Issues*; Volume 8 *Private Fostering and Miscellaneous*; Volume 9 *Adoption Issues*; Volume 10 *Index* (London: H.M.S.O.)

D.H. (1992) *Manual of Good Practice for Guardians ad Litem and Reporting Officers* (London: H.M.S.O.)

D.H. (1993) Department of Health Local Authority Circular LAC (93) 1 *The Children Act and Day Care for Young Children: Registration*

D.H. (1993) Department of Health Local Authority Circular LAC (93) 13 *Guidance on Permissible Forms of Control in Children's Residential Care*

D.H. and W.O. (1993) Department of Health and Welsh Office *Children Act Report 1992* Cm. 1244 (London: H.M.S.O.)

D.H.S.S. (1974) *The Family in Society: Dimensions of Parenthood* (London: H.M.S.O.)

D.H.S.S. (1977) Local Authority Circular L.A.C. (77) 1, *Children and Young Persons Act 1969—Intermediate Treatment* (London: D.H.S.S.)

D.H.S.S. (1982) *Child Abuse: A Study of Inquiry Reports, 1973–81* (London: H.M.S.O.)

D.H.S.S. (1985) *Social Work Decisions in Child Care—Recent Research Findings and their Implications* (London: H.M.S.O.)

D.H.S.S. (1986) *Children in Care in England and Wales, March 1984* (London: D.H.S.S.)

D.H.S.S. (1986) *Legislation on Human Infertility Services and Embryo Research: A Consultation Paper* Cm 46 (London: H.M.S.O.)

D.H.S.S. (1987) *The Law on Child Care and Family Services* Cm 62 (London: H.M.S.O.)

D.S.S. (1992) *Notes for Advisers—Child Support: A New Approach* (London: Department of Social Security)

Dickens, B.M. (1981) "The Modern Function and Limits of Parental Rights (1981) 97 *Law Quarterly Review* 462

Dickens, J. (1993) "Assessment and the Control of Social Work: An Analysis of Reasons for the Non-Use of the Child Assessment Order [1993] *J. Social Welfare and Fam. Law* 88

Dingwall, R., Eekelaar, J.M. and Murray, T. (1983) *The Protection of Children—State Intervention and Family Life* (Oxford: Blackwell)

Dodds, M. (1983) "Children and Divorce" [1983] *Journal of Social Welfare Law* 228

Douglas, G. (1992) *Access to Assisted Reproduction: Legal and Other Criteria for Eligibility: Report of a survey funded by the Nuffield Foundation* Cardiff Law School

Douglas, G. (1991) *Law, Fertility and Reproduction* (London: Sweet and Maxwell)

Dunlop, A.B. (1980) *Junior Attendance Centres* Home Office Research Studies No. 60 (London: H.M.S.O.)

Eekelaar, J.M. (1973) "What are Parental Rights?" (1973) 89 *Law Quarterly Review* 210

Eekelaar, J.M. and Clive, E. (1977) *Custody after Divorce* (Oxford: Centre for Socio-legal Studies)

Eekelaar, J.M. (1982) "Children in Divorce: Some Further Data" (1982) 2 *Oxford Journal of Legal Studies* 62

Eekelaar J.M., Dingwall, R. and Murray, T. (1982) "Victims or Threats? Children in Care Proceedings" [1982] *Journal of Social Welfare Law* 68

Eekelaar, J.M. (1986) "The Emergence of Children's Rights" (1986) 6 *Oxford Journal of Legal Studies* 161

Eekelaar, J.M. and Maclean, M. (1986) *Maintenance after Divorce* (Oxford: Clarendon)

Eekelaar, J. and Dingwall, R. (1990) *The Reform of Child Care Law—A Practical Guide to the Children Act 1989* (London: Routledge)

Elfer, P. and Beasley, G. (1991) *Registration of Childminding and Day Care: Using the Law to Improve Standards* (London: H.M.S.O.)

Elliott, B.J. (1991) "Divorce and adult health: the mediating effects of gender", Child Care and Development Group, University of Cambridge

Elliott, B.J. and Richards, M. (1991) "Children and divorce: educational performance and behaviour, before and after parental separation" (1991) 5 *Int. J. Law and the Family* 258

Emergy, R.E. (1982) "Interparental conflict and the children of discord and divorce" (1982) 2 *Psychological Bull.* 310

Emery, R.E. (1988) *Marriage, Divorce and Children's Adjustment* (California: Sage)

European Convention on Human Rights (Strasbourg: Council of Europe)

Family Rights Group (1982) *Accountability in Child Care—Which Way Forward?* (London: Family Rights Group)

Family Rights Group (1986) *Promoting links: keeping families and children in touch* (London: Family Rights Group)

Farmer, E. and Parker, R. (1985a) *A Study of Interim Care Orders* (Bristol: University of Bristol)

Farmer, E. and Parker, R. (1985b) *A Study of the Discharge of Care Orders* (Bristol: University of Bristol)

Ferri, E. (1976) *Growing Up in a One-Parent Family* (Windsor: N.F.E.R. Publishing)

Feversham, Earl of (1960) *Report of the Departmental Committee on Human Artificial Insemination* Cmnd. 1105 (London: H.M.S.O.)

Field-Fisher, T.G. (1974) *Report of the Committee of Inquiry into the Care and Supervision provided in relation to Maria Colwell* (Chairman: T.G. Field-Fisher Q.C.) (London: H.M.S.O.)

Finer, M. and McGregor, O.R. (1974) "The History of the Obligation to Maintain" *Appendix 5 to the Report of the Committee on One-Parent Families* (Chairman: The Hon. Mr. Justice Finer) Cmnd. 5629–I (London: H.M.S.O.)

Finer, Sir M. (1974) *Report of the Committee on One-Parent Families* (Chairman: The Hon. Mr. Justice Finer) Cmnd. 5629 (London: H.M.S.O.)

Fisher, M., Marsh, P. and Phillips, D. with Sainsbury, E. (1986) *In and Out of Care—The Experiences of Children, Parents and Social Workers* (London: Batsford/B.A.A.F.)

Fisher, T. (ed.) (1990) *Family Conciliation within the U.K.* (Bristol: Family Law)

Fletcher, R. (1973) *The Family and Marriage in Britain*, 3rd ed. (Harmondsworth: Penguin)

Franklin, B. (ed.) (1986) *The Rights of Children* (Oxford: Blackwell)

Freeman, M.D.A. (1983) *The Rights and Wrongs of Children* (London: Frances Pinter)

Freeman, M.D.A. (1984) "Subsidised adoption" in Bean, P. (ed.), *op. cit.*

Freeman, M. (1992) *Children, Their Families and the Law—Working with the Children Act* (London: Macmillan)

Furstenberg, F.F. and Cherlin, A.J. (1991) *Divided Families* (London: Harvard University Press)

Geach, H. and Szwed, E. (eds.) (1983) *Providing Civil Justice for Children* (London: Edward Arnold)

George, V. and Wilding, P. (1972) *Motherless Families* (London: Routledge)

Goldstein, J., Freud, A. and Solnit, S. (1973) *Beyond the Best Interests of the Child* (New York: Free Press)

Goldstein, J., Freud, A. and Solnit, S. (1980) *Before the Best Interests of the Child* (London: Burnett Books)

Graham, J. and Moxon, D. (1986) "Some trends in juvenile justice" (1986) 22 *Home Office Research Bulletin* 10

Grubb, A. and Pearl, D.S. (1990) *Blood Testing, AIDS and DNA Profiling* (Bristol: Family Law)

Haimes, E. and Timms, N. (1985) *Adoption, identity and social policy: the search for distant relatives* (Aldershot: Gower)

Hall, J.C. (1968) *Arrangements for the Care and Upbringing of Children (section 33 of the Matrimonial Causes Act 1965)* Law Commission Published Working Paper No. 15 (London: Law Commission)

Hall, J.C. (1972) "The Waning of Parental Rights" [1972] *Cambridge Law Journal* 248

Hallett, C. and Stevenson, O. (1980) *Child Abuse: Aspects of Inter-Professional Cooperation* (London: George Allen and Unwin)

Harding, L.M. (1987) "The Debate on Surrogate Motherhood: the Current Situation, Some Arguments and Issues: Questions facing Law and Policy" [1987] *Journal of Social Welfare Law* 37

Haskey, J. (1982) "Widowhood, widowerhood and remarriage" (1982) 30 *Population Trends* 15

Haskey, J. (1987) "Social class differentials in remarriage after divorce: results from a forward linkage study" (1987) 47 *Population Trends* 34

Haskey, J. (1990) "Children of Families broken by Divorce" (1990) 61 *Population Trends* 34

Heywood, J.S. (1978) *Children in Care: the development of the service for the deprived child*, 3rd ed. (London: Routledge)

Hilgendorf, L. (1981) *Social Workers and Solicitors in Child Care Cases* (London: H.M.S.O.)

Hillingdon Council Area Review Committee on Child Abuse (1986) *Report of the Review Panel into the death of Heidi Koseda* (London: London Borough Council of Hillingdon)

Holman, R. (1973) *Trading in Children—A Study of Private Fostering* (London: Routledge)

Holman, R. (1975) "The Place of Fostering in Social Work" (1975) 5 *British Journal of Social Work* 3

Home Office (1965) *The Child, the Family and the Young Offender* Cmnd. 2742 (London: H.M.S.O.)

Home Office (1968) *Children in Trouble* Cmnd. 3601 (London: H.M.S.O.)

Home Office (1970) *Part I of the Children and Young Persons Act 1969—A Guide for Courts and Practitioners* (London: H.M.S.O.)

Home Office, Welsh Office, D.H.S.S. (1980) *Young Offenders* Cmnd. 8045 (London: H.M.S.O.)

Home Office (1991) *Police and Criminal Evidence Act 1984: Codes of Practice* (London: H.M.S.O.)

Home Office (1986a) Statistical Bulletin 14/86, *The Sentencing of Young Offenders under the Criminal Justice Act 1982: July 1983–June 1985* (London: Home Office)

Home Office (1986b) *Custodial Sentences for Young Offenders* (London: H.M.S.O.)

Home Office Circular 102/1988 *Protection of Children: Disclosure of Criminal Background of Those with Access to Children*

Home Office Circular 59/1990 The Cautioning of Offenders

Home Office Circular 30/1992 *Criminal Justice Act 1991: Young People and the Youth Court*

Home Office Circular 72/1992 *Criminal Justice Act 1991: Attendance Centre Orders*

Houghton, Sir W. (1972) *Report of the Departmental Committee on the Adoption of Children* Cmnd. 5107 (London: H.M.S.O.)

House of Commons (1977), Select Committee on Violence in the Family *Violence to Children* Session 1976–77, H.C. 329 (London: H.M.S.O.)

House of Commons (1984), Second Report from the Social Services Committee, Session 1983–84, *Children in Care* H.C. 360 (London: H.M.S.O.)

House of Commons Social Services Committee (1988) *Children in Care* Session 1988–89 H.C. 84 (London: H.M.S.O.)

Human Fertilisation and Embryology Authority (1991; revised 1993) *Code of Practice* (London: H.F.E.A.)

Jackson, B. and Jackson, S. (1979) *Childminder—A Study in Action Research* (London: Routledge)

James, A. and Wilson, K. (1984) "Reports for the Court: The Work of the Divorce Court Welfare Officer" [1984] *Journal of Social Welfare Law* 89

James A.L. and Hay, W. (1992) *Court Welfare Work: Research, Practice and Development* (Hull: University of Hull)

Kahan, B. (1979) *Growing Up in Care* (Oxford: Blackwell)

Kellmer Pringle, M.L. (1974) *The Needs of Children* (London: Hutchinson)

Kids Clubs Network (1989) National Out of School Alliance *Guidelines of Good Practice for Out of School Care Schemes*

Kiernan, K. (1992) "The impact of family disruption in childhood and transitions made in adult life" (1992) *Population Studies*

King, M. (ed.) (1981) *Childhood, Welfare and Justice* (London: Batsford)

Kuh, D. and Maclean, M. (1990) "Women's childhood experience of parental separation and their subsequent health and socio-economic status in adulthood" (1990) 22 *J. Biosocial Sci.* 1

Lambert, L. and Streather, J. (1980) *Children in Changing Families: A Study of Adoption and Illegitimacy* (London: Macmillan)

Law Commission (1979) Working Paper No. 74, *Illegitimacy* (London: H.M.S.O.)

Law Commission (1982) *Report on Illegitimacy* Law Com. No. 118 (London: H.M.S.O.)

Law Commission (1985) Working Paper No. 91, *Review of Child Law: Guardianship* (London: H.M.S.O.)

Law Commission (1986) *Illegitimacy: Second Report* Law Com. No. 157 (London: H.M.S.O.)

Law Commission (1986) Working Paper No. 96, *Review of Child Law: Custody* (London: H.M.S.O.)

Law Commission (1987a) Working Paper No. 100, *Care, Supervision and Interim Orders in Custody Proceedings* (London: H.M.S.O.)

Law Commission (1987b) Working Paper No. 101, *Wards of Court* (London: H.M.S.O.)

Law Commission (1988) *Report on Guardianship and Custody* Law Com. No. 172 (London: H.M.S.O.)

Law Commission (1988a) *Facing the Future: A Discussion Paper on the Ground for Divorce* Law Com. No. 170 (London: H.M.S.O.)

Law Commission (1989) *A Criminal Code for England and Wales* Law Com. No. 177 (London: H.M.S.O.)

Law Commission (1992) *Report on Domestic Violence and Occupation of the Family Home* Law Com. No. 207 (London: H.M.S.O.)

Leete, R. (1978) "Adoption Trends and Illegitimate Births" (1978) 14 *Population Trends* 9

Leete, R. (1979) *Changing Patterns of Family Formation and Dissolution in England and Wales 1964–76*, O.P.C.S. Studies on Medical and Population Subjects No. 39 (London: H.M.S.O.)

Leete, R. and Anthony, S. (1979) "Divorce and Remarriage: A Record Linkage Study" (1979) 16 *Population Trends* 5

Levy, A. and Kahan, B. (1991) *The Pindown Experience and the Protection of Children: The Report of the Staffordshire Child Care Inquiry* (London: H.M.S.O.)

Lord Chancellor and others (1990) *Children Come First—The Government's proposals on the maintenance of children* Cm. 1263 (London: H.M.S.O.)

Lowe, N. (1990) "Freeing Children for Adoption—the Experience of the 1980s" [1990] *J. Social Welfare Law* 220

Lowe, N.V. (1982) "The legal status of fathers: past and present" in McKee, L. and O'Brien, M. (eds.), *The Father Figure* (London: Tavistock)

Lowe, N., Murch, M., Copner, R. and Griew, K. (1991) *Freeing for Adoption—Research Report for the Adoption Law Review* (Bristol: University of Bristol Socio-Legal Centre for Family Studies)

Luepnitz, D.A. (1982) *Child Custody* (Lexington: Lexington Books)

Lyon, C.M. (1985) "Safeguarding Children's Interests?—Some Problematic Issues surrounding Separate Representation in Care and Associates Proceedings" in Freeman, M.D.A. (ed.) *Essays in Family Law* (London: Stevens)

Maclean, M. (1991) *Surviving Divorce: Women's Resources after Separation* (London: Macmillan)

Maclean, M. and Wadsworth, M. (1988) "The interests of children after parental divorce: a long term perspective" (1988) 2 *Int. J. Law and the Family* 155

McGregor, O.R., Blom-Cooper, L. and Gibson, C., (1970) *Separated Spouses* (London: Duckworth)

Macleod A. and Malos, E. (1984) *Representation of Children and Parents in Child Care Proceedings* (Bristol: University of Bristol Family Law Research Unit)

Macleod, A. with Borkowski, M. (1985) *Access after Divorce: The Follow-Up to the Special Procedure in Divorce Project* (Bristol: University of Bristol)

Maddox, B. (1980) *Step-parenting: How to Live with other People's Children* (London: Unwin)

Maidment, S. (1975) "Access Conditions in Custody Orders" (1975) 2 *British Journal of Law and Society* 182

Maidment, S. (1976) "A Study in Child Custody" (1976) 6 *Family Law* 195 and 236

Maidment, S. (1978) "Some Legal Problems Arising out of the Reporting of Child Abuse" [1978] *Current Legal Problems* 149

Maidment, S. (1980) "The Relevance of the Criminal Law to Domestic Violence" [1980] *Journal of Social Welfare Law* 26

Maidment, S. (1981) *Child Custody: What Chance for Fathers?* Forward from Finer No. 7 (London: One Parent Families)

Maidment, S. (1984a) *Child Custody and Divorce* (London: Croom Helm)

Maidment, S. (1984b) "The Matrimonial Causes Act, s. 41 and the children of divorce: theoretical and empirical considerations" in Freeman, M.D.A. (ed.) *State, Law and the Family: Critical Perspectives* (London: Tavistock)

Mair, L. (1971) *Marriage* (Harmondsworth: Pelican)

Mansfield, P. and Collard, J. (1988) *The Beginning of the Rest of Your Life? A Portrait of Newly-Wed Marriage* (London: Macmillan)

Marsden, D. (1967) *Mothers Alone: Poverty and the Fatherless Family* (Harmondsworth: Penguin)

Marsh, P. (1986) "Natural families and children in care: an agenda for practice development (1986) 10 (4) *Adoption and Fostering* 20

Masson, J., Norbury, D. and Chatterton, S.G. (1983) *Mine, Yours or Ours? a study of step-parent adoption* (London: H.M.S.O.)

Masson, J. (1984) "Old families into new: a status for step-parents" in Freeman, M.D.A. (ed.) *State, Law and the Family: Critical Perspectives* (London: Tavistock)

Mayall, B. and Petrie, P. (1977) *Minder, Mother and Child* (London: University of London Institute of Education)

Millham, S., Bullock, R., Hosie, K. and Haak, M. (1986) *Lost in Care—The Problems of Maintaining Links between Children in care and their Families* (Aldershot: Gower)

Millham, S., Bullock, R., Hosie, K. and Little, M. (1989) *Access Disputes in Child-Care* (Aldershot: Gower)

Mitchell, A. (1985) *Children in the Middle* (London: Tavistock)

Mnookin, R. (1975) "Child Custody Adjudication: Judicial Functions in the Face of Indeterminacy" (1975) 39 *Law and Contemporary Problems* 226

Monckton, Sir W. (1945) *Report . . . on the circumstances which led to the boarding-out of Denis and Terence O'Neill at Bank Farm, Minsterley, and the steps taken to supervise their welfare* Cmnd. 6636 (London: H.M.S.O.)

Morgan, D. and Lee, R.G. (1991) *Blackstone's Guide to the Human Fertilisa-*

tion and Embryology Act 1990, Abortion and Embryo Research, the New Law (London: Blackstone Press)

Morgan, P. (1975) *Child Care: Sense and Fable* (London: Temple Smith)

Morris, A., Giller, H., Szwed, E. and Geach H. (1980) *Justice for Children* (London: Macmillan)

Morris A. and Giller, H. (eds.) (1983) *Providing Criminal Justice for Children* (London: Edward Arnold)

Mortlock, B. (1972) *The Inside of Divorce* (London: Constable)

Morton, Lord (1956) *Report of the Royal Commission on Marriage and Divorce* Cmnd. 9678 (London: H.M.S.O.)

Murch, M. and Bader, K. (1984) *Separate Representation for Parents and Children* (Bristol: University of Bristol Family Law Research Unit)

Murch, M. and Howell, L. (1987) *The Length of Care Proceedings: report of a 3 year survey of workloads in 10 juvenile courts, 1st June 1983–31st May 1986* (Bristol: University of Bristol Socio-Legal Centre for Family Studies)

Murch, M. and Hunt, J. (1990) *Speaking Out for Children* (London: The Children's Society)

Murch, M., Hunt J. and Macleod A. (1990) *The Representation of the Child in Civil Proceedings Research Project 1985–89: Summary of Conclusions and Recommendations for the Department of Health* (Bristol: University of Bristol Socio-Legal Centre for Family Studies)

Murch, M., Thomas C. and Hunt, J. (1992) *The Duration of Care Proceedings—a replication study* (Bristol: University of Bristol Socio-Legal Centre for Family Studies)

National Children's Bureau (1991) *Guidelines for Good Practice for Young Children in Group Day Care* (London: National Children's Bureau)

National Childminding Association (1991) *Setting the Standards: Guidelines of Good Practice in Registering Childminders*

Newcastle Conciliation Project Unit (1989) *Report to the Lord Chancellor on the Costs and Effectiveness of Conciliation in England and Wales* (Newcastle: University of Newcastle-upon-Tyne)

Norris, T.L. and Parton, N. (1987) "The Administration of Place of Safety Orders" [1987] *Journal of Social Welfare Law* 1

One Parent Families (1980) *An Accident of Birth—A Response to the Law Commission's Working Paper on Illegitimacy* (London: National Council for One Parent Families)

Owen, D. *et al.* (1986) *A review of the Children Act 10 years on—its effect on foster care policy and practice* (London: National Foster Care Association)

Packman, J. (1981) *The Child's Generation—Child Care Policy in Britain,* (Oxford: Blackwell)

Packman, J. (1986) *Who Needs Care? Social-work Decisions about Children* (Oxford: Blackwell)

Parker, R. (1991) *Looking After Children: Assessing Outcomes in Child Care* The Report of an Independent Working Party established by the Department of Health (London: H.M.S.O.)

Parkinson, L. (1986) *Conciliation in Separation and Divorce* (London: Croom Helm)

Parsloe, P. (1978) *Juvenile Justice in Britain and the United States—The Balance of Needs and Rights* (London: Routledge)

Pettitt, P.H. (1957) "Parental Control and Guardianship" in Graveson, R.H. and Crane, F.R. *A Century of Family Law* (London: Sweet and Maxwell)

Phillips, R. (1988) *Putting Asunder: A History of Divorce in Western Society* (Cambridge; Cambridge University Press)

Plotnikoff, J. (1992) *Timetabling of Care Proceedings before the Implementation of the Children Act 1989* (London: H.M.S.O.)

Pre-School Playgroups Association (1989) *Guidelines: Good Practice for Full Daycare Playgroups* and *Guidelines: Good Practice for Sessional Playgroups*

Priest, J. and Whybrow, J. (1986) *Custody Law in Practice in the Divorce and Domestic Courts* Supplement to Law Commission W.P. No. 96 (London: H.M.S.O.)

Priestley, P., Fears, D. and Fuller, R. (1977) *Justice for Juveniles—The 1969 Children and Young Persons Act: A Case for Reform?* (London: Routledge)

Raynor, L. (1980) *The Adopted Child Comes of Age* (London: George Allen and Unwin)

R.C.C.L. (1985) *Review of Child Care Law: Report to Ministers of an Interdepartmental Working Party* (London: H.M.S.O.)

Reibstein, J. and Richards, M. (1992) *Sexual Arrangements: Marriage and Affairs* (London: Heinemann)

Richards, M. (1982) "Post Divorce Arrangements for Children: A Psychological Perspective" [1982] *Journal of Social Welfare Law* 133

Richards, M. (1986) "Behind the Best Interests of the Child: An Examination of the Arguments of Goldstein, Freud and Solnit Concerning Custody and Access at Divorce" [1986] *Journal of Social Welfare Law* 77

Richards, M. (1987) "Parents and kids: the new thinking" *New Society*, 27 March 1987

Richards, M. (1991) "Children and Parents after Divorce", presented at the Seventh World Conference of the International Society on Family Law, Yugoslavia

Richards, M. and Dyson, M. (1982) *Separation, Divorce and the Development of Children: A Review* (Cambridge: Child Care and Development Group)

Richards, M. and Light, P. (eds.) (1986) *Children of Social Worlds* (Oxford: Polity Press)

Rights of Women (1985) *Lesbian Mothers on Trial. A report on lesbian mothers and child custody* (London: Rights of Women)

Rowe, J. and Lambert, L. (1973) *Children who wait* (London: Association of British Adoption Agencies)

Roman, M. and Haddad, W. (1978) *The Disposable Parent: The Case for Joint Custody* (New York: Penguin)

Rosenbaum, M. and Newell, P. (1991) *Taking Children Seriously: A Proposal for a Children's Rights Commissioner* (London: Calouste Gulbenkian Foundation)

Rowe, J., Cain, H., Hundleby, M. and Keane, A. (1984) *Long- term fostering and the Children Act—a study of foster parents who went on to adopt* (London: British Agencies for Adoption and Fostering)

Rowe, J., Cain, H., Hundleby, M., and Keane, A. (1984) *Long- Term Foster Care* (London: Batsford)

Russell, Lord Justice (1966) *Report of the Committee on the Law of Sucession in relation to Illegitimate Persons* Cmnd. 3051 (London: H.M.S.O.)

Rutter, M. (1971) "Parent-Child Separation: Psychological Effects on the Children" (1971) 12 *Journal of Child Psychology and Psychiatry* 233

Rutter, M. (1972 and 1981) *Maternal Deprivation Reassessed* 2nd ed. with Postscript (Harmondsworth: Penguin)

Rutter, M. and Giller, H. (1983) *Juvenile Delinquency: Trends and Perspectives* (Harmondsworth: Penguin)

Schaffer, R.H. (1990) *Making Decisions about Children: Psychological Questions and Answers* (Oxford: Blackwell)

Scottish Law Commission (1992) *Report on Family Law* Scot. Law Com. No. 135 (Edinburgh: H.M.S.O.)

Sedley, S. (1987) *Whose Child? The Report of the Public Inquiry into the Death of Tyra Henry* (London: London Borough of Lambeth)

Seglow, J., Kellmer Pringle, M.L., and Wedge, P. (1972) *Growing Up Adopted* (Windsor: National Foundation for Educational Research)

Shaw, M. (1984) "Growing up adopted" in Bean, P. (ed.), *op. cit.*

Sinclair, R. (1984) *Decision Making in Statutory Reviews on Children in Care* (Aldershot: Gower)

Smart, C. (1990) *The Legal and Moral Ordering of Child Custody* Department of Sociology, University of Warwick

Smart, C. and Sevenhuijsen, S. (1989) *Child Custody and the Politics of Gender* (London: Routledge)

Snowden, R. and Mitchell, G.D. (1981) *The Artificial Family—A Consideration of Artificial Insemination by Donor* (London: George Allen and Unwin)

Taylor, R., Lacey, R. and Bracken, D. (1979) *In Whose Best Interests? The Unjust Treatment of Children in Courts and Institutions* (London: Cobden Trust/MIND)

Terry, J. (1979) "Childminding: Time for Reform?" [1978–79] *Journal of Social Welfare Law* 389

Thoburn, J. (1990) *Review of Research relating to Adoption* Interdepartmental Review of Adoption Law, Background Paper No. 2 (London: Department of Health)

Thoburn, J., Murdoch, A., and O'Brien, A. (1986) *Permanence in Child Care* (Oxford: Blackwell)

Thorpe, D., Grey, C. and Smith, D. (1983) *Punishment and Welfare: case studies of the workings of the 1969 Children and Young Persons Act* (Lancaster: University of Lancaster Centre of Youth Crime and Community)

Thorpe, The Hon. Mr. Justice (1993) "The assessment of personality: its contribution to judicial decisions in the field of child care and protection" [1993] *Family Law* 293

Tizard, B. (1977) *Adoption: A Second Chance* (London: Open Books)

Triseliotis, J. (1973) *In Search of Origins: The Experiences of Adopted People* (London: Routledge)

Triseliotis, J. (ed.) (1980) *New Developments in Foster Care and Adoption* (London: Routledge)

Triseliotis, J. (1983) "Identity and Security in Adoption and Long-Term Fostering" (1983) 7(1) *Adoption and Fostering* 22

Triseliotis, J. (1984) "Obtaining birth certificates" in Bean, P. (ed.) *op. cit.*

Triseliotis, J. (1989) "Foster care outcomes: a review of key research findings" (1989) 13 (3) *Adoption and Fostering* 12

United Nations Convention on the Rights of the Child (1989)

Vaughan, D. (1987) *Uncoupling: Turning Points in Intimate Relationships* (London: Methuen)

Vernon, J. and Fruin, D. (1986) *In Care—A Study of Social Work Decision-Making* (London: National Children's Bureau)

Wadsworth, M.E.J. (1985) "Parenting skills and their transmission through generations" (1985) 9(1) *Adoption and Fostering* 28

Wagner, G. (1981) *Children of the Empire* (London: Weidenfeld and Nicholson)

Walczak, Y. with Burns, S. (1984) *Divorce: the Child's Point of View* (London: Harper and Row)

Walby, C. and Symons, B. (1990) *Who am I? Identity, adoption and human fertilisation* Discussion Series No. 12 (London: British Agencies for Adoption and Fostering)

Wallerstein, J.S. and Blakeslee, S. (1989) *Second Chances* (London: Bantam)

Wallerstein, J.S. and Kelly, J.B. (1980) *Surviving the Break- Up—How Children and Parents Cope with Divorce* (London: Grant McIntyre)

Warner, N. (1992) *Choosing with Care: the report of the Committee of Inquiry into the Selection Development and Management of Staff in Children's Homes* (London: H.M.S.O.)

Warnock, Dame Mary (1984) *Report of the Committee of Inquiry into Human Fertilisation and Embryology* (Chairman: Dame Mary Warnock DBE) Cmnd. 9314 (London: H.M.S.O.)

Webb, D. (1986) "The Use of Blood Grouping and DNA 'Fingerprinting' Tests in Immigration Proceedings" (1986) 1 *Immigration and Nationality Law and Practice* 53

Weitzman, L. and Maclean, M. (1992) *Economic Consequences of Divorce—The International Perspective* (Oxford: Clarendon Press)

White, R., Carr, P. and Lowe, N. (1990) *A Guide to the Children Act 1989* (London: Butterworths)

Working Together under the Children Act 1989: A Guide to arrangements for inter-Agency co-operation for the protection of children from abuse (1991) Home Office, Department of Health, Department of Education and Science, Welsh Office (London: H.M.S.O.)

INDEX